The
Crisis
of
Zionism

The
Crisis
of
Zionism

PETER BEINART

TIMES BOOKS   HENRY HOLT AND COMPANY   NEW YORK

Times Books
Henry Holt and Company, LLC
Publishers since 1866
175 Fifth Avenue
New York, New York 10010

Library of Congress Cataloging-in-Publication Data

Beinart, Peter.
  The crisis of Zionism / Peter Beinart.
    p. cm.
  Includes bibliographical references and index.
  ISBN 978-0-8050-9412-1
  1. Zionism—United States.   2. Israel and the diaspora.   3. Jews—United States—Politics
and government.   4. United States—Foreign relations—Israel.   5. Israel—Foreign relations—
United States.   I. Title.
  DS149.5.U6.B45 2012
  320.54095694'0973—dc23   2011042021

First Edition 2012
Designed by Meryl Sussman Levavi
Map by Gene Thorp/Cartographic Concepts, Inc.

Printed in the United States of America
10 9 8 7 6 5 4 3 2 1

To My Parents

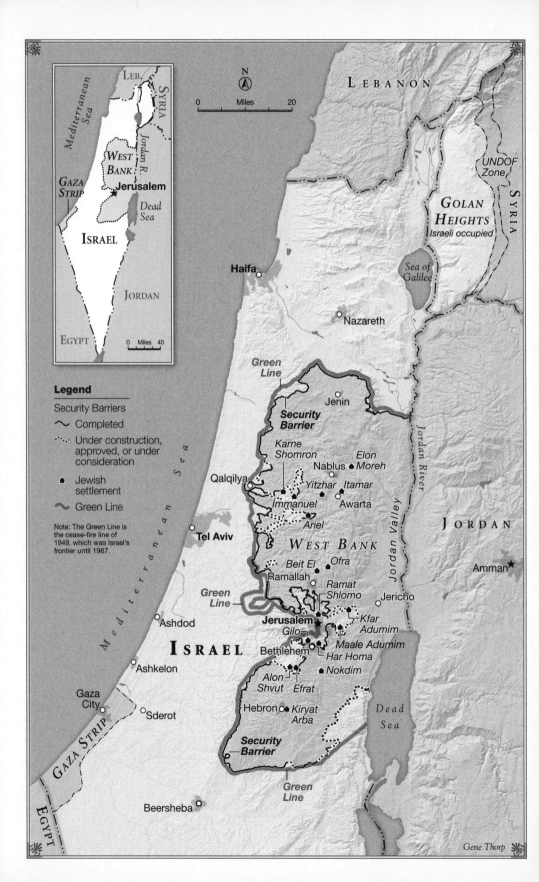

N

Miles
0   20

LEB.
SYRIA
Mediterranean Sea
Jordan R.
WEST BANK
GAZA STRIP
★ Jerusalem
Dead Sea
ISRAEL
JORDAN
EGYPT

0   Miles   40

LEBANON

UNDOF Zone

GOLAN HEIGHTS
Israeli occupied

SYRIA

Sea of Galilee

Haifa

Nazareth

Green Line

Jenin

Security Barrier

Karne Shomron

Elon Moreh

Nablus

Qalqilya

Yitzhar   Itamar

Immanuel

Awarta

Jordan River

Ariel

WEST BANK

JORDAN

Jordan Valley

Beit El   Ofra

Ramallah

Ramat Shlomo

Jericho

Amman

Green Line

Jerusalem

Kfar Adumim

Gilo

Maale Adumim

Ashdod

Bethlehem

Har Homa

ISRAEL

Nokdim

Ashkelon

Alon Shvut

Efrat

Gaza City

Hebron

Kiryat Arba

Dead Sea

Sderot

GAZA STRIP

Security Barrier

EGYPT

Green Line

Beersheba

Gene Thorp

Contents

The
Crisis
of
Zionism

Introduction

I WROTE THIS BOOK BECAUSE OF MY GRANDMOTHER, WHO MADE ME a Zionist. And because of Khaled Jaber, who could have been my son.

I remember walking back with my grandmother one night from synagogue, past the loquat trees of Sea Point, South Africa, the most beautiful Jewish ghetto in the world. I was a kid, and boasting about the United States, the country to which her daughter—my mother—had immigrated. She grew annoyed. "Don't get too attached," she announced. "The Jews are like rats. We leave the sinking ship. One day, please God, we'll all join Isaac in Israel."

Isaac was her brother. They had parted ways four decades earlier, as the ancient Jewish community of Alexandria, Egypt, broke under the strain of economic depression, Arab nationalism, and world war. My grandmother's family were Sephardic Jews. They took their name, Albeldas, from a Spanish town cleansed of Jews five hundred years ago. From Spain, her ancestors crossed the Mediterranean. Her father hailed from Izmir in what is now Turkey, her mother from the Isle of Rhodes in what is now Greece. When the Jewish community of Alexandria collapsed, everyone in the family except Isaac went south, to a corner of the Belgian Congo where Jews from Rhodes were congregating. A few years later, the Jews who still remained in Rhodes found themselves under Nazi rule. The Nazis rounded them up, stole their possessions, extracted their gold teeth, stripped them naked to search for hidden jewelry, starved them, and put them in cargo ships and sealed cars for the two-week trip to Auschwitz. Virtually the entire community—which dated from the second century B.C.E.—was murdered. Now there were no more Jews there either.

When the war ended, my grandmother moved again, this time to South Africa, where she met my grandfather. Fifteen years later, the Congo erupted in civil war, and the Jews there fled. Now, in her old age, racial violence was bloodying South Africa, too, and all around her, Jews were again packing their things. Only later did I realize: My grandmother had spent her life burying Jewish communities. So had her parents. She suspected I would do the same.

Yet she was at peace, because of Israel. She never joined Isaac, who ran a store in Haifa. But Israel's existence calmed her, comforted her, rooted her. It made her feel that Jewish history was more than an endless cycle of estrangement and dislocation; it actually led somewhere. It made her feel that not all Jewish homes need be temporary, that all the running had not been in vain.

My life has been very different from my grandmother's. But I have seen enough to understand how she feels. When I was thirteen, I watched footage of thousands of emaciated Ethiopian Jews, isolated from the rest of their people since the days when the First Temple stood, trekking through the Sahara to reach the planes that the Jewish state had sent to take them home. When I was fourteen, I saw a squat, bald Russian named Anatoly Sharansky—fresh from eight years in a Soviet jail—raise his hands in triumph as he descended the steps at Ben-Gurion Airport. In those soul-stirring scenes, I saw my grandmother's Zionism—the Zionism of refuge—play out before my eyes. It became my Zionism, too. Like her, I sleep better knowing that the world contains a Jewish state.

———+———

But not any Jewish state. Roughly eighteen months ago, an Israeli friend sent me a video. It was of a Palestinian man named Fadel Jaber, who was being arrested for stealing water. His family had repeatedly asked Israeli authorities for access to the pipes that service a nearby Jewish settlement. But the Jabers have little influence over the Israeli authorities: like all Palestinians in the West Bank, they are subjects, not citizens. Partly as a result, West Bank Palestinians use roughly one-fifth as much water per person as do Jewish settlers, which means that while settlements often boast swimming pools and intensive irrigation systems, Palestinians fall far below the World Health Organization's recommended daily water consumption rate.

In the video, Israeli police drag Fadel toward some kind of paddy wagon. And then the camera pans down, to a five-year-old boy with a striped shirt and short brown hair, Khaled, who is frantically trying to navigate the thicket of adults in order to reach his father. As his father is pulled away, he keeps screaming, "Baba, Baba."

As soon as I began watching the video, I wished I had never turned it on. For most of my life, my reaction to accounts of Palestinian suffering has been rationalization, a search for reasons why the accounts are exaggerated or the suffering self-inflicted. In that respect, I suspect, I'm like many American Jews. But in recent years, for reasons I can't fully explain, I had been lowering my defenses, and Khaled's cries left me staring in mute horror at my computer screen.

Perhaps it is because my son is Khaled's age. He attends a Jewish school, has an Israeli flag on his wall, and can recount Bible stories testifying to our ancient ties to the land. When he was younger, we thought he would call me *Abba*, the Hebrew word for father. But he couldn't say Abba, so he calls me Baba, the same name Khaled calls his father.

One day, when they're old enough to understand, I'll tell his sister and him how my grandmother made me a Zionist. And one day, if they see a video like this, I'll tell them that unless American Jews help end the occupation that desecrates Israel's founding ideals, this is what Zionism will become, a movement that fails the test of Jewish power.

——+——

The shift from Jewish powerlessness to Jewish power has been so profound, and in historical terms so rapid, that it has outpaced the way many Jews think about themselves. One hundred years ago, Jews in Palestine lived at the mercy of their Ottoman overlords; Jews in Europe endured crushing, often state-sponsored, anti-Semitism; Jews in the Muslim world were frequently consigned to second-class status; and Jews in the United States lived at the margins of American life. Even fifty years ago, none of Israel's Arab neighbors recognized its right to exist, and some of those neighbors seemed to enjoy military parity with, if not superiority over, the Jewish state. Most of the Jews still in Europe lived under a tyrannical, anti-Semitic Soviet regime, and even in the United States, some Ivy League universities still limited the number of Jewish students who could attend.

Today, we inhabit a different world. Israel has made peace with two of its Arab neighbors, and all the Arab countries have offered to make peace if Israel ends its occupation of the West Bank and Gaza Strip, returns to the lines that prevailed before the 1967 Six-Day War, and reaches a "just" and "agreed upon" solution to the Palestinian refugee issue. Israel's defense budget easily exceeds those of its four immediate neighbors combined; it is the world's fifth-largest exporter of arms, and it is the only country in the Middle East with nuclear weapons.

In Europe, although anti-Semitism persists, the transformation of Jewish fortunes has been equally dramatic. Most Jews have left the former Soviet Union, and the vast majority of European Jews now live in democracies that ensure religious liberty. In Britain in recent years,

Jews have run Oxford and Cambridge universities, the Conservative Party, the Labor Party, and *The Times* of London. In France, the president proudly proclaims his Jewish ancestry, as did his first foreign minister. The foreign minister of Poland—Poland!—has a Jewish wife.

But even that pales in comparison to the United States, where in the last two decades Jews have served as secretary of state, secretary of the treasury, national security adviser, House majority leader, and White House chief of staff, and have held the presidencies of Harvard, Yale, and Princeton. Of the last six editors of *The New York Times*, four have been Jews. On the Supreme Court, Jews currently outnumber Protestants three to zero. A Jew recently married the daughter of a former president while wearing a tallis. According to polling by the Harvard political scientist Robert Putnam, Jews are now the most esteemed religious group in the United States.

Privately, American Jews revel in Jewish power. But publicly, we often avoid discussing it for fear of feeding anti-Semitic myths. The instinct is understandable but the consequences are grave. Because we don't talk much about Jewish power, we rarely grapple with the potential for its abuse. Instead, we tell ourselves that we are still history's victims, whose primary responsibility is merely to survive. Consider the language of prominent Jewish leaders. In 2009, the national director of the Anti-Defamation League, Abraham Foxman, declared that "global anti-Semitism [is] . . . reaching a peak this year that we haven't seen since the tragic days of World War II." In 2010, House Majority Leader Eric Cantor devoted his entire speech at the American Israel Public Affairs Committee (AIPAC) policy conference to an extended analogy with the Nazi era. That December, Malcolm Hoenlein, the powerful executive vice chairman of the Conference of Presidents of Major American Jewish Organizations, gave a speech entitled "Is It 1939?" (In a 2007 speech subtitled "Is It 1938 Again?" Hoenlein claimed, "There are no analogies that are perfect but there are similarities.")

But the rhetoric of American Jewish leaders hints at a deeper problem. Consider the way American Jews discuss our holidays. We tell the story of Chanukah as the story of the Jewish return to sovereignty. The Syrian Greeks tried to outlaw Judaism; the Maccabees rose in rebellion; they liberated and rededicated the Temple; God made the menorah's oil last for eight days. Then we eat our latkes. But what did Jews do after we gained power? What happened after we survived? The historical record tells us much about the Hasmonean dynasty—the last experiment in Jewish sovereignty before our time—much of it chilling. Yet we don't talk about that.

It's the same with Purim. Ask most American Jews how the Purim story ends and they will tell you that Haman tried to kill the Jews, but Esther and her uncle Mordechai foiled his wicked plan. But that isn't how the Purim story ends. It ends with the king giving Persia's Jews license to do to Haman's people what Haman wanted to do with them—and the Jews slaughtering seventy-five thousand souls. We don't talk about that either, because we begin our stories with victimhood and end them with survival. We talk about what the Egyptians did to us when we were slaves, but we rarely talk about what Joseph did to the Egyptians when Pharaoh put him in charge of the nation's grain. We discuss the Exodus, but we rarely discuss what happened afterward, when the Jews struggled to rule themselves in the desert. Again and again, we silence our tradition just when it becomes most relevant to our age. And so, as the joke goes, many American Jews think the lesson of Jewish history is "They tried to kill us; we survived; let's eat."

Given the fragility of Jewish life in the twentieth century, it is not surprising that American Jews—especially older ones—emphasize stories of persecution. But perpetual victimhood is not a narrative that can answer the two great Jewish challenges of our age: how to sustain Judaism in America, a country that makes it easy for Jews to stop being Jews, and how to sustain democracy in Israel, a country that for two-thirds of its existence has held the West Bank, a territory where its democratic ideals do not apply. Today, we are failing both challenges.

In city after city, American Jews have built Holocaust memorials. The Jewish schools in those cities are often decrepit, mediocre, and unaffordable, but there is no shortage of places to learn how Jews died. When a community builds better memorials than schools—when it raises children more familiar with Auschwitz than with Simchat Torah—the lesson of those memorials cannot be: *Honor the dead by leading informed, committed Jewish lives.* Nor is the lesson: *Honor the dead by acting justly toward those non-Jews who live under Jewish rule,* since mainstream Jewish organizations rarely grapple with the injustice inherent in occupying land in which Jews enjoy citizenship and non-Jews do not. Instead, the implicit lesson is: *Honor the dead by preventing another Holocaust, this time in Israel.* That lesson is reinforced by the vast sums that American Jewish groups spend on "Israel advocacy," on teaching young American Jews to defend the Jewish state against the viciously anti-Semitic climate that supposedly pervades their college campuses and the world.

But the Israel advocacy generally fails. For one thing, it is difficult to teach Jewish students to defend the Jewish state when they have not been taught to care much about Judaism itself. Second, it is intellectually insulting to tell young Jews who have been raised to think for themselves that they should start with the assumption that Israeli policy is justified, and then work backward to figure out why. Third, since young American Jews—more than their elders—take Jewish power for granted, the victimhood narrative simply doesn't conform to what they see in their own lives or in the Middle East.

For the most part, young American Jews don't experience their campuses as hostile or anti-Semitic. In 2008, when researchers at Brandeis asked students at eight universities whether it was easy to be Jewish on campus, 84 percent said yes and only 7 percent said no. To the contrary, Jewish students frequently befriend Muslims, Arabs, or Palestinians—communities that were far less present on campus in their parents' day—and thus develop an empathy that their elders often lack. They also realize that as a mostly white, native-born, upper-middle-class population, they occupy a position of privilege. When they look at the Middle East, they see Israel as powerful, too. American Jewish leaders often call Israel a democracy threatened with destruction by its neighbors, and that story line feels authentic to many older Jews who remember an Israel that did not hold the West Bank and Gaza, and faced Arab armies that seemed to enjoy military parity with the Jewish state. But younger American Jews have never known Israel as a full democracy. For forty-four years, twice a college student's life span, they have seen Israel control territory in which millions of Palestinians lack citizenship. And since the 1980s, they have seen Israel fight wars not against Arab armies but against terrorists nestled amid a stateless and thus largely defenseless Palestinian population. Thus, they are more conscious than their parents of the degree to which Israeli behavior violates democratic ideals, and less willing to grant Israel an exemption because it stands on the brink of destruction. The more the American Jewish establishment forces today's realities onto the procrustean bed of 1939 or 1967, the more young liberal-minded American Jews turn away.

We need a new American Jewish story, built around this basic truth: We are not history's permanent victims. In a dizzying shift of fortune, many of our greatest challenges today stem not from weakness but from power. If non-Orthodox American Jewish life withers in the coming generations, it will be less because gentiles persecute Jews than because they marry them. And if Israel ceases being a democratic Jewish state, it is less likely to be because Arab armies invade the West Bank than because Israel permanently occupies it.

The fact that Israel wields power does not mean it faces no external threats. But it does mean that Israel plays a larger role in shaping those threats than American Jewish leaders generally admit. Yes, the Islamist groups Hamas and Hezbollah traffic in anti-Semitism and murder Jews, but they gain strength when Israel—by subsidizing West Bank settlement and meeting nonviolent protesters with tear gas, rubber bullets, and military courts—discredits those Palestinians willing to live in peace. Yes, the populism sweeping the Middle East has unleashed frightening hostility against the Jewish state. But this hostility feeds off Israeli policy. As recently as 2005, the same government that rules Turkey today was signing military deals with Israel. In 2008, it tried to broker an Israeli-Syrian peace. Turkey only began shunning the Jewish state after Israel's 2009 war in Gaza, and after Israeli troops killed eight Turkish militants who tried to break Israel's blockade of the strip in 2010. Similarly, the Egyptian leaders who have emerged in Hosni Mubarak's wake are not generally calling for Israel's destruction, let alone promising to take up arms in that cause. But they are exploiting widespread anger that more than thirty years after the Camp David Accords, which called for Israel to grant Palestinians full autonomy in the West Bank and Gaza Strip, Israel still directly controls most of the West Bank and has subsidized hundreds of thousands of its people to move there. There is, of course, real anti-Semitism in today's Middle East. But by too often ascribing criticism of Israel to a primordial hatred of Jews, American Jewish leaders fail to grapple with Israel's own role in its mounting isolation. And by ignoring the fact that Jews today enjoy far more power to define their relationships with their neighbors than did Jews in the past, they imply that the Jewish condition has not fundamentally changed.

Accepting that the Jewish condition has fundamentally changed requires looking to our tradition for guidance about how Jews should treat the people we rule, not just how we should endure treatment from the people who rule us. That guidance will not always be comfortable: Jewish tradition offers no simple lessons for how to wield power, and the lessons it does teach can sometimes be hard for modern liberals to stomach. But it is striking that when describing the previous two times that Jewish sovereignty failed—the Kingdom of Judah's destruction by the Babylonian empire around 586 B.C.E. and the Hasmonean dynasty's destruction by the Romans more than five hundred years later—our tradition insists that physical collapse was preceded by ethical collapse.

Again and again, Jewish texts connect the Jewish right to sovereignty in the land of Israel to Jewish behavior in the land of Israel. In the words of Jeremiah, "If ye oppress not the stranger, the fatherless, and the widow, and shed not innocent blood in this place, neither walk after other gods to your hurt: Then will I cause you to dwell in this place, in the land that I gave to your fathers, for ever and ever."

Today, too, Israel's physical survival is bound up with its ethical survival. Whether or not Israel's nuclear weapons and antimissile shields can protect it from Iran, Hezbollah, and Hamas, they will be of no use on the day that hundreds of thousands of Palestinians march, nonviolently, to demand the very "equality of social and political rights" that Israel promises in its declaration of independence. And if American Jewish leaders continue to defend the Israeli government at the expense of Israeli democracy, they may find their own children and grandchildren cheering those protesters on.

I will try to give my son and daughter a sense of the immensity of what they have been given, of the agony that prior generations endured so that Jews could have a state. And I will tell them that their duty is to help ensure that this time, Jewish sovereignty does not fail. I will tell them, if they see that video of Khaled Jaber calling for his father, that I learned of his story because brave young Israelis chronicled it, Israelis who believe in the promise of Israel's independence declaration, which envisions a nation that pursues "freedom, justice, and peace as envisaged by the Hebrew Prophets." I will tell them that that pledge, made when the stench of Jewish death still hung over Europe, and amid a war for Israel's very existence, is their patrimony. If Israel betrays that promise, it will be a stain upon their lives. I will tell them about their great-grandmother, who spent her life fleeing sinking ships. And tell them that today Israel—democratic Israel—is the ship that must not sink. The birthright they must not squander. The dream that must not die.

1

The Crisis in Israel

A S A ZIONIST, I BELIEVE THAT AFTER TWO MILLENNIA OF HOME-
lessness, the Jewish people deserve a state dedicated to their
protection in their historic land, something enjoyed by many peoples
who have suffered far less. As a partisan of liberal democracy, I believe
that to honor that history of suffering, a Jewish state must offer equal
citizenship to all its inhabitants. In the spirit of Hillel, it must not do to
others what Jews found hateful when done to them. Are these principles
in tension? Absolutely. There will always be tension between Israel's
responsibility to the Jewish people and its responsibility to all its people,
Jewish and non-Jewish alike. But as the scholars Alexander Yakobson
and Amnon Rubinstein have noted, "Tension between values, in and of
itself, is no indication that one of the competing values is illegitimate."
If there is tension between Zionism and liberal democracy, there is also
tension between economic development and environmental protection,
or government spending and fiscal discipline, or civil liberties and
national defense, or many other goals that governments rightly pursue.

At the heart of the Zionist project is the struggle to reconcile these two valid but conflicting ideals. If Israel fails in that struggle, it will either cease being a Jewish state or cease being a democratic one. Today, it is failing, and American Jews are helping it fail.

Theodor Herzl would be distraught, but not surprised. The man who founded the Zionist movement did not merely want a Jewish state. He wanted a Jewish state that cherished liberal ideals. And he knew that to create such a state, Jews would have to wage a battle for its soul. In 1902, he wrote a novel called *Altneuland* (*Old New Land*) about a future Jewish country. Herzl's Jewish country is an impressive place. It guarantees freedom of speech and freedom of religion; rabbis enjoy "no privileged voice in the state." The book's hero, a presidential candidate named David Littwak, speaks Arabic, and one of his closest allies is an Arab engineer from Haifa. In their political party, Littwak tells a visitor, "We do not ask to what race or religion a man belongs. If he is a man that is enough for us."

But, Littwak admits, "there are other views among us." Their foremost proponent is a Rabbi Geyer, who seeks to strip non-Jews of the vote. Herzl modeled Geyer on an anti-Semitic demagogue in his native Austria, thus raising the specter that once Jews enjoyed power they might persecute others in the same way gentiles had persecuted them. The novel ends with the campaign between Littwak's party and Geyer's. "You must hold fast to the things that have made us great: To liberality, tolerance and love of mankind," one of Littwak's supporters tells a crowd. "Only then is Zion truly Zion!" In his final words, the outgoing president declares, "Let the stranger be at home among us." After a fierce contest, Littwak's party wins, Geyer leaves the country, and in the novel's epilogue, Herzl implores readers to make his Zionist dream come true.

As a vision of the Zionist future, *Altneuland* has its problems. While Herzl believed deeply in equality for individual Arabs, he could not imagine an Arab national movement demanding a state in Palestine of its own. (His rival, the cultural Zionist Ahad Ha'am, knew better, insisting that "This land is also their national home . . . and they have the right to develop their national potential to the best of their ability.") Still, for all its flaws, *Altneuland* shows that while Zionism was a nationalist movement, it was also, from the beginning, a liberal one. (Even those early Zionists who identified themselves as socialists mostly shared a liberal conception of freedom of conscience and equality under the law.) Zionism's founding fathers—men like Herzl, Moses Hess, and Leon Pinsker—were children of the Enlightenment. Earlier in their lives, each had hoped that as the nations of Europe dedicated themselves to the rights of man they would eventually extend those rights to Jews. When anti-Semitism refused to climb into history's grave, and instead reincarnated itself in racial, pseudoscientific form, the Zionist intellectuals lost faith in Europe and decided that only in their own state could Jews live safe, full lives. But they did not lose faith in Enlightenment ideals; they transplanted them. "We don't want a Boer state," wrote Herzl in his diary, expressing revulsion at racist Afrikaner nationalism. "But a Venice."

But Herzl knew that a tolerant, cosmopolitan republic like Venice was not preordained, that Jews were entirely capable of birthing a Boer state. This conflict, between the desire to build a Jewish state premised on liberal democratic principles and the temptation to flout those principles in the name of Jewish security and power, runs throughout the Zionist enterprise. It is the battle every Zionist generation wages against itself. In May 1948, in "The Declaration of the Establishment of the State of Israel," the state's founders promised "complete equality of social and political rights to all its inhabitants irrespective of religion, race or sex." Yet in the war that preceded and followed those majestic words, Zionist forces committed abuses so terrible that David Ben-Gurion, Israel's first prime minister, declared himself "shocked by the deeds that have reached my ears." In the town of Jish, in the Galilee, Israeli soldiers pillaged Arab houses, and when the residents protested, took them to a remote location and shot them dead. During the war, roughly 700,000 Arabs left Palestine, and irrespective of whether most left their homes voluntarily or were forced out, Israel refused to let them return.

In the struggle to build a Jewish state in the face of implacable foes, the liberal ideals outlined by Israel's founders were brutally flouted. But the fact that those liberal ideals existed at all created space for demo-cratic struggle. When the war of independence ended, Israel gave citizen-ship to the Arabs still living within its territory, which was more than the refugees gained in most of the Arab countries to which they fled. The rights of Israeli Arabs were curtailed, to be sure: in Israel's first decades, most lived under martial law. But Arab and Jewish Israelis joined together to protest this blatant discrimination, and in 1966 martial law was lifted. Massive inequities remained, but it was possible to believe that, slowly and fitfully, the gap between Zionism and liberalism was narrowing, that Israel was moving in the direction of Herzl's dream.

Then, in 1967, the Six-Day War turned history's trajectory upside down. With its Arab neighbors poised to attack, Israel struck first, fought brilliantly, conquered the West Bank of the Jordan River, among other territories, and began to settle the land (a process made easier by the Arab world's apparent refusal to offer peace, even if Israel gave the new territories back). For a country built by pioneers, this was natural. Set-tling land—especially land as rich with biblical meaning as the West Bank—was in the Zionist DNA. The problem was that this time, liberal ideals did not tether the Zionist project. A year after it eliminated its most flagrant discrimination against its own Arab citizens, Israel made itself master of millions of Palestinian Arabs who enjoyed no citizen-ship at all. Suddenly, Rabbi Geyer had a kingdom of his own.

———✦———

It is as if *Altneuland*'s election had ended with each party governing part of the land. In David Littwak's Israel, the Israel born in 1948, lib-eral Zionism, to some extent, exists. Israel's Arab citizens enjoy indi-vidual rights like freedom of speech, assembly, and worship. They sit in Israel's parliament, the Knesset, and on its Supreme Court. Arab Israe-

lis also enjoy the kind of group rights for which many ethnic and religious minorities yearn. They maintain their own religious courts and
their own, state-funded, Arabic-language schools and media. Indeed,
Arabic is one of Israel's official languages. Arab citizens have also made
dramatic educational and economic gains under Israeli rule. The political scientists Ilan Peleg and Dov Waxman note that in 1948 the illiter-
acy rate among Israeli Arabs was 80 percent. By 1988, it was 15 percent.

In a nation that has lived since its creation with the ever-present
threat of war—a strain that would have turned countries less nourished
by liberal ideals into police states—these are impressive accomplishments. The very anti-Zionist critics who attack Israel most ferociously
often rely on the work of Israeli historians, Israeli journalists, Israeli
human rights activists, and Israeli lawyers. Yet they rarely acknowledge
that the ability of Israelis, including Arab Israelis, to damn their government in the harshest of terms—and rarely see the inside of a prison
cell—says something admirable about the Zionist project. It is far from
clear that, under similar circumstances, any of the democracies that
criticize Israel's human rights record would have done better. Arab
Israelis, after all, share an ethnicity with the states and organizations
against which Israel has repeatedly gone to war. And some—though not
most—Arab Israelis sympathize with those adversaries. Certainly, no
American familiar with the way the United States government treated
German Americans during World War I, Japanese Americans during
World War II, or even Muslim Americans during the "war on terror"—
during wars that, unlike Israel's, mostly took place thousands of miles
from America's shores—has any cause for sanctimony.

Still, as important as it is to honor Israel's accomplishments, it is
even more important to deepen them. And while liberal Zionism is not
a fantasy within Israel's 1967 lines, it is far from a fully fledged reality.
The Or Commission, tasked by the Israeli government with investi-
gating conditions for Arab Israelis in 2003, found that "government
handling of the Arab sector has been primarily neglectful and discriminatory." This is especially true when it comes to social services. In

part because of historic restrictions on Arab access to Israeli public land, Arab citizens today own less than 4 percent of Israel's land even though they constitute almost 20 percent of its population. A 2010 study by the Organization for Economic Cooperation and Development found that Israel spends one-third more per Jewish Israeli student than per Arab Israeli student.

There are other inequities, too. While Arab political parties do serve in the Knesset, by long-standing tradition Israeli prime ministers do not include them in their governing coalitions. Most Arab Israelis do not serve in the Israel Defense Forces, a key vehicle for advancement in Israeli society. (Though a small Arabic-speaking religious minority, the Druze, and some Bedouin, do.) And perhaps most fundamentally, Israel's flag features a Jewish star, its national anthem speaks of "the Jewish soul," and its immigration policy grants Jews, and only Jews, instant citizenship. Israel is not unique in these respects. The British, Australian, New Zealand, Swiss, Greek, Slovak, Swedish, Norwegian, Finnish, and Danish flags all feature crosses. Germany, Ireland, Finland, Greece, Poland, Hungary, Bulgaria, Slovakia, Slovenia, Croatia, and the Czech Republic—all democracies—maintain immigration policies that favor members of the state's dominant ethnic group. But all this is cold comfort to Arab Israelis, most of whom feel like second-class citizens, and in important respects, truly are.

Reconciling Zionism and liberal democracy within Israel's 1967 lines requires two kinds of changes. First, it requires eliminating those inequities that are not inherent to Zionism itself. Being a Jewish state does not require Israel to pursue discriminatory land policies or to spend more on its Jewish citizens than on its Arab ones. To the contrary, such policies violate the "full and equal citizenship" promised Arab Israelis in Israel's declaration of independence. Similarly, maintaining a Jewish state should not prevent Arab parties from joining government coalitions. While it is true that the major Arab parties do not endorse Zionism, neither do some ultra-Orthodox Jewish parties that regularly sit in the Israeli cabinet. And while it is unrealistic to expect most Arab Israelis to serve in the military (an obligation from which ultra-Orthodox Jews are also largely exempt), the Israeli government should encourage, and eventually even require, them to perform some form of national service, making it clear that greater service to the state and better treatment from it go hand in hand. Finally, as Herzl makes clear in *Altneuland*, there is nothing in the Zionist project that requires Israel to cede control over marriage to clerics, thus forcing Jews who marry in Israel to be married by a rabbi and Christians or Muslims to be married by a minister or imam. Instituting civil marriage, and thus giving Arabs and Jews the right to marry inside Israel across religious lines, would not only mean greater liberty for Israel's Arab citizens but for its Jewish ones as well.

Accomplishing all this would be extremely difficult, but not impossible. In fact, one Israeli prime minister moved in exactly this direction. During his second stint in office, between 1992 and 1995, Yitzhak Rabin doubled spending on education for Arab Israelis, ended the discrepancy between the amount the government paid Jewish and Arab families per child, and built dozens of health clinics in Arab Israeli communities. He introduced affirmative action to boost the number of Arab citizens in Israel's civil service and, while he didn't formally include Arab parties in his government, he did rely on their support in the Knesset, and thus gave them an unofficial role.

But even if future Israeli leaders were to follow Rabin's path, they still would not eliminate the inequity in Zionism itself. As a Jewish state, Israel's anthem, flag, and Jewish right of return would still afford Jewish Israelis a sense of national belonging and national refuge that Arab Israelis lack. This fundamental tension between Zionism and liberal democracy cannot be fully resolved within Israel's borders. But it can, to some extent, be resolved outside them. Were Israel to permit the creation of a Palestinian state that enabled a Palestinian right of return and expressed Palestinian identity in its anthem and flag, Arab Israelis, like diaspora Jews, would have a country that expressed their special character as a people, even if they chose not to live there. The struggle for a liberal democratic Zionism, therefore, cannot be merely a struggle to afford Arabs individual and even group rights inside a Jewish state. It must also be a struggle to satisfy the Palestinians' national yearning for a state of their own. If Israel's founders endorsed the first goal in May 1948, when they created a Jewish state that pledged "complete equality of social and political rights to all its inhabitants irrespective of religion, race or sex," most Zionist leaders endorsed the second in November 1947, when they embraced the United Nations' plan to partition British Mandatory Palestine between a Jewish and Arab state. In recent decades, however, the struggle to achieve both these goals has been crippled by Israel's behavior in the land it conquered in 1967. For the past forty-four years, on the very land on which Palestinians might establish their state—the state that could help fulfill the liberal Zionist dream—latter-day Rabbi Geyers, secular and religious alike, have forged an illiberal Zionism that threatens to destroy it.

—⊣⊢—

The boundary between David Littwak's Israel and Rabbi Geyer's winds vertically from just below Nazareth in the north to just above Beersheba in the south. To the west of that line, Israel is a flawed but genuine democracy. To the east, it is an ethnocracy. In the Israel created in 1948, inequities notwithstanding, citizenship is open to everyone. In the Israel created in 1967, by contrast, Jews are citizens of a state whose government they help elect; Palestinians are not. Jews carry identity cards with blue covers, which allow them to travel freely among the West Bank, Jerusalem, and the rest of Israel. West Bank Palestinians carry identity cards with orange or green covers, which deny them access to East Jerusalem, large chunks of the West Bank, and the rest of Israel unless they gain a special—and hard-to-obtain—permit. Jews in the West Bank who violate Israeli law go before civilian courts that afford them the full measure of due process. Palestinians who violate Israeli law go before military courts where, according to a 2007 study by the Israeli human rights group Yesh Din, defendants are often held for months or even years before trial and where fewer than 1 percent are found innocent. This boundary, between a nation where Jewish power is restrained by democratic ideals and a territory where Jewish power runs wild, is called the "green line." Its existence is what keeps the possibility of liberal Zionism alive.

But the green line is fading. In 1980, around twelve thousand Jews lived east of democracy, with another seventy thousand or so in East Jerusalem, where Palestinians can seek Israeli citizenship but are not born with it. Today, that number is three hundred thousand (with roughly two hundred thousand more in East Jerusalem), and the Jewish population of the West Bank is growing at three times the rate of the Israeli population inside the green line. In 1980, the Knesset did not contain a single Jewish settler. Today, Israel's foreign minister lives halfway across the West Bank. Over time, democratic and nondemocratic Israel have become Siamese twins. They share the same telephone system, bus system, road system, rail system, water system, and electricity grid. In 2010, Prime Minister Benjamin Netanyahu called Ariel, a settlement that stretches thirteen miles into the West Bank, "the heart of our country." Many Israeli maps and textbooks no longer show the green line at all.

"The moment of truth," warns former Knesset speaker Avraham Burg, "is coming very fast." One day, maybe five years from now, maybe fifteen, maybe it has already happened, the green line will disappear: West Bank settlers will have grown so numerous and so entrenched within the Israeli government, rabbinate, and army that it will be impossible to remove enough of them to create a viable Palestinian state with a border near the green line. When that happens, Zionism as a liberal democratic project will die. If Israel honors the promise in its declaration of independence to provide "full equality of social and political rights" to all the people under its domain, a country of roughly 6 million Jews and 1.5 million Arabs will add close to 2.5 million new Arab citizens in the West Bank and another 1.5 million in the Gaza Strip, which, according to international law and the United States government, Israel still occupies even though no more Jewish settlers live there. And those new Arab citizens will have a population growth rate almost 50 percent higher than Israel's Jews. By honoring the democratic promises of its founders, Israel will commit suicide as a Jewish state.

Some on the far left yearn for that day. They believe that given the inequality inherent in Zionism, the only truly liberal option is a secular, binational state on all the land between the Jordan River and the Mediterranean Sea. But binationalism barely works in placid countries like Canada and Belgium. (It failed in Czechoslovakia, where in 1993 the Czech and Slovak populations opted for divorce.) Jews and Palestinians, by contrast, have spent much of the last century at war. Only a fantasist can imagine that the army they shared would be anything but a cloak for rival militias. Make Israel, the West Bank, and the Gaza Strip one country and you will resurrect the Jewish-Arab conflict of the 1930s, when Palestine was under British control. Except this time the British won't be there to play referee. The result won't be liberal democracy; it will be civil war.

If, on the other hand, Israel occupies the West Bank in perpetuity without granting citizenship to its Palestinian inhabitants, it will remain a Jewish state, but become an apartheid one. That prophecy may grate on Jewish ears, but it comes from two former Israeli prime ministers, Ehud Barak and Ehud Olmert, both of whom have warned that this will be Israel's fate if it permanently rules, but does not enfranchise, the Palestinians beyond the green line. In theory, Israel could remain a democracy within its 1967 lines even as it forever denied Palestinians in the occupied territories the right to vote. But as Abraham Lincoln famously observed, countries that try to practice freedom and despotism side by side generally "become all one thing or all the other." Or as Israel's finance minister, Pinchas Sapir, warned soon after the Six-Day War, "If we keep holding the territories, in the end the territories will hold us."

Every day, Sapir's prediction grows more true. On the one hand, within the green line, the struggle to fulfill the liberal democratic vision outlined at Israel's birth has continued. In the 1990s, the Knesset passed two "Basic Laws" that put legal scaffolding on the human rights guarantees in Israel's independence declaration, and in a series of stirring decisions, the Supreme Court has used those laws to bar the Israeli security services from practicing torture and from sentencing suspects who are not present at trial. These rulings, declared Chief Justice Aharon Barak, represent a "constitutional revolution," and there have been other liberal "revolutions" as well. In recent decades, Israeli historians have challenged cherished myths about Israel's founding, documenting that Israelis were victimizers, as well as victims, at their nation's birth.

But at the same time, Rabbi Geyer's Zionism has infected democratic Israel, stunting the growth of liberal values and spawning authoritarian ones in their stead. Take the prohibition on the use of violence to resolve political disputes, one of liberal democracy's most basic prerequisites. In the West Bank, that prohibition barely applies. "Settler attacks on Palestinians in the Occupied Territories," reports the Israeli human rights group B'Tselem, "have become routine." Some militant settlers, in fact, have formalized this violence in something called the "price tag" policy. For every Israeli government attempt to restrict settlement growth, they vandalize Palestinian homes, torch Palestinian fields, beat Palestinian men. For every act of law, a little pogrom.

Palestinians attack Jews in the West Bank, too, of course. In March 2011, for instance, two Palestinian men from the village of Awarta broke into the nearby settlement of Itamar and murdered Ehud and Ruth Fogel and three of their children, Yoav, Elad, and Hadas, in their beds. Elad, aged four, was strangled to death. Hadas, aged three months, was decapitated. The murderers later said that had they found the Fogels' three other children, they would have killed them, too.

But what distinguishes Palestinian terrorism and settler terrorism is the Israeli government's response. The Fogels' murder sparked a massive manhunt, which resulted in the killers serving five consecutive life terms in jail. Indeed, when Palestinians attack Jews, the Israeli army often puts entire villages under curfew, and perpetrators sometimes have their homes bulldozed. By contrast, according to a 2011 study by Yesh Din, fewer than 10 percent of reported settler attacks against Palestinians even result in indictments, let alone convictions. "For all practical purposes," explains the Israeli newspaper *Haaretz*, "the law is not the law, the settlers are the sovereign."

This culture of impunity would be dangerous enough were it confined to the West Bank. But people who grow habituated to lawlessness and violence do not shed those tendencies when they cross a line on a map. In 1996, a settler drove his car into one carrying Yossi Sarid, a cabinet minister from the dovish Meretz Party, trying to force it into a nearby ditch. The settler was later made a representative of the official settler body, the Yesha Council. In 2002, Hebrew University classics lecturer Amiel Vardi was shot while trying to help Palestinian farmers harvest their vineyards. The settler who shot him went free. In 2006, Baruch Marzel, a settler and the leader of the far-right Jewish National Front Party, declared at a campaign rally that the government should "carry out a targeted killing against [anti-occupation activist] Uri Avnery and his leftist collaborators." Marzel currently serves as an aide in the Knesset. In August 2008, a prominent rabbi in the settlement of Alon Shvut argued that members of the dovish group Peace Now might be eligible for the death penalty under Jewish law. The following month, Hebrew University professor Ze'ev Sternhell—a Holocaust survivor, veteran of four of Israel's wars, internationally renowned scholar of fascism, recent winner of the prestigious Israel Prize, and impassioned critic of the occupation—was wounded when a pipe bomb exploded at his home. Near the scene, police found flyers offering one million shekels to anyone who killed a member of Peace Now.

After the attack on Sternhell, Prime Minister Ehud Olmert warned that "an evil wind of extremism, of hate, of maliciousness, of violence, of losing control, of lawbreaking, of contempt for the institutions of state, is passing through certain sections of the Israeli public." This "evil wind" emanates from only a small minority of settlers. But in the words of General Gadi Shamni, who oversaw Israeli forces in the West Bank from 2007 to 2009, that small minority enjoys "the backing of part of the [settler] leadership, both rabbinical and public, whether in explicit statements or tacitly." For instance, Dov Lior, the head of the West Bank's rabbinical council, has called Baruch Goldstein, who murdered twenty-nine Palestinians at Hebron's Cave of the Patriarchs in 1994, "holier than all the martyrs of the Holocaust." In the mid-1990s, Lior and other prominent settler and pro-settler rabbis implied that Prime Minister Yitzhak Rabin's willingness to cede land to the Palestinians made him a *rodef* (pursuer) or *moser* (traitor), a transgression they claimed was punishable by death. Emboldened, one of their disciples, Yigal Amir, murdered Rabin as he was leaving a peace rally. Since then, Israel's internal security service, the Shin Bet, has repeatedly warned of new assassination plots against Israeli leaders suspected of being willing to give up parts of the West Bank.

———+———

But violence is only the most obvious way in which the antidemocratic culture of the West Bank menaces the culture of democratic Israel. Another is racism. The polling on Israeli Jewish attitudes toward Arabs is shocking. Seventy percent of Jewish Israelis, according to a poll by the Israel Democracy Institute, oppose appointing Arab Israelis to cabinet posts. A survey by the Friedrich Ebert Foundation found that 49 percent of Jewish Israelis aged twenty-one to twenty-four would not befriend an Arab. (Among Arab Israelis of the same age, 19 percent said they would not befriend a Jew.) Fifty-six percent of Jewish Israeli high school students, according to a survey by Tel Aviv University's School of Education, do not believe that Arab citizens should be allowed to run for the Knesset. And a poll by the Truman Institute at the Hebrew University reported that 44 percent of Jewish Israelis believe that Jews should avoid renting apartments to Arabs. (All of these polls were conducted in 2010.)

As painful as it is for Jews to admit that race hatred can take root among a people that has suffered so profoundly from it, the ground truth is this: occupying another people requires racism, and breeds it. It is very difficult to work day after day at a checkpoint, making miserable people bake in the sun, or to blow up a family's house as they watch, or to cut off water to a village in the Jordan Valley because Palestinians are barred from living in most of that section of the West Bank, and still see the people you are dominating as fully human. In democracies, too, of course, governments sometimes subject citizens to intrusive, even degrading, forms of control: people wait in endless lines for a document from some tyrannical clerk or watch the police tow away their car because they have not paid their parking tickets. But as citizens, they are not powerless. They can take legal recourse, even scream that they will get the offending official fired, and thus remind their tormentors that they are equals in the eyes of the law. In so doing, they not only assert their own dignity, they force the people in power to acknowledge it, too. In the West Bank, however, where Palestinians are barred from citizenship, that human leveling rarely occurs. When Israelis perform tasks that invite them to see Palestinians as less than fully human, and those Palestinians lack the power to prove them wrong, the result, in the words of the Israeli novelist David Grossman, is that "we set up a sort of 'block' in our souls . . . we accustom ourselves to relations like those between master and slave."

Research by the Hebrew University social psychologist Ifat Maoz has shown that the less Jewish Israelis interact with Arabs as equals, the less they support Arab and Palestinian rights. That is true for settlers, who in a 2010 Truman Institute poll were less than half as likely as other Jewish Israelis to cite democracy as Israel's most important value. But it is also true for many younger Jewish Israelis, who are less likely than their elders to have had an Arab acquaintance and thus more likely to have interacted with Palestinians in a sustained way only during their military service in the West Bank. Demographic changes also help explain why young Jewish Israelis are more intolerant than their elders. Still, it is no coincidence that the segment of Israeli Jewry most supportive of granting Arab citizens equal rights are the very people old enough to remember an Israel where every Arab actually was a citizen.

But the occupation breeds hatred even among Jewish Israelis who never set foot in the West Bank. The reason is that it breeds fear. Palestinians held for decades as noncitizens by an occupying army will periodically rebel, sometimes in dignified and nonviolent ways, sometimes in grotesque and unforgivable ways. And every time Palestinians in the West Bank commit violence, it foments hatred inside the green line. When Jewish Israelis are dying in terrorist attacks, they grow enraged at their fellow Arab citizens, whom they suspect of sympathizing with the enemy. And when Arab Israelis see the Israeli army killing their cousins—and they are often, literally, cousins—across the green line, they grow enraged at the Israeli government, and thus exhibit exactly the militancy that Jewish Israelis suspect them of.

There is a basic tension between Arab and Jewish Israelis. The Jewish Israelis want Israel to be a Jewish state; the Arab Israelis don't. But when the occupation recedes, Arab Israelis grow less hostile to the Jewish state, Jewish Israelis grow less hostile to Arab Israelis, and reconciling liberal democracy and Zionism becomes easier. It is no coincidence that the "golden age" of Jewish-Arab relations inside the green line took place under the prime ministership of Yitzhak Rabin in the 1990s, at the very time that he was launching the Oslo Accords. As Jewish Israelis grew less afraid of West Bank Palestinians, it became politically easier for Rabin to reach out to the Arab citizens of Israel. And as those Arab citizens saw movement toward greater equality inside the green line and toward a Palestinian state beyond it, they became more loyal to Israel. According to the sociologist Sammy Smooha of the University of Haifa, the percentage of Arab Israelis who rejected Israel's right to exist dropped from more than 13 percent in 1988, during the first intifada, to less than 7 percent by 1995, Rabin's last year in office. Over that same time span, the percentage of Jewish Israelis who opposed the right of Arab citizens to vote dropped from almost 43 percent to less than 31 percent.

Since then, this virtuous cycle has turned into a vicious one. When the second intifada erupted in the West Bank in 2000, Arab Israelis joined in, throwing stones, burning tires, and torching buildings. The Israeli police responded by killing thirteen Arab citizens. For many Jewish Israelis, it was confirmation that Arab Israelis were a fifth column, attacking the Jewish state just when it was most vulnerable. For Arab Israelis, it was confirmation that Jewish Israelis saw their lives as cheap. Since then, both sides have done their best to exacerbate the fears of the other. Arab Israelis are growing more radical. The percentage who reject Israel's right to exist, having dropped from 13 percent in 1988 to less than 7 percent in 1995, spiked to 24 percent in 2009. In 2003, Sheikh Ra'ed Salah, head of the "northern wing" of the Islamist movement in Israel, was arrested on suspicion of raising money for Hamas. In 2006, Arab Knesset member Azmi Bishara traveled to Lebanon, where he praised Hezbollah.

Many Jews have responded by embracing Avigdor Lieberman, who has rocketed to political power by targeting what he calls the "enemy within." Lieberman, whose Yisrael Beiteinu Party has grown from four Knesset seats in 1999 to fifteen today, is the political incarnation of the anti-Arab racism that the occupation breeds. He spent a brief period of his youth in Meir Kahane's Kach Party, which advocated expelling Arabs from Israel and criminalizing sex between Arabs and Jews. More recently, key members of Yisrael Beiteinu have called for amending Israel's Basic Law that promises equal marriage rights to Jews and non-Jews in order to deny citizenship to Arabs from outside Israel who marry Israel's Arab citizens. In 2006, Lieberman proposed revoking the citizenship of anyone who did not swear loyalty to the Israeli state, flag, and national anthem, and in 2009 he led an effort—which the leaders of the Likud, Kadima, and Labor parties also backed—to ban two anti-Zionist Arab parties from running for the Knesset. That same year, *Haaretz* reported that when Yisrael Beiteinu held its annual conference in the Galilee, a region where many Arab Israelis live, throngs of party activists chanted "Death to Arabs" at passing cars. In the 2009 elections, Lieberman's party came in third. In the mock voting held in Israeli high schools, it came in first.

Lieberman is currently Israel's foreign minister. He is joined in Benjamin Netanyahu's cabinet by housing minister Ariel Attias from the Sephardi ultra-Orthodox party, Shas, who in 2009 said he regards it "as a national duty to prevent the spread of a population that, to say the least, does not love the state of Israel"—in other words, Israel's Arab citizens. In the same speech, Attias volunteered that he does not "think that it is appropriate [for Arabs and Jews] to live together." Given those sentiments, it's no surprise that in 2011 the Knesset passed a law giving small Israeli communities greater latitude to bar Arab Israelis from moving in. Or that prominent lawmakers from Yisrael Beiteinu, Likud, and Kadima have all endorsed a law removing Arabic as one of Israel's official languages. "No other Knesset," notes *Haaretz*, "has submitted so many bills under the guise of 'preserving state security' that show open preference to Jews over Arabs in all walks of life."

This vicious cycle, in which the illiberal Zionism beyond the green line destroys the possibility of liberal Zionism inside it, not only breeds intolerance toward Arab Israelis; it also breeds intolerance toward dissident Jewish Israelis. The more Israel entrenches the occupation, the more isolated it grows around the world. And the more besieged Israelis feel by criticism from without, the less tolerant they become of criticism from within. In Israel today, it is not only Arab citizens who are routinely described in the language of treason, so are Jews who actively oppose Israel's policies in the West Bank. In 2011, according to the Israeli Democracy Institute, 53 percent of Jewish Israelis said "a speaker should be prohibited from harshly criticizing the Israeli government in public." In 2010, according to Tel Aviv University's Steinmetz

Center for Peace Research, 57 percent of Jewish Israelis said that human rights groups that expose "immoral" conduct by the state should not be permitted to operate freely, a ten-point increase since 2003. The message of the study, warned the Tel Aviv University social psychologist Daniel Bar-Tal, is that "the Israeli public is not tolerant or pluralistic."

Benjamin Netanyahu's government has exploited these sentiments, and fanned them, in an effort to cripple organizations that criticize the occupation. In early 2010, a right-wing group called Im Tirtzu claimed that the United Nations Commission led by Judge Richard Goldstone that harshly criticized Israel's conduct during the 2009 Gaza war had relied heavily on research by Israeli human rights organizations. A Knesset member from Netanyahu's Likud Party promptly charged the New Israel Fund, which funds some of those human rights groups, with treason, and a Knesset member (and settler) from Yisrael Beiteinu launched an investigation into Im Tirtzu's claims. The result was a bill to dramatically increase the administrative burden on Israeli human rights groups that receive funding from foreign governments. After an international uproar, the bill failed. But in 2011, Netanyahu endorsed new legislation, introduced by a Knesset member from Yisrael Beiteinu, to impose a special tax on Israeli human rights groups that receive foreign government funding. And that same year, the Knesset passed a law making it illegal for Israelis to boycott not only Israel as a whole, but even individual settlements, a practice advocated by prominent Israeli writers like David Grossman, Amos Oz, and A. B. Yehoshua. The terrible irony is that even as Israel's leaders defend the Jewish state against international isolation by invoking its liberal democratic character, their own policies are eroding it.

The vicious cycle is becoming a downward spiral. In 1988, after Meir Kahane advocated the forced "transfer" of Israel's Arab citizens from the country, his party was banned. In 2010, in a speech before the United Nations, Israel's foreign minister, the former Kahane disciple Avigdor Lieberman, proposed "right-sizing the state" by "moving borders to better reflect demographic realities." In other words, redrawing

Israel's border so as to exile hundreds of thousands of its Arab citizens against their will. When asked about his foreign minister's proposal, Benjamin Netanyahu said Lieberman's speech had not been coordinated with him, but did not disavow its substance.

"Population transfer," warns left-wing Knesset member Dov Khenin, "has turned from a nightmare into an operational plan." In 2009, Daniel Gordis, senior vice president of the Shalem Center, an Israeli think tank with close ties to the Netanyahu government, declared that while "on the surface, there are almost innumerable reasons to denounce transfer . . . the picture is not nearly as one-sided as it is often portrayed . . . population transfers do not need to be catastrophic for those moved." Perhaps, Gordis mused, Arab countries could be enticed to take in those Arab citizens that Israel expelled. "Alternatively, perhaps the international community could raise sufficient funds and offer massive cash settlements to those Israeli Arabs willing to relocate." Raising the subject, Gordis declared, "has filled me with . . . pain," but Israelis must "finally confront head-on the *kinds* [his italics] of choices that they will soon have to make." Many, it seems, are ready. A 2010 poll by the Israeli Democracy Institute found that 53 percent of Jewish Israelis want their government to encourage Israel's Arab citizens to leave.

Just one politician, one commentator, one poll. But in the words of retired Israeli judge Boaz Okon, "Like in a children's connect-the-dots coloring book, where connecting random dots creates a picture, so in Israel, if you connect a number of horrifying, multiplying incidents, you begin to see a monster." The Israelis most committed to liberal democracy see Herzl's dream slipping away. And here in the United States, the most powerful leaders of the American Jewish establishment insist on seeing almost nothing at all.

2

The Crisis in America

DAVID STEINER: Don't have many left. Everybody got . . .

CHAIM KATZ: Let me tell you. The same with me. Let me tell you, my parents were the only ones who came out. Let me tell you, my . . .

STEINER: You're a Holocaust survivor?

KATZ: Yeah, no, not me, my parents.

STEINER: That's some experience, I've got two cousins, I've got one in Israel and one in France that came out of Mauthausen, I'll tell you, and everybody else dead on my father's side . . .

KATZ: Right. Let me tell you that, you know what my father always says? My father was a rich man in Poland, and he says, he says, "Economic power is very good. You have to have money, but if you just have economic power and you don't have political power . . ."

STEINER: You've got nothing.

KATZ: You've got nothing.

STEINER: If we had AIPAC in the '30s and '40s, we would have
saved millions of Jews. We would have the political power. But
Jews were afraid to open their mouths. They didn't know how.

> —Conversation between American Israel Public Affairs
> Committee (AIPAC) president David Steiner and
> New York real estate developer Chaim Katz, October
> 22, 1992

THE AVERAGE LARGE DONOR TO A MAJOR AMERICAN JEWISH
organization is in his fifties, sixties, or seventies. He has worked
hard in his life and achieved status and wealth. Now partially freed
from the burden of making money, he can devote some of his time to
the things he cares about most. And what he cares about most, upon
reflection, is the Jewish people. He remembers a time when he was not
so wealthy and esteemed, when being an American Jew was not all
sweetness and light. He remembers his parents, shaking with fear, in
1967, in the run-up to the Six-Day War, when it seemed that Israel might
be destroyed. He does not remember the Holocaust; he is too young for
that. But he has immersed himself in it. He has read more books about
it, watched more movies about it, had more conversations about it, than
about any other aspect of Jewish history, by far. When he goes to synagogue, he is often bored. When he goes to a Holocaust memorial, by
contrast, he is overcome. And now, in the autumn of his life, he is
playing his own role in the great struggle for Jewish survival. In the
1940s, when the Jews of Europe cried out from their ghettos and cattle
cars, the Jews of America did little. Those Jews—he grew up around
them—were tailors and shopkeepers; they were marginal, fatalistic,
timid. What could you expect of them? Now the Jewish people, he
believes, are again imperiled, this time in the very homeland created to
give Jews refuge. But this time, their American brethren are people like
him. They are not powerless and they are not afraid. If he goes to an
AIPAC event, he may hear this story: In 1945 an American Jewish soldier helped liberate a concentration camp. Seeing his name tag, one of

the survivors asked the soldier if he was Jewish. The soldier answered yes, expecting a tearful embrace. Instead, the survivor slapped him and said, "You're too late." I have heard this story many times at AIPAC functions. The room goes silent. The donor thinks to himself: "Not this time." And he writes his check.

I feel I know this large donor. I know him, and like other younger Jews, I owe him. Through his tenacity, he has helped fling open America's doors to us. His devotion to the Jewish people is earnest and admirable; I wish it were shared by more of my peers. But he is living a double tragedy. He wants nothing more than to ensure Jewish survival. Yet the real struggle for Jewish survival is taking place in his own family, where his children are producing non-Jewish grandchildren. And why shouldn't they? If he was bored at synagogue, so were they. If he knows little about Judaism, and finds in it little meaning or joy, they find even less. He had no choice but to live separately as a Jew; in his day, Christian girls were still shiksas. But his children do have a choice, and they are availing themselves of it. When he tries to enlist them in the grand drama of Jewish victimhood that has replaced Judaism in his own life, they look at him like he's from Mars. Isn't Israel taking the Palestinians' land? they ask, to his dismay. And can he please stop talking about anti-Semitism in front of Kristin and the kids?

This is his private Jewish tragedy. Meanwhile, he is contributing to a public Jewish tragedy halfway across the world. What he is buying for Israel, with his check, is American indifference—indifference to Palestinian suffering and indifference to the principles in Israel's declaration of independence. When Israel subsidizes Jews to move across the green line or imprisons Palestinians for protesting nonviolently in the West Bank or makes it illegal to boycott settlement goods, he helps ensure that the American government will not care. At home, he is losing the struggle for Jewish survival, and with his check, he is helping to ensure that Israel loses the struggle for Jewish democracy.

At the core of the tragedy lies the refusal to accept that in both America and Israel, we live in an age not of Jewish weakness, but of

Jewish power, and that without moral vigilance, Jews will abuse power just as hideously as anyone else. American Jewish organizations do not deny that Jews wield power; privately, they exult in it. Emotionally, power is what groups like AIPAC sell: the power to be a modern-day Esther, whispering in the ear of the king and saving your people from destruction. What they don't acknowledge is what happens at the end of the Purim story. By discussing power only as a means of survival, the American Jewish establishment implicitly denies that Jews can use power for anything *but* survival. They deny that Jews, like all human beings, can use power not merely to survive, but to destroy. A few years ago, a journalist reported that Malcolm Hoenlein, the influential executive vice chairman of the Conference of Presidents of Major American Jewish Organizations, had a photo in his conference room of Israeli F-15s flying over Auschwitz. It is a photo of a fantasy. Israeli jets never bombed Auschwitz and never will. What they have bombed, in recent years, is the Gaza Strip, a fenced-in, hideously overcrowded, desperately poor slum from which terrorist groups sometimes shell Israel. Hoenlein, in other words, has decorated his conference room not with an image of the reality that he helps perpetuate, but with an image of the fantasy he superimposes on that reality. In this way, he embodies the American Jewish establishment, which, by superimposing the Jewish past on the Jewish present, is failing the challenge of a new age.

——————

There is a terrible irony here. Perhaps no group of Jews has ever made liberalism—the belief in individual freedom and equality of opportunity, irrespective of gender, religion, race, or creed—as central to their identity as have American Jews. For close to a century, despite growing ever richer, American Jews have baffled political scientists by voting every four years for the major presidential candidate most likely to give their money to the poor. In 2008, they supported Barack Obama, a black man with a Muslim father, at roughly twice the rate of white Christians, and at a higher rate than did women, Hispanics, or lesbians and gays. In 2004, when asked by the American Jewish Committee what best defines their Jewish identity, as many Jews chose "social justice" as chose "religious observance" and "support for Israel" combined. In 2011, according to Gallup, American Jews were the religious group most likely to say that American Muslims face widespread discrimination—more likely, even, than American Muslims themselves.

How did a Jewish community famed for its liberalism create a communal leadership so reluctant to defend liberal democracy in the Jewish state? The answer is simple: today's American Jewish establishment was not born from American Jewish liberalism; it was born as a reaction against it. America's major Jewish organizations are less and less representative of most American Jews, they do not champion democracy within Israel, they have retreated from the struggle for a more equal democracy in the United States, and all too often, they justify this by claiming it is 1939. They are, in important ways, exactly what the founders of American Zionism did not want American Zionism to be.

The founders of American Zionism were mostly liberals, broadly defined. They saw Zionism as roughly akin to the progressive causes that they championed in the United States. Louis Brandeis, the most important American Zionist leader of the early twentieth century, often remarked that he came to his Zionism through his Americanism. He saw in the kibbutz movement the chance to build a society free from the corporate monopolies that he believed had perverted democracy in the United States. "It is democracy that Zionism represents," Brandeis told a Boston crowd in 1915. "It is social justice which Zionism represents, and every bit of that is the American ideals of the twentieth century." At around the same time Brandeis's ally, Henrietta Szold, created Hadassah, the Women's Zionist Organization of America, whose efforts at improving health care for both Arabs and Jews in Palestine mimicked the work that progressives like Jane Addams were doing in poor neighborhoods in the United States. The man who became American Zionism's public face after Brandeis joined the Supreme Court, Rabbi Stephen Wise, was a famed campaigner for women's suffrage, labor rights, and the minimum wage. And the man who supplanted him in the 1940s, Rabbi Abba Hillel Silver, described the movement for a Jewish state as treading "the common ground between Zionism and liberalism, Judaism and America." In the words of the historians Deborah Dash Moore and S. Ilan Troen, "From Louis Brandeis around World War I to Abba Hillel Silver after World War II, Zionism has been defined as a form of American liberalism."

Central to that liberalism was the belief that not only should a Jewish state be democratic, but American Jewish organizations should be democratic, too. In the first years of the twentieth century, when wealthy, anti-Zionist German Jews dominated the powerful American Jewish Committee, Brandeis and Wise resented what they considered the Committee's effort to squelch open debate about the desirability of a Jewish state. Railing against "the undemocratic, un-American, un-Jewish method of dictation from above," Wise—with Brandeis's support—in 1918 helped create the democratically elected American Jewish Congress, which gave voice to the poor, Zionist masses flooding in from Eastern Europe. "The time is come," Wise declared, "for a leadership by us to be chosen, a leadership that shall democratically and wisely lead rather than autocratically command."

With the exception of Szold and Hebrew University founder Judah Magnes, whose fears about Jewish-Arab coexistence led them to support a secular, binational state, most early American Zionist leaders did not focus on how to meld their democratic vision with the national aspirations of the local Arab population. And by the 1930s, when riots destroyed the naive belief that Palestinian Arabs would welcome a Jewish state, many American Zionists were too focused on the desperate struggle to help Jews escape Europe to take much note of Arab concerns. But for all their ignorance of, and condescension toward, the local Arab population, most early American Zionists genuinely believed that democracy lay at the heart of the Zionist idea, and they were not afraid to criticize Zionist leaders who threatened that vision. In 1935, Wise denounced Vladimir Jabotinsky's Revisionist Zionism, with its hostility to territorial compromise and glorification of military power, as "a species of fascism," a view that Silver echoed three years later. In 1964, a report by the American Jewish Committee declared, "in our support for Israel, our guiding principle has always been that such support be consistent . . . with the rights of the individual, be he Jew or non-Jew. As Americans, we have not hesitated to withhold this support or to disagree publicly when Israel's actions appeared to depart from the principle." In 1969, Nahum Goldmann, president of the World Jewish Congress and one of the founders of the Conference of Presidents of Major American Jewish Organizations, criticized the Israeli government for having "become committed to demands, both tactical and fundamental, that even the most moderate of Arabs can hardly be expected to accept."

If American Jewish leaders agitated for a democratic Jewish state, they also agitated for a more democratic United States. In the half-century between World War I and the Six-Day War, American Jewish organizations repeatedly linked the struggle for Jewish acceptance to the broader struggle for a more just and tolerant America, even when that meant allying with the most despised and brutalized groups in American life. The Anti-Defamation League, founded in 1913, paired its mission "to stop . . . the defamation of the Jewish people" with a campaign against "unjust and unfair discrimination against and ridicule of any sect or body of citizens." In the 1920s, the presidents of the American Jewish Committee and American Jewish Congress both served on the board of the NAACP. In the 1940s, the American Jewish Congress employed seven attorneys to fight segregation, more than either the NAACP or the Department of Justice. In the 1950s, the American Jewish Committee funded the research by African American psychologist Kenneth Clark that helped sway the Supreme Court in *Brown v. Board of Education*. In 1956, Israel Goldstein, president of the American Jewish Congress, declared that both the "fulfillment of the American dream" and the "fulfillment of the Zionist dream" required addressing "the problem affecting the American Negro."

This was not pure altruism, to be sure. As a conspicuous minority, Jews reasoned that a more inclusive America would also benefit them. But if Jewish support for civil rights and civil liberties was self-interested, it was self-interest of the most enlightened kind. For the most powerful American Jewish organizations of the mid-twentieth century—the ADL, American Jewish Committee, American Jewish Congress, Council of Jewish Federations (American Jewry's philanthropic arm), Union of American Hebrew Congregations (representing the Reform movement), United Synagogues of America (representing the Conservative movement), and Synagogue Council of America (an umbrella for Reform, Conservative, and Orthodox Jews)—Zionism was one component of a broad liberal agenda, as it had been for Brandeis, Wise, and Silver. By contrast, AIPAC, which took no interest in the liberal domestic agenda, was, on the eve of the 1967 war, obscure and nearly bankrupt.

Then, in the aftermath of the Six-Day War, American Jewish liberalism and organized American Zionism began drifting apart. It didn't look that way at first. In the terrifying days before the war, when Egypt, Syria, Iraq, and Jordan massed their armies and announced their intention to wipe out the Jewish state, American Jews rallied behind Israel as never before. A fund-raising lunch in New York netted $15 million in fifteen minutes. A small congregation in Oklahoma sold its synagogue building and sent Israel the proceeds. American Jewish organizations raised so much money in such a short time that their bookkeepers could not keep up.

When Israel won a shocking, lightning victory, American Zionism hit fever pitch. Between 1968 and 1971, the number of American Jews immigrating annually to Israel rose by a factor of eight. But if Israel's victory increased its power, it did not bring global acceptance. To the contrary, most of the Soviet bloc broke diplomatic relations with the Jewish state, and, partnering with leftist regimes in the third world, in 1975 pushed a resolution through the United Nations General Assembly equating Zionism with racism. A parallel trend occurred in the United States, where African American and other leftist activists who had previously marched with Jews for civil rights and against the Vietnam War began denouncing Israel as an artifact of Western imperialism.

Watching these trends with dismay, American Jewish leaders hit upon an explanation: the world was turning against Jews because it no longer saw them as victims. In 1974, Benjamin Epstein, the national director of the Anti-Defamation League, coauthored *The New Anti-Semitism*, a book whose argument proved so influential that in 1982 his successor, Nathan Perlmutter, echoed it in a book entitled *The Real Anti-Semitism in America*. Epstein's argument was that for a period after World War II, guilt over the Holocaust had kept anti-Semitism at bay. But with memories of the Holocaust fading, anti-Semitism had returned, largely in the form of hostility to Israel, because Israel represented Jewish power. "Jews are tolerable, acceptable in their particularity, *only* [his emphasis] as victims," wrote Epstein and his ADL colleague Arnold Forster, "and when their situation changes so that they are either no longer victims or appear not to be, the non-Jewish world finds this so hard to take that the effort is begun to render them victims anew."

Epstein and Forster understandably felt that much of the criticism of Israel was excessive. But if Israel's critics were unfairly judging the way Israel exercised its newfound might, Epstein and Forster ducked the question altogether. At exactly the moment that Israel's occupation of the West Bank and Gaza Strip made it essential for American Jews to reckon with the ethical challenges of Jewish power, American Jewish leaders began insisting that to even acknowledge the misuse of Jewish power was to deny Jewish victimhood and thus victimize Jews anew. The argument caught on: in the 1970s, victimhood, especially as a strategy for defending Israel, supplanted liberalism as the defining ideology of organized American Jewish life.

Before 1967, in keeping with their effort to link the struggle against anti-Semitism to the struggle against bigotry more generally, American Jewish groups had frequently universalized the lessons of the Holocaust. In 1960, when Israel arrested and tried the former Nazi official Adolf Eichmann, the ADL insisted that the trial was "not a case of special pleading for Jews" because "what happened to the Jews of Europe . . . can very well happen to other peoples." The American Jewish Committee declared that the trial was aimed at combating all forms of "hatred and totalitarianism . . . and their continued presence in the world today." But in the 1970s, American Jewish organizations began hoarding the Holocaust, retelling it as a story of the world's eternal hatred of Jews, and linking it to criticism of Israel. In 1973, the ADL embarked on a "new international mission" to combat "Arab anti-Israel propaganda" and four years later created a Center for Holocaust Studies. In 1980, the ADL's Oscar Cohen advised the National Conference of Christians and Jews to link its Holocaust programming "to Israel and the dangers which confront" it. The following year, as part of its bid to prevent the Reagan administration from selling AWACS surveillance planes to Saudi Arabia, AIPAC sent a copy of the novel *Holocaust* to every member of Congress.

This new emphasis on Jewish victimhood was aimed not only at gentiles; it was also aimed at young Jews. Since the 1960s, American Jewish leaders had been growing increasingly worried about intermarriage, which had spiked dramatically in the postwar years. In 1972, when CBS began airing *Bridget Loves Bernie*, a sitcom about the exploits of a Jewish cabdriver married to a Catholic teacher, Jewish groups demanded that it be canceled. In 1976, the American Jewish Committee held its first national conference on intermarriage and followed up with its first nationwide study. By 1979, the associate editor of the American Jewish Committee's annual publication, *The American Jewish Yearbook*, was calling intermarriage "the single most pressing problem confronting the organized Jewish community."

Victimhood offered an answer. Young American Jews' "lack of a sense of 'being Jewish,'" declared American Jewish Committee president Bertram Gold in 1970, stemmed from the fact that the Holocaust was not "seared into the memory of a generation born after World War II." In 1972, the magazine of the American Jewish Congress warned that young Jews "depreciate ethnic or group loyalties" because "they didn't live through the period of the Holocaust . . . and they don't pay much attention to history." In the 1970s, Holocaust education exploded in Jewish schools, with curricula often featuring texts, and even simulations, designed to help children imagine that they were experiencing the trauma firsthand. "Why? Two generations later, why does the memory of the Holocaust loom larger for Jews?" asked the ADL's Nathan Perlmutter and his wife, Ruth Ann, in 1982. In part "so that our children will know who they really are, so that they will not mistake the comfortable facts of their acculturation for the uncomfortable truth of their vulnerability."

In its embrace of victimhood as a strategy for dealing with gentiles and younger Jews, the American Jewish establishment was turning away from the universalism that had defined it for a half-century. Jews were not alone in this regard. To some degree, they were copying African American activists, whose decision to spurn alliances with white liberals allowed Jews to begin turning inward as well. As the civil rights coalition collapsed in the late 1960s and 1970s, Jewish charities began redirecting their money toward exclusively Jewish causes. The American Jewish Committee, which before 1967 had been so universalistic that it considered dropping the word "Jewish" from its name and calling itself the Institute for Human Relations, began sending its entire staff to a month-long Zionist education program in Israel. The group least able to make the switch, the American Jewish Congress, which still reflected Brandeis's and Wise's passion for civil liberties and equality of opportunity, began a decline that would culminate in its dissolution. Liberalism was out; tribalism was in. American Jews, wrote the American Jewish Committee's research director, Milton Himmelfarb, had "relearned the old truth that you can depend only on yourself. . . . We relearned the old, hard truth that only you can feel your own pain."

———+———

But who, exactly, was "we"? Even as the American Jewish establishment lurched right, the mass of American Jews remained as liberal as ever. In the presidential elections of 1972 and 1976, Jews voted for George McGovern and Jimmy Carter at higher rates than they had voted for Adlai Stevenson in 1952 and 1956. One reason was that most American Jews simply did not believe that the world was turning against them. Although bothered by international condemnation of Israel, American Jews also saw the Jewish state emerging—via its territorial acquisitions in 1967 and its burgeoning alliance with the United States—as a regional superpower. And while suspicious of the far left at home, most American Jews did not feel menaced by a "new anti-Semitism"; to the contrary, the barriers to their acceptance into the highest echelons of American life continued to fall. That, in a way, was the whole point. As they integrated further into American society, American Jews had less need for exclusively Jewish organizations. While in the 1950s a liberal-minded Jew concerned about race relations or separation of church and state might have expressed her activism through the American Jewish Congress, by the 1970s Jews were eminently comfortable operating through the American Civil Liberties Union or the National Organization for Women. Beginning in the 1970s, the number of American Jews donating to Jewish groups sharply fell. American Jews, in other words, weren't abandoning liberalism. Rather, they were removing their liberalism from an explicitly Jewish context, leaving Jewish organizations disproportionately in the hands of those who believed that gentiles didn't care about Jews and that Jews had little obligation to care about them.

In the 1980s, the ideological gulf widened between American Jews and the organizations that claimed to represent them. When Jabotinsky's heir, Likud leader Menachem Begin, became Israel's prime minister in 1977, and Ronald Reagan entered the White House in 1981, even the attenuated liberalism of groups like the American Jewish Committee and the ADL became a liability. How could organizations rooted in American liberalism and Labor Zionism effectively influence the Revisionists governing Jerusalem and the Christian conservatives governing Washington? Suddenly AIPAC, whose indifference to liberal values in the United States had once contributed to its marginality, took center stage. AIPAC's executive director, Tom Dine, was a former aide to Senator Ted Kennedy. But after the elections of Begin and Reagan, he recruited a cluster of conservative donors and used AIPAC's ties to the American and Israeli right to outpace the older organizations in influence. He succeeded all too well. By 1993, those conservative donors had ousted him, and in 1996 they installed an official from the Republican Jewish Coalition in AIPAC's top job. Similarly, in 1986, the Conference of Presidents of Major American Jewish Organizations, the umbrella group deputized since the 1950s with lobbying the executive branch on Israel policy, hired Malcolm Hoenlein, an activist with ties to the settler movement, as its top staffer. America's Jewish communal leaders, declared the Jewish journalist J. J. Goldberg, were becoming "ever more incomprehensible to the majority of their fellow Jews."

—————

Israel's policies deepened the rift. With the exception of the waning American Jewish Congress, mainstream American Jewish organizations still described Israel as a victim-state, besieged by aggressors. But to many American Jews, Begin's 1982 invasion of Lebanon looked more like reckless adventurism than self-defense. A 1983 American Jewish Committee poll found that 48 percent of American Jews were "often troubled by the policies of the current Israeli government." In 1986, 63 percent said that American Jews had the right to criticize Israeli actions. In 1989, more than half of American Jews told an American Jewish Committee survey that they disagreed with Israel's response to the first intifada. By the late 1990s, almost two-thirds supported establishing a Palestinian state and a large majority supported halting settlement growth. In 2005, three-quarters of American Jews said they supported U.S. pressure on both Israel and the Palestinians if it would help bring a peace deal.

Those numbers have held steady in the years since. American Jews are not left-wing on Israel: they generally distrust Palestinian intentions and support Israel's wars, at least initially. And as with all polling, much depends on how one asks the question. But in their support for a halt to settlement growth and their comfort with public criticism of Israeli policy, the mass of American Jews are to the left of the organizations that speak in their name, organizations that almost always oppose U.S. pressure on Israeli leaders and blame the Palestinians almost exclusively for the lack of Middle East peace.

But it doesn't really matter because American Jewish organizations are not accountable to the mass of American Jews. Brandeis's and Wise's vision of a democratized Jewish community may have been unrealistic. But before the 1970s, when a higher percentage of American Jews participated in Jewish organizations, and those organizations pursued a liberal agenda that mirrored the community's general political outlook, Jewish organizations were at least broadly representative. Today, by contrast, as the pool of donors to specifically Jewish causes has shrunk, and escalating income inequality has left rich Americans exponentially richer, America's major Jewish groups have come to resemble the "American Jewish peerage" that Wise warned against. Far more than in the past, a small number of large donors now sustain American Jewish groups, and far more than in the past, they set the agenda.

As a result, American Jewish leaders can afford to dismiss—and even mock—the opinions of most American Jews. Consider this 2009 interview with Malcolm Hoenlein conducted by a right-leaning Jewish talk-show host named Nachum Segal:

SEGAL: The majority of Jews in the United States are for a two-state solution.

HOENLEIN: That's true, too, even though they couldn't define it.

SEGAL (*laughing*): Or tell us the implications of it.

HOENLEIN: Or understand what it means.

In the words of Yossi Beilin, a shrewd Israeli observer of American Jewry, "The American Jewish community may be characterized as a sort of plutocracy, dominated by its most affluent members." And since the 1970s, when liberal donors began exiting Jewish philanthropy, it has been anti-Semitism and Israel—especially anti-Semitism *directed at* Israel—that convinces those affluent members to open their wallets. The ADL still does valuable work promoting tolerance in the United States, but that work has been so eclipsed by its focus on defending Israel against alleged anti-Semitism that one former longtime staffer calls the group's current anti-discrimination work "window dressing." A major reason is fund-raising. The "ADL is first and foremost a fund-raising organization," explains another former official. "[National director] Abe [Foxman] and his inner circle are beholden to no one else but the philanthropic dollar." And "the big donors are the Palm Beach retirees who think there's an anti-Semite behind every door." At the American Jewish Committee, the dynamic is similar. In 2009, a top AJC official told a regional representative, "Your little Christian-Jewish dialogue is very nice but remember, whatever you do with your inter-group relations, the end game is always Israel." While the Committee has a laudable program promoting global human rights, a former staffer concedes that it "doesn't bring in money." What donors are "interested in is Iran, anti-Semitism and something that someone said about Israel that was bad." The American Jewish Congress learned this lesson the hard way. When the group finally dissolved in 2010, the Jewish Tele-graphic Agency reported that while it "was doing important work, focusing on issues of religious freedom in the United States, free speech and women's rights, those simply did not resonate with donors who show more interest in Israel and anti-Semitism."

Donors inclined to see Israel as perpetually besieged by Jew-haters are disinclined to wrestle with the occupation's impact on Israeli democracy. And that unwillingness is built into the fund-raising models of the groups themselves. In significant measure, what large donors to mainstream American Zionist organizations get for their money is access to top Israeli officials. As Tom Dine puts it, "These guys live to tell stories about how I had dinner with so and so." Among American Jewish groups, competition for such meetings is intense, and publicly criticizing a sitting Israeli government is an excellent way not to procure them. In 2009, when the liberal Jewish advocacy group J Street was founded with the goal of challenging Israeli policy in the West Bank, it was denied meetings with the Israeli ambassador in Washington and with the Foreign Ministry in Jerusalem.

The need to curry favor with Israeli leaders also influences American Jewish groups in more subtle ways. When these groups take donors to Israel, they do so as guests of the Israeli government, which heavily influences who and what they see. As a former ADL official puts it, "They feel it's a betrayal of your hosts if you meet with too many Palestinians." In 2011, a group of Jewish officials from Britain canceled a trip to the West Bank under reported Israeli government pressure. As a result, even donors who travel to Israel frequently rarely get a ground-eye view of the occupation. After traveling in the West Bank with Encounter, a nonprofit that exposes American Jews to Palestinian life, one senior Federation official commented, "I felt like I had never been to Israel before, and I am considered a professional Israel expert who travels to Israel several times a year."

Ignorance of Palestinian suffering breeds indifference, if not contempt. Call them "Arabs, not Palestinians," instructed the pollster Frank Luntz in a 2005 report to American Jewish leaders. "The term 'Palestinians' evokes images of refugee camps, victims and oppression," while

"Arab says wealth, oil and Islam." A former American Jewish Committee employee remembers being struck by the "visceral hostility to Palestinians" he encountered among his coworkers, and their delight at uncovering evidence that some Palestinians in the Gaza Strip—a place where the unemployment rate nears 50 percent—have swimming pools.

———+———

When it comes to Israel, there are today two kinds of mainstream American Jewish organizations: those whose tolerance for the occupation is warping their historic commitment to democratic ideals and those with no commitment to democratic ideals at all. The ADL and the American Jewish Committee fall into the former category. At times, they try earnestly to fulfill their stated missions of battling "unfair and unjust discrimination" (ADL) and advancing "human rights and democratic values" (AJC), including in the Jewish state. In 2006, both joined an American Jewish task force aimed at improving the lives of Arab Israelis. In 2009, AJC leaders warned that Avigdor Lieberman's proposed loyalty oath bill "would chill Israel's democratic political debate." In 2011, the ADL said that the Knesset law outlawing boycotts of Israel and Israeli settlements "may infringe on basic democratic rights." But these laudable efforts to defend the rights of Israeli citizens make it all the more extraordinary that neither organization publicly challenges the occupation, which denies millions of Palestinians any citizenship at all.

Ethically, the ADL and AJC are caught between the liberalism that defined organized American Jewish life before 1967 and the tribalism that has dominated it since. The result is schizophrenia. The ADL has created a widely praised curriculum aimed at fostering awareness of genocide. But in 2007 the organization refused to back a congressional resolution declaring that Turkey had committed genocide against the Armenians—a decision the ADL's own New England regional director called "morally indefensible"—for fear that doing so would undermine relations between Turkey and Israel. Foxman has eloquently condemned anti-Muslim bigotry. But in 2010, when that bigotry ran wild during the debate over a plan to build a Muslim community center near the site of the World Trade Center, he concluded that the religious freedom of Muslims must bow to the sensitivities of anti-Muslim bigots. The American Jewish Committee has been equally incoherent. It was slightly more supportive of the community center near Ground Zero. But it has commissioned studies and sponsored op-eds aimed at proving that the American Muslim population is smaller than Muslim leaders claim. One can only imagine how the Committee would react if a Muslim advocacy group commissioned a study aimed at proving that American Jewish leaders are exaggerating the number of American Jews.

The ADL and the American Jewish Committee are transitional organizations, rooted in a liberalism that for decades has been fading from institutional American Jewish life. But when it comes to Israel, they are increasingly eclipsed by organizations that have no connection to that liberal tradition at all. AIPAC and the Presidents' Conference need not reconcile their support for Israeli policy with a historic commitment to battling bigotry and promoting human rights. Supporting Israeli policy *is* their mission. The organizations do not phrase it that way. Instead, each says that its mission is to strengthen the U.S.-Israel "relationship." But since both groups view strengthening that relationship as compatible with public criticism of the American government yet incompatible with public criticism of the Israeli government, supporting the U.S.-Israel relationship and supporting the policies of the Israeli government end up being largely the same thing.

Because their allegiance is to the Israeli government, and not to Zionism as a set of ideals, AIPAC and the Presidents' Conference are not troubled by the growing illiberalism in Israeli public life. During Avigdor Lieberman's rise to prominence following the 2009 elections, Foxman tried to explain why his ascendance did not threaten democratic values. The lay head of the Presidents' Conference did not even bother. He simply asserted that Lieberman's rise was an internal Israeli matter, on which American Jewish leaders should take no public position.

Similarly, AIPAC and the Presidents' Conference need not square their support for Israeli policy with a commitment to tolerance inside the United States. In 2007, the AIPAC Policy Conference made the evangelist John Hagee—who the previous year had called Hurricane Katrina God's retribution against New Orleans for a planned gay pride march— a featured speaker.

One hundred years ago, when America's major Jewish organizations were battling child labor, or fifty years ago, when they were battling segregation, the leaders of American Jewry would have been horrified to imagine a day when the most powerful Jewish organizations were indifferent to whether democratic values governed American life and whether those values governed the Jewish state. For Louis Brandeis and Stephen Wise, as for Theodor Herzl and the framers of Israel's declaration of independence, Jewish sovereignty was precious not only as a means of Jewish survival, but as a means of achieving liberal ideals. The pursuit of Jewish power was twinned with the recognition of Jewish obligation. Today, American Jews have created a communal establishment more adept at amassing political power than Brandeis and Wise could ever have dreamed, and less interested in fulfilling Jewish ethical obligation than they would ever have believed.

3

---◄+◆+◄-►---

Should American Jews Criticize Israel?

AMERICAN JEWISH LEADERS OFFER TWO SETS OF ARGUMENTS for why American Jews should not publicly challenge the occupation that threatens to extinguish the liberal ideals of Zionism's founders. The first set isn't specifically about the occupation. It is a series of claims about why diaspora Jews should not criticize the Jewish state at all.

At their bluntest, American Jewish leaders say that American Jews should not publicly criticize Israeli policy—or at least should not publicly criticize Israeli security policy—because they don't live there. As Abraham Foxman has put it, "I'm not a citizen [of Israel], I don't bear the consequences of my opinions." This argument harnesses the guilt at the heart of American Zionism, a guilt born of the fact that American Jews have never immigrated to the Jewish state in large numbers, largely because life in America is easier. American Jews, particularly those involved in Zionist organizations, feel pampered and even vaguely effeminate when they contemplate the hardships endured by

Israelis who huddle in shelters during rocket attacks and send their children off to war. Supporting the Israeli government balms this insecurity. Challenging the Israeli government exacerbates it.

But for all its emotional currency, the argument that American Jews should not publicly criticize Israeli policy because they don't live there is incoherent. For one thing, the reticence only applies to one side. If American Jews don't live in Tel Aviv or Sderot, neither do they live in Ramallah or Gaza City. Yet American Jewish groups constantly demand that Palestinian leaders change their policies, even though American Jews would not endure the consequences of those policy shifts either. In fact, American Jewish leaders have spent recent decades criticizing government policy in a bevy of countries where American Jews do not live, from the former Soviet Union to Syria to Iran. If taken seriously, the claim that American Jews must live in a country in order to publicly criticize its government would eliminate all public moral judgment of policies outside the United States. In fact, it would circumscribe judgment even within the United States. After all, if American Jews can't criticize the Israeli government because they don't live under threat of Palestinian terrorism, why should New Yorkers be able to criticize Arizona's harsh immigration laws when they don't live near the Mexican border?

The second reason American Jewish organizations give for not publicly criticizing Israeli policy is that Israel is a democracy, and therefore American Jews should respect the procedural legitimacy of its policies. In Foxman's words, "Israeli democracy should decide; American Jews should support." This, too, is a principle that American Jewish groups apply only to Israel, since they frequently criticize democratic governments in Europe and Latin America, often for their policies toward Israel. Mainstream American Jewish groups also paid little heed to the procedural legitimacy of Hamas's victory in the 2006 election for the Palestinian Legislative Council, even though a report by the Congressional Research Service noted that the election "was widely considered to be free and fair." To the contrary, they supported an Israeli blockade aimed at undoing that victory via economic pain.

But beyond the question of consistency, there is something perverse about citing Israeli democracy to condone an occupation that imperils Israeli democracy. Within the green line, one might conceivably argue that Israeli policies are beyond reproach because they enjoy popular consent. Israeli policy in the occupied territories, by contrast, enjoys no such thing. To the contrary, the occupation relies on Palestinian disenfranchisement. Were Israel to allow Palestinians in the West Bank and Gaza Strip to vote in its elections, Israeli policy in the West Bank and Gaza would shift radically. Even if Israel merely restricted voting to those Jews whose non-Jewish neighbors can also vote—that is, Jews within the green line—Israeli policy would substantially change. Without settler votes, for instance, Benjamin Netanyahu would have lost to Shimon Peres in 1996 and would have found it harder to create a right-wing coalition government in 2009.

—◆—

The final reason American Jewish leaders give for why American Jews should not publicly criticize Israeli policy is perhaps the most important because it goes to the heart of the victimhood narrative they have made central to American Zionism. They argue that because Israel's very existence is being "delegitimized" around the world, American Jews must stand in its defense, not join the lynch mob. But this claim rests on a basic fallacy. There are, to be sure, left-wing activists and Islamist militants who oppose Israel's existence as a Jewish state. But they are marginal compared to the much broader and more influential swath of people who seek to "delegitimize" not Israel, but its occupation. As the distinguished Israeli political theorist Shlomo Avineri has observed, no government that maintains diplomatic relations with Israel—even those that criticize its policies in the West Bank and Gaza Strip the most harshly—has questioned its right to exist. In 2010, when

University of Maryland professor Shibley Telhami asked respondents from Egypt, Saudi Arabia, Morocco, Lebanon, Jordan, and the United Arab Emirates whether "even if Israel returns all 1967 territories, Arabs should continue to fight," only 12 percent answered yes. Even Palestinian Authority president Mahmoud Abbas's 2011 bid for United Nations recognition of a Palestinian state, which American Jewish groups repeatedly called an exercise in Israel's delegitimization, was no such thing. As Abbas himself said, "We do not want to isolate Israel or to delegitimize it. On the contrary, we want to coexist with it." By asking the UN to recognize a Palestinian state in the West Bank, the Gaza Strip, and East Jerusalem, in fact, Abbas was simultaneously asking it to *legitimize* Israel's existence within the green line.

What the American Jewish establishment doesn't grasp is that Israel's legitimacy is bound up with its democratic character. The best way to preserve that legitimacy, therefore, is to preserve Israeli democracy, and thus marginalize those who oppose even a democratic Jewish state. Entrenching the occupation, by contrast, will gradually bring what American Jewish leaders most fear: the delegitimization of Israel as a Jewish state. The less democratic Zionism becomes in practice, the more people across the world will question the legitimacy of Zionism itself.

But acknowledging that Israel bears some responsibility for the criticism directed against it requires acknowledging that Jews can abuse power rather than merely use it to survive. And that threatens the edifice of victimhood upon which American Jewish leaders have tried to construct American Jewish identity. Israel has real enemies, some of which spew the vilest anti-Semitism. But to sustain its claim that most criticism of Israel constitutes anti-Zionist or anti-Semitic "delegitimization," American Jewish leaders ignore an astounding number of inconvenient facts. In 2009, for instance, an ADL ad in *The New York Times* declared that "settlements are not the impediment [to peace]. The issue is simple: the Arab and Palestinian rejection of Israel's right to exist." There are, of course, Arab and Palestinian leaders who reject Israel's right to exist. But the ADL did not even acknowledge that in 2002 and again in 2007, the Arab League—representing every Arab government—declared that it would recognize Israel if Israel withdrew to the 1967 lines and reached a "just" and "agreed upon" settlement of the Palestinian refugee issue. Not only did the ADL not mention the Arab League offer in its ad, it doesn't mention it in the eighty-nine-page "Guide for Activists" it issued in 2010.

Similarly, when American Jewish organizations discuss the ideology of Hamas, they dwell almost exclusively on the organization's anti-Semitic 1988 charter, which calls for Israel's destruction. In his "Global Language Dictionary"—a guide for how American Jewish leaders should speak about Israel—the pollster Frank Luntz urges them to "Read from the Hamas Charter. . . . Don't just 'quote' from it. Read it. Out loud. Again and again. Hand it out to everyone. Stop and ask them to read it. Draw arrows to the most offensive parts." Discussing the Hamas charter is important; people should read it. But listening to American Jewish organizations, one would never know that Hamas has in recent years issued several new documents, which are more compatible with a two-state solution. Nor would one know that in 2010, Hamas's two top leaders, Khaled Meshal and Ismail Haniyeh, each declared that if the Palestinian people vote to endorse a two-state solution, Hamas will accept the results. Should these newer documents and statements be accepted at face value? Of course not, especially since Hamas continues to make statements hostile to Israel's existence. But it is striking that while the Hamas Charter is discussed endlessly, one can search the websites of AIPAC, the Conference of Presidents, the American Jewish Committee, and the ADL and find barely any acknowledgment that Hamas's public statements about a two-state solution have evolved at all.

One sees the same omissions in the way American Jewish groups describe Israel's critics outside the Middle East. Again and again, non-Jews who harshly criticize Israel's occupation are described as irrationally, viciously, pathologically hostile to Israel's very existence, if not to

Jews per se, while information that complicates this narrative is simply ignored. In 2009, American Jewish organizations condemned the White House's decision to award the Presidential Medal of Freedom to Mary Robinson, the first female president of Ireland, because she had criticized Israeli policies in the West Bank and Gaza and chaired a UN conference in Durban, South Africa, which produced a draft report accusing Israel of "racial discrimination against the Palestinians." AIPAC declared that Robinson harbors a "bias against the Jewish state." The ADL denounced her "anti-Israel bias." What neither AIPAC nor the ADL mentioned was that Robinson had helped expunge the language about racial discrimination from the Durban conference's final report, thus angering Syria and Iran. Nor did they mention that after discovering that an Arab nongovernmental organization at the parallel NGO forum across the street was displaying anti-Semitic cartoons, Robinson offered an impassioned public denunciation of anti-Semitism, declaring, "When I see something like this, I am a Jew." For these reasons, and others, seven Israeli human rights groups issued a joint statement in Robinson's defense. But in their attacks on her, AIPAC and the ADL didn't mention that, either.

That same year, after the television commentator Bill Moyers linked Israel's invasion of the Gaza Strip to Moses's call to kill the inhabitants of the land of Canaan, Abraham Foxman wrote a public letter accusing Moyers of "anti-Semitism." What Foxman's letter didn't acknowledge was that in the very same commentary, Moyers had declared, "Every nation has the right to defend its people. Israel is no exception, all the more so because Hamas would like to see every Jew in Israel dead." Nor did Foxman mention that Moyers had warned that "attacks on Jews in Europe are escalating" or that Moyers had condemned "a radical stream of Islam now seek[ing] to eliminate Israel from the face of the earth." Evidently Foxman didn't consider these statements relevant to Moyers's alleged hatred of Jews.

Robinson and Moyers are not necessarily correct in all their criticisms of Israel. But the fact that Israel receives unfair criticism is no excuse for American Jewish leaders to call Israel's critics anti-Israel or anti-Semitic when contrary evidence stares them in the face, something they do all too often. According to AIPAC, Human Rights Watch exhibits an "anti-Israel bias," even though it devotes only about 15 percent of its Middle East reporting to Israel and has been so critical of Palestinian rocket fire against Israeli civilians that in 2009 a Hamas spokesman called its work "lacking [in] objectivity and impartiality." Former president Jimmy Carter is "bigoted" for having warned that Israel risks becoming an apartheid state if it doesn't relinquish the occupied territories, even though two former Israeli prime ministers, Ehud Barak and Ehud Olmert, have said largely the same thing. An Amnesty International report on Israel's killing of civilians in the 2006 Lebanon war was "bigoted, biased and borderline anti-Semitic" because it did not discuss Hezbollah's attacks on Israel, even though Amnesty issued an entire report condemning Hezbollah attacks a few weeks later. The influential blogger Andrew Sullivan, who harshly criticizes Israel's policies while supporting its right to exist, and who has called anti-Semitism "an eternal toxin for which my own Church bears a huge amount of responsibility and which needs to be confronted wherever it appears," is called "an example of someone who is educated and an anti-Semite."

By traditional definitions, the claim that Sullivan, Moyers, Carter, and the leaders of Amnesty International are anti-Semitic is absurd. After all, if they really hated Jews, wouldn't they express that hatred in some form other than criticism of Israeli policy? But for prominent American Jewish leaders, any harsh criticism of Israel that is not accompanied by equally harsh criticism of other countries constitutes anti-Semitism. As Foxman puts it, "Most of the current attacks on Israel and Zionism are not, at bottom, about the policies and conduct of a particular nation-state. They are about Jews. . . . When other countries and people pursue policies that are similar (or far worse than) those of Israel, do the critics condemn them? If so, do they condemn them with the same fervor as they condemn Israel? If not, it's hard to deny that anti-Semitism explains the discrepancy."

Actually, it's not hard to deny at all. There are several, non-anti-Semitic reasons that one might focus on Israel's misdeeds and pay less attention to those of other nations. A Jew might do so because he simply cares more about Israel than about other countries. Take, for example, me. If Egypt fails to become a democracy, I will consider it unfortunate. If Israel ceases to be a democracy, I will consider it one of the greatest tragedies of my life. Foxman never contemplates that disproportionate criticism of Israel's policies might reflect a disproportionate attachment to Israel itself.

An American might pay more attention to Israel's misdeeds because the United States, as Israel's foremost benefactor, is so deeply implicated in them. Countries like North Korea, Iran, Myanmar, Zimbabwe, and Sudan certainly violate human rights more egregiously than does Israel, but in part for that reason, America does not underwrite their behavior. To the contrary, America imposes sanctions. There's nothing wrong with an American focusing her ire on the world's worst human rights offenders. But neither is it wrong to focus on those human rights offenders over which the American government wields the most leverage. And by that standard, it is perfectly reasonable to focus on Israel's policies in the occupied territories, which would likely be unsustainable without American financial, military, and diplomatic support. In fact, although American Jewish organizations don't acknowledge it in the case of Israel, we all intuitively understand the rationale for focusing on those offenses over which we have more control, even if they are not the most egregious. If that weren't the case, how could an American justify focusing her attention on the misdeeds of the government of the United States?

But what about all those non-Jewish non-Americans who seem disproportionately angered by Israel's occupation? Here the explanation is more complex. Israel receives disproportionate abuse from people on the global left for the same reason it receives disproportionate love from Americans on the Christian right: because it is considered part of the West. It is no secret that for many on the left, imperialism is the defining evil of the modern world. Leftists in Asia, Africa, and Latin America revile imperialism because their nations suffered from it. Leftists in Europe revile imperialism because their nations committed it. And both groups believe that imperialism is alive and well, as reflected in America's wars in Afghanistan and Iraq and in the policies of the International Monetary Fund and World Bank in the developing world. Is the war in Iraq worse than the war in Congo? Are the IMF's economic policies worse than North Korea's? No, but they get more attention because they fit the left's mental image of the world. Think back to the 1980s, when no country received more international condemnation than apartheid South Africa. Was South Africa, for all its horrors, the world's worst human rights offender? No, but it was the worst human rights offender that fit the imperial lens.

Israel is not South Africa, not by a long shot. But the same principle applies. Like South Africa, Israel is seen by the global left as a Western, imperialist imposition, and thus its crimes strike a chord. There is much that's wrong with this view. Unlike the British in India or the Afrikaners in South Africa, Jews have ancient roots in the land of Israel. And close to half of Israel's Jews hail from Middle Eastern countries like Iraq and Morocco rather than from Europe. The left's obsession with imperialism gets Israel wrong, and sometimes blinds leftists to human rights abuses by postcolonial regimes that deserve their fury. But ideological blindness does not constitute anti-Semitism, even when it affects Jews. The main reason Israel generates disproportionate criticism from leftist academics, artists, and labor unionists, not to mention the General Assembly of the United Nations, is not because it's a Jewish state but because it's perceived as a Western one. And ironically, it is that very conceit—that Israel is a Western outpost in the Middle East—that accounts for much of its support among conservatives in the United States.

There is still anti-Semitism in the world and it should never be tolerated, no matter what the context. But in their effort to inoculate Israeli policy from criticism, American Jewish organizations have stretched anti-Semitism's definition to the point of absurdity. And many in the organized Jewish world know it. "On a daily basis," notes Jodi Ochstein, who worked in the ADL's Washington office from 2006 to 2010, "people thought it [the charge of anti-Semitism] was over the top. It would be one of those eye-rolling days; you were embarrassed to be working there on those days." But rarely does embarrassment translate into empathy for people unfairly charged with one of the most damning epithets in contemporary America. All too often, Jews assume that gentiles, because they are powerful, can take it, and that Jews, because of our history of persecution, can play fast and loose in the Israeli government's defense. This moral promiscuity constitutes a terrible abuse of the authority that Jewish leaders enjoy as a result of the history of Jewish suffering. It constitutes a kind of desecration, analogous to taking a sacred object and putting it to profane use. But most of all, it represents an unwillingness to accept that the world has changed, that although Israel still faces threats and anti-Semitism still exists, Jews today wield power, both in Israel and the United States. With power comes the temptation to abuse it, and using the charge of anti-Semitism to shield Israel from criticism is the best way to ensure that Israel does exactly that.

4

———❈———

Is the Occupation
Israel's Fault?

I F THE FIRST SET OF ARGUMENTS FOR WHY AMERICAN JEWS SHOULD
not publicly challenge the occupation focuses on the legitimacy of
Diaspora criticism of Israel, the second set focuses on the occupation
itself. According to American Jewish leaders, the occupation is either a
moral right or a security necessity or a burden that Israel would love to
relinquish but cannot because Palestinians don't really want a state
alongside Israel at all.

Many American Jewish leaders see no problem with Jews settling
the West Bank. David Harris, the executive director of the American
Jewish Committee, has called a West Bank without Jews "Judenrein,"
thus implicitly comparing the evacuation of settlers to the Nazi effort
to rid Germany of Jews. In Malcolm Hoenlein's words, "Jews have a
right to live in Judea and Samaria [the biblical names for the West
Bank], part of the ancient Jewish homeland—just as they have a right
to live in Paris or Washington." Yes, they do. What they don't have is
the right to live in "Judea and Samaria" under a different law from

their non-Jewish neighbors. If Jews want to live as equal citizens in a Palestinian state, as they do in France or the United States, they should be able to (something Palestinian leaders have repeatedly said they would allow). But until a Palestinian state is created, Jewish leaders who encourage Jewish migration to the West Bank are playing with fire. After all, if Jews have the right to move to the West Bank, their "ancient homeland," why don't Palestinian refugees have the right to move to pre-1967 Israel, where they lived not in ancient times, but as recently as 1948? Hoenlein's rhetoric about freedom of movement sounds liberal, but it's actually profoundly illiberal, since he wants it to extend only to Jews. If he doesn't—if he believes in freedom of movement for everyone under Israeli rule—then he's advocating an unrestricted Palestinian right of return and the likely end of Israel as a Jewish state.

A narrower version of this argument holds that even if Jews don't have the right to live in the entire West Bank, they have the right to live anywhere in Jerusalem, Judaism's most sacred city. As AIPAC executive director Howard Kohr told the organization's Policy Conference in 2010, "Jerusalem is not a settlement." But if you define a settlement as a place where Jews and non-Jews live under a different law, then East Jerusalem is indeed a settlement, since the Jews who live there are born with Israeli citizenship and the Palestinians are not (although, unlike their brethren in the West Bank, they can acquire it). What's more, suggesting that Israel has the right to control all of Jerusalem because for millennia Jews pined to return to it raises a basic question: What is Jerusalem? Until well into the nineteenth century, Jerusalem was defined as the Old City alone. When the Jordanians controlled the eastern half of the city between 1949 and 1967, they defined it as spanning six square kilometers. Then, after Israel conquered the West Bank in 1967, it expanded East Jerusalem's borders more than tenfold, to seventy square kilometers. In the process, Israel incorporated twenty-eight Palestinian towns and villages that had never been considered part of Jerusalem before, some of which are actually closer to Bethlehem or Ramallah than to the Old City. American Jewish leaders like Kohr imply that because those neighborhoods are now part of this enlarged municipality of Jerusalem, ceding them to a Palestinian state would violate the sacred Jewish attachment to the city. It's like extending the borders of Rome all the way to Naples and then insisting that because of the city's sanctity to Catholics, the entire territory must remain under Vatican control.

Beyond the question of Jewish rights to the West Bank and East Jerusalem, some American Jewish leaders say that occupying them is necessary for Israeli security. In his "Global Language Dictionary," Frank Luntz advises American Jewish leaders to claim that settlements "provide a security buffer." But a security buffer against what? Historically, Israeli military strategists saw the West Bank as a bulwark against attack from the east, a way to guard against the combined assault by Jordanian, Syrian, and Iraqi forces that Israel faced in 1948 and 1967. By this logic, the West Bank gave Israel—which within the 1967 lines is only nine miles wide at its narrowest point—the territorial depth to withstand an attack. The West Bank was considered particularly valuable because the mountain range that runs down its spine overlooks the Jordan Valley to the east, thus offering Israel high ground from which to repel an assault.

But when analyzing the security consequences of relinquishing the West Bank, it's worth remembering what actually happened before Israel occupied it. In 1967, Arab forces outnumbered Israel's three to one. Egypt, Syria, and Iraq were being armed by the Soviet Union. Jordan controlled the mountain ridge that overlooks Israel's narrow coastal plain. And despite all this, Israel won the war in six days. Since then, Israel's strategic position has dramatically improved. The Soviet Union's collapse and Israel's ever-tighter military relationship with the United States have enhanced its technological advantage over its neighbors. What's more, Jordan has made peace with the Jewish state and America has invaded Iraq, in the process constructing a military with ties to the United States. For its part, the Syrian regime of Bashar al-Assad is struggling simply to stay in power. Judging by the negotiations that took place during the prime ministerships of Ehud Barak and Ehud Olmert, it is also likely that if Israel did permit the creation of a Palestinian state, the West Bank would be demilitarized and Israel would have access to its airspace and telecommunications spectrum, would operate early warning stations on the mountain ridge, and would enjoy the benefit of an international peacekeeping force in the Jordan Valley, all advantages it did not have in 1967. All of which helps explain why Major General Aharon Ze'evi-Farkash, a former head of Israeli military intelligence, has declared, "There is no longer an eastern front."

For the foreseeable future, Israel's greatest external threats will come not from conventional armies but from rockets and terrorists. But occupying the West Bank is a poor way to guard against them. While a Palestinian state in the West Bank could put all of Israel within range of rocket fire, the harsh truth is that all of Israel is already within range. Between them, Iran, Syria, and Hezbollah have missiles that can hit every inch of Israel. That doesn't mean that Israel need not worry about potential rocket fire from the West Bank. It does mean, however, that the best way to combat that threat is through sophisticated missile defense systems like the recently installed Iron Dome; through a credible deterrent so that Hezbollah, Hamas, Syria, and Iran know they will pay a severe price for bloodying the Jewish state; and ultimately, through peace deals like the ones Israel reached with Egypt and Jordan. Occupying the West Bank, by contrast, offers less protection at much higher cost.

The occupation is not the best way to combat terrorism either. In recent years, two factors have dramatically reduced Palestinian suicide bombings. The first is the security barrier that Israel has built in the West Bank, which makes it harder for terrorists to cross the green line. The problem with the security barrier is that because sections of it cut deep into the West Bank, it disrupts Palestinian life and sparks international outrage. It also doesn't protect those Jews who live in more remote settlements, who are currently most at risk of terrorist attack. Were Israel to negotiate a border with a Palestinian state, consolidate Jewish settlements within it, and reroute the security barrier so it ran along that internationally recognized border, the barrier would become a more effective and more sustainable defense against terrorism than it is today.

The other factor that in recent years has reduced terrorism against Israelis is security cooperation with the Palestinian Authority. Since Salam Fayyad became the Palestinian Authority's prime minister in 2007, he has built an American-trained security force that works closely with Israel to prevent Palestinian attacks. Israelis understandably worry that if the Palestinians create a state, especially one in which Hamas freely contests elections, this security cooperation will erode. But it is even more likely to erode if the Palestinians remain under occupation. Politically, Fayyad has justified his crackdown on terrorism by telling Palestinians that he is showing Israel and the world that the Palestinians can be trusted to govern themselves. As a Palestinian policeman told the International Crisis Group, "Before I go to bed at night, I look at myself in the mirror with pride, as I know that what I am doing is the only way to an independent Palestinian state." The less likely a Palestinian state appears, the more Palestinian security officers will be seen as lackeys of the occupation, and the less able they will be to jail and kill Palestinian terrorists.

Since very few Israelis want to go back to the days before the Palestinian Authority's creation, when Israeli troops directly patrolled Palestinian villages and towns, it is virtually inevitable that Israel will place some of its security in Palestinian hands. In the long run, Palestinians will do a better job of safeguarding that security if they have their own state than if they are subcontractors of the Israeli occupation. They will do a better job for the same reason Egypt and Jordan have done a reasonably effective job of combating anti-Israel terrorism since they recognized the Jewish state: because when you have a state, you enjoy more of the benefits of peace. And the more you enjoy the benefits of peace, the easier it is to combat those in your own society who jeopardize it.

This view is widely held inside the Israeli security establishment. As the journalist J. J. Goldberg has noted, five of the six living former chiefs of staff of the Israel Defense Forces support the creation of a Palestinian state near the 1967 lines. So do all of the former heads of the Shin Bet (Israel's internal security service) and the Mossad (Israel's external security service) who have taken a public position. The eminent Israeli military historian Martin van Creveld recently argued, "Israel can easily afford to give up the West Bank. Strategically speaking, the risk of doing so is negligible." Van Creveld is too glib. No matter the guarantees in a peace agreement, by allowing the creation of a Palestinian state Israel will be surrendering most of its control over what happens in the West Bank and Gaza Strip, territories populated by millions of people who, in their ideal world, would rather Israel not exist. With revolution sweeping the Middle East, it is also conceivable that governments could emerge in Egypt and Jordan that abandon peace with Israel, thus increasing the strategic dangers that a Palestinian state would pose. The greater the regional turmoil, the more American Jewish leaders will defend the occupation on security grounds, arguing that it would be reckless to push Israel to relinquish the West Bank when fury is mounting against the Jewish state. But since a key driver of that fury is the occupation itself, entrenching it is like trying to contain a brush fire by dousing it with gasoline. Whether or not true democracy comes to Egypt and Jordan, what is rising throughout the Middle East is populism, a climate in which governments defer less to the United States and more to their domestic street. More than ever before, therefore, Israel's security depends on its relationship not merely with the Middle East's leaders, but with its people. Making the occupation permanent will poison that relationship beyond hope of repair while destroying the dream of a democratic Jewish state. Given that reality, it makes little sense to ask American Jews to silence their criticism of Israel's policies in the West Bank and Gaza Strip in the face of regional uncertainty. Whatever risks American Jews are asking Israel to take, they pale before the risk of perpetuating the status quo.

———+———

Since the collapse of the Oslo peace process in 2001, American Jewish leaders have added another explanation for why American Jews should not criticize the occupation: it's not Israel's fault. According to this argument, successive Israeli governments have tried mightily to hand over the West Bank and Gaza Strip, but have failed because Palestinians don't want a Palestinian state if it means having to accept a Jewish one. "Since the 1993 Oslo Accords," writes the American Jewish Committee's David Harris, the Palestinians have "spurned every offer—from left-of-center, right-of-center, and centrist Israeli governments—for a two-state deal."

There is some truth to this argument. Two Israeli prime ministers, Ehud Barak and Ehud Olmert, did offer proposals that would have created a Palestinian state, and Palestinian leaders—especially Yasser Arafat—do bear part of the responsibility for the failure of those negotiations. But when American Jewish leaders blame the Palestinians for Israel's occupation, they ignore one gaping fact: whatever the Palestinians' sins, they are not the ones paying Jews to move to the West Bank. That must be laid at the feet of successive Israeli governments, who by designating many settlements Preferred Development Areas, eligible for a host of subsidies, have made it cheaper to live beyond the green line than within it. Even if you believe that the Palestinians have proved themselves unready to accept a two-state solution right now, that still doesn't exonerate Israel from swallowing up more and more of the West Bank, thus eventually foreclosing a two-state solution *ever*.

But beyond that, it's simply not true that Israeli leaders have offered the Palestinians everything they could reasonably want, only to see their efforts scorned. Start with the famous summit at Camp David in the summer of 2000. By the time Yasser Arafat and Ehud Barak arrived at the Maryland presidential retreat, the trust that was supposed to have developed during the previous seven years of the Oslo peace process had dissipated because both sides—the Palestinians and the Israelis alike—had repeatedly violated the pledges they made. Palestinian leaders had not done nearly enough to stop the terrorism that traumatized Israel. At times, in fact, they had actively abetted it. But as several Israeli officials later admitted, Israel had not fully carried out the territorial withdrawals that Oslo required, and Barak had refused to implement the final withdrawal outright. Furthermore, although it did not violate Oslo's terms, the dramatic growth of Jewish settlement in East Jerusalem and the West Bank—which nearly doubled, from about 200,000 in 1990 to roughly 360,000 ten years later—embittered Palestinians every bit as much as terrorism embittered Israelis. Largely because of settlement growth, notes the Palestinian pollster Khalil Shikaki, the percentage of Palestinians who believed the Oslo process would bring them a state dropped during Oslo's final four years from 44 percent to 24 percent. Camp David failed, in other words, at least partly because the groundwork was not effectively laid, and the responsibility for that falls not only on Palestinian shoulders, but on Israeli ones as well.

There remains some dispute about what exactly Barak offered Arafat at Camp David, largely because Barak's ideas were conveyed orally, and often presented as American rather than Israeli proposals, in order to give him plausible deniability. But it is safe to say that his final offer, while courageous and far-reaching compared to past Israeli positions, was less generous than it has come to be remembered in the minds of prominent American Jews. In his final offer at Camp David, Barak proposed that Israel annex the 9 percent of the West Bank that included the largest settlement "blocs" while offering in return an area one-ninth as large inside the green line. Nine percent may not seem like much, but as some Israel officials have since conceded, annexing settlements like Ariel, which stretches thirteen miles beyond the green line, would have severely hindered Palestinian travel between the northern and southern halves of the West Bank. It also would have left Israel in control of much of the West Bank's water supply. Moreover, Barak insisted on maintaining sovereignty for up to twelve years over part of the Jordan Valley, which comprises another 25 percent of the West Bank. No wonder Shlomo Ben-Ami, a key Israeli negotiator at Camp David, has since declared, "If I were a Palestinian I would have rejected Camp David as well."

If there is a dispute about the terms and significance of Barak's offer, there is a dispute about whether Arafat made any offer at all. In the words of the lead U.S. negotiator, Dennis Ross, "Whether the Israelis put a generous offer on the table [at Camp David] is not the issue. The issue is, did Yasser Arafat respond at any point?" But according to Gilead Sher, who served as Israel's co-chief negotiator at Camp David, Arafat did indeed respond. As detailed by Sher and other Israeli negotiators—along with American and Palestinian officials—the Palestinians proposed that Israel annex roughly 2.5 percent of the West Bank in exchange for an equal amount of equal-quality land inside the green line. They also reportedly accepted an international force, but not an Israeli one, in the Jordan Valley, and Israeli sovereignty over the Jewish neighborhoods of East Jerusalem and the Western Wall, but not the Temple Mount that overlooks it.

Although much remains shrouded in ambiguity, it is more accurate to say that Barak and Arafat had very different visions of what a Palestinian state would look like than that Barak offered Arafat a fully fledged state and the Palestinian leader refused to accept it. One area of blunt disagreement was Jerusalem. Barak offered the Palestinians sovereignty in some, but not all, of the Palestinian neighborhoods of East Jerusalem. Arafat, in return, conceded Israeli sovereignty over East Jerusalem's Jewish neighborhoods, the Jewish quarter of the Old City, and the Western Wall. But the two men clashed over the Temple Mount (which Muslims call Haram al-Sharif, or Noble Sanctuary), with Barak demanding that Israel retain sovereignty over the site and Arafat saying that granting it would betray Muslims worldwide.

The two parties also deadlocked on the issue of Palestinian refugees. Palestinian negotiators said that only after Israel acknowledged the right of refugees to return to pre-1967 Israel could the two sides discuss the practicalities of how many would actually return. For their part, Barak's negotiators accepted some limited reunification of Palestinian families, but denied that there was any Palestinian right of return. At least two of Barak's aides, Gilead Sher and Yossi Beilin, believed that if Israel conceded refugee return in principle, the Palestinians would largely abandon it in practice, particularly if they gained sovereignty over the Temple Mount. But it is impossible to know if Arafat would ultimately have made such a deal, and even if he had, whether he could have sold it to his people. He had not prepared them for that wrenching concession, and given his corrupt and tyrannical rule—which by 2000 had alienated many Palestinians—he may have lacked the moral authority to convince them to make painful compromises. When American Jewish groups say that at Camp David the Palestinian leaders wanted a Palestinian state but not a Jewish one, the refugee issue is the best evidence they have.

But if the Camp David talks raise questions about the Palestinian willingness to abandon a large-scale right of return, they also eviscerate the American Jewish establishment's oft-repeated claim that, in the words of the 2009 ADL ad, "The Problem Isn't Settlements." At Camp David, one of the biggest problems was, indeed, settlements. With Yitzhak Rabin's assassination still fresh in his mind, Barak was extremely concerned about a confrontation with the settlers, and insisted that he needed to annex the land on which 80 percent of them lived in order to avoid grave domestic strife. To achieve that, he proposed an annexation that would have created serious contiguity problems for the nascent Palestinian state. Arafat reportedly countered with a land swap that would have allowed Israel to incorporate 35 percent of the settlers—not in broad settlement "blocs," but in thin "ribbons" that would have less significantly impeded Palestinian travel but would have proved extremely difficult for Israel to defend. The same issue bedeviled talks eight years later between Ehud Olmert and Arafat's successor, Mahmoud Abbas. Olmert proposed a roughly 6 percent land swap; Abbas offered roughly 2 percent, and "kept coming back," in Olmert's words, to the need to dismantle Ariel.

Settlements are not the only important barrier to a two-state solution. But the historical record clearly shows that, contrary to the American Jewish establishment's twin insistences that Israel tried to give back virtually the entire West Bank, and that settlements are not a major obstacle to peace, it was precisely because Israel insisted on retaining most of the settlers that it could not offer the Palestinians virtually the entire West Bank. In the words of the former Palestinian negotiator Nabil Shaath, "Probably the settlement issue was the single most important destroyer of the Oslo agreement."

Two months after the Camp David summit failed, all hell broke loose. For major American Jewish groups, the second intifada has become another part of the rationale for why Israel doesn't deserve criticism for the occupation. Not only did Ehud Barak try to make peace, they argue, but Yasser Arafat responded with war. But key Israeli officials like Ami Ayalon, who ran the Shin Bet from 1996 and 2000, reject this story as too simple. At its deepest level, the second intifada erupted because while many Israelis genuinely believed that Barak was trying to end the occupation, Palestinians felt it closing in on them. After years of settlement growth and repeated Israeli closures of the border, which devastated the economies of the West Bank and Gaza Strip, Palestinian support for violence, which had stood at only 20 percent in 1996, reached more than 50 percent by 2000. "How would you feel if on every hill in territory that belongs to you a new settlement would spring up?" declared the Palestinian militant leader Marwan Barghouti, a key instigator of the second intifada. "I reached a simple conclusion. You [Israel] don't want to end the occupation and you don't want to stop the settlements, so the only way to convince you is by force."

By 2000, many Palestinians were ready for war. And that fall, Israeli leaders lit the fuse. In September, despite pleas from American, Palestinian, and even Israeli security officials, Barak allowed opposition leader Ariel Sharon—a hated figure among Palestinians for his role in the massacre of Palestinian refugees during the 1982 Lebanon war—to travel to the ultrasensitive Temple Mount accompanied by one thousand Israeli police. Palestinians began throwing stones, one of which struck Jerusalem's chief of police in the head. Israel forces responded with rubber bullets, killing six. In the days that followed, the Palestinians escalated to Molotov cocktails and Israeli forces kept firing, discharging over a million bullets in the first three weeks of violence. On October 12, two Israeli reservists were detained by Palestinian police in a Ramallah police station. A mob stormed the jail, beating and stabbing the Israeli soldiers to death, and gouging out their eyes. In response, Israeli air force helicopters shelled Palestinian Authority buildings in the West Bank and Gaza.

Soon, militants like Barghouti—hoping to emulate Hezbollah's success in forcing Israel to withdraw earlier that year from southern Lebanon, and hoping to overthrow Arafat, whom they viewed as tyrannical and corrupt—began launching terrorist attacks. Arafat, fearing he might lose a confrontation with this younger guard, acquiesced.

Given the suffering that the second intifada visited on both Israelis and Palestinians, and its devastating impact on the prospects for peace, Arafat's decision to ride the tiger of Palestinian violence was no small offense. Indeed, it was a crime. Still, it was not the second intifada's sole cause. A commission led by former U.S. senator George Mitchell spotlighted both Arafat's acquiescence and Israel's overreaction to the stone throwing as key reasons for the descent into bloodshed. Israeli major general Yaakov Or, the man who oversaw the West Bank, blamed the occupation itself. Without tangible steps toward Palestinian self-determination, he argued, "an explosion could be expected."

Once the blood began to flow, public support for a deal collapsed on both sides. But Israeli and Palestinian officials kept negotiating, and in

December 2000 President Bill Clinton outlined parameters that went well beyond Barak's proposal at Camp David. Under Clinton's parameters, the Palestinians would establish a state in 94 to 96 percent of the West Bank with a 1 to 3 percent land swap and sovereignty over the Palestinian neighborhoods of East Jerusalem. Israel would have three years to leave the Jordan Valley, during which time its soldiers there would be replaced by an international force. Israel would acknowledge the Palestinian right to return to pre-1967 Israel, but retain control over how many refugees, if any, it would actually accept. Finally, Israel and the Palestinians would choose from several compromise arrangements regarding sovereignty over the Western Wall and the Temple Mount.

Arafat accepted the Clinton parameters in principle, but then offered reservations that rendered his acceptance virtually meaningless. For his part, Barak got the Israeli cabinet to endorse Clinton's vision, but then sent the White House a letter with his own list of reservations, in which he insisted that Israel annex 8 percent of the West Bank and that any international force in the Jordan Valley include Israeli troops. Nevertheless, in January 2001, negotiators met at the Egyptian resort of Taba and came closer than ever before to a deal. The Israelis inched down to a 6 percent annexation (plus 2 percent more they hoped to lease); the Palestinians inched up to between 3 and 4.5 percent. The two sides also moved closer on Jerusalem, the Jordan Valley, and refugees. But it was too late. By this time, Barak led a minority government. He enjoyed the support of only 42 of the 120 members of the Knesset, and his own attorney general and military chief of staff had publicly denounced the talks. Weeks later, Sharon defeated him in a landslide and broke off negotiations.

The claim that Barak had tried to give away virtually the entire West Bank but Arafat would not take it did not emerge from nowhere. Under a withering right-wing assault, and desperate for political cover as elections approached, Barak himself boasted of having exposed Arafat's rejectionism. Clinton, eager to help Barak politically, echoed the refrain. But over the last decade, as the American Jewish establishment has turned this argument into a kind of catechism, top aides to Clinton and Barak have repudiated it. Aaron David Miller, Clinton's deputy special Middle East coordinator, has said that both Barak and Arafat "in his own way bears responsibility for what happened at Camp David." Martin Indyk, Clinton's ambassador to Israel, argues, "It was not reasonable to expect that Arafat, or any Arab leader for that matter, would agree to an end-of-conflict agreement that left sovereignty over the Haram-al-Sharif in Israeli hands forever." Israeli officials have been even more vehement. "I was part of the 'no-partner' campaign, and it's one of the things I regret most," notes former Barak aide Tal Zilberstein. "Ten years later, there are still people who say, 'We gave them everything at Camp David and got nothing.' That is a flagrant lie." Adds Eldad Yaniv, Barak's former campaign adviser, "I was one of the people behind this false and miserable spin. It may have been justified to a certain extent to stir the Palestinians to revive the negotiations, but it's false."

If American Jewish groups have taken the messy reality of the Oslo process and scrubbed it clean of Israeli culpability, they have done the same with Ariel Sharon's 2005 dismantling of settlements in Gaza, another episode that supposedly shows that Israeli leaders yearned to create a viable Palestinian state. The problem with this argument is that Sharon and his top advisers said exactly the opposite: that the Gaza evacuation was meant not to create a Palestinian state, but to forestall one. By 2004, the second intifada had fizzled, Arafat was dead, and America's sequel to Oslo, the Road Map, was going nowhere. Into the breach came two initiatives. The first was the offer, drafted by Saudi Arabia and endorsed by the entire Arab League, to recognize Israel if it returned to the 1967 lines and negotiated a "just" and "agreed upon" solution for the Palestinian refugees. The second was the Geneva Accord, a model peace agreement signed by former Israeli and Palestinian negotiators that would have required Israel to dismantle major

settlements like Ariel. These moves terrified Sharon, a lifelong opponent of a Palestinian state who feared international pressure to agree to
the kind of deal that Clinton had proposed in December 2000. Warning that "only an Israeli initiative will keep us from being dragged into
dangerous initiatives like the Geneva and Saudi initiatives," Sharon
proposed unilaterally withdrawing from Gaza, a place with far less
biblical significance than the West Bank, a tiny fraction of the settlers,
and which Israeli strategists had long considered a burden. His influential chief of staff, Dov Weissglas, made Sharon's intentions clear.
"The significance of the disengagement plan," he declared in October
2004, "is the freezing of the peace process. And when you freeze that
process, you prevent the establishment of a Palestinian state and you
prevent a discussion on the refugees, the borders and Jerusalem. Effectively, this whole package called the Palestinian state, with all that it
entails, has been removed indefinitely from our agenda."

Given Sharon's history as a patron of the settler movement, his decision to evacuate any settlers at all constituted high drama within Israel,
and led him to form a new political party, Kadima, to implement the
Gaza evacuation. But for all the bitterness occasioned by Sharon's break
from his old colleagues in Likud, he still shared their fundamental opposition to a contiguous Palestinian state. In fact, as *Haaretz*'s Akiva Eldar
has documented, Sharon's preferred solution to the Israeli-Palestinian
conflict was drawn heavily from apartheid South Africa. He envisioned
ten noncontiguous Palestinian "Bantustans"—Sharon reportedly used
the word himself—with Israel occupying the rest of the West Bank.
Despite the Gaza withdrawal, argued former Israeli foreign minister
Shlomo Ben-Ami in 2005, "Sharon's hidden agenda, which he has been
harbouring for years, remains unchanged . . . the confinement of a Palestinian homeland within scattered enclaves surrounded by Israeli settlements, strategic military areas and a network of bypass roads." So
much for the bold move toward a Palestinian state.

American Jewish groups generally ignore Sharon's stated motivation for dismantling the settlements in Gaza. Instead, they argue that if the Palestinians had acted differently once the settlers left, Israelis would have been more willing to repeat the experiment in the West Bank. That is true, but as with Oslo, it is only half the story. If Israel's Gaza withdrawal ended in disaster, Israel—as well as the Palestinians—bears some of the blame.

In 2006, after the Gaza settlers left, the Palestinians held legislative elections, which, to the shock of American leaders, Abbas's Fatah lost and Hamas won. According to Palestinian pollster Khalil Shikaki, the two issues cited most frequently by Hamas voters were Fatah's rampant corruption and its failure to maintain law and order. Most Hamas voters, in fact, said they wanted the group to negotiate with Israel toward a two-state solution. Still, Israelis understandably greeted Hamas's election with alarm. The group's charter, written in 1988, teems with anti-Semitism and demands Israel's destruction. In the 1990s, in the midst of the peace process, Hamas terrorists murdered numerous Israelis in suicide attacks.

But there were hints, at least rhetorically, that Hamas had changed. In its election manifesto, the group did not mention Israel's destruction, instead calling for an "independent [Palestinian] state whose capital is Jerusalem" and referring to the UN resolutions calling on Israel to withdraw from land it conquered in 1967. After the election, when Hamas's leader in Gaza, Ismail Haniyeh, outlined his party's agenda to the Palestinian parliament, he praised the Arab League's 2002 peace offer. In January 2007, Hamas's leader in exile, Khaled Meshal, told Reuters, "I speak of a Palestinian and Arab demand for a state on 1967 borders. It is true that in reality there will be an entity or a state called Israel on the rest of Palestinian land." In 2010, he told the talk-show host Charlie Rose, "If Israel withdraws to the 1967 borders, so that will be the end of the Palestinian resistance." And while Meshal did not himself accept Israel's right to exist, he said that if Palestinians voted to do so in a referendum, Hamas would accept the results.

Israelis can be forgiven for viewing these statements through jaundiced eyes. When Hamas leaders talked about a referendum on a two-state solution, they envisioned allowing Palestinians in refugee camps to participate, a population presumably wedded to the right of return. What's more, it was not always clear if Hamas leaders even believed that a two-state solution would end the conflict, or merely produce a decades-long cease-fire. And, of course, the loathsome Hamas charter still stood.

Nonetheless, Israel faced a choice: risk Palestinian democracy or try to extinguish it. Risking Palestinian democracy would have meant accepting that Hamas had won control of the Palestinian parliament, and supporting a unity government in which Mahmoud Abbas—who had been elected independently the year before—remained president of the Palestinian Authority and chairman of the PLO. Under this deal, which most Palestinians and Hamas itself preferred, Abbas pledged to keep negotiating with Israel on the understanding that any deal he struck be put before Palestinian voters. By participating in a coalition government that was negotiating a two-state solution even though its party charter rejected a two-state solution, Hamas would have been in a position oddly analogous to today's Likud, whose own platform explicitly rejects a Palestinian state, but which leads a coalition that has pledged to put any deal creating one to a popular vote.

When American Jewish leaders say that the Gaza withdrawal shows that Israel once again sought peace and the Palestinians once again chose war—and thus, that the occupation is not Israel's fault—this is the choice they ignore. Israel's choice, rather than supporting a unity government and negotiating a cease-fire, was to boycott Hamas until the group recognized Israel, unilaterally renounced violence, and abided by past peace agreements. (The third criterion was particularly bizarre since during the Oslo peace process, as Shlomo Ben-Ami notes, "every new Israeli government asked for a revision of the agreements signed by the previous government.") In fact, Israel and the United States not only opposed a Palestinian unity government; they encouraged Fatah strongman Mohammed Dahlan to violently overturn the election results, a move that backfired when Hamas won the battle of arms and took control in its stronghold of Gaza. When that failed, Israel—with the support of the United States, and to some extent Hosni Mubarak's Egypt, which feared Hamas's ties to its own Islamist opposition—imposed a blockade designed not only to prevent Hamas from importing weapons, but to punish Gazans for electing it. Since the vast majority of Gaza's exports and imports passed through Israel, the blockade shattered its economy. By 2008, 90 percent of Gaza's industrial companies had closed. Lacking fuel, garbage trucks stopped running in a majority of Gazan towns. With Gaza's border with Israel largely sealed except for humanitarian goods, Hamas built tunnels underneath Gaza's border with Egypt. And while the tunnels did little to relieve the misery of average Gazans, they left Hamas in almost total control of the Strip's economy and armed with even more sophisticated weapons than they had possessed before the blockade. Thus, a policy meant to weaken Hamas by immiserating the people of Gaza achieved the latter goal but not the former.

Against this backdrop, Hamas and other terrorist groups fired thousands of rockets and mortars from Gaza into southern Israel, traumatizing border cities like Sderot. To say that Israel's embargo caused the rocket fire would be unfair, since Hamas had been killing Israeli civilians since the 1990s and launching rockets since the start of the second intifada in 2001. But while Israel's policies did not cause the rockets, they provided Hamas a rationalization to keep launching them. Hamas leaders, after all, repeatedly named their price for ending the rocket fire: a lifting of the blockade and a halt to Israeli attacks inside Gaza. In the summer and early fall of 2008, in fact, when Hamas believed it had reached a deal along these lines, it not only ceased its own rocket attacks but largely prevented other Palestinian organizations from launching them as well.

In November 2008, the cease-fire began to unravel, with Hamas claiming that Israel had not significantly lifted the blockade and Israel demanding a complete halt to attacks by all Palestinian groups before it did so. Hamas was not innocent in all this: it had abducted an Israeli soldier, Gilad Shalit, and refused to release him until Israel released Palestinians in its jails (a deal finally carried out in 2011). But the basic point remains: the Israeli government did not do everything it could to find a diplomatic solution that would have quieted Hamas's guns. It was neither politically creative nor politically brave. And as a result, it gave Hamas what the group's most militant members wanted anyway: war.

In December 2008, after the cease-fire collapsed, Israel invaded the Gaza Strip. The invasion took thirteen Israeli and fourteen hundred Palestinian lives. Despite Israel's genuine efforts to limit civilian damage, the war partially or completely destroyed 14 percent of Gaza's buildings, including sixteen hospitals, thirty-eight health clinics, and 280 schools, some of which were in session when the bombs fell. After the war, the United Nations Development Program reported that 61 percent of Gazan children suffered from "severe" or "very severe" post-traumatic stress disorder. Some were too afraid to return to school; others went completely mute, but began screaming when they heard loud noise. Psychologists have noticed similar patterns in Sderot, where children exposed to rocket fire sometimes refuse to leave their homes and grow hysterical upon hearing loud noise.

The war cowed Hamas, which between early 2009 and late 2011 permitted far less rocket fire from Gaza than it had before. And in the summer of 2010, under international pressure following its killing of Turkish militants seeking to reach Gaza by sea, the Israeli government eased the blockade on civilian goods. But Gaza remains a place of brutal suffering: According to a 2011 report by the World Food Programme, more than half its households are "food insecure," which means they lack "access to sufficient food to meet their dietary needs." And while Hamas bears part of the blame for its people's misery, so does Israel, which by barring most Palestinians from roughly one-third of the arable land *inside* the Strip, remains Gaza's occupying power.

In Arafat and Hamas, Israel has been unlucky in its adversaries.

But accepting the ethical responsibilities of power requires accepting the way that the occupation has shaped the behavior of those adversaries. To ignore those ethical responsibilities constitutes political and moral blindness. And blindness is the opposite of what American Jews owe the Jewish state.

5

The Jewish President

I F STEPHEN WISE WERE TRANSPORTED TO THE OVAL OFFICE TO WIT-
ness a meeting between the leaders of the American Jewish establishment and the president of the United States, he would find only one
person whose view of Jewish identity, and of the Jewish state, approxi-
mated his own. He would find only one person who espoused the liberal Zionism that he championed in his own time. And it would be the
black man with the Muslim name: Barack Hussein Obama.

To understand how Obama came to embody the Jewish liberalism
that America's leading Jewish organizations have abandoned, one must
understand his relationship with a rabbi named Arnold Jacob Wolf.
And to understand Arnold Jacob Wolf, one must understand *his* relationship with Rabbi Abraham Joshua Heschel.

Heschel arrived in the United States in 1940, having spent most of
his life in the cloistered embrace of Hasidic Poland. He walked off a
boat in New York City and saw a black man shining a white man's shoes.
It was the first black man he had ever seen, and he identified with him

fiercely, as a Jew. Over the next three decades, Heschel—with his unruly hair and snow-white goatee—became America's image of a Hebrew prophet. Again and again, he invoked God to challenge unjust human power. Heschel denounced McCarthyism, marched with Martin Luther King Jr., and erupted in anger during a meeting with Robert McNamara at the height of the Vietnam War. Again and again, he chided Americans, and American Jews, for their smug indifference to the evil done in their name. "Above all," he wrote, "the prophets remind us of the moral state of a people: Few are guilty, but all are responsible."

At Hebrew Union College, where he was studying to be a rabbi, Arnold Wolf served as Heschel's private secretary, frequently accompanying him to the movies, which Heschel attended in hopes of losing his Yiddish accent. A Reform Jew and a fourth-generation American whose grandmother had seen Abraham Lincoln campaign, Wolf's background was worlds away from that of his mentor. But he sponged Heschel's prophetic example. In 1957, Wolf established Temple Solel on Chicago's North Shore and began causing trouble. He brought Martin Luther King Jr. to speak; he took congregants to Selma to march for voting rights; he picketed a Jewish hospital on behalf of striking black workers even though some of Temple Solel's most prominent members served on the hospital's board. He so passionately denounced the Vietnam War that in 1967 FBI agents infiltrated the synagogue and recorded one of his antiwar sermons.

A short, round, bearded man whom one observer compared to a troll, Wolf was a most unusual rabbi: In 1969, after Judge Julius Hoffman gagged and shackled Black Panther Bobby Seale to prevent outbursts in his Chicago courtroom, Wolf stationed a gagged and shackled man outside the synagogue during services, which led some members of Temple Solel to quit. In the spring of 1970, one enraged congregant denounced Wolf in the synagogue newsletter, to which Wolf retorted, "One should not believe all one reads" in the synagogue newsletter. With his biting, confrontational style, Wolf stood at the vanguard of the liberal activism that helped shape organized American Jewish life.

As one former synagogue member explained, "The core teaching of the Torah for him had to do with justice and one sometimes had to speak about that in ways that people didn't care to hear."

Abraham Joshua Heschel died in 1972, just as American Jewish organizations were turning against the prophetic liberalism he embodied. In his declining years, he had grown increasingly anguished by Israel's occupation of the West Bank and Gaza Strip and Arnold Wolf turned that anguish into a crusade. Like his mentor, Wolf was a committed Zionist: For twelve straight years, Temple Solel paid for its Hebrew school graduates to spend the summer in Israel; on the eve of the 1967 war, Wolf mortgaged the synagogue's building and sent Israel the money. But by the 1970s, Wolf's devotion to Israel was leading him toward a confrontation with its government. In 1973, he helped start Breira ("Alternative"), the first American Jewish group to endorse a Palestinian state in the West Bank and Gaza. The reaction from the organized American Jewish community was savage. Benjamin Epstein, coauthor of *The New Anti-Semitism*, urged the ADL's parent organization, B'nai B'rith, to fire employees who associated with Breira. The Conservative movement's Rabbinical Assembly denied Wolf—who had branched beyond Reform Judaism—a seat on its executive council. Members of Meir Kahane's Jewish Defense League attacked Breira's inaugural conference, trashing the hall and beating conferees.

For Wolf, it was the beginning of a feud with the American Jewish establishment that would last to the end of his days. Breira, after all, was not merely challenging Israeli policy; it was challenging organized American Jewry. Echoing Brandeis and Wise a half-century earlier, the group demanded that "Jewish organizations and communal structures must be democratic and egalitarian." Wolf also challenged the narrative of perpetual victimhood that underpinned American Jewish institutional life. In 1979, in an essay entitled "Overemphasizing the Holocaust," he lamented that in "Jewish school or synagogue . . . one does not now learn about God or the *Midrash* or Zionism nearly as carefully as one learns about the Holocaust." Worse, he continued,

American Jewish leaders were using "the Shoah as the model for Jewish destiny" with the result that "'Never again' means nothing more or less than 'Jews first—and the devil take the hindmost.'" In 1993, he objected to building a Holocaust museum on Washington's National Mall. Given that it was Native Americans who had experienced genocide on U.S. soil, Wolf argued, a Native American museum would better capture the true purpose of Holocaust memory, which was "not to give us Jews special rights or special roles, but to make us sensitive to the outrages that marred all of Western history and to the tasks of human rescue and succor that still remain." Wolf loathed the way Jewish communal leaders used the Holocaust to perpetuate the idea that Israel would always be besieged by anti-Semites, thus fostering "a Zionism that sees all mankind as enemies." For him, Zionism was not an alibi for whatever Jews did with power; it was a test of whether Jews could wield power in keeping with Judaism's ethical commands. "I love Israel as the Prophets did," Wolf explained, which meant "demanding that Israel be the Covenant people."

—•—

What does all this have to do with Barack Obama? Actually, quite a bit. Far more than any previous president, Obama spent his adulthood in the company of Jews. His most important professional mentors were Jews; most of his big donors were Jews; many of his neighbors were Jews; his chief political consultant was a Jew. As Wolf himself would later say, Obama was "embedded in the Jewish world."

But Obama was not embedded in *the* Jewish world; he was embedded in one specific Jewish world—a world of Jews who in the 1960s had opposed segregation and the Vietnam War and after 1967 applied the same liberal democratic principles when it came to Israel. Woven into the life stories of many of the Jews who most influenced the young Barack Obama was a bitter estrangement from the see-no-evil Zionism of the American Jewish establishment. In Chicago, those Jews constituted a geographic and moral community, a community that bred in Obama a specific, and subversive, vision of American Jewish identity and of the Jewish state. And at the heart of it all was Arnold Jacob Wolf.

In 1985, twenty-four-year-old Barack Obama answered an ad in *The New York Times*. Three white community organizers, two of them Jewish, were looking for an African American colleague to give them credibility on Chicago's largely black South Side, and Obama answered the call. Their leader was Jerry Kellman, who as a Jewish teenager in New Rochelle, New York, had petitioned the school board to stop teaching *Little Black Sambo* and had boycotted his high school graduation in protest against the Vietnam War. While working with Kellman, Obama gravitated toward Reverend Jeremiah Wright's Trinity Church, partly because of the church's deep commitment to social justice, partly because it offered him the authentic African American experience he craved, and partly because it provided him a potential power base in black Chicago. But despite his yearning to be accepted in African American circles, and despite jeers from black nationalists, Obama always kept his community organizing work multiracial. As his biographer David Remnick has noted, he had come to Chicago not merely to find a black community, but to find a latter-day civil rights movement, and that movement, he believed, required whites, and especially Jews.

After community organizing, Obama attended Harvard Law School, where he became president of the law review. Accounts of Obama's law school career sometimes describe Harvard as a place of bitter racial tensions, which Obama helped to soothe. But on law review, where Obama spent much of his final two years, there was also considerable ideological harmony. Some of Obama's associates on law review were black, many were white, many of the whites were Jews, and with the exception of a few marginal conservatives, liberalism reigned across the color line. In his campaign for president of the law review, Obama's main rival was David Goldberg, a Jewish New Yorker who, if anything, stood slightly to Obama's left. "On the law review," remembers one of Obama's colleagues, "the black-Jewish alliance was intact." Blacks and Jewish liberals "saw the world in pretty much the same way."

When Obama returned to Chicago after law school, he settled in Hyde Park, whose largest synagogue, KAM Isaiah Israel, was led by Arnold Jacob Wolf. Hyde Park was, in its way, a lot like the *Harvard Law Review*. It was intellectual (the neighborhood's largest employer was the University of Chicago), it was racially integrated, it was heavily Jewish, and it was hegemonically liberal. It had not always been that way. In the 1950s, crime and decay so menaced the neighborhood that university administrators considered moving the campus to the suburbs. But the university stayed, and with the help of Mayor Richard J. Daley, built Hyde Park into a class cocoon, an oasis for black and white professionals alike. "Everyone got along . . . everyone listened to NPR," remembers Dayo Olopade, a child of Nigerian doctors who grew up in the neighborhood while Obama lived there. Olopade went to summer camp at the local Jewish Community Center, where she remembers making the blessing over challah bread on Fridays. Obama's own daughters attended preschool at Hyde Park's Akiba-Schechter Jewish Day School.

So as in his community organizing, and as on the *Harvard Law Review*, Obama found himself not merely in the company of Jews, but Jews who, like him, wished to reconstruct the civil rights coalition. When Obama ran for the Illinois state senate in 1996, Wolf was one of his earliest and most prominent supporters. By the time he ran for president twelve years later, Obama had moved across the street from KAM Isaiah Israel, and the synagogue took a proprietary interest in his campaign. "This is a congregation," explained Darryl Crystal, who became the rabbi after Wolf retired, "where the question wasn't, 'Are you going to vote for Obama?' The question was, 'What state are you going to help canvass?'"

The Jews of Hyde Park, in Wolf's words, were "interfaith, left, liberal, integrationist." In fact, Wolf had come to KAM Isaiah Israel after a stint as the rabbi at Yale University precisely because he wanted to lead a progressive Jewish community in an integrated neighborhood. And the synagogue's progressivism enabled an extraordinary degree of interracial and interreligious harmony. It's not just that as a state senator Obama spoke at KAM Isaiah Israel. Or that a small black congregation holds weekly services there. Or that the Catholic Theological Union uses the synagogue for its graduation ceremonies. Or even that Rashid Khalidi, the Palestinian historian who befriended Obama, spoke at KAM Isaiah many times. Even more revealing, as a window into the ethos of Hyde Park, is that Khalidi regularly came to KAM Isaiah Israel to attend the bar and bat mitzvahs of his children's friends.

If Arnold Wolf stood at the geographic center of Obama's Jewish world, he stood near the center in other ways as well. One of Obama's key mentors at Harvard Law School was Martha Minow, whom Obama would later call the "teacher who changed my life." Minow was a native Chicagoan, and her family had been members of Temple Solel, where Wolf introduced her to the writings of Heschel, and where, she recalls, she "grew up not understanding there was a difference between religion and politics." The two reconnected when Wolf worked at Yale, where Minow was attending law school. When Minow got married, Wolf performed the ceremony.

In 1989, near the end of Obama's first year at Harvard Law School, Minow called her father, Newton Minow, a partner at the Chicago firm of Sidley and Austin, and urged him to give Obama a job. Obama spent only a summer at Sidley, but he met his wife there, and Newt Minow became a key mentor, a bridge to many in the city's legal and business elite. As personalities, Minow and his longtime rabbi, Arnold Wolf, were acres apart. Wolf was incendiary; Minow was formal and discreet, the kind of man to whom the rich entrust their affairs. But ideologically, the two had much in common. In the 1950s and 1960s, Minow had been an establishment liberal, a protégé of Adlai Stevenson who chaired the Federal Communications Commission under John F.

Kennedy. But in the early 1980s, a few years after Wolf formed Breira, Minow began his own break with the major American Jewish organizations over Israel. During the Lebanon war, which he opposed, Minow told a meeting of the American Jewish Committee that while American Jews should donate to Israel, they should also "tell Israel our opinions about world affairs. Where did we get this idea we needed to keep our mouths shut?" The crowd, he recalled, "almost threw me out." Minow never attended another AJC event.

Over time, as the American Jewish establishment shifted right, Minow grew even more alienated. In 2003 he appeared at a press conference organized by Americans for Peace Now and later joined the advisory council of J Street. He repeatedly took to the local papers to criticize the Israeli government for expanding settlements and to criticize the "American Jewish leadership for failing to distinguish between supporting the State of Israel and supporting whoever happens to be in the current, transitory government of Israel." No wonder he had felt so comfortable at Temple Solel.

One of Minow's closest friends was Judge Abner Mikva, who was born four days after him in their mutual hometown of Milwaukee. When Obama graduated from law school, Mikva offered him a clerkship. Obama turned it down, but Mikva became another important mentor. While Minow introduced Obama to the city's legal and business world, Mikva, a former state representative and member of Congress, tutored him on Chicago politics. Mikva was also a former congregant of Wolf's, in his case at KAM Isaiah Israel. And just as Wolf had influenced Minow's daughter Martha, he also profoundly influenced Mikva's daughter, Rachel. From 1990 to 1994, in fact, Rachel Mikva served as KAM Isaiah Israel's associate rabbi and director of religious education.

Not surprisingly, Rachel Mikva, who currently serves in J Street's rabbinic cabinet, shared Wolf's views on Israel. So did her father. Like Minow and Wolf, Abner Mikva was exhilarated by Israel's victory in 1967 but disquieted by its occupation, a disquiet that alienated him from the major institutions of American Jewry. In 1969, he visited

Israel for the first time. "It was a very moving experience," he remembered, "but as excited as I was, and the people were after their victory, we went to an Arab town and you could see that the Jews weren't treating them very well." In 1977, Mikva traveled to Israel again as part of a congressional delegation that met newly elected prime minister Menachem Begin, and came away disturbed by Israel's rightward drift. He is no more enamored of Israel's current Likud prime minister, about whom he quipped, "Netanyahu speaks excellent English and that's the only positive thing I can say about him." In 2010, Mikva and a number of other prominent, left-leaning American Jews issued a public statement declaring, "We abhor the continuing occupation that has persisted for far too long; it cannot and should not be sustained." Abraham Foxman denounced the statement as "sophistry."

In 1992, Obama took his first step toward electoral politics by directing the Illinois chapter of Project Vote, a nationwide effort to register poor and African American voters. There he grew close to yet another politically connected Chicago Jew who was profoundly alienated from the American Jewish leadership over Israel: Bettylu Saltzman. Saltzman's father, Philip Klutznick, had been a legendary figure in organized Jewish circles. A wealthy real estate developer, he began in the 1950s to devote his time to Jewish communal work, at various times heading B'nai B'rith, the United Jewish Appeal, and the World Jewish Congress, as well as helping to found the Conference of Presidents of Major American Jewish Organizations. In 1957, Israeli finance minister Levi Eshkol tasked him with building Ashdod, a new city on Israel's southern coast.

But like his longtime lawyer, Newt Minow; his mentor in Jewish communal affairs, Nahum Goldmann; and his friend, Arnold Wolf, Klutznick began to break with the Israeli government in the 1970s. Upon returning from a trip to Israel following the Yom Kippur War, he warned that Israel's occupation was unsustainable because "any government of military occupation is an imposed government whose decisions—even the most nobly intended—always arouse suspicion and provoke opposition and revolt." By the late 1970s, his views on Israel were straining relations with other American Jewish leaders. And many of those relations ruptured completely in 1982 when Klutznick, Goldmann, and the former French premier Pierre Mendes-France publicly called on Menachem Begin to halt Israel's invasion of Lebanon and negotiate with Yasser Arafat's PLO. "That was the end of my dad in the Jewish community," remembers Saltzman. "They lambasted him." That fall, when Klutznick delivered a speech at the Jewish Community Center in Omaha, Nebraska, where he had attended law school, local Jewish groups organized a boycott. At the Chicago Federation, the local Jewish community's fund-raising arm, word went out that Klutznick was never to be honored, nor even publicly mentioned. In 1984, when AIPAC led a campaign to oust Senator Charles Percy of Illinois, who as chairman of the Foreign Relations Committee had helped shepherd the Reagan administration's sale of AWACS surveillance planes to Saudi Arabia, Klutznick, then nearing eighty, wrote a letter in Percy's defense. The man who had spent most of his adult life as the quintessential communal insider was, by its end, a near pariah in the organized Jewish world.

All this made a deep impression on Klutznick's eldest daughter, Bettylu, who still seethes with hostility toward the mainstream Jewish groups that assailed her father. The "AJC used to be a nice organization," she says of the American Jewish Committee, until it began focusing so much on Israel. As for the Presidents' Conference, her father would "blow up the organization today. What it's turned out to be would make him sick at heart." When the head of the Chicago Federation asked her to serve on the board, she refused because "I didn't like what they did [on Israel]." Instead, she became vice president of the New Israel Fund, which helps American Jews fund human rights and other progressive Israeli groups. Like Minow, she has worked with Americans for Peace Now and sits on the advisory council of J Street.

Saltzman met Obama when she was working on Bill Clinton's 1992 presidential campaign and he was registering voters. Like Minow and Mikva, she became a conduit to the wealthy North Shore Jews who helped fund his state senate, House, and U.S. Senate campaigns. In 2002, it was Saltzman and Marilyn Katz, another veteran progressive activist who currently serves on J Street's advisory council, who organized the rally against the Iraq War where Obama proclaimed his opposition to an American invasion.

Saltzman also introduced Obama to the man who would become his closest political adviser, David Axelrod. For Axelrod, who considered Robert Kennedy's assassination one of the defining events of his youth, reassembling the civil rights alliance was an obsession. As a political consultant, he specialized in helping African American candidates win white votes. Like many of Obama's early Jewish supporters, Axelrod put the "progressive social justice tradition" at the core of his Jewish identity, and in his view, "Obama was very much a part of that and was very much a product of it." That tradition also informed Axelrod's relationship to Israel; every year from 1991 to 2002, he and his wife donated to the New Israel Fund. In 1994, Axelrod went on an AIPAC-sponsored trip to Israel. He remembers someone in the group asking three Israeli leaders the same question: "What would you tell the settlers if there is a peace deal?" Labor Party stalwart Shimon Peres answered: "I would tell them they can live in the West Bank." Benjamin Netanyahu, then a rising star in Likud, replied: "I wouldn't tell them to leave." Finally, the questioner asked Prime Minister Yitzhak Rabin. "I'd tell them," Rabin replied wearily, "peace has a cost; too many children have died." It's clear which answer impressed Axelrod the most.

———+———

How did all this shape Obama's view of Israel? In his pre-presidential career, the answer is clear: Obama saw Israel in much the same way Minow, Mikva, Saltzman, Axelrod, and Wolf did. In 2000, he reportedly told a Palestinian American activist named Ali Abunimah that he supported American pressure to make Israel change its policies, a view with which most of his Jewish friends would have concurred. During his run for the U.S. Senate in 2004, in response to a questionnaire from the *Chicago Jewish News*, he criticized the barrier built to separate Israel and its major settlements from the rest of the West Bank, a remarkable statement given that that same year, after the International Court of Justice condemned the barrier, 361 members of the House backed a resolution supporting it. When his U.S. Senate campaign—at the request of local Jewish activists—submitted a position paper on Israel, the activists deemed it too weak, and obtained a rewrite.

Obama's description of the Israeli-Palestinian conflict in his 2006 book, *The Audacity of Hope*, is also telling. In the one paragraph Obama devotes to the conflict, his central theme is the similarity between Israelis and Palestinians. He describes talking "to Jews who'd lost parents in the Holocaust and brothers in suicide bombings" and hearing "Palestinians talk of the indignities of checkpoints and reminisce about the land they had lost." Flying by helicopter over Israel and the West Bank, he says he "found myself unable to distinguish Jewish towns from Arab towns, all of them like fragile outposts against the green and stony hills." While such rhetoric is hardly radical, it subtly contradicts the view of major American Jewish leaders, who usually reject any equivalence between Jewish and Palestinian suffering. The American Jewish establishment generally stresses the moral *dissimilarity* between Israelis and Palestinians; Obama in *The Audacity of Hope* does the opposite.

Perhaps most revealing of all, as an insight into Obama's view of Israel's occupation, is the fact that he read, and vividly remembers, David Grossman's 1988 book, *The Yellow Wind*. Grossman is not only one of Israel's leading novelists, he is among its leading intellectual doves, and *The Yellow Wind* is his searing account of the occupation, as he witnessed it during seven weeks on assignment in the West Bank for an Israeli newsweekly. It is difficult to read *The Yellow Wind* without being profoundly disturbed by its portrait of Palestinian life under Israeli rule. That Obama read it, along with the novels of another famed Israeli dove, Amos Oz, lends further credence to Arnold Wolf's claim that in his pre-presidential years, Obama "was on the line of Peace Now."

—|—

Jews were not the only influence on Obama's views of Israel. Unusually for an American politician, he spent a great deal of his early life in the presence of Muslims. Not only did Obama live in Indonesia from ages six to ten, but at both Occidental College and Columbia University, he developed close friendships with students from Pakistan, a country he visited in 1981. Obama also took a keen interest in colonialism. He attended a class at Columbia taught by the famed Palestinian literary critic Edward Said, and in his autobiography, he wrote at length about the impact of British rule in Kenya, his father's native land. In Hyde Park, Obama grew friendly with Rashid Khalidi and other Palestinian intellectuals. And, of course, he spent two decades as a parishioner in the church of Jeremiah Wright, a man bitterly hostile to the Jewish state.

Despite Obama's interactions with people who saw Israel as a colonial venture, however, there is no evidence that he ever echoed those views. He did sometimes criticize Israeli and American Jewish leaders. But far from questioning Zionism itself, Obama generally criticized those leaders for not living up to the liberal aspects of Jewish and Zionist tradition that he admired, the aspects embodied by Israelis like David Grossman and American Jews like Arnold Wolf. In a May 2008 interview with the journalist Jeffrey Goldberg, Obama mentioned his "great affinity for the idea of social justice that was embodied in the early Zionist movement and the kibbutz." He later added, "What I also love about Israel is the fact that people argue about these issues, and that they're asking themselves moral questions. . . . My staff teases me sometimes about anguishing over moral questions. I think I learned that partly from Jewish thought." While presented as a compliment,

Obama's comments were subtly subversive since neither the Israeli government nor its supporters in the American Jewish leadership were noted for "anguishing over moral questions."

In another bit of damning praise, Obama told a Cleveland crowd in February 2008 that "one of the things that struck me when I went to Israel was how much more open the debate was around these issues in Israel than they are sometimes here in the United States." Two months later, in Philadelphia, he repeated the point, declaring, "One of the things I loved about visiting Israel was to see Israelis argue among themselves. There is just a healthy debate that takes place that sometimes is not as open . . . in the United States." With those statements, Obama challenged one of the core contentions of the American Jewish establishment: that the American debate over Israel should be more constrained than the debate inside Israel, since it is up to Israelis—not Americans—to determine their government's policies. Obama, by contrast, not only insisted that Americans have the right to openly debate Israel's actions, but allied himself with one side in that debate, the side more concerned with "social justice" and more prone to "moral anguish." In Cleveland, he remarked, "There is a strain within the pro-Israel community that says unless you adopt an unwavering pro-Likud approach to Israel that you're anti-Israel," implicitly revealing his view of Benjamin Netanyahu's party.

After the talk, a woman asked Obama to sign his autograph for her two sons. While he wrote, she began sounding out their names: "Meyer, M-E-Y-E-R," she spelled, and "Heschel, H- . . ."

Obama interrupted her. "Like Abraham?" he asked.

———

Over the course of his presidential campaign, Obama accumulated a broader array of Chicago Jewish supporters, including some, like billionaire businessman Lester Crown, lawyer Alan Solow (who would later become chairman of the Presidents' Conference), and venture capitalist Lee Rosenberg (who would later assume the presidency of

AIPAC), with more establishment views on Israel. But unlike many national politicians, whose first sustained experience with Jews comes via groups like AIPAC, Obama befriended supporters like Crown only after having developed an inner circle of Jewish advisers like Minow, Mikva, Saltzman, and Axelrod, whose views on Israel leaned left. And that meant that he was repeatedly reminded, in a way most American politicians are not, that when it comes to Israel, many American Jews disagree with their communal leaders. In the summer of 2008, for instance, Crown organized a meeting between Obama and roughly a dozen of his prominent Chicago Jewish supporters, most of them people with establishment views. The supporters took turns detailing the Iranian nuclear threat and insisting that the Israeli government be spared U.S. pressure. But when it came Newt Minow's turn to speak, he declared, "These guys don't speak for me; they don't speak for most American Jews. They think they do—I'm not questioning their sincerity—but no one elected them. Most American Jews support Israel but think it should get the hell out of the settlements." Abner Mikva, who also attended the meeting, told Obama he agreed.

Not surprisingly, the Obama campaign and the American Jewish establishment viewed each other with suspicion. In the spring of 2008, Obama attended a Passover Seder organized by some of his Jewish campaign staff. He was no stranger to the custom, having attended Seders for the previous nine years. But this Seder, like those he had attended with Mikva and other Jewish friends in Chicago, stressed broad themes of persecution and liberation. It reflected, in other words, the universalism that the American Jewish leadership has turned against. The event, which Obama continued once in office, featured many black as well as Jewish staff. At the 2011 White House Seder, Obama read the Emancipation Proclamation. No Jewish communal leaders were ever invited to attend.

The universalism of the Obama Seder annoyed some in the Jewish organizational world. ("You've got ten people, seven of whom are not Jewish," quipped one staffer at a major Jewish group. "That's not a

Seder. That's dinner with matzah ball soup.") But the distrust ran much deeper. In January 2008, the Jewish newspaper *The Forward* published excerpts of an internal American Jewish Committee memo, later disavowed, which warned that Obama "appears to believe the Israelis bear the burden of taking the risky steps for peace." Malcolm Hoenlein declared that there is "a legitimate concern over the zeitgeist around the campaign" and later hired a campaign adviser of Sarah Palin's to run a group created by the Presidents' Conference to oppose a nuclear Iran. In private, a congressional staffer and an Obama campaign adviser each heard Hoenlein call Obama "anti-Israel." Hoenlein denies ever having made such a statement and emphasizes that if he considered Obama to be "anti-Israel," he would have said so in his many public speeches.

In public, AIPAC remained neutral during both Obama's primary battle with Hillary Clinton and his general election campaign against John McCain. People close to the organization stress that internally, staff are warned to avoid even the appearance of partisan favoritism. And in their personal capacities, prominent AIPAC lay leaders supported each of the major candidates. Still, some Washington Democrats believed that AIPAC was subtly sending anti-Obama messages. At one point during the presidential primaries, a half dozen or so large AIPAC donors expressed anxiety about Obama to top congressional Democrats in what struck one congressional aide as a coordinated campaign. In the race between Clinton and Obama, notes the aide, "Every Jewish member [of Congress] knew where AIPAC was." Nor did the suspicion end when Clinton left the race. At a rooftop reception during the Democratic National Convention in August, one party official accused AIPAC staffers of disseminating anti-Obama material.

———

Among actual Jewish voters, Obama held his own in the Democratic primaries, losing the Jewish vote to Hillary Clinton in states with older and more Orthodox Jewish populations like New Jersey, Arizona,

Nevada, and Florida, but winning it in states like Massachusetts, Connecticut, and California, where the Jewish population skewed younger and less observant. But by the spring of 2008 it was clear that while Obama might wax dovish when speaking without a script, his campaign was determined to reassure American Jewish leaders that his views on the Israeli-Palestinian conflict differed little from those of his opponents. After Obama told an Iowa crowd that "nobody is suffering more than the Palestinian people," a campaign spokesman explained that what he really meant was that "the Palestinian people are suffering from the Hamas-led government's refusal to renounce terrorism." In his first address to AIPAC, in May 2007, Obama had ventured that Israel would have to take "heavy and tough" steps in the search for peace. But by June 2008, when he addressed the organization again, this time as the presumptive Democratic nominee, he was so eager to dispel any peacenik reputation, that he vowed never to permit the re-division of Jerusalem, a statement so baldly hostile to a two-state solution that the campaign had to retract it the following day. In July, the Obama campaign hired a former AIPAC staffer to lead its Jewish fund-raising effort.

That same month, Obama journeyed to Israel as part of an eight-country tour designed to burnish his foreign policy credentials. Hours before he arrived, a Palestinian man in Jerusalem slammed his truck into several cars and a bus, injuring twenty-four people. The Israel Defense Forces retaliated by ordering the man's home bulldozed (a decision that was later reversed). The advisers traveling with Obama drafted a statement that took no issue with Israel's response. Obama told them he disagreed, saying he doubted that bulldozing houses deterred terrorism and that the man's relatives were being punished for a crime in which they played no part. But then he added, "I'm not going to say that" in public.

As Obama's public statements on Israel grew more conventional, so did the ideological character of his Middle East advisers. A key reason is that those advisers were judged not merely on their policy acumen, but on their ability to assuage the organized Jewish community's fears.

Advisers who aggravated those fears were dealt with ruthlessly. In February 2008, a right-leaning website called American Thinker attacked Obama foreign policy adviser Samantha Power for her past criticisms of Israeli behavior. In response, the Obama campaign noted that she was not an adviser on the Middle East. After the website assailed former national security adviser Zbigniew Brzezinski for, among other offenses, advocating that the United States talk to Hamas, the Obama campaign volunteered that Obama had not spoken to him in months. Harshest was the treatment of Robert Malley, a former Clinton administration National Security Council staffer who had infuriated Jewish leaders by meeting with representatives of Hamas and claiming that Israel bore part of the blame for the failure of the Camp David peace talks. Not only did a campaign aide promise that Malley would not receive a job in an Obama administration, but the campaign distributed an article by Martin Peretz, the hawkish editor in chief of *The New Republic*, which praised Obama while calling Malley "a rabid hater of Israel." Malley discovered what the campaign had done when the mass e-mail arrived in his inbox.

But even advisers who were not publicly rebuked paid a price for crossing the Jewish establishment. The Obama campaign's first full-time adviser on Israeli and Palestinian affairs was a young former congressional aide named Daniel Shapiro. From the beginning, Shapiro's duties were described as both Middle East policy and Jewish outreach, and he performed the latter in part by avoiding controversial statements on the former, despite what associates call personally dovish views. More troubled was the experience of Daniel Kurtzer, who joined the campaign near the end of 2007. A former ambassador to Egypt and Israel, Kurtzer was more senior than Shapiro. But despite being a Hebrew-speaking Orthodox Jew, Kurtzer had alienated American Jewish leaders by too openly confronting the Israeli government about settlement growth during his ambassadorship and by later suggesting that the Clinton administration had worried too much about the domestic constraints faced by Israeli leaders and not enough about the domestic pressures on their Palestinian counterparts. In April 2008, *American Thinker* warned that Kurtzer's record "may displease many supporters of the American-Israel relationship." And while the campaign never repudiated Kurtzer, the attacks limited his utility as an emissary to the organized American Jewish world. "They hid Dan Kurtzer during the campaign," noted one Washington observer. "They didn't send him to [Jewish events] in Florida; they didn't even send him to New Jersey, where he lived."

As it turned out, Kurtzer's predicament shaped Middle East policy not only during the Obama campaign, but during the Obama administration. Given his stature, and the fact that he had endorsed Obama when other senior Middle East policy experts were either staying neutral or supporting Hillary Clinton, Kurtzer might have become the dominant Obama adviser on Israeli and Palestinian affairs. But his inability to reassure an anxious American Jewish leadership left a void, which in the summer of 2008, Dennis Ross began to fill.

Kurtzer and Ross had once been friendly. They had worked together on Middle East policy in the Reagan administration, and when Ross became the State Department's director of policy planning under George H. W. Bush, he helped Kurtzer gain an appointment as deputy assistant secretary of state for Near East affairs. The break came in the Clinton years, when Ross became the administration's dominant Middle East adviser, in part through his relationship with Secretary of State Warren Christopher's powerful chief of staff, Tom Donilon. Bureaucratically, Ross marginalized Kurtzer, who eventually left Washington to become ambassador to Egypt and then Israel. The two men fell out ideologically as well, with Kurtzer disapproving of what he considered Ross's excessive deference to the Israeli government. For that very reason, Abraham Foxman later praised Ross as a *"melitz yosher"*—an ancient Hebrew term for advocate—"as far as Israel is concerned."

Even many of Ross's critics conceded that he came by his views honestly. He sincerely believed that reassuring Israel, rather than pressuring it, would usually prove more successful in advancing Israeli-Palestinian peace. But his views also proved politically convenient. After leaving the Clinton administration, Ross took a senior position at the Washington Institute for Near East Policy, a think tank founded as an offshoot of AIPAC. He also published a 2004 memoir that placed less blame on Israeli leaders for the failure of the Camp David talks than did his colleagues on the Clinton Middle East team. In tandem, these moves transformed Ross into a favorite of the American Jewish establishment, a transformation that further alienated Kurtzer. In 2008, Kurtzer coauthored a book on the peace process peppered with blind hostile quotes about Ross, the gist of which was that Ross was not "an honest broker" because he "tilted too much towards the Israelis."

After Hillary Clinton exited the race, Ross moved aggressively to join the Obama team. His involvement worried some Obama loyalists, who appreciated Ross's value as a campaigner but warned against rewarding him with an administration job given the discrepancy between his views and Obama's. Ironically, however, it was precisely that discrepancy that made Ross so useful as an emissary to the organized Jewish community. "Dennis Ross was the biggest tool in the toolkit that the campaign used to push back the sense that Obama was going to be soft," explains one executive at a Jewish organization. Among the elderly, and often hawkish, Jews of Florida, the only Obama surrogates whose appeal exceeded Ross's were a group of Jewish doctors from Sloan-Kettering who promoted Obama's position on stem cell research. By contrast, Kurtzer, who had publicly expressed views that more closely reflected Obama's own, was, for that very reason, of limited political value.

In large measure, Obama's inoculation strategy worked. As the fall progressed, American Jewish groups muted their criticism, partly because Obama looked increasingly likely to win, but also because Obama had muted his own criticisms of Israeli policy and the American Jewish establishment. His campaign had succeeded: on the Israeli-Palestinian issue, it had made him safe. With their friend on the verge of the presidency, many of Obama's longtime Jewish backers were euphoric. But there was a discordant note. In October, the *Chicago Jewish News* asked Rabbi Arnold Wolf to reflect upon what Obama's election would mean for Jews and Israel. Wolf, now eighty-four years old, and only two months from death, was oddly somber. "He's going to go very cautiously and not do anything that shakes up the Jewish community," Wolf said about his famous neighbor. "I'm not sure I agree with that, but that's what's going to happen."

6

—+++—

The Monist Prime Minister

BENJAMIN NETANYAHU DOESN'T TRUST BARACK OBAMA, AND probably never will. The reason is simple: Obama reminds Netanyahu of what Netanyahu doesn't like about Jews.

Understanding what Netanyahu doesn't like about Jews requires understanding what Vladimir Jabotinsky didn't like about Jews. For if Obama's Jewish lineage runs through Arnold Jacob Wolf to Abraham Joshua Heschel, Netanyahu's runs through his father, Benzion, to Jabotinsky, the spellbinding, romantic, brutal founder of Revisionist Zionism.

What Jabotinsky didn't like about Jews was their belief that they carried a moral message to the world. In his telling, the story of Jewish history went roughly like this. Once upon a time, when they still lived on their land, the Jews had been warriors, renowned for their fierce resistance to the empires of the day. Jabotinsky wrote an entire novel about Samson, the giant muscleman who killed a thousand Philistines with the jawbone of an ass. The Revisionist youth movement, Betar, took its name, in part, from the location of the last Jewish revolt against Roman rule. Abba Achimeir, one of Jabotinsky's most militant disciples, wrote glowingly about the battlefield exploits of biblical leaders like Joshua and King David.

The problem began, according to Jabotinsky and the Revisionists, with the prophets. Achimeir was particularly hostile to Isaiah, who challenged the Judean kings to "seek justice, relieve the oppressed." The Revisionists, while devouring the Bible's accounts of Jewish political and military life, often scorned those passages suggesting that Jews were tasked with a special ethical mission. "The Bible says 'thou shalt not oppress a stranger; for ye know the heart of a stranger, seeing ye were strangers in the land of Egypt,'" wrote Jabotinsky in 1910. "Contemporary morality has no place for such childish humanism."

When the Jews had land, an army, and a state, the Revisionists argued, nationalism held this emasculating moralism in check. But when the Jews were dispersed, they turned weakness into a virtue by valorizing religious ethics and religious ritual at the expense of military power. They adopted, as the writer Dov Chomsky explained in Betar's monthly journal, *Madrich*, "the dangerous and weakening belief that Israel is different from all other nations . . . that the Jews were scattered all over the world in order to advance humanity and spread the humanistic teachings of the prophets."

Zionism should have solved this, since it focused on reclaiming land, sovereignty, and—for the Revisionists especially—military power. But Jabotinsky feared that Labor Zionism—the movement's dominant strand—had not fully exorcised the prophetic curse. While Labor Zionists also believed that Diaspora life had made Jews passive and weak, they were less likely to blame that passivity on Jewish morality. To the contrary, many Labor Zionists insisted that the character of Jewish life in Palestine, and of the eventual Jewish state, was as important as the creation of the state itself. Truly realizing the Zionist dream, they argued, required modeling various liberal or socialist principles for the world. As David Ben-Gurion explained, "Two basic aspirations underlie all our work in this country: to be like all nations, and to be different from all nations."

Such thinking was dangerous, Jabotinsky insisted, because the belief that a Jewish state could be judged by any external moral standard implied that Zionism was not moral in and of itself. "We hold that Zionism is moral and just," he wrote in 1923. "There is no other morality." Jabotinsky was not indifferent to how a Jewish state should be run. He often called himself a nineteenth-century liberal, devoted to individual rights and parliamentary government. But he subordinated those beliefs to Zionism itself. "We do not forbid any person from nurturing in the depth of his soul alongside of the Zionist ideal also a world outlook, opinions or even subsidiary ideals of another kind. These are the private affair of each individual," Jabotinsky explained, "but in accord with our Herzlian world outlook we do not recognize the permissibility of any ideal whatsoever apart from the single ideal: a Jewish majority on both sides of the Jordan as a first step towards the establishment of the State. That is what we call 'monism.'"

Jabotinsky claimed that Theodor Herzl had been a monist as well, that he, too, denied there was any universal moral benchmark against which Zionism could be judged. But much of Herzl's writing suggests the opposite. Whereas Jabotinsky mocked the idea that Jews have a special responsibility to the stranger as "childish humanism," *Altneuland* climaxes with the president of Herzl's fictional Jewish state declaring, "Let the stranger be at home among us." For Herzl, the character of Jewish nationalism was crucial. Repelled by the racial doctrines of South Africa's Afrikaners, he insisted, "We don't want a Boer state, but a Venice." Jabotinsky, by contrast, praised the Boers, who had not only achieved statehood, but developed a reputation as fierce fighters. He also admired key figures in the Ukrainian nationalist movement, even though their xenophobia and anti-Semitism repelled many Zionists. What Jabotinsky admired about the nationalism of the Ukrainians, and of the Latvians, Germans, and Poles, was precisely their lack of a prophetic moral tradition. Jabotinsky, argues the historian Yaacov

Shavit, sought "to reconstruct a Jewish national existence on the model of a neighbouring nationalism . . . untainted by any universalist and socialist ideas."

—+—

At times, this reverence for nationalism—any nationalism—bred in Jabotinsky a gruff respect for those Arabs who claimed Palestine as their national home. "Every native population, civilised or not, regards its lands as its national home," Jabotinsky admitted in 1923. But Jabotinsky drew a sharp distinction between the nationalisms of the West, which he saw as modern and civilized, and the nationalisms of the East, which he saw as savage. He twisted himself in a pretzel claiming that the Jews had always been a Western people. Hebrew, he argued, although superficially similar to Arabic, was actually a European language best rendered in Latin script. "We Jews," he wrote in 1933, "have nothing in common with what is denoted 'the East' and thank God for that."

In keeping with his pro-imperial worldview, Jabotinsky expressed openly racist views of Arabs and Muslims. Islamic civilization, he declared, represents the "complete antithesis to European civilization, which distinguishes itself by intellectual curiosity, free investigation, dynamism and a minimum of interference of religion in everyday life." The Arabs, he added, "are five hundred years behind us." Jabotinsky's most radical disciples, like Abba Achimeir and Avraham Stern, founder of Lehi (also called the Stern Gang), which took up arms against the British authorities who ran pre-state Palestine, regularly referred to Arabs as a slave race, inherently inferior to Jews. "The word 'Arab' became for the [Zionist] Right a symbol of negative human qualities," argues Shavit. Labor Zionists expressed anti-Arab attitudes, too, but they also saw Arabs as workers, whose common class position gave them an identity of interests and even values with Jews. "Only among the Right," observes Shavit, "did the 'Arab' take on major demonological dimensions within the framework of a political and cultural tradition."

Jabotinsky's view of Arabs was interwoven with his view of how to build the Jewish state. Labor Zionists, in keeping with their belief that they were building a workers' haven, sometimes suggested—naively—that the Arabs of Palestine would embrace the quest for Jewish self-determination. They were also more willing to compromise Jewish ambitions in order to gain Arab and international support, either by pursuing statehood more cautiously or by accepting partition of the land. Revisionists, by contrast, fervently opposed any restraints on the Jewish pursuit of statehood, and insisted that such a state encompass both sides of the Jordan River: not only what today comprises Israel and the West Bank, but also the East Bank, which comprises modern-day Jordan. Revisionists generally understood that these demands made a political settlement with the Arabs impossible in the near future. But they embraced another solution—force—which many believed was the only language Arabs understood anyway. For more extreme Revisionists like the Stern Gang, force meant "transfer": the Arabs would be deported to another country—Iraq was a popular suggestion—perhaps in exchange for the Jews of Arab lands moving to Palestine. Jabotinsky himself wavered on transfer, sometimes praising the idea, at other times denouncing it.

For the most part, however, he envisioned Arabs living in a Jewish state with individual rights and cultural autonomy. But that could only happen once Palestine's Arabs abandoned their own nationalist dreams, and that could only happen, in Jabotinsky's view, once they had been militarily and psychologically crushed. This required building up Jewish military might and using it without scruple—no matter what the moralists said—for as long as it took to make the enemy submit. Labor Zionists used force ruthlessly as well, but they were more troubled by it. During Israel's war of independence, members of the Stern Gang and the larger Revisionist militia, the Irgun, massacred more than one hundred Arabs, many women and children, in the village of Deir Yassin. The following year, Yaakov Meridor, a Revisionist member of the Knesset, proclaimed, "Thanks to Deir Yassin we won the war."

A leftist member, Aharon Cizling, scolded him: "Don't boast about Deir Yassin."

To which another Revisionist interjected: "There's nothing to be ashamed of."

Which prompted another leftist member to exclaim, "For your sakes, I should like to say that I don't believe you're not ashamed of Deir Yassin."

But for Revisionists, not being ashamed was the whole point. Wielding power without shame was the key not only to building a Jewish state, but to reclaiming the true, long-suppressed spirit of the Jews. By crushing the Arabs, Revisionists believed, Jews would also crush a malignant part of themselves.

In 1939, Vladimir Jabotinsky cabled the thirty-year-old former editor of a Revisionist newspaper in Palestine, Benzion Netanyahu, and summoned him to New York. Netanyahu complied and, until Jabotinsky's death the following year, worked as his private secretary. For the next eight years, Netanyahu served the Revisionist cause in America, including by editing a Revisionist newspaper in New York called *Zionews*. Netanyahu eventually returned to Israel and traded journalism for academia, before returning to the United States to teach. But over the following half-century, his views remained remarkably constant and remarkably faithful to the man he served. He also proved remarkably successful in transmitting them to his middle son, Benjamin.

Jabotinsky's influence permeates Benzion Netanyahu's writing. First, the yearning to recover the lost glory of Jewish militarism: "The prowess of Jewish youth in Palestine should serve as a warning that the blood of the old warrior race is still alive in the Jewish people," exulted an unsigned *Zionews* editorial during Netanyahu's time as editor. Second, the belief that Diaspora life had turned Jews against their martial heritage: "In antiquity we were a nation known for its superior capacity to 'resist,'" argued Netanyahu in 1981, in a lecture on the one hundredth anniversary of Jabotinsky's birth. "Our capacity for resistance was retained also during our first few centuries of Exile; but it gradually diminished and was worn down until it virtually disappeared . . . the unwillingness to offer resistance, which had been regarded as a 'curse' of the Diaspora, came gradually to be viewed as a worthy trait." And finally, the claim that this moralistic impotence had infected Zionism itself: "An ideology which glorified this passivity . . . even penetrated the ranks of the national movement."

Jabotinsky's greatness, argued Netanyahu, lay partly in his willingness to cast off this prophetic shackle and assert "the full and total justice of our claims," irrespective of broader moral concerns. And what Zionism claimed, in Netanyahu's view, was both banks of the Jordan. Throughout his career, Netanyahu mourned the cleaving of the East Bank—which in 1922 had become the Arab state of Transjordan (now simply Jordan)—and fiercely opposed the return of any more land. While many Labor Zionists accepted international partition plans, first in 1937 and then in 1947, a 1944 editorial in Netanyahu's *Zionews* declared, "The partition of the land itself is an utter impossibility." More than three decades later, Netanyahu bitterly attacked Prime Minister Menachem Begin, himself a Revisionist, for betraying his ideological heritage and ceding the Sinai Peninsula to Egypt in the Camp David Accords. (In response, Begin called Netanyahu a rightwing extremist.) In 1993, Benzion Netanyahu called the Oslo Accords "the beginning of the end of the Jewish state." And in 2009, at the age of ninety-nine, he told the Israeli newspaper *Maariv* that Israel should retake the Gaza Strip, from which it had withdrawn four years earlier. "We should conquer any disputed territory in the land of Israel," Netanyahu declared. "Conquer and hold it, even if it brings us years of war. . . . You don't return land."

Despite his monism, Jabotinsky had a liberal streak, a belief in individual rights for all people, as long as those rights did not endanger a Jewish state on both banks of the Jordan. And among contemporary Revisionists like Deputy Prime Minister Dan Meridor and Knesset

Speaker Reuven Rivlin, that liberal tradition lives on to this day. But it is notably absent from the writings of Benzion Netanyahu. Netanyahu, in fact, admired those more radical Revisionists who disparaged the very idea of liberal democracy. In 1944, a *Zionews* editorial called a member of the Stern Gang convicted of trying to kill British police a "hero." *Hayarden*, the newspaper Netanyahu edited in Palestine, campaigned for the release of Abba Achimeir, a man who openly called himself a fascist. More than six decades later, Netanyahu gave a lecture in Jerusalem in Achimeir's honor.

Like the Stern Gang, Netanyahu promoted the physical "transfer" of Palestine's Arab population. In 1939, in the introduction to a book by the British Zionist Israel Zangwill, he endorsed Zangwill's call for encouraging Arab emigration from Palestine. Four years later, he helped create the American Resettlement Committee for Uprooted European Jewry, which urged freeing up space in Palestine for Jewish refugees by resettling Palestine's Arabs in Iraq. The committee, noted a *Zionews* editorial, would "transfer those Arabs of Palestine who prefer to live in a purely Arab state to one of the rich and underpopulated Arab territories in the Middle East, preferably to Iraq." The editorial called this "a sound and far-reaching plan."

Even in his dotage, Benzion Netanyahu still seemed attracted by the idea. In a 2003 book on Zionism's founders, he lavished praise on Zangwill and described his proposals for relocating the Arabs of Palestine "to Arabia, Iraq, Syria—anywhere—as long as they will get out of the land of Israel," without a word of criticism. "The Jews and the Arabs are like two goats facing each other on a narrow bridge. One must jump into the river," Netanyahu told *Maariv* in 2009. "What does the Arab's jump mean?" asked the interviewer, trying to decipher the metaphor. Netanyahu explained: "That they won't be able to face the war with us, which will include withholding food from Arab cities, preventing education, terminating electrical power and more. They won't be able to exist and *they will run away from here*." [My emphasis.]

Unsurprisingly, racism pervades Benzion Netanyahu's writing. In an essay in 1943, he called the Arabs "a semi-barbaric people, which lacks any democratic traditions and is fired by religious fanaticism and hatred for the stranger." Later, during Netanyahu's editorship, an unsigned editorial in *Zionews* described the Arabs as "Ishmael, the wild man of the desert." Netanyahu conjured the same image sixty-six years later, when asked by *Maariv* why he didn't like Arabs. "The Bible finds no worse image than this of the man from the desert," the old man replied. "And why? Because he has no respect for any law. Because in the desert he can do as he pleases. The tendency towards conflict is the essence of the Arab. He is an enemy by essence. His personality won't allow him any compromise or agreement. It doesn't matter what kind of resistance he will meet. His existence is one of perpetual war."

There is an irony here, for while Benzion Netanyahu reviles the Arabs for their warlike "essence," he urges Jews to recapture that essence themselves. And given his twin beliefs that force is the only method Arabs understand, and force is the best method for reawakening the Jewish spirit, his policy prescriptions are predictable: meet any inkling of Palestinian nationalism with brutal violence.

"Is there any hope of peace?" asks the *Maariv* interviewer.

"Out of agreement? No," replies Netanyahu. But "the other side might stay in peace if it understands that doing anything [else] will cause it enormous pain." Later in the interview, he advises threatening the Palestinians with "enormous suffering."

Netanyahu has a model in mind for all this: Ottoman rule. Under the Ottoman Empire, he notes, "every little thing they [the Arabs of Palestine] did brought mass killings and hangings in town squares." He doesn't advise public hangings, Netanyahu adds, but withholding food, electricity, and education is fine. The parallels with his mentor are clear. Just as Jabotinsky looked to the Afrikaners and Ukrainians to craft a Zionism unencumbered by the moralism of the prophets, Benzion Netanyahu looks to the Ottoman Turks. By mimicking gentiles and recasting Jewish history, Netanyahu, too, hopes to realize the Revisionist dream: a dream in which Jewish ethics no longer hinder Jewish power.

Israeli prime minister Benjamin (Bibi) Netanyahu has dismissed talk of his father's ideological influence as "psychobabble." But throughout his political career, friends and advisers have testified to it. "Bibi's father had a substantial influence over him," noted Hagai Ben-Artzi, Netanyahu's brother-in-law, in 1998. "His father has a huge influence on him. Huge," a former adviser told *Newsweek* in 2010. "Always in the back of Bibi's mind is Ben-Zion," a family friend told the *Atlantic* that same year. "He worries that his father will think he is weak."

Netanyahu has said so himself. After shaking hands with Yasser Arafat during his first stint as prime minister in the late 1990s, he acknowledged his anxiety about his father's reaction. In 2001, he told settlers that he had consulted his father before withdrawing Israeli troops from most of Hebron. In 2005, when he resigned from Ariel Sharon's cabinet to protest the dismantling of Israeli settlements in Gaza, he declared, "From you I've learned, father."

The influence is also unmistakable in Netanyahu's writing, which often reads like a paraphrase of both his father and Jabotinsky. First, the glorification of the ferocious Jews of antiquity. "Jews in ancient times were not known as docile victims," wrote Netanyahu in his 1993 book, *A Place Among the Nations*, which was reissued with minor changes in 2000 as *A Durable Peace*, and again, as an electronic book, in 2009. "Jews may not have been loved in antiquity, but they were respected for their determination and capacity to resist assaults." Then the descent into moralism. "Slowly and surely, through the centuries of exile, the image and character of the Jew began to change. . . . Not a trace could be found of the grudging admiration that the peoples of antiquity had harbored for Jewish courage and tenacity. Worse, a substantial segment of Jewish opinion assimilated this disparaging image of the Jew. . . . That the Jews 'would not' (could not) resort to arms, that they would not 'demean' themselves by 'stooping to violence,' was taken to be a clear sign of their moral superiority over other peoples." Finally, the impact of this pathology on Zionism and Israel. "The visions of Isaiah and the other Jewish prophets were principally intended to teach us what to strive for—and not necessarily what to expect next week. But whereas many other peoples have been able to distinguish between the ideal vision of human existence and the way the affairs of nations must be conducted in the present, the Jewish people has had a harder time accepting this separation. The Jews have such an acute sense of what mankind should be that they often act as though it is virtually there already."

At first glance, Benjamin Netanyahu's monism seems dated. When Jabotinsky argued that Jewish morality threatened Jewish survival, the Jews were a stateless people, millions of whom lived at the mercy of their increasingly genocidal neighbors. Today, Jews have birthed not merely a state, but a regional superpower. Surely now, Jews can temper the single-minded pursuit of power with a concern for that power's ethical character.

For Netanyahu, however, the Jewish condition has not fundamentally changed. Since Jews still live on the knife edge of extinction, any ethical standard outside of Zionism itself still endangers Jewish survival. It is always 1938. After Prime Minister Yitzhak Rabin and Foreign Minister Shimon Peres signed the Oslo Accords in 1993, Netanyahu called Peres "worse than [Neville] Chamberlain," the British prime minister who appeased Hitler. In *A Durable Peace*, Netanyahu repeatedly compares the West Bank to the Sudetenland, which the Nazis cleaved from Czechoslovakia en route to overrunning the entire country. Dismantling Jewish settlements, he argues, would mean a "*judenrein*" West Bank and a "ghetto-state" within Israel's 1967 borders.

If it is 1938, then Jews have no moral responsibility except to survive. In the Warsaw Ghetto, you don't agonize about how you treat the Nazis. And if the Palestinians are Nazis, compromise is fruitless because the enemy understands only force. By repeatedly comparing Palestinians to Nazis, Netanyahu dehumanizes them, turning them into little more than irrational, genocidal Jew-haters. But he also dehumanizes them in a more old-fashioned way, the way his father and

Jabotinsky did: by calling them savages. One of the remarkable features of *A Durable Peace* is Netanyahu's tendency to approvingly quote imperialists expressing racist views of Arabs. He quotes Winston Churchill as saying, "Left to themselves, the Arabs of Palestine would not in a thousand years have taken effective steps toward the irrigation and electrification of Palestine." He cites Colonel Richard Meinertzhagen, Britain's chief political officer in Palestine after World War I, as opining, "The Arab is a poor fighter, though an adept at looting, sabotage and murder." (Like Churchill, Meinertzhagen is one of Netanyahu's favorite historical figures. In *A Durable Peace*, he praises Meinertzhagen's "remarkable character.")

But Netanyahu doesn't merely use former colonial officials as his ventriloquist dummies. He has expressed similar sentiments himself. In 2009, in a meeting with American diplomats, Palestinian negotiator Saeb Erekat complained that Netanyahu had called him a "wild beast of a man," an echo of his father's tirade against "Ishmael, the wild man of the desert." In 1988, in his first political campaign, Netanyahu declared, "The Arabs know only force." And in *A Durable Peace*, he writes that "for much of the Arab world, peace is a coin with which one pays in order to get something else . . . peace can be signed one day and discarded the next . . . much to the astonishment of Westerners." It's worth noting that Netanyahu isn't referring to one Arab leader, one Arab political party, or even one Arab country—he's referring to Arabs per se.

What Benjamin Netanyahu learned from his father, he seems to have transmitted to his son. In 2011, *Haaretz* reported that on his Facebook page, nineteen-year-old Yair Netanyahu had written, "Terror has a religion and it is Islam." Two years earlier, the teenager ran a Facebook group that urged boycotting Arab products and businesses.

—+—

In 482 pages, much of it a history of the Arab-Israeli conflict, Benjamin Netanyahu's *A Durable Peace* contains barely a word about Palestinian suffering. Indeed, when he refers to those gullible observers who actually do empathize with the Palestinians' "plight" and the way they "have suffered," Netanyahu puts the phrases in quotation marks. How does Netanyahu explain away the suffering of the roughly seven hundred thousand Palestinians who lost their homes during Israel's war of independence? By claiming that their departure was overwhelmingly voluntary. Indeed, he insists that in many cases Jews pleaded with their Palestinian neighbors to stay. Given the more than two decades of scholarship—mostly by Israeli scholars using Israeli archives— documenting that many Palestinian refugees were either coerced or frightened into leaving, Netanyahu's historical account is silly. But it is also deadly serious, because if there was no moral problem with transfer in the past, there is no moral problem with transfer in the present. And top Netanyahu advisers have flirted with exactly that.

Uzi Arad served as Netanyahu's chief foreign policy adviser during his first term as prime minister and as national security adviser during his second. In between, he published an article proposing that in a final settlement with the Palestinians, Israel should seriously consider either redrawing its border so as to reduce its number of Arab citizens or pursue "population transfers without land exchanges": in other words, encouraging or coercing "Israeli Arabs and Bedouins living in the Galilee and Negev to [leave their homes and] settle in Palestine." Avigdor Lieberman, who served as chief of staff during Netanyahu's first prime ministership and whom Netanyahu in 2009 appointed foreign minister, has also proposed redrawing Israel's border to exile hundreds of thousands of Israel's Arab citizens. And Netanyahu has not publicly repudiated the idea. In 2010, the Israel Prisons Service conducted a drill based upon a hypothetical Israeli move to redraw the border, which provoked hypothetical riots among those Israeli Arabs exiled from the country. When the Association for Civil Rights in Israel asked Netanyahu to pledge that he would not take such a step, the organization received no response.

None of this means that Netanyahu would physically expel Israel's

Arabs, or even redraw the border so as to deposit them on the other side. He may well find such ideas impractical. But there is no evidence that he considers them immoral, since as a monist, he subordinates external moral considerations to Zionism itself. Consider the following exchange. In 2007, Netanyahu declared that one of the "positive" effects of the cuts in child welfare programs he enacted as Ariel Sharon's finance minister "was the demographic effect on the non-Jewish public, where there was a dramatic drop in the birth rate." *Jerusalem Post* columnist Larry Derfner objected, arguing that it was racist for an ex-government official to celebrate his success at reducing a particular ethnic group's birth rate. In response, Ron Dermer—who would later become Netanyahu's most influential aide—said that Derfner was "mistaken in calling Bibi a bigot. He is only a Zionist." Dermer's meaning was clear: maintaining Israel's Jewish majority, by whatever means necessary, is Zionist, and thus beyond reproach. Of course, there are—and always have been—Zionists who believe in a Jewish state with a Jewish majority but who are restrained in their pursuit of such goals by universal principles like nondiscrimination. But for Dermer, as for Jabotinsky and Benzion Netanyahu, such people are not true Zionists, but rather Jews emasculated by moralism, Jews who refuse to do what it takes to ensure that the Jewish people survives.

As a commentator, Benjamin Netanyahu has remained strikingly faithful to the principles of his father and of Jabotinsky. And as a politician, he has remained faithful, too, even if he sometimes obfuscates those principles for fear that they will be considered too extreme. "Bibi might aim for the same goals as mine," Benzion told *Maariv*, "but he keeps to himself the ways to achieve them, because if he expressed them, he would expose his goals. . . . I am talking about tactics regarding the revealing of theories that people with different ideology might not accept."

What are those goals? Above all, preventing the establishment of a viable Palestinian state. To understand Netanyahu's perspective, it is important to understand that, like his father and Jabotinsky, he believes that Zionists have already made vast, gut-wrenching—indeed, foolish—territorial concessions. The most important of these came in 1922, when the socialists who led the Zionist movement acquiesced in Britain's decision to carve Transjordan from Palestine and deny Jews the right to settle there. As a result, Netanyahu argues, modern-day Israel—even including the West Bank and Gaza Strip—encompasses a mere "scrap" of the land on which the Jews should have built their state. Thus, while international observers frequently note that establishing a Palestinian state in all of the West Bank and Gaza would still leave Israel in control of 78 percent of British mandatory Palestine, Netanyahu's calculations are radically different. Since the Jews relinquished 80 percent when Transjordan was created, he argues, they currently control only "20 percent" of their rightful land. Ceding the West Bank and Gaza would reduce that to "15 percent . . . a truncated ghetto-state squeezed onto a narrow shoreline."

As that statement suggests, Netanyahu has made holding the West Bank and Gaza a cornerstone of his political career. Among his key supporters when he first ran for the Knesset in 1988 was the Likud leader in the northern West Bank settlement of Ariel, and in one of his first statements as a candidate for the Knesset, Netanyahu stressed the West Bank's importance to Israeli security, a topic to which he devotes an entire chapter of *A Durable Peace*. Not surprisingly, he opposed the 1993 Oslo Accords, telling his advisers, "It is against my principles and my conscience." The accords, he told a rally several days after they were signed, are based upon "an enormous lie." Two years later, he attacked Oslo at length in a book about terrorism. These attacks strengthened Netanyahu's alliance with the settler movement, and when he ran for prime minister against the Labor Party's Shimon Peres in 1996, settlers formed his activist base. After a campaign in which he told rallies, "We are here to prevent the establishment of a Palestinian state," and in which he relentlessly accused Peres of planning to divide Jerusalem,

Netanyahu orchestrated a stunning upset, winning by one percentage point. Had the election been held only within the green line, he would have lost by five points.

———‡———

If the settler movement played a key role in Netanyahu's rise to power, so did the leaders of American Jewry. In the 1980s and 1990s, Netanyahu did not merely forge close ties to the American Jewish establishment; he helped to create it.

Netanyahu's familiarity with American culture is legendary: he attended high school in the United States, attended college in the United States, attended graduate school in the United States, was first married in the United States, got his first full-time job in the United States, and held American citizenship until he was in his thirties. He also began his governmental career in the United States, when, in 1982, he became a political attaché in the Israeli embassy in Washington. The 1980s were a hinge decade in organized American Jewish life. With Republicans in the White House and Likud prime ministers in Israel, the venerable, civil-rights-minded Jewish institutions—the American Jewish Congress, American Jewish Committee, and Anti-Defamation League—were losing power to AIPAC and the Conference of Presidents of Major American Jewish Organizations, which lacked any connection to domestic liberalism. Netanyahu, with his perfect English, inspiring family story (his older brother, Yonatan, had been the only Israeli commando to die in the famed 1976 hostage rescue mission at Entebbe Airport in Uganda), and facility on American television, became a star of the American Jewish lecture circuit. And as a Revisionist with no ties to Zionism's socialist heritage, he was perfectly placed to build ties to the conservative Jews who were gaining influence in an American Jewish establishment newly freed from its own left-liberal roots. In Washington and then in New York, where he served as Israel's ambassador to the UN, Netanyahu grew close to Malcolm Hoenlein, who in 1986 became the top staffer at the Presidents' Conference. He also developed friendships with the cosmetics heir Ronald Lauder and the real estate magnate Mortimer Zuckerman, both of whom went on to chair the conference; with the casino mogul Sheldon Adelson, one of the largest donors to AIPAC and the more right-leaning Zionist Organization of America; and with Irving Moscowitz, a major funder of settler and pro-settler groups in Israel and the United States. To be sure, Netanyahu's American circle represented only a subset of the broader community of large donors to major Jewish organizations. But it was unparalleled among Israeli politicians. When Netanyahu first ran for the Knesset in 1988, he was virtually unknown in Israel but already a celebrity among activist American Jews.

When Netanyahu returned to Israel to run for office, he and his American Jewish backers maintained their symbiotic relationship. Lauder and Moscowitz poured money into Netanyahu's campaigns. Lauder and Adelson helped to fund the Shalem Center, a think tank that reflects Netanyahu's hawkish views. Lauder employed Netanyahu's aides, and even his ex-wife. And Lauder introduced Netanyahu to the Republican political consultant Arthur Finkelstein, who ran his 1996 campaign for prime minister.

Netanyahu proved generous in return. In 1991, he reportedly arranged for Adelson to hold his wedding reception at the Knesset. (Netanyahu has denied the Knesset speaker's claim that he made the request.) On May 29, 1996, the night he was first elected prime minister, Netanyahu spent election eve in a room at the Tel Aviv Hilton with his American backers, who had flown in to watch the returns. Four months later, as a Yom Kippur gift to Moscowitz, he opened the entrance to a passageway under the Temple Mount. (The move sparked Palestinian rioting that left twenty-six Israelis and more than one hundred Palestinians dead.)

Above all, Netanyahu and his American Jewish allies worked together to undermine the effort to create a Palestinian state. As the leader of the Likud in the mid-1990s, Netanyahu lobbied aggressively in Washington against Prime Minister Yitzhak Rabin's agenda. While Rabin supported American aid to the Palestinian Authority, Netanyahu urged members of Congress to oppose it. His effort paid off in 1995, when New York's Republican senator Alfonse D'Amato—a fellow Finkelstein client—introduced legislation banning direct U.S. assistance to the Palestinians.

Quietly, AIPAC and the Presidents' Conference subverted Rabin's efforts, too. In the ten months after Rabin's September 1993 handshake with Arafat on the White House lawn, the Presidents' Conference did not issue a single press release supporting his peace efforts. Colette Avital, Rabin's consul general in New York, grew so frustrated with the Conference's lack of support that she convened a meeting of American Jewish liberals to plot a response. After Rabin's assassination, the Israeli government decided to organize a commemorative concert at Madison Square Garden. Hoenlein, according to Avital, insisted that Netanyahu be invited to speak. When the Israelis refused, Avital says that Hoenlein began finding excuses to cancel the event. Hoenlein denies that there was any controversy about Netanyahu's participation or that he tried to undermine the event—which the Presidents' Conference helped to arrange—in any way.

The story was similar at AIPAC, where, according to former staffer Keith Weissman, key figures in the organization "were sucking at the teat of Likud." Neal Sher, AIPAC's executive director from 1994 to 1996, believed AIPAC had a responsibility to support Rabin's agenda. But as he later admitted, "Getting AIPAC to support Oslo, and what the Israeli government wanted to do, was like pulling teeth." Knowing that Rabin privately opposed efforts to move the U.S. embassy in Israel from Tel Aviv to Jerusalem because he feared antagonizing the Palestinians, Sher tried to downplay the issue. But his deputy, Howard Kohr, who had come to AIPAC from the Republican Jewish Coalition, and a powerful AIPAC board member, Robert Asher—in tandem with Netanyahu and Jerusalem mayor Ehud Olmert—lobbied GOP leaders in Congress in favor of the embassy move. In May 1995, hours after arriving in Washington to address the AIPAC Policy Conference, Rabin was ambushed by news that Robert Dole, the Senate majority leader, would use his own AIPAC speech to announce legislation moving the embassy. Despite Rabin's private rage, AIPAC and the Presidents' Conference endorsed Dole's bill. A year later, Sher resigned, reportedly at the insistence of AIPAC's board. He was replaced by Howard Kohr.

———+———

AIPAC's most powerful board members, according to one former staffer, spent the Rabin years "waiting for Bibi to ascend." And when Netanyahu did win the prime ministership in 1996, he and his allies in the American Jewish establishment switched from undermining Rabin's peace efforts to undermining Clinton's.

Upon becoming prime minister, Netanyahu—under American pressure—pledged to continue the Oslo process. But as he later told settlers, his real strategy was "to interpret the accords in such a way that would allow me to put an end to this galloping forward to the '67 borders." In a speech to Likud's central committee a few months after taking office, Netanyahu flatly declared, "There will never be a Palestinian state between the Mediterranean and the Jordan."

To make good on that pledge, Netanyahu created a government dominated by parties hostile to the peace process, and repeatedly used their hostility as an excuse for avoiding the steps that Oslo required. But the coalition was a prison of Netanyahu's own making. He could have forged a national unity government with Labor and thus created the political basis for bolder moves toward a peace deal. But he refused, telling Dennis Ross that a leader must never abandon those ideological stalwarts who constitute "his tribe."

If Netanyahu used his coalition partners as one pretext for not implementing Oslo, he used the Palestinians as another. He endlessly charged that the Palestinians were not fulfilling their obligations, and thus, that Israel need not fulfill its own. Some of what Netanyahu said about Palestinian infractions was true. Arafat's PLO did not stop hateful anti-Israel propaganda, collect illegal weapons, limit the size of the

Palestinian police force, or consistently combat the terrorism that took scores of Israeli lives. But Netanyahu's own violations, according to Ron Pundak, director general of the Shimon Peres Center for Peace in Tel Aviv, were even "more numerous." Netanyahu refused to fully honor Israel's pledges to withdraw from parts of the West Bank, to release Palestinian prisoners, to allow safe passage for Palestinians from Gaza to the West Bank, or to transfer the tax money that the Israeli government had collected from Palestinians. He also reinstated the subsidies for settlement building that Rabin had eliminated and oversaw increased construction in the West Bank, moves that, while not a formal violation of Oslo, added to the atmosphere of distrust. During Netanyahu's first year in office, the percentage of Palestinians who believed Oslo would bring them a state fell from 44 to 30 percent.

More fundamentally, Netanyahu's strategy of using (and sometimes even inventing) Palestinian transgressions as a rationale for shirking Israel's own obligations ran counter to Oslo's basic logic, which was that the two sides would build trust by taking parallel steps toward peace. Instead, Netanyahu destroyed that trust by demanding that the Palestinians fully meet their obligations while consistently minimizing Israel's own. By late 1995, for instance, Rabin's government had transferred 27 percent of the West Bank to partial or full Palestinian control, and had led the Palestinians to believe that they would receive substantially more land in three additional withdrawals. But when Netanyahu took office, he found a loophole. Under Oslo, Israel was permitted to exempt military bases from the land from which it withdrew. As Netanyahu later boasted, he defined the entire Jordan Valley—roughly one-quarter of the West Bank—as the equivalent of a military base, and thus dramatically reduced the land available for transfer. Ultimately, in the 1998 Wye River Memorandum, he agreed to relinquish an additional 10 percent of the West Bank (with another 3 percent set aside for nature reserves), while insisting that the third and final withdrawal would comprise no more than an additional 1 percent. But even then,

Netanyahu made a halfhearted effort to convince his cabinet to ratify Wye, and as a result, only part of the promised withdrawal was carried out.

—————✦—————

Netanyahu's defenders argue that for a Likud prime minister to hand back any territory at all constituted a momentous break with Revisionist ideology. And on the hard right, Netanyahu's deviations did produce cries of betrayal. When Netanyahu handed over most of Hebron to the Palestinians in 1997, his cabinet approved the move by a vote of only eleven to seven, and Menachem Begin's son, Benjamin, resigned his ministership in disgust. In 1998, the cabinet approved the Wye Memorandum eight to four, but five ministers abstained.

But in Netanyahu's mind, these tactical deviations from Revisionist ideology—made under American pressure—served a broader Revisionist goal: retaining as much of the West Bank as possible. The point of giving back most of Hebron, he later told settlers, is that "it is better to give two percent than to give one hundred percent." Or as he wrote in *A Durable Peace*, "My principal objective at Wye was to limit the extent of further interim Israeli withdrawals so as to leave Israel with sufficient territorial depth for its defense."

In fact, Netanyahu had a clear vision of where he hoped Oslo would lead. Over the course of the 1990s, he detailed this vision in books and op-eds; he drew maps on napkins; he even presented a plan to his cabinet. Under Netanyahu's plan, the Palestinians would live in four disconnected cantons: one encompassing Jenin, Nablus, and Ramallah in the north; a second encompassing Bethlehem and Hebron in the south; a third encompassing Jericho in the east; and a fourth encompassing Qalqilya in the west. Together, these cantons would comprise roughly 40 percent of the West Bank. Israel would control the other 60 percent. This would include most Jewish settlements, and all "the open (and largely unpopulated) land" in the West Bank. Since the West Bank's rural land would be annexed to Israel, it could not be used to resettle

Palestinian refugees, who under Netanyahu's plan would remain permanently in those Arab countries to which they fled in 1948. These four Palestinian cantons would not constitute a state—indeed, even they would be bisected by Israeli roads—but within them, Palestinians would enjoy autonomy over education, health care, and the like.

Netanyahu's vision left American negotiators dumbfounded. "No Palestinian alive will accept that," exclaimed Dennis Ross. But Netanyahu was not seeking Palestinian acceptance; he was seeking Palestinian submission. In 1923, in perhaps his most famous essay, Jabotinsky had argued that while the Arabs of Palestine would never willingly accept a Jewish state—or abandon hopes for one of their own—they would acquiesce once they had repeatedly smashed up against the "iron wall" of Zionist military power. Benzion Netanyahu had suggested something similar when he told *Maariv* that although there was no hope of peace "out of agreement . . . the other side might stay in peace if it understands that doing anything [else] will cause it enormous pain." The same concept underlay Netanyahu's cantons scenario. While many liberal Zionists agreed that Israel needed an "iron wall" to show Palestinians that they could not destroy the Jewish state, Netanyahu took the metaphor farther, arguing that an "iron wall" must stand between the Palestinians and their own statehood aspirations as well. "I am often asked: Would the Palestinian Arabs accept autonomy?" he wrote in 1994. "My answer is that they would accept it if they knew Israel wouldn't give them an independent state." In other words, once Israel crushes their spirit, the Palestinians will take whatever they get.

Not surprisingly, given Netanyahu's hostility to a Palestinian state, many in the Clinton administration felt hostile toward him. According to Aaron David Miller, the Clinton administration's Middle East team "saw Bibi as a kind of speed bump that would have to be negotiated along the way until a new Israeli prime minister came along who was more serious about peace." In the words of Miller's boss, Dennis Ross, "neither President Clinton nor Secretary Albright believed that Bibi had any real interest in pursuing peace."

But every time the Clinton administration tried to drag Netanyahu in the direction of a viable Palestinian state, Netanyahu rallied American Jewish groups and conservative Republicans to his defense. In January 1998, with the White House pushing him for a larger territorial withdrawal, Netanyahu flew to Washington just days after the news broke about Bill Clinton's affair with Monica Lewinsky and addressed a rally organized by Clinton foe Jerry Falwell and the Adelson-backed Zionist Organization of America. After Netanyahu's speech, the crowd chanted, "Not one inch." Falwell later said the event "was all planned by Netanyahu as an affront to Mr. Clinton."

Some mainstream American Jewish leaders were taken aback by Netanyahu's brazenness. But most still supported his efforts to resist U.S. pressure. In May 1998, with the Clinton administration mulling a public proposal about the amount of land from which Israel should withdraw as part of its Oslo obligations, Netanyahu confidant Dore Gold, who was serving as Israel's ambassador to the UN, complained to the Presidents' Conference that Secretary of State Madeleine Albright was delivering an "ultimatum." On cue, the American Jewish Committee's executive director, David Harris, declared himself "uneasy" that "Israel is being given a public ultimatum." House Speaker Newt Gingrich also attacked the administration's "public ultimatum."

Then, in December, with Clinton about to travel to Gaza to witness the PLO revoke the clauses in its charter demanding Israel's destruction, Gold—fearful that Clinton was boosting Arafat's stature—urged the Presidents' Conference to publicly condemn the Palestinian leader's anti-Israel incitement and his threat to unilaterally declare a Palestinian state. The Conference's more liberal members objected, fearing that Netanyahu was using them to undermine Clinton's trip. But Netanyahu's conservative allies went along. Later, Netanyahu would tell settlers that "I wasn't afraid to confront Clinton" because "America is something that can be easily swayed."

In 1999, after failing to fully implement the Wye Accords, Netanyahu's government fell. It would take him ten years to return to the prime minister's office, and there is no evidence that his views about the Palestinians changed much during that time. In 2001, Netanyahu criticized the new Likud prime minister, Ariel Sharon, for not responding harshly enough to the terrorism of the second intifada, proposing—in language reminiscent of his father—that Israel "hit them. Not simply a single hit, many painful hits so that the price will be too heavy to bear." In 2005, he resigned as Sharon's finance minister to protest Israel's dismantling of settlements in Gaza. That same year, Netanyahu's old confidant, Dore Gold, outlined a proposal for Israel's permanent borders based on assumptions similar to those underlying the cantons plan Netanyahu had laid out in the 1990s. "All the events that happened subsequent to his first premiership only reaffirmed and strengthened his beliefs," explained Naftali Bennett, Netanyahu's chief of staff from 2006 to 2008. Bennett, it's worth noting, went on to become director general of the Yesha Council, the umbrella organization for the settler movement.

True to form, when Netanyahu ran for prime minister in late 2008 and early 2009, he held to his longstanding view that a Palestinian state was incompatible with Israeli security. He vowed not to evacuate settlements, or to negotiate a final settlement with the Palestinians, but instead to focus on "economic peace." And what would "economic peace" look like? In October 2008, a *Financial Times* reporter saw Netanyahu sketch it in green marker on a white board: in Netanyahu's map, "the West Bank [would be] divided into a collection of disconnected [Palestinian] economic zones" with Israel controlling the land in between.

Nearing sixty years old, more than two decades into his political career, and on the verge of his second stint as prime minister, Benjamin Netanyahu remained very much his father's son.

7

——+┼+——

The Clash

T HE CLASH BETWEEN BARACK OBAMA AND BENJAMIN NETAN-
yahu began before each was even elected. During the 2008 presidential primaries, Obama had criticized the view that "unless you adopt
an unwavering pro-Likud approach to Israel that you're anti-Israel,"
thus leaving little doubt as to where on the Israeli political spectrum his
sympathies lay. Many of the Clinton administration veterans who populated the Obama campaign still nursed resentments from Netanyahu's
first prime ministership, resentments captured by former White House
press secretary Joe Lockhart, who called Netanyahu "one of the single
most obnoxious individuals you're going to come into [contact with]—
just a liar and a cheat."

For their part, Netanyahu and his allies clearly favored Obama's
Republican opponent, John McCain. In their two private meetings before
taking office—one at Reagan National Airport in Washington and the
other at Jerusalem's King David Hotel—Obama and Netanyahu had

gotten along well, with each stressing to the other that he was a pragmatist. But privately, Netanyahu told associates that Obama knew little
about the Middle East, put too much faith in the power of speeches,
and might take Israel for granted while he reached out to the Arab
world. In September 2008, Yoram Ettinger, a Likud activist who had
lobbied Congress against Yitzhak Rabin's pro-Oslo agenda during
Netanyahu's first prime ministership, wrote that "Obama's passive
approach [to fighting terrorism] adrenalizes the veins of terrorists and
intensifies Israel's predicament, while McCain's approach bolsters the
US' and Israel's war on terrorism." At around the same time, the historian and commentator Michael Oren, whom Netanyahu would later
appoint ambassador to the United States, published a study warning
that while "McCain's priorities are unlikely to ruffle the U.S.-Israel
relationship, Obama's are liable to strain the alliance." The public and
private criticism grew so blatant that prominent Democrats warned
Netanyahu's supporters to stop.

Netanyahu and Obama also took office buoyed by the belief that
their fellow countrymen and women had ratified their view of the
world. Netanyahu was propelled to power by an election in February
2009 that not only swelled the parliamentary ranks of his own Likud,
but turned Avigdor Lieberman's Yisrael Beiteinu into a second major
right-wing party. As a result, throughout his prime ministership,
Netanyahu's hawkish instincts were reinforced by the fear that if he
compromised them, he might forfeit his leadership of the Israeli right.

For his part, Obama had won 78 percent of the Jewish vote, a
remarkable testament to the gulf between American Jewry and many
of its communal leaders. The results confirmed what Obama's personal
experience had taught: that most Jews were liberal, even on Israel. And
that belief, combined with his healthy self-confidence in his persuasive
powers, led him to believe that he could risk a public confrontation
with the Israeli government and still retain the support of American
Jews. As during the campaign, Obama's initial inclination was toward

a liberal democratic Zionism that challenged Israel's occupation of the West Bank. And as during the campaign, when this inclination clashed with political reality, political reality won.

—＊—

At the behest of Hillary Clinton, his new secretary of state, Obama chose former Senate majority leader George Mitchell as his envoy for the peace process. Clinton believed that Mitchell's stature, and his success in brokering a peace deal in Northern Ireland, would demonstrate the Obama administration's commitment to Israeli-Palestinian peace. But the choice also sent a more subtle signal. In 2000, Bill Clinton had asked Mitchell to investigate the causes of the second intifada, an investigation that led Mitchell to write a report calling on Israel to freeze settlement construction. The report also demanded that the Palestinians more aggressively fight terrorism—indeed, it was scrupulously "evenhanded," a phrase often used to describe Mitchell's relationship to the conflict. But the phrase itself suggested that his appointment signified a break with the Clinton and Bush administrations' perceived deference to Israel, an implication grasped immediately by Israeli and American Jewish leaders. In a paper for the Jerusalem Center for Public Affairs, a think tank led by Netanyahu ally Dore Gold, a former AIPAC official and Netanyahu aide named Lenny Ben-David wrote that Mitchell's "committee [had] attempted—even at the risk of straining credibility—to split the blame for the crisis." After conceding that Mitchell was known for his "neutrality," Abraham Foxman added acidly that the "Swiss were neutral" in World War II.

Mitchell took office on January 22, 2009, four days after the end of Operation Cast Lead, Israel's war to quell Hamas rocket fire from Gaza into southern Israel. When Mitchell arrived in the region, he encountered a Palestinian leadership in the West Bank terrified that, having stood by while Israel invaded Gaza, they looked like lackeys of the Jewish state. Palestinian Authority president Mahmoud Abbas and Prime Minister Salam Fayyad had dramatically improved security cooperation with Israel. Mitchell and his aides wanted to show the Palestinians that they were getting something in return, and what the Palestinians wanted in return was a halt to settlement construction. Given past U.S. behavior, even thinking in these terms represented a shift. As Daniel Kurtzer had pointed out, the Clinton and Bush administrations had often tailored their initiatives to Israeli domestic politics. Now, working through Mitchell, Obama was tailoring his initiatives to Palestinian domestic politics.

But the motivation was not only instrumental; it was emotional, too. In March 2009, Hillary Clinton, Mitchell, and a few aides traveled from Jerusalem, where they had met with Israeli officials, to Ramallah. As they sped through the West Bank, passing boulders that blocked Palestinian villages from accessing settler-dominated bypass roads, the Americans became palpably uncomfortable. "There was a kind of silence and people were careful," remembers one former senior State Department official, "but it was like, my God, you crossed that border and it was apartheid." In meetings in Washington, Obama spoke bluntly about Palestinian suffering. One longtime capital insider noted that in all his years of going to the White House, he had never heard Clinton, Reagan, or either Bush speak the same way.

——+——

The Obama team deferred any policy announcements until late March, when Netanyahu formed his government. Then, when Netanyahu requested two months to do his own policy review, they deferred again. But there was little doubt as to Netanyahu's inclinations. During his own election campaign, he had refused to endorse the idea of a Palestinian state and had made it clear that he considered negotiations with the Palestinians aimed at creating one to be a waste of time. Instead, he had proposed "economic peace," an effort to turn attention away from Palestinian statehood and toward Palestinian economic development. Those views did not change when he finished his policy review. As top Netanyahu aide Ron Dermer explained in May 2009, "There is no way now where you have on the Palestinian side a willingness to make the sorts of compromises that will be required for a deal on the core issues but yet despite that the previous government just decided to negotiate and negotiate and negotiate and to focus on that, to bang their head against the wall.... What Netanyahu will do is ... to work to change the reality on the ground." Netanyahu's national security adviser, Uzi Arad, added, "It will be difficult to reach a true Israeli-Palestinian agreement that does away with the bulk of the conflict. I don't see that in the coming years." In mid-May, when Netanyahu first met Obama at the White House, he said he was ready to begin peace talks, but still refused to endorse a Palestinian state.

Ironically, Netanyahu's hard line helped convince the White House to push for a settlement freeze. Abbas was eager to carry on the negotiations he had been pursuing with Netanyahu's predecessor, Ehud Olmert, negotiations in which, Olmert would later say, "we were very close." Had Netanyahu agreed to pick up where those talks left off, some former U.S. officials believe, the White House might have convinced Abbas to shelve his demand for a settlement freeze. (Abbas had, after all, been negotiating with Olmert in the absence of such a freeze.) But Netanyahu's evident disdain for Olmert's concessions convinced Palestinian leaders that even if the new prime minister did enter negotiations, they would drag on inconclusively, thus giving Israel cover to seize more and more of the West Bank. So the Palestinians, buttressed by the Arab states, held firm in their insistence on a halt to settlement growth. And the Obama administration, doubtful that Netanyahu and Abbas would enter meaningful negotiations in the current climate, decided to link the demand for a settlement freeze to a push for Arab governments to move toward diplomatic recognition of Israel. Together, the White House reasoned, these moves might build trust and allow serious talks to begin.

Inside the Obama administration, the call for a settlement freeze sparked little internal dissent. After all, Mitchell had demanded a freeze back in 2001, and two years later, by accepting the Bush administration's "Road Map" to peace, Israel had actually agreed to one, although it was never carried out. National security adviser James Jones had himself written an unpublished 2008 study that reportedly criticized Israeli policy in the West Bank. And Rahm Emanuel, the White House chief of staff, was particularly enthusiastic about the idea. Although his Israeli-born father had once fought in the Revisionist militia, the Irgun, Emanuel had a record of opposing settlement growth. In 2003, he had been one of only four Jewish members of Congress to sign a letter endorsing the Road Map. Privately, he told associates that the Bush administration had coddled Israel, and that it was time for Israel's American friends to speak more frankly to the leaders of the Jewish state. When Netanyahu tried to establish back-channel discussions with Emanuel, bypassing Mitchell, Obama's chief of staff refused.

Younger White House aides also backed the push for a settlement freeze. Close observers noted an ideological affinity among four key staffers: Daniel Shapiro, the National Security Council's senior director for the Middle East and North Africa; Mara Rudman, Mitchell's chief of staff; chief foreign policy speechwriter Ben Rhodes; and National Security Council chief of staff Denis McDonough, the foreign policy aide personally closest to Obama. Shapiro, Rudman, and McDonough had all previously worked for Lee Hamilton, the former chairman of the House Foreign Affairs Committee, a man with distinctly dovish views on the conflict. After retiring from Congress in 1999, Hamilton had advocated that the United States support a dialogue with Hamas. He had also cochaired the Iraq Study Group, whose final report urged an aggressive U.S. push for Arab-Israeli peace and, controversially, claimed that Israel's 2006 bombing of Lebanon had increased hostility to U.S. troops in Iraq. The report's coauthor was Ben Rhodes.

Among the few administration skeptics of the push for a settlement freeze was Dennis Ross, who considered it deeply unrealistic given the nature of Netanyahu's government. But Ross was working at the State Department, not the White House, and his job description was restricted to Iran. He had tried to broaden his mandate during the transition, arguing that in order to effectively craft Iran strategy he needed the freedom to dabble in every aspect of Middle East policy, including the peace process. A memo by Ross's former employer, the Washington Institute for Near East Policy, had even declared that he would be working on a "wide range of Middle East issues, from the Arab-Israeli peace process to Iran." But Jones promised Mitchell that Ross would not meddle in his work, and when a State Department spokesman announced Ross's appointment, he insisted that Ross "in terms of negotiating, will not be involved in the peace process." Whether Ross abided by that pledge while at the State Department is a matter of sharp dispute among former and current Obama officials. But either way, he did not control the Israel-Palestinian portfolio. Not yet.

On May 5, Vice President Joseph Biden told AIPAC that in keeping with its obligations under the Road Map, Israel must "not build more settlements." On May 18, after his first meeting with Netanyahu at the White House, Obama declared, "Settlements have to be stopped in order for us to move forward."

Netanyahu was livid. Before going to Washington, he had told advisers that he planned to explain to the president that the Palestinian issue was not central to the problems in the Middle East. And in a bout of wishful thinking, he had predicted that the White House would downplay the settlements issue and instead focus on Iran's nuclear program. After the trip, when it became clear that the White House was serious about demanding a settlement freeze, Netanyahu told advisers that Emanuel and Hillary Clinton had turned Obama against him. It was just like during the Clinton administration, he fumed. "They want to throw me under the bus." Associates of the prime minister believed the United States was using the settlement freeze to try to topple his government. One well-placed Israeli heard Ron Dermer, Netanyahu's top aide, and Dore Gold, a close outside adviser, privately refer to the president as Barack *Hussein* Obama. Dermer and Gold vehemently deny the charge.

Israeli and American Jewish officials immediately marshaled arguments against the proposed freeze. First, they claimed that in expanding settlements, Israel was merely accommodating the "natural growth" of the people already living there. How, they asked, could the Israeli government tell a family that it could not build an addition to its house to accommodate a new child? But as the dovish Israeli group Peace Now has documented, close to 40 percent of the "natural growth" in the settlements in recent years has stemmed from new residents moving in, often with the help of government subsidies. What's more, there is no inherent right to live in the same community when your family expands, as many former city dwellers now living in the American suburbs can attest. And in accepting the Road Map, Israel had previously committed to a freeze that included "natural growth."

Second, critics assailed the Obama administration for lumping small, remote settlements together with large, closer-in ones that they contended would be incorporated into Israel in the event of a peace deal. They also claimed that the Bush administration had promised to support Israel's right to annex "major Israeli population centers" in the West Bank in any final deal. But even George W. Bush had said such annexations must be "mutually agreed" to by the Palestinians, and in the absence of a peace agreement, it was impossible to know which West Bank "population centers" the two sides would allow Israel to retain. In fact, some of the settlements that Israel's supporters insisted it would ultimately annex—such as Ariel—were vehemently opposed by Palestinian leaders who said they would destroy the contiguity of their future state. And even if it did make sense to exempt some close-in settlements from a freeze, doing so would have required Netanyahu to identify other settlements where the freeze would apply, something he refused to do.

Finally, critics claimed that by demanding a settlement freeze, despite the fact that the Palestinians had negotiated without one during the Clinton and Bush years, the Obama administration was making Palestinian leaders intransigent, since they could not be seen as softer on settlements than the president of the United States. But in truth, as documents leaked to the Arabic cable news network Al Jazeera would later reveal, it was the Palestinians who had demanded the settlement freeze, in part because they believed that the lack of one was a major reason the Oslo process had failed. Palestinian negotiators stressed that, unlike the Israelis, they had met their obligations under the Road Map. As even Israeli officials acknowledged, they had dramatically improved security cooperation against terror, even though doing so had left them open to charges of collaborating with the occupation. Now Palestinian leaders feared that if they entered talks without a settlement freeze, particularly given Netanyahu's opposition to a Palestinian state, they would hemorrhage domestic support. "If Israel doesn't recognize the two-state solution and continues settlements," Palestinian negotiator Saeb Erekat told Mitchell, "it will be the last nail in Abu Mazen's [Mahmoud Abbas's] coffin if we send him to negotiate."

———+———

Given the inclinations of Obama and his advisers, it is easy to see why they wanted a settlement freeze. But they badly misjudged the difficulty of achieving one. Top administration officials believed that merely by publicly asserting his wishes, Obama would create so much political pressure inside Israel that Netanyahu would have to acquiesce. After all, they noted privately, Netanyahu had lost his prime ministership in 1999—as had his Likud predecessor Yitzhak Shamir in 1992—after alienating an American president. Moreover, they assumed that what Netanyahu cared about most was U.S. support for a hard line against Iran. To ensure that, they reasoned, he would give ground on the Palestinian question, even if it meant shifting to a more centrist coalition.

But much of this was wishful thinking. Obama was popular in many countries, but not in Israel, where according to one 2009 poll, 39 percent of Jewish Israelis considered him a Muslim. He further undermined his reputation among Israelis by traveling to Turkey in April and to Egypt in June without stopping in the Jewish state, an affront to Israelis who had grown accustomed to presidential attention in the Clinton and Bush years. It didn't help that in its broadcast of Obama's Cairo speech on June 4, Israel's public television station identified him as Barack Hussein Obama, thus emphasizing his Muslim heritage. As a result, a public standoff with the American president didn't hurt Netanyahu's domestic standing at all.

What's more, Netanyahu helped deflect American pressure when, in a June speech at Bar-Ilan University, he reversed course and endorsed a Palestinian state—thus prompting AIPAC to applaud his "strong desire to reach peace." But a close look at Netanyahu's Bar-Ilan speech showed that his vision of a Palestinian state bore little resemblance to what most people meant by the word. For starters, Netanyahu insisted that Jerusalem must remain "the united capital of Israel," thereby distinguishing his vision from that of former prime ministers Ehud Barak and Ehud Olmert, both of whom had offered to make East Jerusalem the capital of a Palestinian state. Then he demanded that Palestinian leaders not merely recognize Israel, which the PLO had done in 1993, but recognize it as a Jewish state, even though Egypt and Jordan had not done so when they made peace. "To vest this declaration with practical meaning," Netanyahu added, the Palestinians must concede that there would be no return of Palestinian refugees to pre-1967 Israel, and thus no threat to Israel's Jewish character. But even those Palestinians who privately conceded that there would be no substantial refugee return vehemently rejected making that concession up front, since they—along with some former Israeli negotiators—believed that the final element of any peace deal would be a trade in which the Palestinians abandoned a large-scale return of refugees in exchange for a capital in East Jerusalem and some control over the Temple Mount. Netanyahu almost certainly knew that. As his father, Benzion, explained when asked about his son's Bar-Ilan speech, "He doesn't support [a Palestinian state]. He supports the sorts of conditions that they [the Palestinians] will never accept."

Even more revealing were Netanyahu's hints about the borders of his envisioned Palestinian "state." Never in the speech—nor in any subsequent interview—did he endorse territorial contiguity inside the West Bank. To the contrary, at Bar-Ilan he said that a Palestinian state must leave Israel with "defensible borders," a phrase he had previously defined as requiring that Israel hold roughly half the West Bank. More striking still, he devoted a full two paragraphs of the speech to the folly of territorial withdrawal. "A great many people are telling us that withdrawal is the key to peace with the Palestinians," he declared. "But the fact is that all our withdrawals were met by huge waves of suicide bombers. We tried withdrawal by agreement, withdrawal without an agreement, we tried partial withdrawal and full withdrawal. . . . The argument that withdrawal would bring peace closer did not stand up to the test of reality."

One interpretation of Netanyahu's speech is that he believed that this time—if the Palestinians agreed to a "demilitarized" state, a long-term Israeli troop presence in the Jordan Valley, and other tough security arrangements—a large-scale Israeli territorial withdrawal might not lead to disaster. In other words, between his first and second prime ministerships, his perspective on a Palestinian state in almost all of the West Bank had fundamentally changed. The problem with this analysis is that Netanyahu had spent years arguing that those tough security arrangements were impossible. "Demilitarizing an entire sovereign state," he insisted in *A Durable Peace,* is "unheard-of in the annals of nations and for good reason: It cannot be sustained." Netanyahu reiterated those words when *A Durable Peace* was reissued in electronic form in October 2009—four months *after* his Bar-Ilan speech.

The more plausible interpretation of Netanyahu's speech is that his real view had not changed at all. He still believed that a Palestinian state would inevitably threaten Israeli security and thus, that there was no way Israel could withdraw from the bulk of the West Bank. But he could no longer say that. So under heavy international pressure to utter the words "Palestinian state," he simply affixed those words to his old map. This explains how he could simultaneously endorse a Palestinian state and denounce territorial withdrawal: because in his vision, creating a Palestinian "state" would not require any substantial territorial withdrawal.

———+———

Buoyed by Netanyahu's apparent moderation, American Jewish and right-wing Christian groups pushed back hard against Obama's call for a settlement freeze. AIPAC convinced 329 House members to sign a letter urging the administration to work "privately"—in other words, cease making public demands—in its dealings with Israel. In June, Malcolm Hoenlein warned, "President Obama's strongest supporters among Jewish leaders are deeply troubled by his recent Middle East initiatives." Abraham Foxman added, "The administration is putting too much weight on solving the conflict." In a replay of his speech to a rally organized by Jerry Falwell during the Monica Lewinsky scandal, Netanyahu addressed a Christians United for Israel conference and basked as the group's head endorsed "Israel's sovereign right to grow and develop the settlements of Israel as you see fit and not yield to the pressure of the United States government."

Still, influential congressional Democrats backed the White House, not wanting to defy a popular president from their own party. John Kerry, the chairman of the Senate Foreign Relations Committee, called for "demonstrating—with actions rather than words—that we are serious about Israel freezing settlement activity in the West Bank." In May, when Netanyahu had breakfast with Jewish members of Congress the day after his White House meeting with Obama, he was—in the words of Representative Robert Wexler—"taken aback" by members' insistence that Israeli settlement policies had to change. "Most of the Jewish members feel very uncomfortable with the settlement policy and with Netanyahu personally," explains one Democratic strategist. But members of Congress also worried that the administration did not fully grasp what it had gotten itself into. "If you're going to pick a fight with a bully," explained a congressional staffer who works on Israel policy, "you need to win."

The American Jewish groups, recounts one former Obama campaign Middle East adviser, were "scared to death." Another adds that "when the Israelis thought Obama would go to the mat [on settlements] they were terrified." But Obama did not go to the mat. Asked by Mitchell for advice, Daniel Kurtzer said that had he been asked before the president made a public demand, he would have advised against making a settlement freeze including natural growth a precondition for negotiations. However, Kurtzer argued, now that the president had announced the policy, he had to succeed. When Mitchell responded that success would be hard to achieve, Kurtzer replied that it might be necessary to examine policy options that had long been considered in private, such as exempting settlement goods from the U.S.-Israeli free trade agreement or closing the IRS loophole that allows Americans to receive tax deductions for money they donate to settler groups. Another outside expert circulated an unofficial document called a "non-paper" to Obama Middle East officials, which listed a variety of carrots and sticks the administration could deploy, including recalling the U.S. ambassador in Israel for consultations, canceling an Israeli military delegation's visit to the Pentagon, and letting it be known that the United States would not veto a UN resolution criticizing settlements.

There were precedents for all these moves. After Israel attacked Iraq's Osirak nuclear reactor in 1981, the Reagan administration had not only supported a UN resolution condemning Israel, it had delayed various arms sales. Between 1990 and 1992, George H. W. Bush's administration had not only conditioned loan guarantees on a settlement freeze, it had backed six UN Security Council resolutions criticizing the policies of the Jewish state. In 2004, after Israel repaired and upgraded an unmanned aerial vehicle it had sold to China, the Pentagon had demanded the resignation of the director general of the Israeli Defense Ministry. Even George W. Bush had refused to veto a 2009 resolution demanding that Israel cease its military operations in Gaza.

It is impossible to know how Netanyahu would have responded to tangible pressure as opposed to mere public disagreement. Given Obama's relative unpopularity in the Jewish state, Israelis might have blamed him rather than Netanyahu for the standoff. But even so, George H. W. Bush had been unpopular in Israel, too, and his tough stance had still helped dethrone Shamir as prime minister. Agreeing to anything like a full settlement freeze might have shaken Netanyahu's right-wing coalition, but in the centrist Kadima Party he had an alternative partner that could have kept him in power.

It remains a theoretical question because when challenged by Netanyahu and his American Jewish allies, Obama did what he had done during the campaign: he retreated. His Israel policy would never be the same. For starters, Obama's backpedaling undermined Mitchell and his young allies, Mara Rudman and Daniel Shapiro. (McDonough and Rhodes, whose portfolios spanned the globe, were less affected.) Their strategy had only made sense when accompanied by presidential pressure. When Obama refused to apply that pressure, he needed a new strategy, one premised upon his unwillingness to confront Netanyahu. To craft it, in June he brought Ross to the National Security Council to serve as senior director for the Central Region, which essentially meant everything from Morocco to Iran, Israel and Palestine included. It was a job for which Kurtzer had been considered during the transition, but had not received, in part because Jewish organizational officials lobbied against him and in part because top Obama aides knew that given Kurtzer's relationship with Ross, they could not hire them both. It was an eerie echo of the campaign. Once again Ross was overshadowing Shapiro and supplanting Kurtzer, and once again his power derived in large measure from his ability to help Obama retreat from the views he actually held.

Soon, reports surfaced about a power struggle between Ross, on the one hand, and Mitchell and his deputy, Mara Rudman, on the other. It was no contest. For one thing, Ross now worked at the White House, in close proximity to the president, while Mitchell spent most of his time either in the Middle East or at his home in New York. Second, given the weakness of James Jones, Tom Donilon—Ross's old ally from the Clinton administration—had become the de facto national security adviser. Finally, Ross had much closer ties to the Israeli government—which had been trying to bypass Mitchell from the outset—and to the American Jewish establishment. As in the campaign, the capacity to reassure American Jewish leaders had become a crucial test of a staffer's effectiveness, and in that contest Ross had no equal. Even more attractive, from Obama's perspective, Ross sincerely argued that a strategy of mollifying Israel was the best way to advance the peace process. In the words of one outside expert, "Dennis is very good at telling politicians why they don't have to do what they don't want to do anyway."

——+——

If the settlement freeze had been designed to strengthen Abbas and Fayyad, the Obama administration's retreat from it had the reverse effect. The accounts of meetings between American and Palestinian officials during Obama's settlement climbdown are excruciating. Urged on September 16 by Mitchell's deputy, David Hale, to accept a temporary freeze riddled with exceptions, Erekat predicted, "This will mean more settlement construction in 2009 than in 2008." "Let me be candid," he declared the next day, "you made a great effort to get a settlement freeze and you did not succeed. . . . Therefore, no settlement freeze at all, not for 1 hour. More construction in 2010 than 2009. You know this." Hale responded, "We cannot force a sovereign government," prompting Erekat to reply, "Of course you could."

In his prediction about settlement construction, Erekat was wrong, but only barely. In November, Israel and the United States agreed to a settlement freeze that exempted East Jerusalem, exempted all public buildings "essential for normal life," exempted all buildings whose foundations had already been laid, and was set to expire in ten months. Key was the exemption for construction already under way. As several Israeli newspapers reported, settlers had spent the months preceding

November busily laying the foundations of new houses, which they then built upon during the "freeze." Then, when the freeze expired, they began laying more foundations. All in all, according to Peace Now, construction began on 1,518 West Bank housing units in 2008. In 2009, the number was 1,920. In 2010—the year of the "freeze"—it was 1,712.

Under pressure from the United States, various Arab governments had in 2009 contemplated steps toward normalization with Israel: the United Arab Emirates had discussed allowing cell phone links, Bahrain had considered opening (and Qatar had considered reopening) trade offices, Morocco had mused about allowing overflight rights. (Saudi Arabia—the biggest prize—offered nothing itself, but promised not to block the others.) It is impossible to know how serious these offers were. But when they saw the explosion of new settlement building before the temporary freeze began, the Arab governments pulled back.

Publicly, the Obama administration put on a brave face, with Hillary Clinton calling the settlement freeze "unprecedented." Privately, the mood was darker. As Mitchell told Erekat, "We know what you think of us because we failed."

—•—

Once the administration abandoned its demand for a full settlement freeze, it needed to force the Palestinians to do so as well. To make that more palatable, American negotiators promised that Israel would not launch high-profile construction projects in areas of East Jerusalem that the Palestinians considered especially sensitive. But having learned that he could defy Obama with impunity, Netanyahu felt little need to be conciliatory. "This government has shown that you don't always need to get flustered, to surrender and give in," crowed Avigdor Lieberman. Once Netanyahu "realized that Obama was not willing to twist his arm," explained *Haaretz* columnist Akiva Eldar, "he got more chutzpah. He saw that Obama was a paper tiger."

On November 17, eight days before the partial settlement freeze began, the Israeli government moved forward with the expansion of the East Jerusalem neighborhood of Gilo. On December 29, it issued tenders for new construction in three more Jewish neighborhoods of East Jerusalem, including Har Homa, which particularly outraged the Palestinians because it impedes direct access between East Jerusalem and Bethlehem.

Finally, in early March 2010, under intense American and European pressure, the Palestinians agreed to take part in indirect talks. In announcing the negotiations on Monday, March 8, Mitchell urged both sides "to refrain from any statements or actions which may inflame tensions or prejudice the outcome of these talks." The same day, Vice President Biden arrived in Jerusalem on a visit that was supposed to herald a new spirit of goodwill between the Obama and Netanyahu governments. While he was there, the Israeli interior ministry announced that it was almost doubling the size of the Jewish East Jerusalem neighborhood of Ramat Shlomo.

Biden, who was accompanied on the trip by Ross and Shapiro, responded mildly. He said he "condemn[ed] the decision," which "undermines the trust we need right now," and as a further protest, he arrived ninety minutes late for a dinner with Netanyahu. But that Thursday, Biden gave a conciliatory speech at Tel Aviv University that mentioned the construction only briefly. U.S. officials say that, privately, the Israelis promised to permit no more new construction in Ramat Shlomo for the next two years. The crisis, it seemed, had passed.

While Ross and Shapiro were on a commercial flight back to Washington, however, and thus briefly incommunicado, Hillary Clinton held her weekly meeting with President Obama—with Emanuel, Jones, and Donilon sitting in—and the White House decided that it could no longer tolerate Netanyahu's affronts. On Friday, Clinton harangued the Israeli leader on the phone for forty-three minutes. Two days later, Axelrod publicly called it "an insult" that Israel had announced the Ramat Shlomo construction during Biden's visit. When Netanyahu visited the White House nine days later, Obama refused him the courtesy of a joint press conference or photo op.

The divergent responses reflected, in part, the ongoing battle
between Ross and Mitchell. One administration official complained to
Politico that Ross was advocating "pre-emptive capitulation to what he
described as Bibi's coalition's red lines." Ross, in turn, waged what one
close observer called "a ruthless campaign against George Mitchell,"
repeatedly suggesting that he was spending too much time at home in
New York and not enough in Washington and the Middle East.

But by now, the political wind was strongly at Ross's back. Having
largely supported Obama's call for a settlement freeze in 2009, only to
see him retreat, congressional Democrats were wary of doing so again.
It was also an election year, and members of Congress reported that
Obama's criticism of Netanyahu, in tandem with his criticism of Wall
Street, was hurting donations to the Democratic campaign committees. In April, AIPAC convinced seventy-six senators to sign a letter
urging Obama to "diligently work to defuse current tensions" with
Israel. And as it had done during the Clinton administration, Netanyahu's government helped shape the American Jewish response. In
May 2010, at a meeting at the Council on Foreign Relations in Washington hosted by Elliott Abrams, a prominent American Jewish hawk,
Israeli vice prime minister Moshe Ya'alon called Obama the "least pro-
Israel president in American history." The following month, when former congressman Robert Wexler, a close White House ally, arranged a
meeting between American Jewish officials and Abbas, Israeli officials
called the American Jewish leaders and urged them not to attend.

The Obama administration's rage after the Biden trip did succeed
in ending the provocations in East Jerusalem. Although he made no
official pledge, Netanyahu halted new government construction for the
duration of the freeze, which allowed indirect talks to resume, talks
that gave way to direct talks that fall. The problem was that in those
negotiations, Netanyahu refused to discuss the borders of a Palestinian

state, the status of Jerusalem, or the problem of refugees. Just about the only major issue he would discuss was the security arrangements that would accompany a peace deal.

From the Israeli government's perspective, this made sense. After all, how could they know how much land it was safe to relinquish until they knew what arrangements would be in place to safeguard Israeli security? But the Israeli unwillingness to discuss borders confirmed Palestinian suspicions that Netanyahu's real map had not changed much since the 1990s. In fact, when Palestinian negotiators calculated how much of the West Bank would be left for a Palestinian state once all of Netanyahu's security demands were met, they told *Newsweek* that it came out to only 60 percent.

U.S. officials wanted the two sides to discuss borders and security simultaneously. But the Israelis refused, and as a result, the talks sometimes verged on the absurd. At a September 15, 2010, meeting at Netanyahu's home in Jerusalem, Mahmoud Abbas tried to hand the Israeli prime minister the position papers and maps that the Palestinians had given Ehud Olmert, papers that envisioned Israel annexing 1.9 percent of the West Bank in return for equal territory inside the green line. Nine days later at the Waldorf-Astoria Hotel in New York, Palestinian negotiator Saeb Erekat tried to hand the same documents to Netanyahu's chief negotiator, Yitzhak Molho. Both times, the Israelis refused to read the documents, or even touch them. This was exactly what the Palestinians had feared when they refused to negotiate with Netanyahu absent a settlement freeze.

Getting Netanyahu to discuss the borders of a Palestinian state would have required tougher measures. But inside the administration, the word had gone out: no more public fights. By the second half of 2010, the Obama administration wasn't primarily focused on progress toward a two-state deal. It was primarily focused, as it had been in the second half of 2008 and again in the second half of 2009, on making amends for pursuing the policies in which Barack Obama actually believed. Yet again, the problem was not Obama's popularity among actual American Jews. An August Gallup poll found that while the president's popularity among Jews had slipped since Election Day, as it had with voters as a whole, the margin between Jews and other religious groups was virtually unchanged. In the November 2010 midterm elections, the Democratic candidate for U.S. Senate in Pennsylvania—the state in which Republicans tried most aggressively to make Israel an issue—won 76 percent of the Jewish vote, only two points below Obama's percentage in 2008.

Nevertheless, the White House launched an apology tour. Rahm Emanuel told a group of rabbis that the White House had "screwed up the messaging" on Israel. Daniel Shapiro told a senior Jewish organizational official that the administration should not have allowed a settlement freeze to become a precondition for talks. Dennis Ross said he hoped American Jewish leaders "had seen the manifestations of the change" in the administration's tone.

By the fall of 2010, with the partial settlement freeze about to expire and the Palestinians promising to break off negotiations once it did, the administration appealed to Netanyahu to extend the freeze. But the Israelis refused. As they saw it, Abbas—by refusing to recognize Israel as a Jewish state and by not assuaging Israel's security concerns—had shown himself uninterested in truly ending the conflict. The Arab states, by not taking steps toward diplomatic normalization, had also shown themselves unwilling to take political risks for peace. Convinced it had no true partner on the other side, the Netanyahu government refused to extend the settlement freeze, which would have entailed a nasty confrontation with its own political base.

So once again, the White House was rebuffed, and once again it did not seriously consider applying pressure. To the contrary, Ross—who was now firmly in control of Israel policy—tried to bribe the Israelis. In exchange for a three-month extension of the partial settlement freeze, the Obama administration reportedly offered to sell Israel twenty F-35 jets, to veto a declaration of Palestinian statehood at the UN, to offer long-term security guarantees in the event of a peace deal, and to never request another extension again. Kurtzer was amazed. "Previously U.S. opposition to settlements resulted in penalties, not rewards," he wrote in *The Washington Post*. Ross's offer, by contrast, would represent "the first direct benefit that the United States has provided Israel for settlement activities that we have opposed for more than 40 years." A White House that had taken office determined to take a harder line against settlements than its predecessors was now offering to reward Israel for them in a way no administration ever had. For Barack Obama, the retreat from the liberal Zionism he had learned in Chicago had only just begun.

8

⊰╾┼╼┼╾╼⊱

The Humbling

B Y NOVEMBER 2010, BOTH THE PEACE PROCESS AND THE OBAMA administration's Israel policy had collapsed. Realizing that there was little chance of a peace deal even if Israel continued its partial settlement freeze for three more months, the White House abandoned its effort to bribe the Netanyahu government into extending it. Negotiations were now officially dead. That same month, the voters handed Republicans control of the House of Representatives. Nine days later, Eric Cantor, the incoming House majority leader, met Benjamin Netanyahu in New York and declared that when it came to Israel, "The new Republican majority will serve as a check on the administration." Netanyahu and the American Jewish establishment looked stronger than ever, and a Palestinian state looked farther than ever away.

In his frustration, Mahmoud Abbas began to take diplomatic revenge: bypassing the United States in favor of the United Nations, and thus threatening not only to isolate Israel internationally, but to isolate America as well. In December 2010, the Palestinians announced that they would seek a United Nations Security Council resolution demanding that Israel "immediately and completely cease all settlement activities," language that—to underscore American hypocrisy—they borrowed from a statement by Hillary Clinton. The move coincided with the Arab Spring: a cascade of uprisings against the region's authoritarian regimes. With the Arab masses apparently taking control of their political destiny, some on the Obama foreign policy team feared that vetoing a resolution on settlements would put the United States on the wrong side of Arab public opinion at the worst possible time.

The old battle lines inside the administration re-formed. Ross and Donilon argued for a U.S. veto, with Ross insisting that the demonstrators filling Arab streets cared about their own plight, not the plight of the Palestinians. Hillary Clinton, Defense Secretary Robert Gates, Ambassador to the United Nations Susan Rice, and Deputy National Security Adviser Ben Rhodes argued against a veto. Everyone's preference, however, was for the Palestinians to withdraw the resolution, and thus spare America from having to make the choice. In that effort, the Obama administration promised the Palestinians that if they backed down, the United States would support sending a Security Council fact-finding mission to the region and publicly declare its support for a peace deal based upon the 1967 lines with mutually agreed land swaps. According to the Palestinians, the White House also made threats. In a fifty-five-minute phone conversation on February 17, Abbas told *Newsweek*, Obama warned that if the Palestinians followed through at the UN, the United States might pursue a "list of sanctions" including eliminating aid to the Palestinian Authority. (The White House denied Abbas's account.) It was ironic. Having refused to threaten sanctions against Israel for building settlements, Obama was now reportedly threatening sanctions against the Palestinians for trying to stop them.

But the Palestinians held their ground, and so after waiting until the last possible minute, the White House gritted its teeth and vetoed a resolution that clearly echoed Obama's own beliefs. The Security Council vote was fourteen to one. The new government of Egypt, having come to power just days earlier when Hosni Mubarak resigned, warned that the veto would "lead to more damage to the United States' credibility on the Arab side as a mediator in peace efforts." Anti-American protests broke out across the West Bank.

It was a practice run. In May, the Arab League announced that the Palestinians would return to the United Nations in September to request international recognition of a Palestinian state along the 1967 lines. With that move, Abbas succeeded in doing what he had been unable to do in 2009 and 2010: pressure the United States. However much the White House wished to avoid another confrontation with Netanyahu and his American allies, it found the prospect of being internationally isolated once again—this time in a far more public way, at the very moment that America's influence in the Arab world hung in the balance—almost unbearable to contemplate. Senior administration officials also worried that if the Palestinians won greater recognition at the UN, they would gain standing to sue Israel in the International Criminal Court and the International Court of Justice, which would provoke Israel into harsh retaliatory measures and perhaps permanently destroy the peace process.

The Obama foreign policy team had already been mulling a speech about the Arab Spring, and now a two-pronged debate broke out inside the administration. First, should the speech discuss the Israeli-Palestinian issue? And if so, should the president do what he had been considering since negotiations collapsed in the fall of 2010: offer his own parameters for solving the conflict? Initially, Ross and Donilon argued against including Israel-Palestine in the Arab Spring speech. Then, after losing that argument, they opposed laying out specific parameters. Gates, Mitchell, and Clinton, by contrast, argued that only by laying out parameters could the United States hope to launch negotiations serious enough to make Abbas abandon his bid for UN recognition. Gates and Mitchell wanted Obama to outline the American position on all four key issues—borders, security, Jerusalem, and refugees—or as administration insiders dubbed it, "the full monty." Top State

Department officials were divided over whether to outline all four or to discuss only borders and security, with Clinton herself arguing each position at different times. Eventually, Ross and Donilon agreed to the "half monty" position, and it was decided that Obama would outline his vision on "security"—which meant the gradual withdrawal of all Israeli forces from a non-militarized Palestinian state—and "borders"—which meant the 1967 lines plus mutually agreed land swaps. In policy terms, outlining an American position on borders without outlining one on Jerusalem didn't entirely make sense, since it is impossible to establish the borders of a Palestinian state without establishing the borders of the city that Palestinians want to be its capital. But top Obama officials believed that if the president mentioned dividing Jerusalem, the response from Netanyahu, the Republicans, and the American Jewish organizations would be too ferocious to bear.

Originally, the plan was to deliver the speech in late March. But that was shelved when the United States went to war in Libya, and Obama had to address the nation on that subject instead. Then the speech was scheduled for May 4, but postponed again because of the assassination of Osama bin Laden two days earlier. Finally, the White House settled on May 19. Two events made the timing urgent. First, Obama was due to fly to Europe four days later, and administration officials feared that if the United States did not propose a plan for relaunching peace talks, the Europeans might either offer their own plan, or worse, embrace the Palestinians' statehood bid. Second, John Boehner, the new Republican Speaker of the House of Representatives, had invited Netanyahu to address a joint session of Congress. Yet again, the Israeli prime minister was using his influence in Congress to box Obama into a corner. As one administration official had noted in 2010, Netanyahu "sets up his meetings on Capitol Hill before he even schedules his meetings with us. It's like we're in a subsidiary, secondary position, as if he has more influence on Capitol Hill than we do." To have any chance of restarting peace talks, Obama officials realized, they would need to set the agenda before Netanyahu did.

By the Monday preceding Obama's Thursday speech, White House staffers had crafted the language the president would use to discuss Israel and the Palestinians. But they were so worried that his statement about the 1967 lines would leak—and spark a pressure campaign by Netanyahu and his American allies—that when White House speech-writers began circulating drafts inside the administration, they left the Israel section blank. Thirty-six hours before the speech, National Secu-rity Council officials told Netanyahu's aide Ron Dermer what Obama would say. On Thursday morning, Hillary Clinton informed Netan-yahu himself. The Israelis urged changes: they wanted Obama to rule out the return of Palestinian refugees or call for the Palestinians to recognize Israel as a Jewish state, which implied the same thing. The administration refused.

The fight over the speech revealed the ideological gulf between the Obama and Netanyahu governments. Top White House officials did not believe that the president was saying anything particularly new. After all, Obama's formulation—the 1967 lines plus mutually agreed upon land swaps—had underpinned the parameters Bill Clinton had laid out in 2000, and the negotiations between Olmert and Abbas in 2008. Moreover, the White House had been musing about formalizing those parameters since the breakdown of negotiations in 2010, and had told the Israelis as much. As one Washington insider noted, specula-tion about whether Obama would discuss the 1967 lines in his speech had been rampant in the Israeli press. So when Israeli officials declared themselves shocked by what Obama was planning to say, their Ameri-can counterparts concluded they were simply lying.

From the Israeli government's perspective, however, the speech looked different. Netanyahu and his top aides had never accepted the legitimacy of the Clinton parameters or the Olmert-Abbas talks. Their very different point of departure was George W. Bush's 2004 letter to Ariel Sharon, which declared, "In light of new realities on the ground, including already existing major Israeli population centers, it is unrealistic to expect that the outcome of final status negotiations will be a full and complete return" to the 1967 lines. Another favored Netanyahu precedent was the American and Israeli refusal to negotiate with the Hamas leadership in Gaza until it renounced violence, accepted past peace agreements, and accepted Israel's right to exist. Given Abbas's recent decision to sign a unity agreement with Hamas, which Netanyahu considered a profoundly hostile act, the Israeli prime minister thought it exactly the wrong time to try to force Israel into negotiations based upon the 1967 lines. Netanyahu aides had also been deeply disturbed by a recent march on Israel's borders by Palestinian refugees, a march that, in their view, dramatized the importance of America coming out squarely against any refugee return. Even the Obama administration's section on security left the Israelis underwhelmed, since it envisioned a "full and phased" withdrawal of Israeli troops from the Jordan Valley, which the Netanyahu government was unwilling to concede, absent fundamental changes in the Middle East.

Given its very different ideological assumptions, the Netanyahu team really did see Obama's parameters as a dramatic shift in U.S. policy, one they were being presented with at the last possible moment, in violation of the tradition that an American president should not undertake major policy shifts without consulting Israel first.

At lunchtime on Thursday, May 19, Obama delivered his Arab Spring speech at the State Department. At the heart of the Israel section lay a classic liberal Zionist formulation: "The dream of a Jewish and democratic state cannot be fulfilled with permanent occupation." And in a warning to Israel about the Palestinians' efforts to win statehood at the UN, Obama added, "The international community is tired of an endless process that never produces an outcome."

Abbas called Obama's speech "a foundation with which we can deal positively." Netanyahu, by contrast, declared diplomatic war. As the

Israeli leader departed for Washington, his office announced, "Prime Minister Netanyahu expects to hear a reaffirmation from President Obama of U.S. commitments made to Israel in 2004, which were overwhelmingly supported by both Houses of Congress. Among other things, those commitments relate to Israel not having to withdraw to the 1967 lines which are both indefensible and which would leave major Israeli population centers in Judea and Samaria beyond those lines." The most remarkable part of the statement was the word "expects," a verb usually used by the United States to dictate to smaller powers. Now Netanyahu was using it to dictate to Obama. "Expects," according to Ron Dermer, was actually a mistranslation—done in haste as the Netanyahu team was boarding the plane for Washington—of the Hebrew word *metzapeh*, which given the context would have been better translated as "anticipates." But the Israelis made their displeasure known in nonverbal ways as well. That same day, the Israeli interior ministry announced the approval of new construction in Har Homa, the Jewish neighborhood of East Jerusalem that most damages the contiguity of a future Palestinian state. It was merely the beginning of one of the most extraordinary humiliations of a president by a foreign leader in modern American history.

On Friday, May 20, Netanyahu and Obama met at the White House, and after a one-hour-and-forty-minute private meeting, they appeared together before the cameras. Obama spoke first, and downplayed his differences with the Israeli prime minister, noting, "Obviously there are some differences between us in the precise formulations and language, and that's going to happen between friends." Then Netanyahu took the floor and bluntly reprimanded the president. "Remember," Netanyahu declared, "that, before 1967, Israel was all of nine miles wide. It was half the width of the Washington Beltway. And these were not the boundaries of peace; they were the boundaries of repeated wars, because the attack on Israel was so attractive. So we can't go back to those indefensible lines, and we're going to have to have a long-term military presence along the Jordan."

Privately, Obama was enraged. As one administration official put it, he "felt the office of the presidency, the dignity of the office was insulted." On Saturday, Tom Donilon and White House chief of staff William Daley expressed their deep displeasure to Netanyahu's aides. When the Israelis, concerned about the way the media were portraying Netanyahu's behavior, asked for a second meeting with the president to mend fences, the White House refused. Netanyahu did, however, meet Joseph Biden in the vice president's office the following Monday, where Biden reprimanded the Israeli leader for his tone, and especially for his use of the word "expects."

But publicly, the White House had no choice but to endure the abuse. In their fear that the Israel-Palestine section of Obama's speech would leak, White House staffers had given the president's supporters no instructions on how to defend it. One White House ally received calls from members of Congress who wanted to defend the president, but did not know what to say. Meanwhile, Netanyahu's denunciation of a return to the 1967 lines—which brazenly ignored Obama's language about mutually agreed upon land swaps—was recycled endlessly. Former AIPAC spokesman Josh Block declared Obama's speech "an ambush" that would "further undermine the trust of Israelis, not to mention their elected officials, that this president can be trusted with their security." Thirty senators cosponsored legislation opposing any return to the 1967 lines. One administration official received a call from his sister, a Hebrew school teacher, demanding to know why he was helping push Israel back to the indefensible 1967 lines. A White House staffer received gloating e-mails from American Jewish leaders asking him if he regretted having allowed discussion of the 1967 lines into the president's speech.

It got worse. Two days later, on Sunday, May 22, Obama went before AIPAC and tried to make his formulation about the 1967 lines palatable to the American Jewish establishment, declaring, "The parties themselves—Israelis and Palestinians—will negotiate a border that is different than the one that existed on June 4, 1967. That's what mutually agreed-upon swaps means. . . . It allows the parties themselves to account for the changes that have taken place over the last 44 years." But the applause for the president was tepid compared to the thunderous reception that greeted Netanyahu's address. Even more humiliating was the audience's response to Senate majority leader Harry Reid, who declared, "No one should set premature parameters about borders." As the most powerful Democrat in Congress repudiated the president, the AIPAC crowd responded with a standing ovation.

The final act came on Tuesday, May 24, when Netanyahu addressed the joint session of Congress. Ever since the Israeli prime minister's rejection of Obama's parameters the week before, commentators had been speculating about his reasons for so harshly attacking the president's speech. Some suggested that Netanyahu was playing to his right-wing domestic base, a suspicion confirmed by the fact that his advisers did extensive polling to gauge Israeli reaction to his behavior in Washington. But Netanyahu's address to Congress also suggested another interpretation: the Israeli prime minister had repudiated negotiations based upon the 1967 lines because his vision for how to solve the conflict still differed radically from those laid out by Bill Clinton and Barack Obama, Ehud Barak and Ehud Olmert. For starters, Netanyahu in his speech reiterated that Jerusalem must remain unified under Israeli control and that the Palestinians must recognize Israel as a Jewish state, the very conditions his father had called poison pills when he outlined them two years earlier at Bar-Ilan. Moreover, he demanded a "long-term military presence along the Jordan" River, thus rejecting the transition to an international force envisioned in both the 2000 Clinton parameters and Olmert's 2008 negotiations with Abbas.

When it came to the borders of a Palestinian state, Netanyahu said Israel was willing to relinquish "parts" of the West Bank. He even said that a Palestinian state "must be big enough to be viable." Unlike Obama, however, he still did not promise that it would be contiguous in the West Bank, though according to one interpretation his refusal to promise contiguity had less to do with the West Bank itself than with his fear of contiguity *between* the West Bank and the Gaza Strip. Netanyahu also insisted that Israel would annex "the vast majority" of settlers, which former Israeli foreign minister Shlomo Ben-Ami had said made true Palestinian contiguity extremely difficult. But then Netanyahu went even further, declaring that Israel would also retain "other places of critical strategic and national importance." What those other places were—and how much of the West Bank would be left for the Palestinians once Israel retained them—was anyone's guess, since Netanyahu had refused to discuss borders, even in private. And as a result, it was still impossible to know—more than two years into his second prime ministership—whether Netanyahu had truly broken with the vision he had outlined in the 1990s: a Palestinian archipelago on roughly half of the West Bank.

But the audience did not seem to care. Each member of Congress had been allotted one ticket for the gallery seats above the House floor. With the AIPAC Policy Conference still in session nearby, most members gave their seat to one of their large AIPAC donors. As a result, AIPAC activists constituted roughly 90 percent of the crowd. Many had come straight from the conference and were still wearing their name tags. As the AIPAC faithful watched from above, members of Congress gave Netanyahu twenty-nine standing ovations. Whenever Republicans rose to applaud Netanyahu's more controversial statements, Democratic representative Debbie Wasserman Schultz of Florida would turn to her party colleagues and raise her arm, thus signaling them to stand as well. One White House staffer called the event a "cartoon scene."

—————

The May 2011 clash over the 1967 lines proved to be the last time President Obama publicly articulated the liberal Zionism that he had learned in Chicago. After that, he effectively adopted Benjamin Netanyahu's monist Zionism as his own.

After the president's May 19 speech, articles began to appear suggesting that Jewish donors were refusing to support his reelection bid. One of Obama's largest fund-raisers told *New York* magazine, "There's no question. We have a big-time Jewish problem." According to one

Jewish leader, "about $10 million evaporated in that speech." Among actual Jewish voters, there was still no evidence that Obama's Israel policy was undermining his support. Obama's popularity among Jews had certainly declined since the early days of his presidency, as it had among the public at large. But a Gallup poll in September 2011 found that the gap between Jews and other Americans had not narrowed at all.

The Obama political team, however, was anxious. White House officials told Washington insiders that Tom Donilon and William Daley believed that the president had already paid a high enough price for his Israel policy. It was now time to get reelected. When the campaign began polling Jews, it found—as have other surveys—that fewer than 10 percent make Israel their primary voting issue. But the campaign's polling also found that convincing Jews that Obama's policies were benefiting Israel was hard. Praise from Jewish members of Congress or from the leaders of American Jewish groups didn't help. For American Jews, the only effective validators of Obama's Israel policy were Israelis themselves. Soon, the Obama campaign began trumpeting supportive statements by Israeli officials. On August 5, David Axelrod sent out a mass e-mail quoting defense minister Ehud Barak as saying, "I can hardly remember . . . a better period of [American] support" for Israel. In September, the campaign posted on its website a clip of Danny Ayalon, the deputy foreign minister from Avigdor Lieberman's Yisrael Beiteinu party, declaring, "We've never had a better friend than President Obama." The White House also distributed a transcript of Netanyahu praising Obama for his help in rescuing Israeli officials during an attack on the Israeli embassy in Cairo.

A strategy of using Israeli government officials to reassure American Jews about Obama's pro-Israel credentials effectively ruled out another confrontation with the Israeli government. And so, after May, Obama's policy toward the occupation largely mimicked Netanyahu's. Instead of asking the Quartet to endorse the president's May 19 parameters, American diplomats proposed new parameters that took account of the "new demographic realities" in the West Bank and required the

Palestinians to recognize Israel as a Jewish state. But key European governments rebelled, refusing to codify the Obama administration's retreat from the 1967 parameters, and the Russians balked at demanding that the Palestinians recognize Israel as a Jewish state. Top administration officials suspected that the Russians didn't actually want a Quartet statement that restarted negotiations because they relished forcing America to veto the Palestinian statehood bid at the UN and thus reducing America's influence in the Middle East. For their part, some European diplomats wondered if perhaps the Obama administration secretly wanted to cast a veto, since it would demonstrate to American Jewish leaders that the president was defending Israel against the world.

So the summer passed and the Quartet failed to launch any initiative for restarting negotiations, thus leaving the Obama administration to oppose the Palestinian UN bid without any credible alternative. It was a depressing exercise. One State Department official remarked that after personally lobbying 150 different foreign diplomats against the Palestinian effort, "sometimes I feel like I work for the Israeli government."

American diplomats told Abbas that since the statehood bid would not change anything on the ground, he was raising expectations among his people that he could not fulfill. They also warned him that Congress might retaliate by slashing aid to the Palestinian Authority. Palestinian officials responded that going to the UN was not their first choice. But having launched the UN bid, they would not abandon it without assurances that Netanyahu would do what he had not done in 2010: conduct serious negotiations aimed at creating a Palestinian state near the 1967 lines. During the spring and summer of 2011, Abbas had quietly tested that proposition. He had held two secret meetings with Israeli president Shimon Peres—the first in London in March and the second in Rome in June—aimed at seeing whether the Israeli government would embrace the parameters set out by Clinton in 2000, embraced by Olmert in 2008, and reaffirmed by Obama in 2011. It did not. Netanyahu had authorized Peres to talk, but not to talk about the borders of a Palestinian state. One Obama administration official speculated that Netanyahu's caution stemmed from his fear that whatever Peres told the Palestinians would leak to the press. Others suggested that with the United States pushing the Quartet to make the Palestinians trade a declaration about the 1967 lines for recognition of Israel as a Jewish state, it made no sense for Netanyahu to authorize Peres to accept those lines as the basis of negotiations without getting anything in return. For whatever reason, Peres cancelled his third meeting with Abbas—scheduled for late July in Amman, Jordan— because Netanyahu, he said, had left him "empty handed." Abbas met privately with Ehud Barak as well, with no better result. And so the Palestinians pushed ahead at the UN.

By September, the United States was badly isolated. On September 12, former Saudi ambassador Turki al-Faisal published an op-ed in *The New York Times* warning that if America vetoed the Palestinians' UN bid it would "lose an ally" in Saudi Arabia. Nine days later, French president Nicolas Sarkozy publicly broke with the United States and proposed upgrading the Palestinians to "observer" status at the UN General Assembly. France's move, suggested *The New York Times*, "underscored a stark new reality: the United States is facing the prospect of having to share, or even cede, its decades-long role as the architect of Middle East peacemaking."

On September 21, Obama went before the United Nations and publicly abandoned the critique of Israel's occupation that he had been making since his days in Hyde Park. In his speech to the UN in 2009, he had said, "America does not accept the legitimacy of continued Israeli settlements." In 2010, he had called for extending the settlement freeze. In 2011, by contrast, he did not mention settlements at all. Nor did he defend his May 19 call for negotiations based upon the 1967 lines plus mutually agreed upon land swaps. Instead, he merely noted, "I put forward a new basis for negotiations in May of this year," without even explaining what that new basis was. Moreover, in a sharp departure from his pattern of acknowledging the pain and dignity of both sides, Obama talked about Jewish suffering and Jewish fear while barely mentioning the fear and suffering of the Palestinians. Israel, Obama declared, "look[s] out at a world where leaders of much larger nations threaten to wipe it off of the map. The Jewish people carry the burden of centuries of exile and persecution, and fresh memories of knowing that six million people were killed simply because of who they are." In so doing, Obama perfectly echoed the description of Jews favored by Netanyahu and the American Jewish establishment: forever persecuted and licensed by their fears to worry only about themselves. As one Israeli commentator quipped, Obama's words "appeared as though they were faxed to his office by the Israeli Prime Minister's Office."

Hours before Obama's speech, three White House aides had held a conference call to drum up support among American Jewish leaders. It worked. AIPAC, which had expressed "concern" about aspects of Obama's May 19 speech, now gushed with praise. So did the Israeli government. Avigdor Lieberman declared that he would "sign the speech with both hands." Netanyahu remarked, "There's been a great closing of the ranks between Israel and the United States in the last few months." Meanwhile, anti-Obama protests broke out in the West Bank. After traveling to Ramallah, one Israeli journalist observed that the Palestinians now hated Obama more than they had hated George W. Bush. PLO general secretary Yasser Abed Rabbo declared that the United States could no longer serve as the primary mediator between the two sides.

Rabbi Arnold Wolf's prediction about his old neighbor had proven correct. Ultimately, Obama's personal views had proven irrelevant. When it came to Israel, he had accommodated himself to American political reality, a political reality largely created by American Jews. In a sense, Obama had made the same prediction himself. In May 2007, at a fund-raiser in Montclair, New Jersey, someone had asked him how he would achieve a just peace between Israel and the Palestinians. Obama had responded with a story. The great African American labor leader

A. Philip Randolph had once poured out his heart to Franklin Roose-velt about the plight of black America, and pleaded with the president to address it. FDR had said he agreed entirely, but had a request of his own: "Make me do it." The same was true, Obama explained, for end-ing Israel's occupation and creating a Palestinian state. "Make me do it," he told the crowd. It was a not-so-subtle warning to American Jews: If you don't care about saving Israeli democracy, why should I?

9

⸺✛✛✛⸺

The Future

S O FAR, BARACK OBAMA'S PLEA TO THOSE AMERICAN JEWS WHO wish to save Israeli democracy—"Make me do it"—has gone largely unanswered. Despite the emergence of J Street and other liberal Jewish groups that seek to end the occupation, American Jewish politics remains dominated by an establishment that defines support for Israel more as support for the policies of the Israeli government than as support for the principles in Israel's declaration of independence.

But that American Jewish establishment is dying, literally. The typical large American Jewish organization is run by a man in his sixties, who when he meets his large donors, is among the youngest people in the room. The "ADL's big supporters are eighty-year-olds in Florida and New York and they're dying and their kids are not involved at the same level," explains one former staffer. "If you look at the people who come to the Presidents' Conference," notes a prominent Jewish journalist, "it looks like the day room at the old-age home."

This generational crisis is a product of the radically different life experiences of older and younger American Jews. Abraham Foxman, national director of the ADL, is a Holocaust survivor. The Presidents' Conference's Malcolm Hoenlein, AIPAC's Howard Kohr, and Morton Klein, president of the right-wing Zionist Organization of America, are the children of Holocaust survivors. Tom Dine, the man who made AIPAC the behemoth it is today, remembers being savagely beaten by Catholic boys in Cincinnati in the 1940s. David Harris, the executive director of the American Jewish Committee, was twice detained by Soviet authorities while trying to aid oppressed Russian Jews. All were near their teens or twenties—the stage of life when worldviews are forged—during the agonizing days preceding the Six-Day War, when Israel's existence seemed to hang in the balance. All have built their careers on stories of Jewish victimhood and survival. None accept that we live in a new era in Jewish history in which our challenges stem less from weakness than from power.

As a result, American Jewish leaders often speak a language that strikes many younger Jews—even inside their own organizations—as alien. "With the younger staff—anyone under fifty, forty—it was like, it's not 1967 anymore, dude," notes another former ADL official. When a particularly scaremongering Foxman article or interview was e-mailed to the ADL staff, one young staffer would go into the office of a young colleague, close the door, and share a laugh.

Compared to their elders, especially their elders who populate Jewish organizations, young American Jews are far less likely to build their identity around victimhood. According to a 2006 American Jewish Committee study, Jews under forty are just over half as likely as Jews over sixty to see anti-Semitism in the United States as a "very serious problem." That does not mean, however, that young American Jews are poised to answer Obama's plea. For the most part, young Jews are not redefining American Zionism. They are abandoning American Zionism. In so doing, they are ceding Jewish organizations to a minority within their generation, drawn heavily from the Orthodox world, which is even less committed to Israeli democracy than its elders. If organized American Jewry has in recent decades failed to adequately defend the principles in Israel's declaration of independence, it may soon stop espousing those principles altogether. And if that happens, American Jews may well serve as undertaker as Israeli democracy dies.

———+———

When it comes to Israel, young American Jews can be divided into three groups. The first are the Orthodox, a population that is fast remaking American Jewish life. Not long ago, the phrase "Orthodox Jew" conjured an elderly man with a Yiddish accent. Today it conjures a young family pushing a stroller. This change in image reflects a massive demographic surprise: Orthodoxy, the Jewish movement once associated with a fading past, is today the one with the brightest future. The Orthodox get married younger than other American Jews, have double or triple the number of children, and intermarry far less. As a result, their share of the American Jewish population is skyrocketing. While the Orthodox constitute only around 10 percent of American Jews, they constitute 21 percent of families affiliated with a synagogue and 40 percent of the children in such families, which suggests how dramatically the demography of committed American Jewry may change in the years to come.

Roughly three-quarters of American Orthodox Jews are "Modern Orthodox," which means they seek to reconcile strict religious observance with active participation in the larger world. Modern Orthodox Jews have long been more intensely committed to Israel than have other American Jews, largely because they are more intensely committed to Jewish enterprises in general. But the gap is widening. According to the 1990 National Jewish Population Survey, Orthodox Jews over the age of sixty were just over twice as likely as their Reform counterparts to feel "extremely" or "very" attached to Israel. Among Jews under forty, the ratio was four to one.

This is partly the result of education. The days when Orthodox Jewish children—like the future U.S. senator Joseph Lieberman—attended public school are long gone. Since roughly the 1970s, the bulk of American Orthodox Jews have sent their children to Orthodox Jewish schools where Israel is a constant presence. In these schools, students learn Hebrew, often from Israeli teachers, and they learn Zionist history, often in courses aimed more at instilling devotion than critical thought. In at least one prominent Modern Orthodox school, the elementary school classes are named for Israeli cities, and a clock near the middle school entrance displays the time of day in Israel. Even more important, most Modern Orthodox high school graduates now spend a year or two studying in an Israeli yeshiva (seminary) before college. Most deepen their attachment to the country; some never come back. The Orthodox share of Americans who immigrate to Israel has risen from about 40 percent in the early 1970s to roughly 80 percent today.

Not surprisingly, Orthodox Jews play a much larger role in the organizations that advocate for Israel in the United States than they did in the past. An Orthodox journalist who worked at the ADL in 1970 remembers being denied permission to leave work early on Friday to observe the Jewish Sabbath. Former AIPAC analyst Keith Weissman remembers that when he started working at the organization in 1993, it did not consistently serve kosher food. Today, such stories are unimaginable, largely because of the increased presence of Orthodox Jews. In 2006, AIPAC chose its first Orthodox president. And among AIPAC's younger Jewish activists, the Orthodox are not merely present, they represent close to a majority. At AIPAC's biannual Saban Leadership Seminar for college students, a large share of the most committed Jewish participants are now Orthodox. At AIPAC's annual Schusterman Advocacy Institute High School Summit, which draws heavily from Jewish schools, the Orthodox constitute over 50 percent. In fact, it is precisely because AIPAC has succeeded in cultivating young Orthodox

Jews (as well as conservative evangelical Christians) that it is likely to endure the erosion of its more secular activist base far better than groups like the ADL and the American Jewish Committee.

—◆—

There is much to admire in Modern Orthodoxy, which more than any other religious movement in the American Jewish world insists upon high standards of both secular and Jewish learning. For many years, my own family has attended Modern Orthodox synagogues, and found in them both intellectual stimulation and communal warmth. The love of Israel that Modern Orthodox Jews instill in their children is an outgrowth of their success in instilling a love of Judaism, an accomplishment from which non-Orthodox Jews have much to learn.

But politically, there is a problem. The problem is that compared to the more secular Jews who have historically dominated American Jewish groups, Orthodox Jews are even less likely to define their devotion to Israel as devotion to Israeli democracy. According to a 2006 poll by the American Jewish Committee, three-quarters of Orthodox Jews under forty oppose the creation of a Palestinian state, close to twice the figure among their non-Orthodox counterparts. But that only hints at a deeper divide. In 2009, when Brandeis sociologist Theodore Sasson asked American Jewish focus groups about the Israeli-Palestinian conflict, he found that Conservative, Reform, Reconstructionist, and unaffiliated Jews often said that ordinary Palestinians wanted peace but had been ill-served by their leaders. The Orthodox participants, by contrast, were more likely to depict the Palestinian people themselves as the enemy, and to deny any commonality of interests or values between Palestinians and Jews. Asked to describe the mood in his community about the Israeli-Palestinian conflict, one Orthodox educator quipped, "Esau hates Jacob." In other words, gentiles have hated Jews since biblical times, and always will. Seeking peace, or even understanding, with Palestinians is a waste of time.

This Manicheanism can shade into racism. And while there is no evidence that most American Orthodox Jews hold bigoted views of Palestinians, Muslims, or Arabs, there is ample evidence that Orthodox institutions indulge such bigotry, even when it incites violence. The Orthodox Union is arguably the preeminent Modern Orthodox organization in the United States. In June 2010, its representative in Israel posted an essay on its website entitled "Reflections on a True Gadol [great person]," which lovingly eulogized the late Israeli chief rabbi Mordechai Eliyahu. Left unmentioned was Eliyahu's notorious ruling that since God gave Jews the entire land of Israel, settlers have the right to steal Palestinian crops. Eliyahu, a close associate of Meir Kahane, also declared, "A thousand Arabs are not worth one yeshiva student." When a tsunami struck Southeast Asia in 2004, he said God was punishing Asian governments for supporting Ariel Sharon's proposed evacuation of settlements in Gaza. None of these statements received even a pro forma condemnation from the Orthodox Union official, who praised Eliyahu's "love and care toward every other Jew in the world" without so much as acknowledging his disrespect for—indeed, hatred of—those non-Jews who live under Israel's domain.

Sadly, there are many such examples. In 2006, both the Orthodox Union and the National Council of Young Israel, another prominent American Orthodox group, expressed concern that too high a percentage of American Jewish funds aimed at helping Israel recover from Hezbollah rocket fire were going to assist Israel's Arab citizens. In 2007, the Israel Day Concert in Central Park, an event cosponsored by the National Council of Young Israel, featured as its keynote speaker retired Israeli general Effie Eitam, who the year before had publicly proposed disenfranchising Israel's Arab citizens and physically expelling most Palestinians from the West Bank. In May 2010, Young Israel's executive vice president traveled to the settlement of Yitzhar in the West Bank. He extolled the settlement's yeshiva, which he called "a beautiful center of Torah and Tefillah [prayer]" and praised its leader, Rabbi Yitzhak Shapira, for teaching "students for many years that every Jew must be 'mutually responsible' for every other Jew." He neglected to mention that Yitzhar is the epicenter of the "price tag" policy, in which settlers respond to Israeli government restraints on settlement growth by terrorizing their Palestinian neighbors. Nor did he mention that Shapira, in a 2009 book widely discussed in the Israeli press, declared it religiously permissible to kill gentile children because of "the future danger that will arise if they are allowed to grow into evil people like their parents." Once again, by judging Israeli leaders and institutions purely on their commitment to the Jewish people, American Orthodox officials proved brazenly indifferent to Israel's commitments to all of its people, Jewish and non-Jewish alike.

This indulgence of anti-Arab racism stems from two sources. The first is the radicalization of the Modern Orthodox—or "National Religious"—population in Israel. In the years since Israel conquered the West Bank in 1967, many in the National Religious community have come to believe that by conquering and settling the West Bank, a place saturated with biblical meaning, Jews can hasten the messianic age. This fosters a view of Palestinians not as people with their own legitimate ties to the land, but as imposters who by their presence impede God's will. It also produces a frighteningly schizophrenic view of the Israeli government, a government that is considered holy when it aids the settlement process and potentially satanic when it impedes it.

In the "Orthodox global village" created by modern communications and transportation, these toxic currents are imported to the United States and then reexported back to Israel. Thus, in 1994, after Brooklyn-born settler Baruch Goldstein—a follower of Brooklyn-born Meir Kahane—massacred twenty-nine Palestinian worshippers in Hebron, he became a hero among a radical fringe of Israeli settlers. A year later, after extremist Modern Orthodox rabbis in Israel and the United States speculated that Prime Minister Yitzhak Rabin might be a traitor to the Jewish people punishable by death under Jewish law for his willingness to cede parts of the West Bank to the Palestinians, a National Religious Israeli named Yigal Amir took Rabin's life. The feedback loop continues to this day. Hershel Schachter is among the most powerful rabbis at Yeshiva University, the flagship educational institution of American Modern Orthodoxy. In 2008, he was caught on video advising yeshiva students in Jerusalem, "If the army is going to give away Yerushalayim [Jerusalem], then I would tell everyone to resign from the army—I'd tell them to shoot the *rosh hamemshala* [prime minister]." Schachter later apologized for his remarks.

To grasp the moral perversion that Schachter's comments reflect, one must understand that he derives his stature in part from having been a student of Rabbi Joseph Ber Soloveitchik, the dominant American Modern Orthodox rabbi of the twentieth century. In the years following Israel's conquest of the West Bank, Soloveitchik was repeatedly asked whether Jewish law permitted ceding land, and he repeatedly said that Jewish law is silent on the question, which should be answered by national security experts, not rabbis. If such experts determined that it would save Jewish lives, Soloveitchik declared in 1967, he would support giving back the Western Wall itself. "The life of a young Israeli," he added in 1975, "overrides the entire Torah." In 1982, after Israeli troops permitted their Lebanese Christian allies to massacre roughly one thousand Palestinians at the Sabra and Shatila refugee camps, Soloveitchik warned that unless Mizrachi, the organization of religious Zionists, supported a government investigation, he would resign his membership.

The moral descent from Soloveitchik to Schachter partly reflects changes among the National Religious in Israel, whose militant turn has reverberated across the ocean. But it also stems from changes inside the United States. It is no coincidence that Schachter, in addition to musing about shooting the prime minister for trying to divide Jerusalem, has in recent years said that "the *neshama* [soul] of the Jew and the *neshama* of the non-Jew are made of different material" and that God "forbids us to display any interest in any other religion. . . . We may not study works of or about any other religion, watch films about them, or study any pieces of religious art." This represents a sharp departure from Soloveitchik's vision of Modern Orthodoxy, which meant observing Jewish law while also finding truth and beauty in the broader world. Yeshiva University's very motto, after all, is *Torah Umadda* (Torah and Secular Knowledge). There are still Modern Orthodox rabbis—at Yeshiva University and even in the West Bank—who uphold that creed. But panicked by the growing permissiveness of contemporary culture, many Modern Orthodox leaders in recent decades have abandoned that intellectual openness in favor of an insularity that bespeaks both fear and arrogance: fear that Orthodox Judaism cannot survive a dialogue with the outside world and arrogance that the outside world can add nothing of value to the world of Torah. Thus, Schachter's contempt for a secular Israeli prime minister who gives away land is of a piece with his contempt for gentile art and, indeed, for the gentile soul.

When leading Orthodox rabbis preach that Jews and non-Jews are intrinsically different, and that Jews should be indifferent to non-Jewish culture, it is no surprise that prominent Orthodox organizations often appear indifferent to non-Jewish dignity. And if young men and women raised in that environment gain preeminence in America's Jewish organizations, we should not be surprised if those organizations become even more indifferent to the pledge of "complete equality irrespective of race, religion and sex" in Israel's declaration of independence than they are today. In 2002, American Jews glimpsed that future. At the height of the second intifada, the Presidents' Conference convened a pro-Israel rally on the Washington Mall. Up and down the East Coast, Orthodox schools bused in their students. The crowd was young and, according to one estimate, as much as 70 percent Orthodox. When Deputy Secretary of Defense Paul Wolfowitz told the rally that "innocent Palestinians are suffering and dying in great numbers as well," he was booed.

—=+=—

If the illiberal Zionism of young Orthodox Jews seems increasingly likely to define organized American Jewry in the coming years, it is partly because so many other young American Jews feel so little Zionist attachment at all. The distancing of young, non-Orthodox American Jews from Israel has troubled Jewish sociologists and philanthropists since at least the 1980s. But it conflates two entirely different phenomena. One large chunk of non-Orthodox Jews cares less and less about Israel because they care less and less about Judaism. A second, smaller, but more influential cadre cares deeply about Judaism but cannot reconcile its version of Judaism with Israel's policies. Thus, these young Jews are building a vibrant American Judaism that averts its gaze from the Jewish state. Both groups, in different ways, are contributing to liberal Zionism's demise in the United States.

The harsh truth is that for many young, non-Orthodox American Jews, Israel isn't that important because being Jewish isn't that important. American Jews are an extremely secular bunch. According to a 2005 study by the American Jewish Committee, Jews were less than half as likely as other Americans to say that they know God exists and less than one-third as likely to attend religious services every week. Among older American Jews, however, this lack of religiosity is often counterbalanced by a passionate ethnicity. It is common to find older American Jews who rarely set foot in synagogue but feel an intense tribal bond to their fellow Jews. Among younger non-Orthodox Jews, by contrast, secular tribalism is in steep decline. While almost three-quarters of American Jews aged sixty-five and older say they feel "a strong sense of belonging to the Jewish people," that figure drops to less than one-half among Jews under thirty-five. Close to 90 percent of American Jews who wed before 1970 married other Jews. For Jews marrying today, the figure is roughly 50 percent.

One reason for this shift is that older American Jews generally came of age in an era when a Jew—no matter how secular—was still barred from full entry into the non-Jewish world. That era is gone. As a result, secular Jewish culture has become less distinct from broader American culture. From food to language to comedy to politics, young secular Jews are abandoning the less translatable elements of Jewish ethnicity, and America is assimilating the rest. Thus, Jews rarely eat bialys anymore, but McDonald's now serves bacon, egg, and cheese bagels. Few Jews still speak Yiddish, but in 2011, Republican presidential candidate Michele Bachmann, an evangelical Christian, accused Barack Obama of "chutzpah" (which she pronounced "choot-spa") for refusing to cut government spending. Borscht Belt humor is gone, but for much of the 1990s, Jerry Seinfeld and Larry David produced the most popular comedy on TV. The socialist and militant labor politics that Jews brought with them from Eastern Europe is a distant memory, but in the 1980s, a young Barack Obama read Saul Alinsky on Chicago's South Side.

Increasingly, what remains of secular Jewish identity is a set of values and tastes that other Americans—especially well-educated, secular, blue-state Americans—share. Politically, these values include nonviolence, nondiscrimination, and free expression. Young secular American Jews may genuinely feel that there is something Jewish about these values, but since the values are universal, they do not produce any particular solidarity with the Jewish state. Older American Jews— because of their greater commitment to the Jewish people and their greater fear of anti-Semitism—more often segregate Israel from their general liberal outlook. They apply one standard to Israel and another to everything else. Young secular Jews, for the most part, don't. Thus, the same inclination toward nonviolence that made them skeptical of America's invasion of Iraq made them skeptical of Israel's wars in Lebanon and Gaza. The same belief in equality under the law that makes them sympathetic to gays and lesbians in the United States makes them sympathetic to Palestinians in the West Bank.

As a result, young American Jews are more critical of Israeli policy than are their elders. According to a 2007 study by the scholars Steven M. Cohen and Ari Kelman, non-Orthodox American Jews under thirty-five were roughly twenty percentage points less likely than those over sixty-five to disagree with the statement "Israel occupies land belonging to someone else." According to a study by four scholars at Brandeis, 59 percent of American Jews over the age of sixty—but only

33 percent under thirty—strongly agreed with the Israeli government's account of its confrontation with the Turkish flotilla that sought to reach Gaza in 2010.

But it would be wrong to imagine that young, secular American Jews seethe with outrage at Israel's policies. For the most part, they do not care enough to seethe. The same process of assimilation that leads them to view Israel through the same ideological lens that they view other nations prevents them from caring much more about Israel than about other nations. They are less alienated than indifferent. According to Cohen and Kelman, non-Orthodox American Jews under thirty-five are almost half as likely as those over sixty-five to say they feel "very emotionally attached to Israel." They are thirty percentage points less likely to say that "Israel's destruction would be a personal tragedy" in their lives. In the 2008 presidential election, they were almost half as likely to say the Israeli-Palestinian conflict had a "high" or "very high" salience in their choice of candidate.

A minority of scholars believe that this gap will close over time, that younger American Jews will become more attached to Israel as they marry and raise children. But were that the case, surveys would show rising attachment to Israel as American Jews enter their thirties and forties and a flattening after that. Instead, the data show a straight drop: as you descend generationally, every age cohort becomes less attached to Israel than the one above it. The scholars who argue that distancing is a product of life cycle rather than generation—and thus will remedy itself over time—cite polls showing that as a whole, American Jews are about as connected to Israel as they were in past decades. This sounds reassuring. But these polls are misleading because they include only those Jews who identify by religion, and a growing number of the least Israel-attached young American Jews identify only culturally. (They will tell a pollster they are Jewish but, if asked their religion, will answer "none.") When these young Jews are included, the supposed stability in American Jewish attachment to Israel over time collapses. As the researchers Laurence Kotler-Berkowitz and Jonathan

Ament observed in a recent review of the debate over Israel attachment, the clear "conventional wisdom" among academics is that non-Orthodox American Jews are growing more distant from Israel. In the words of one prominent Israeli commentator, "We're losing them."

———+———

But there is another "them." Young American Jews are not merely divided between Orthodox Jews who don't care much about Israeli democracy and secular Jews who don't care much about Israel. There is a third camp: young Jews who care deeply about being Jewish and, precisely because they do, find Israel's policies agonizing. Outside of the Orthodox world (and even among a sliver on the Orthodox left), it is these young women and men who will lead American Jewry in the coming decades, although not necessarily through its existing organizations. They are not assimilating; they are reconciling liberal values and Jewish commitment in remarkable ways. The question is whether they will bring those values and that commitment to the struggle for Israeli democracy or build an American Judaism that averts its eyes from the Jewish state. Their alienation from Zionism reflects the American Jewish establishment's failure. In the United States, overcoming that alienation is liberal Zionism's greatest hope.

The odd thing about the younger generation of non-Orthodox American Jews is that while purely ethnic Judaism is dying, religious Judaism is undergoing something of a renaissance. The two phenomena are related. Terrified by the statistics on intermarriage, American Jewish philanthropists in the past two decades have finally begun investing in Jewish education. In 1992, there were fifteen hundred students in non-Orthodox Jewish high schools in the United States. By 2009, that number had almost quadrupled. There are today far more opportunities for young, progressive American Jews to pursue religious study than in the past. The most committed and talented products of these schools and programs are not entering traditional Jewish organizations; they are creating their own. And they are doing so from a position of much greater religious knowledge. In 2010, when the Avi Chai Foundation asked younger "nonestablishment" Jewish leaders and the older leaders of the established American Jewish organizations if they could interpret a sacred text in the original Hebrew, it found that the members of the younger group were almost twice as likely to say they could.

The striking thing about the institutions these young Jews are creating is that they fuse religious commitment and liberal values. Those institutions come in two broad types. The first are independent minyanim: communities of Jewish prayer and study that are led by the participants, not by rabbis, and do not associate with any existing stream of Judaism. In 2001, the first independent minyan was born. Today, there are roughly one hundred. Every Friday night and Saturday morning, often in dingy rented halls, these minyanim overflow with Jews in their twenties and thirties while ornate Conservative and Reform synagogues in the same city struggle to attract any young people at all. The independent minyan movement now has a yeshiva and a biannual conference. Soon, insiders speculate, it may begin establishing schools.

What attracts young people to these communities is telling. Many of the participants grew up Reform or Conservative, but through Jewish school, summer camp, or adult study, they gained a level of religious literacy far beyond that of most Reform or Conservative Jews. Thus, they desire a style of worship that is more demanding and more participatory than one finds in many Reform or Conservative synagogues. The independent minyanim also attract young men and women who were raised Orthodox but desire greater intellectual openness and equal participation for women, lesbians, and gay men. From different backgrounds, these young people are converging. Learned young Reform and Conservative Jews want greater religious commitment; open-minded young Orthodox Jews want greater egalitarianism. As a result, at certain independent minyanim one can find Reconstructionist, Reform, Conservative, and even left-leaning Orthodox rabbinical students, all of whom would rather pray with committed, egalitarian

Jews of their own generation than in the synagogues they will one day lead.

The second kind of institution to which committed young non-Orthodox Jews are also flocking is Jewish social justice groups. Recent decades have witnessed an explosion of Jewish organizations that confront injustice in the broader world: from Hazon, which promotes Jewish environmentalism, to Avodah, which brings young Jews to ravaged parts of urban America for a year of service and study, to the American Jewish World Service, which helps Jews volunteer in developing countries. It is important to note that these organizations are not just Jewish in name only; many integrate the study of Jewish texts into their work. And it is in this effort to fuse religious commitment and liberal values that they resemble the independent minyanim. The minyanim seek religious commitment that honors liberal ideals; the social justice organizations see their good works as an outgrowth of religious commitment. In different ways, both express what one study calls the "religious traditionalism and social progressivism" that defines committed young non-Orthodox Jews.

As important as what these engaged young Jews stress is what they don't stress: victimhood. "In interviews," notes one researcher, "young nonestablishment leaders scoffed at the 'circle-the-wagons' approach to Jewish life. They do not feel threatened by anti-Semitism." Another study notes that for members of independent minyanim, "the twin pillars of the inherited Jewish collective identity—the Holocaust and the founding of the State of Israel—are history, rather than memory. Emergent leaders are far more likely to invoke collective memories of the civil rights movement, the labor movement." In contrast to the American Jewish establishment, this rising counter-establishment of young Jewish leaders takes for granted not just Jewish power, but the ethical responsibilities that come with it. The independent minyan movement, in the words of Rabbi Elie Kaunfer, one of its founders, seeks a Judaism that "knows it has moral responsibility for the major

crises of our modern age." For its part, the Jewish social justice movement seeks to confront those crises through service. While mainstream
American Jewish organizations often emphasize communal survival,
these young Jews stress spiritual meaning and ethical obligation. And
yet, in an extraordinary irony, their efforts to meet the moral challenge
of Jewish power are proving more effective than the Holocaust rhetoric
of their elders at keeping young American Jews Jewish. In the 2010 Avi
Chai study, young nonestablishment leaders were less than half as
likely as their older establishment counterparts to say they were "very
worried" about high intermarriage rates. But while the children of those
older leaders frequently intermarry, members of independent minyanim
marry other Jews at a rate of 93 percent. What ensures Jewish continuity, in other words, is not victimhood, but Jewish knowledge as a vehicle
for Jewish meaning. And outside of the right-wing Orthodox world,
young American Jews are finding that meaning not by evading the obligations that come with power but by facing them head-on.

---·|·---

All of which raises the question: Why are so many of these committed,
progressive young Jews absent from the struggle for Israeli democracy?
For them, unlike for their more secular counterparts, Israel is not
just another country. More than 90 percent of young nonestablishment
Jewish leaders have traveled to Israel. Fifty-six percent have lived there
for more than four months at a time, which is almost double the rate of
older establishment leaders. But unlike most young Orthodox Jews,
they are deeply troubled by Israel's policies. Seventy-seven percent of
younger nonestablishment leaders believe that Israel should freeze settlement growth; only 23 percent of the members of independent minyanim say they always feel proud of Israel. In 2007, the sociologist
Steven M. Cohen and the Stanford historian Arnold Eisen, who was
about to become chancellor of the Jewish Theological Seminary, convened a meeting of young Jewish innovators on Israeli Independence

Day. At the end of the meeting, when Cohen and Eisen suggested that the group rise and sing "Hatikvah," the Israeli national anthem, the young Jews refused.

But when Cohen later asked some of the same individuals to join him in publicly opposing settlement growth in the West Bank, they refused that request, too. Alienation from the Israeli government, in other words, does not necessarily spur committed, progressive young American Jews to action. More often, it makes them turn away. One reason is fear. In the organized American Jewish world, left-leaning young Jews often rely on establishment Jewish institutions for financial support. And publicly criticizing Israel is an excellent way to endanger that support. That was the reason the young Jewish innovators gave Cohen for not publicly opposing settlement growth, and it substantially inhibits young rabbis as well. According to a 2011 study commissioned by the Jewish Theological Seminary, students studying to be Conservative rabbis were sixteen percentage points more likely to view J Street favorably than to view AIPAC favorably. (Their older colleagues, by contrast, preferred AIPAC by a margin of forty-eight percentage points.) But close to one-third of younger Conservative rabbis said they would not express their views about Israel publicly.

Professional survival, however, is only one reason for this generational silence. Another is that religiously committed young non-Orthodox Jews don't see Israeli politics as a vehicle for Jewish meaning. The sense of purpose that older, less observant American Jews find in Zionism, they find in Judaism itself. Indeed, many in the independent minyan movement grew alienated from the Reform and Conservative synagogues of their youth precisely because those synagogues substituted AIPAC-style Israel advocacy for serious Jewish study and prayer. When it comes to their religious communities, and to social justice in the broader world, these committed young Jews are idealists. But when it comes to the American Jewish discourse about Israel—a discourse they find vicious, propagandistic, and shallow—they are jaded. While they may appreciate Israeli culture, they do not see engagement with

Israeli politics as a path to spiritual or moral fulfillment, and they are finding that fulfillment in other ways. The 2010 Avi Chai study found that although younger nonestablishment leaders had spent more time in Israel than their elders and were more likely to speak Hebrew, only 32 percent strongly agreed that Israel was a very important part of their Jewish identity, compared to 56 percent of the older cohort.

"It is increasingly the case," notes Rabbi Shai Held, cofounder of Mechon Hadar, the yeshiva that grew out of the independent minyan movement, "that you can meet young religious Jews who say 'I am passionately religious but Zionism doesn't mean anything to me.'" Blessed by conditions more favorable than any Diaspora generation has ever known, committed, progressive young American Jews are creating a religious life perfectly tailored to their values and tastes. Focusing on the nasty, messy, frightening debate over Israel's future only disrupts the dream.

It is a lovely dream, and an abdication. Even on purely religious grounds, as Held observes, "it makes no sense to say, 'I'm going to pray all the time for Jerusalem but the fact of Jews in Jerusalem in a way that it is unprecedented for thousands of years doesn't interest me.'" Jewish liturgy itself, if taken seriously, requires wrestling with what Jews make of their return to the land of Israel. So does Jewish honor. It is not enough to care about Haiti and Darfur and New Orleans. Acting ethically in an age of Jewish power means confronting not only the suffering that gentiles endure but the suffering that Jews cause. For Jews who espouse liberal principles, indifference to whether the Jewish state remains a democracy constitutes as deep a betrayal of the bonds of peoplehood as indifference to whether there remains a Jewish state at all. Israel cannot be tucked away in the attic, left to degrade while progressive, committed Jews live their religious and ethical ideals in the United States. A disfigured Jewish state will haunt not only American Zionism but American Judaism. And the American Jews who try to avert their eyes will be judged harshly by history, no matter how laudable their soup kitchens and how spirited their prayer.

Conclusion

ON MARCH 27, 1949, WITH DEATH CLOSING IN, RABBI STEPHEN Wise reviewed his life before a Boston crowd. He had spent it agitating for an America in which women could vote, workers could unionize, dissenters were not jailed, and African Americans were not lynched. And he had spent it dreaming that after two thousand years of exile, Jews would make those same "egalitarian and democratic" principles the basis of a state. Ten months earlier, such a state had announced its birth, pledging in its declaration of independence to ensure "complete equality of social and political rights to all its inhabitants irrespective of religion, race or sex" and to pursue "freedom, justice and peace as envisaged by the Hebrew prophets." In its founding document, Israel had pledged not merely to safeguard the Jewish people but to cherish democratic ideals, and Wise told his audience that he could now meet his creator a contented man. "I have lived to see the Jewish state," he declared. "I am too small for the greatness of the mercy which God has shown us."

In those words, Wise captured the immensity of Israel's birth, the immensity of a Jewish state that—in the shadow of the greatest assault on human dignity in Jewish history—promised equal dignity to all its inhabitants, irrespective of religion, race, or sex. Now, more than six decades later, American Jews must face the immensity of the fact that, in our lifetimes, that kind of Jewish state may die.

The day is not far off. We tell ourselves that Israel is a democracy, but in the West Bank it is an ethnocracy, a place where Jews enjoy citizenship and Palestinians do not. We tell ourselves that Israel's occupation of the West Bank is temporary, but it has lasted for more than four decades, two-thirds of the life of the state. We tell ourselves that the Israeli government has no desire to hold the West Bank, but it has subsidized hundreds of thousands of Jews to move there and built a bus system, a road system, a rail system, a water system, a telephone system, and an electricity grid that treat democratic Israel and settler Israel as one and the same. We tell ourselves that since most settlers live near the green line, Israel can draw a border that incorporates them while still offering the Palestinians a viable state. But to annex the land on which 80 percent of settlers live—as Ehud Barak demanded at Camp David—Israel would have to annex settlements like Ariel, Immanuel, Kfar Adumim, Ofra, and Beit El, which sit deep in the heart of the West Bank. And close observers fear that if Israel tried to incorporate many fewer than 80 percent of the settlers, the result might be civil war.

For a long time, we have evaded these painful truths by evading Palestinians. Rarely do American synagogues, American Jewish organizations, American Jewish newspapers, or American Jewish schools invite Palestinians to write or speak; rarely do American Jewish officials travel to the West Bank, let alone the Gaza Strip, to see the occupation through Palestinian eyes; rarely do American Jewish leaders display any familiarity with Palestinian writing about the conflict, except occasionally in the form of a gotcha quote. At its 2011 Policy Conference, AIPAC hosted panels entitled "Political Earthquakes in the Arab World," "Changing Politics in the Arab World," "The Modern Arab State," "U.S.-Arab Relations," "The Arab-Israeli Conflict," "Transformation and Turmoil in Egypt," "Egypt's Relations with Israel and America," "Syria's Destructive Behavior," "Israel and the Gulf States," "Where Is Turkey Headed?" "The West Bank Model," "Continued Threat from Gaza," "Israel Improving Palestinian Lives," "Terrorism's New Breeding Grounds," and "Confronting Radical Islam"—none of which featured a single Palestinian, Arab, Turkish, or Muslim speaker.

This information bubble has allowed the organized American Jewish community to tell itself that Israel can keep expanding settlements because, ultimately, the Palestinians will accept however much of the West Bank is left. They will accept a state in which settlements like Ariel cut off northern Palestinian towns and villages from the rest of the West Bank, a state in which Jewish settlements largely enclose a Palestinian capital in East Jerusalem, a state without control over the Jordan Valley, a state without control over much of the West Bank's water supply. And if the Palestinians don't accept these things, it is because they don't really want two states. There are, to be sure, many Palestinians who don't want two states and seek Israel's destruction. But the best way to ensure their triumph is to keep eating away at the land on which a Palestinian state might be born. The basic bargain behind a two-state solution has long been clear: the Palestinians abandon their claim to the 78 percent of mandatory Palestine inside the green line in return for a state on the 22 percent that constitutes the West Bank and Gaza Strip, with minor adjustments. It is a bargain that would have made most of Israel's founders—who in 1947 accepted a partition plan that gave Israel a mere 55 percent of the land—cry with joy. Yet the organized American Jewish community pretends that Israel can continually transgress that bargain without bringing the entire two-state paradigm crashing down and, with it, Israel's existence as a democratic Jewish state.

But the American Jewish establishment has laid a trap for itself. American Jewish organizations have long justified their support for Israel by invoking Israeli democracy. But for many older American Jews, especially the ones who populate Jewish organizations, that language is something of a mask. For American Jews raised in the shadow of the Holocaust, and even for many like myself who came of age during the movement to rescue Soviet Jewry in the 1970s and 1980s, the real justification for Zionism is refuge. The character of the Jewish state matters less than the fact that, at the end of the day, a despised and threatened people have somewhere to go.

Younger American Jews, by contrast, are less likely to see Israel as a refuge. Not only can they not imagine needing to flee to a Jewish state themselves, but with the Soviet and Ethiopian exoduses now complete, they see no significant community of Diaspora Jews that does. As a result, they are more likely to genuinely believe that what justifies Zionism is Israel's democratic character. For young American Jews, more than for their elders, the policies of the Israeli government determine the legitimacy of the Zionist project. Zionism is what Israel does.

This generational shift will not mean the end of American Zionism. But it could mean the end of American liberal Zionism. The less democratic Israel becomes, the less young, liberal-minded American Jews will support it. And the more they drift away, the more American Zionism will be dominated by Orthodox Jews and evangelical Christians: groups unlikely to maintain even the pretense that what makes Israel precious is its fidelity to liberal democratic ideals. Already, the need to defend an occupation that violates the rights of millions of Palestinian Muslims is blowing back to our shores, making America's Jewish organizations increasingly hostile to the rights of Muslims in the United States. One can see it in the Anti-Defamation League's 2010 opposition to the building of the "Ground Zero" mosque, the American Jewish Committee's campaign to prove that America contains fewer Muslims than Muslim organizations claim, and the way both AIPAC and Malcolm Hoenlein have feted the anti-Muslim evangelical leader John Hagee. As Israeli democracy falters, so will the Zionist consensus that once undergirded American Jewish life. American Zionism will become the province of people indifferent to liberal democratic ideals, and the American Jews most committed to those ideals will become indifferent, at best, to the Jewish state.

———+———

For those of us who aspire to raise our children as both Zionists and liberals—who believe that the miracle of Jewish statehood is inextricably bound up with the promises of Israel's founders about what kind of Jewish state this would be—the impending collapse of Stephen Wise's dream is a tragedy of incalculable proportions. We must resist it with every fiber of our being. But resisting it will require deepening two different kinds of commitments: not merely our commitment to the universal principles of democracy and human rights but our particular commitment to the Jewish people.

Ironically, the very universalism of many American Jews prevents them from actively defending the universalistic principles in Israel's declaration of independence. Think about it this way. The current intermarriage rate among non-Orthodox American Jews is 50 percent. According to the 2001 National Jewish Population Survey, even those children of intermarriage who identify as Jewish themselves intermarry at a rate of 76 percent. And of those who marry non-Jews, only 7 percent raise their children as Jews. These increasingly assimilated American Jews may not like Israel's occupation of the West Bank, but they are not especially angry about it because they are not especially connected to Israel. And they are not especially connected to Israel because they are not especially connected to being Jewish. This is the core problem facing groups like J Street that agitate for a two-state solution. Plenty of American Jews agree with their perspective, but the Jews who agree with them generally care less than the Jews who don't. The very universalism that makes liberal secular American Jews sympathetic to the rights of Palestinians makes them at least as concerned about global warming, health care, gay rights, and a dozen other issues. Establishment Jewish groups, by contrast, attract people willing to devote most of their political energy to Israel because the same particularism that makes them more concerned about Jews than about Palestinians makes them more concerned about Israel than about almost anything else.

Defending Israeli democracy, therefore, requires ensuring that the American Jews most committed to democratic values remain Jews and pass Judaism on to their children. Liberal American Jews must feel a special commitment to Israel's ethical character because they feel a special commitment to being Jewish. They must see their own honor as bound up with the honor of the Jewish state.

Among the world's Diaspora communities, American Jews have done a singularly bad job of inculcating Jewish commitment in our children. Part of the reason is that Jews have simply been in the United States longer than in some other Diaspora nations, where a higher percentage of Jewish immigrants arrived just before or after World War II. As a result, our process of assimilation is further along. The lure of assimilation is also greater in the United States than in countries like Canada, Argentina, Mexico, Australia, South Africa, Britain, or France, where the melting pot ideal is not as strong. But the single biggest reason that American Jews care less about being Jewish is that we are more ignorant of Judaism. Perhaps no community in Jewish history has educated itself so well about the secular world and so poorly about its own tradition.

In previous generations, it mattered less whether American Jews knew much about being Jewish because to stop being Jewish was hard. Even if you wished to assimilate, gentile America did not always comply. Today, however, the decline of anti-Semitism has made it easy to stop being Jewish. Since the 1970s, American Jewish organizations have often used threats to Israel, sometimes in tandem with the Holocaust, to try to convince younger Jews that anti-Semitism hasn't really declined and that they still live in a fundamentally hostile world. But this effort to combat assimilation via victimhood has failed because it has little relevance to a generation growing up in an age of American Jewish, and Israeli, power.

In recent years, the most high profile American Jewish effort at combating assimilation has been Taglit–Birthright Israel, an organization created in 1999 to give Diaspora Jews in their twenties (most of them American) a free ten-day trip to Israel in hopes that the visit would deepen their attachment not only to the Jewish state, but to Judaism itself. Studies of Birthright alumni do show a rise in Jewish and Zionist commitment. But whether they sustain that heightened commitment over time remains unclear, and according to the Rutgers sociologist Chaim Waxman, "the long-term impact of the program is thus still very much open to question." Even a twenty-five-year-old inspired by her Birthright trip will have trouble building upon it if she has reached adulthood without the skills necessary to meaningfully practice Judaism itself.

——◆——

The best antidote to assimilation, by far, is education. And the best way to educate young Jews about Judaism is through full-time Jewish schools. For decades, American Jewry's dominant mode of religious instruction has been supplementary schools, which meet in the afternoons or on Sundays. But it is difficult to gain much knowledge of Judaism—and much fluency in Hebrew—in a couple of hours a week. An analysis of the 2001 National Jewish Population Survey found that among American Jews who had attended Sunday school for six years or less, only 42 percent married other Jews. Among those who had attended Sunday school for more than six years, the figure was 60 percent. By contrast, of those American Jews who had attended full-time Jewish school for six years or less, 82 percent married other Jews. Among those who had attended full-time Jewish school for more than six years, the figure was 96 percent. Even controlling for home environment and other factors, day school attendance increases a Jewish child's likelihood of marrying another Jew by fourteen percentage points.

Throughout the world, in fact, the intermarriage rate rises as the Jewish school attendance rate declines. In Mexico, where 85 percent of Jewish children attend full-time Jewish schools, the intermarriage rate is 10 percent. In Australia, where 65 percent of Jewish children attend Jewish schools, the intermarriage rate is roughly 20 percent. In Canada, where 55 percent of Jewish children attend Jewish schools, the intermarriage rate is 35 percent. In France, where 40 percent of Jewish children attend Jewish schools, the intermarriage rate is roughly 40 percent. And in the United States, where between 18 and 25 percent of Jewish children attend Jewish schools (the vast majority of them Orthodox), the intermarriage rate is roughly 50 percent.

Historically, American Jews have justified their failure to develop a strong Jewish school system by citing their commitment to public schools. It is an honorable commitment, but if it continues, most non-Orthodox American Jews will produce grandchildren who are not meaningfully Jewish. For me, as a partisan not merely of the United States, but of the Jewish people, this cost is too high. Moreover, the main reason so few American Jews send their children to Jewish schools is not because they believe so fervently in the idea of public education. It is because when it comes to academic excellence and affordability, America's Jewish schools can't compete. Because they need to employ sufficient faculty to teach both a Judaic and a secular curriculum, Jewish schools are expensive. Tuition averages $14,000 a year, with many non-Orthodox schools costing more. But especially outside the Orthodox community, schools are often fledgling. New York City's only non-Orthodox Jewish high school, for instance, is less than a decade old. As a result, Jewish schools rarely have significant endowments or first-rate facilities, and teachers' salaries are generally low. Thus, Jewish parents are asked to pay top dollar for schools with makeshift gymnasiums and antiquated science labs when they can send their children to the best private schools for the same amount of money and the best public schools for almost no money. Most Orthodox parents will accept that trade-off. But most non-Orthodox parents—the ones whose children are most likely to intermarry—will not.

It is easy to denounce American Jewish donors for not doing more to subsidize Jewish schools. The Jewish Federations of North America, American Jewry's philanthropic arm, cover, on average, only about 5 percent of the cost of educating a child in Jewish school. And while individual Jewish philanthropists have taken a greater interest in Jewish schools since the 1990s, their efforts barely make a financial dent. As the Jewish Theological Seminary's Jack Wertheimer has calculated, even offering an annual $2,000 voucher to the roughly 200,000 American children currently enrolled in Jewish schools would require an endowment of more than $8 billion, which is close to three times what the Jewish Federations raise annually for their entire range of programs.

The good news is that economically affordable, academically excellent Jewish schools exist. You can find them in Melbourne, London, Paris, Montreal, and Buenos Aires. The bad news is that they generally receive government money. In most large Diaspora communities with a strong Jewish school system, the government picks up part of the tab, often by covering the cost of the school's secular subjects. And if American Jews want our Jewish schools to flourish, our government will have to start doing the same. For decades, liberal American Jews have vehemently opposed government funding for religious schools. The most common objection is that by intertwining church and state, such funding threatens religious liberty, a natural concern for a religious group that comprises roughly 2 percent of the U.S. population. But Jewish schools receive government aid in Australia, Britain, and most of Canada, and Jews in those countries enjoy as much religious liberty as do their counterparts in the United States. Even in America, state and local governments pay for the cost of special education in religious schools without negatively impacting religious freedom. American Jewish liberals need to recalibrate their fears. They should worry less about whether the government will allow them to practice Judaism and more about why they and their children aren't doing so.

A second objection to government support for religious schools is that it would hurt the children who remain in public schools. It is hard to evaluate that claim, since while there have been various studies of whether vouchers improve the academic performance of their recipients, there is very little conclusive data on their impact on students who remain in public schools. The impact is important, of course, and as responsible citizens, Jews should want all American children to receive the best education possible. But if we want non-Orthodox American Jewry to survive, Jews also have the right, indeed the responsibility, to think about ourselves.

Today, the prospect of substantial government aid to religious schools seems remote, especially given the budgetary crises affecting many states and cities. But the concept has strong support among evangelical Protestants, Catholics, and some African Americans and Latinos. And if the organized American Jewish community—currently a vocal opponent of vouchers—switched sides, the politics of the issue could substantially change. Such aid would likely be challenged in the courts but, depending on how it was delivered, might well pass constitutional muster.

If it did, the impact would likely be profound. A recent experiment in Cleveland shows that making Jewish schools more affordable can dramatically increase enrollment. And as enrollment grew, American Jews would deepen not only their commitment to Judaism but their commitment to Israel. According to the 2001 National Jewish Population Survey, only 12 percent of American Jews who had attended Sunday school for seven or more years said they felt "very attached to Israel." Among those who had attended full-time Jewish school for that same span, by contrast, the figure was 67 percent.

Attachment to Israel does not necessarily mean attachment to Israeli democracy, of course. In fact, the American Jews most likely to send their children to Jewish schools today—the Orthodox—are also the ones least troubled by the occupation. But since most Orthodox Jews already send their children to Jewish schools, the new entrants would come largely from the non-Orthodox population, a population with a strongly liberal political outlook. It is the interaction between that liberal outlook and the Jewish knowledge and commitment that a Jewish education can bring that offers the best hope for liberal Zionism's survival in the United States. It is no coincidence that an informal survey by J Street U—J Street's campus arm—found that its student leaders were three times as likely to have attended Jewish school as were Jewish students overall. In my experience, the young American Jews with the deepest commitment to Israeli democracy are generally those raised with both a strong attachment to the Jewish people and a strong commitment to human rights and who have sought to reconcile the two by spending time not only among Jewish Israelis but among Arab Israelis and West Bank Palestinians as well. Today, the American Jewish community does not adequately facilitate either commitment. We make it hard for American Jewish parents to give their children a strong Jewish education, and then we offer those children a free trip to Israel in which they never meaningfully interact with Palestinians. Thus, we raise children who don't know enough about Judaism to grasp the significance of a Jewish state, and don't know enough about Palestinians to grasp the way that Jewish state blights their lives.

———

Better Jewish education is essential to American Jewish survival, and thus to our ability to fulfill our obligations to the Jewish state. But its impact will be slow, perhaps too slow to stop the settlement process that menaces Israel's future. In the short term, preserving Israeli democracy will require something else: direct action against the occupation. The idea will unnerve many American Jews. It unnerves me. But we must weigh this discomfort against the very real prospect that Israeli democracy will die. The hour is late. We can no longer afford our old comfortable ways.

Since the beginning of the Oslo peace process, American Jews troubled by the occupation have focused mainly on influencing the U.S. government. In 1993, a group of influential American Jewish liberals, many with ties to Bill Clinton, founded Israel Policy Forum to help Clinton broker a two-state solution. In 2008, Jeremy Ben-Ami, a former staffer in the Clinton White House, created J Street to act as Barack Obama's "blocking back" in Congress as he tried to relaunch the peace process. These efforts are important, but in and of themselves they are not enough. Changing Israel policy in Washington is hard because liberal Jews wield little influence in a Republican Party substantially beholden to the Christian right. And even in the Democratic Party, where many members of Congress privately support American pressure on Israel to halt settlement growth and negotiate seriously toward a two-state deal, those members often say the opposite in public. In the last three years, J Street has raised large sums of money for members of Congress willing to speak their minds. But AIPAC and its allies have spent decades making friends on Capitol Hill and making politicians fear the consequences of not being AIPAC's friend. When Obama, a Democratic president genuinely committed to ending the occupation, ends up capitulating to an Israeli prime minister whom many Democrats privately loathe, it is hard to imagine any American president significantly challenging Israeli behavior anytime soon. And thus far no Israeli prime minister, even those more committed to a Palestinian state than Netanyahu, has been able to curb settlement growth on his own.

Liberal Zionists should keep trying to influence American policy. But we must also recognize that the Israeli-Palestinian conflict is increasingly bypassing Washington. Middle Eastern governments like those in Turkey, Egypt, and Saudi Arabia are becoming less deferential to the United States. In the Quartet—which once served mostly as a fig leaf for American policy—the European Union and Russia are challenging American leadership. As Mahmoud Abbas's bid for UN statehood has made clear, Palestinian leaders no longer want the United

States to control the peace process either. In defying the Obama administration, Abbas has caught up to the activists in his own society, who in recent years have turned their attention away from the American-sponsored peace process and toward the struggle for global public opinion. The Palestinian bid at the UN may not change realities on the ground, but it will boost what has since 2004 become a key initiative of the Palestinian national movement: the effort to convince people across the world to boycott, divest from, and sanction (BDS) the state of Israel.

For Palestinians and their supporters, BDS has proved a shrewd tactic. As a nonviolent movement, it turns the world's attention away from terrorism, which has long undermined sympathy for the Palestinian cause. It gives activists frustrated by America's unwillingness to pressure Israel a mechanism to do so themselves. It harnesses the new technologies that empower citizens to organize across national lines. And it capitalizes on the revulsion that many people whose nations were once colonized—or were once colonizers—feel toward an Israeli occupation with clear colonial features. The Israeli government and its American Jewish allies are devoting enormous energy to stopping the BDS movement and improving Israel's public image, but those efforts will likely fail because Israel doesn't have a public relations problem; it has a moral problem. You can't sell occupation in a postcolonial age.

Nonetheless, when Israeli and American Jewish leaders criticize the advocates of BDS for "delegitimizing" Israel, they have a point. Many in the BDS movement are doing just that: challenging Israel's legitimacy as a Jewish state. Officially, the Palestinian civil society groups that coordinate the global BDS campaign take no position on whether the Israeli-Palestinian conflict should culminate in two states near the 1967 lines or one binational state between the Jordan River and the Mediterranean Sea. But prominent figures in the BDS movement openly advocate the latter option. And by targeting all of Israeli society—and frequently comparing their effort to the global antiapartheid struggle—the BDS movement sends the message that just as the apartheid state was dismantled in South Africa, so must the Jewish state be dismantled today.

The tragedy is that Israeli and American Jewish leaders on the one hand, and BDS activists on the other, are unwittingly conspiring to destroy Israel as a democratic Jewish state. Israeli settlement policy is creating a single state between the Jordan River and the Mediterranean Sea, and many in the BDS movement are demanding that this one state be punished until it abandons its Jewish character. The challenge for Zionists who cherish Israeli democracy is to counter this erasing of the green line by reinforcing it: *to delegitimize Israel's occupation while legitimizing Israel itself.*

This task starts with language. Israeli and American Jewish hawks often refer to the territory east of the green line by the biblical names Judea and Samaria, thereby suggesting that it was, and always will be, Jewish land. Almost everyone else calls it the West Bank. But both names are inadequate. If "Judea and Samaria" implies that the most important thing about the land is its biblical lineage, "West Bank" implies that the most important thing about the land is its relationship to the kingdom of Jordan. After all, it was only after Jordan conquered the territory in 1948 that it coined the term "West Bank" to distinguish it from the rest of the kingdom, which falls on the Jordan River's east bank. Since Jordan no longer controls the land—and since neither Palestinians nor the Jordanian government want it to do so in the future—"West Bank" is an anachronism. It says nothing meaningful about the territory today.

What we should call the West Bank is "nondemocratic Israel." The phrase suggests that there are today two Israels: a flawed but genuine democracy within the green line and an ethnically based nondemocracy beyond it. It counters efforts by Israel's leaders to use the legitimacy of democratic Israel to legitimize the occupation and by Israel's adversaries to use the illegitimacy of the occupation to delegitimize democratic Israel. Having made that rhetorical divide, American Jews should look for every way possible to reinforce it. We should lobby the U.S. government to exempt settler goods from its free trade deal with Israel. We should push to end IRS policies that allow Americans to make tax-deductible gifts to charities that fund settlements. We should urge the U.S. government to require Israel to separately mark products from the settlements, as the European Union now demands. Then we should stop buying those products and stop investing in the companies that produce them. Every time Avigdor Lieberman or any other prominent public figure from nondemocratic Israel comes to the United States, he should be met with pickets. Every time any American newspaper calls Israel a democracy, we should urge that it include the caveat: only within the green line.

As I write this, I cringe. When I see a Jew—any Jew—I feel a bond. No matter his politics, he and I share a people, a people whose members have often had little to rely on but one another. I will never forget my grandfather, who spent his entire life in Cape Town, South Africa, looking at the roster of Jewish names on an apartment building in Newton, Massachusetts, a place totally alien to him, and declaring, "I know everyone here." I feel that way, too.

So how can we cut the bonds of peoplehood by shunning Jews just because they live on the wrong side of a geographical line, especially when we live in a superpower and they live in a small, embattled Jewish state? Because peoplehood, precious as it is, is not an end in itself. We were made a people in order to fulfill a certain mission in the world. That mission starts, of course, with monotheism, but it also involves Hillel's injunction to not do to others the things that we would find hateful if done to us. For millennia, what have we found more hateful than being treated as lesser human beings because we were Jews? Jews who live in territory in which their neighbors are treated as lesser human beings simply because they are Palestinian are betraying the sacred mission to which we are called every Yom Kippur by the Prophet Isaiah: to "break every yoke" and "let the oppressed go free." By boycotting settlers and their products, we call upon them to rejoin that mission, either by rejoining democratic Israel or by pledg-ing to live as equal citizens in a Palestinian state. And we yearn for the day when, by recommitting to the principles in Israel's declaration of independence, our people can again be one.

But a settlement boycott, in and of itself, is not enough. It must be twinned with an equally vigorous embrace of the people and products of democratic Israel. We should spend the money we are not spending on settler goods on those from within the green line. We should oppose efforts to divest from all Israeli companies with the same intensity with which we support efforts to divest from companies located in the West Bank. When the partisans of nondemocratic Israel visit Jewish America, they should be met with protests. When we receive visits from Israelis struggling for democracy, we should treat them as heroes. Call this simultaneous effort at delegitimizing the occupation and legitimizing Israel, "Zionist BDS."

—⸙—

Left-wing critics will argue that this distinction between democratic and nondemocratic Israel is artificial. After all, the settlements are not a rogue operation. From the beginning, they have been a project of the Israeli state. What's more, many Israeli and international companies profit from the occupation without being based there. Why shouldn't we boycott them, too? The answer is that boycotting anything inside the green line invites ambiguity about our ultimate goal, about whether we oppose Israel's occupation or Israel's existence. A settlement boy-cott, on the other hand, can be undertaken in solidarity with promi-nent Israelis. While only a tiny fringe of Israeli Jews support boycotting the entire state, acclaimed authors like David Grossman, Amos Oz, and A. B. Yehoshua and former cabinet ministers like Yossi Sarid have endorsed forms of settlement boycott. The most militant Palestinian activists will resent this bid to redefine BDS so as to make it compatible with Zionism, but it is worth noting that the Palestinian Authority itself advocates a boycott only of settler products. In fact, recasting

BDS so that it no longer challenges Israel's legitimacy within the green line offers the best chance of creating a protest movement that brings together significant numbers of Palestinians and Jews.

For their part, mainstream American Jewish organizations will likely level two criticisms at this redefined Zionist BDS. First, they will argue that it is unfair to sanction Israel when there are worse human rights offenders in the world. But in truth, many of those offenders are already sanctioned. The United States currently levies sanctions against the governments of Belarus, Cote d'Ivoire, Cuba, the Democratic Republic of Congo, Iran, Lebanon, Myanmar, North Korea, Somalia, Sudan, Syria, and Zimbabwe, along with the Hamas-led regime in Gaza, even as it treats settler Israel as a free-trade zone. The United Nations currently levies sanctions against the governments of Cote d'Ivoire, the Democratic Republic of Congo, Iran, Lebanon, North Korea, Somalia, and Sudan. Besides, Israeli settlements need not constitute the world's worst human rights abuse in order to be worth boycotting. After all, numerous American cities and religious and professional organizations currently boycott the state of Arizona because of its immigration laws. The relevant question is not "Are there worse offenders?" but rather, "Is there profound and systematic oppression that a boycott might help relieve?" That the oppression of Palestinians in nondemocratic Israel is systematic and profound has been acknowledged even by former Israeli prime ministers Ehud Barak and Ehud Olmert, who have compared Israel's rule there to apartheid. And boycotts could help to change that. Already, the Palestinian Authority–led boycott of settler goods has led at least seventeen West Bank companies to close or move inside the green line. And convincing Israeli companies and people to begin leaving the West Bank, instead of continuing to flock there, is crucial to Israel's capacity to one day reach a two-state deal without provoking civil war.

A second objection is that it is unfair to boycott settlements near the green line, which will likely be incorporated into Israel in the event of a peace deal. But morally, what matters is not the likelihood that a settler will one day live in territory in which her non-Jewish neighbors enjoy citizenship, but the fact that she does not live there now. That's why the boycott should not apply to East Jerusalem and the Golan Heights, both also occupied in 1967, because Palestinians and other non-Jews in those areas at least have the right to acquire citizenship (even if Palestinians in East Jerusalem are not granted this right by birth). If moderate settlers living near the green line resent being lumped in with their fanatical counterparts deep in the West Bank, they should agitate for the two-state solution that will make possible their incorporation into democratic Israel. Or they should in some public way renounce the tribal privilege that they—like the British in India, Serbs in Kosovo, and whites in the segregated South—enjoy but have not earned. Or they should move.

—————+—————

At the heart of our generation's struggle lies this irony. We have been given more than any group of Jews in history: wealth, status, power, the first Jewish state since Roman times. We have been given it by Jews now graying in Melbourne, Toronto, Miami, and Tel Aviv and by their mothers, fathers, brothers, and sisters, who lie beneath the ground in Lithuania, Morocco, Iraq, and Ukraine. Our highest obligation is to ensure that what we do in our moment on Jewish history's stage honors them, that we are worthy of the awesome majesty and unspeakable pain to which we are heirs. But the irony is that the only way to live up to that inheritance is by breaking sharply from the mission laid out for us by those among the older generation who today run the Jewish world. We are being asked to perpetuate a narrative of victimhood that evades the central Jewish question of our age: the question of how to ethically wield Jewish power. And if we embrace that victimhood narrative—and insist that we remain a weak and reviled people struggling merely to survive—we will make the occupation permanent and kill the soul of the Jewish state. The more faithful we are to what the loudest of our elders demand, the more we will destroy their most precious legacy. And the more we will defer the reckoning to our children, who will face a choice far crueler than ours. Either our generation will help Israel reconcile its democratic and Zionist ideals, or we will make our children choose between them.

In *The Kuzari*, written around 1140, the medieval Jewish philosopher Judah Halevi imagined a dialogue between a rabbi and a pagan king. At one point, the rabbi extols the morality of the Jews. Unlike the Christian world—which according to Jewish tradition is called *Edom* (red) because it is soaked with blood—the Jews, he declares, have held themselves to a higher standard.

But the king is unconvinced. Jewish morality, he insists, is merely the byproduct of Jewish weakness. "If you had the power," he retorts, "you would slay."

In Israel, we have our answer to the king. We can finally know whether the ethical traditions that so often made diaspora Jews the conscience of their nations can survive now that Jews have a nation of their own. The standard is not perfection; it is equal citizenship, the same standard laid out by Theodor Herzl and by the Israelis who announced their nation's birth to the world. Since 1967, Israel has taken a grave turn away from that principle, and in the next generation, possibly in the next decade, we will learn if it can find its way back. The struggle to help the Jewish state return to its founding ideals is not a struggle for Israelis alone. It is a struggle that calls all Jews because Israel is the great test of Judaism in our time. If Israeli democracy falls, it will fall for all of us. No matter where we live, we will spend our lives sifting through the political, ethical, and theological rubble.

If, on the other hand, we help Israeli democracy survive, we will have met our obligation to those who come after and those who came before. And like Stephen Wise, we too will be able to say, when we take the full measure of our lives, "I have lived to see the Jewish state. I am too small for the greatness of the mercy which God has shown us."

Notes

A Note on Sources

At times in this book I have relied on anonymous sources. Some people would speak to me only if I disguised their identities. Sometimes, they would not even do that, and so gave me information on the condition that I not attribute it to anyone at all. Often those who requested anonymity were government officials worried about endangering their jobs. Others were people who work in the Jewish world and fear retribution for criticizing powerful institutions in American Jewish life. In official Washington and in the organized American Jewish community, talking frankly about the relationship between American Jewry and Israel makes many people anxious. That anxiety is unhealthy. It inhibits the open and unafraid debate that is necessary in both Israel and America to confront the threat to Israeli democracy. But it is real.

Whenever possible, I have tried to compensate for the difficulty in getting people to speak for attribution by confirming the stories I heard with multiple sources. Overall, I spoke to dozens and dozens of people, and it was upon their combined experiences and insights that I built the arguments in the reported sections of this book. As to whether those arguments are convincing, the reader can be the judge.

Introduction

2 **no more Jews:** Jewish Community of Rhodes, "The History of the Jewish Community of Rhodes," available at http://www.jewishrhodes.org/html/history.php?lang=en.

3 **daily water consumption rate:** Amnesty International, "Troubled Waters—Palestinians Denied Fair Access to Water," 2009, 3, 4, 90, available at http://www.amnestyusa.org/sites/default/files/pdfs/mde150272009en.pdf.

3 **In the video:** Noam Sheizaf, "The Story Behind the Image of the Crying Boy," +972, August 16, 2010, available at http://972mag.com/the-story-behind-the-images-of-the-crying-boy/; Liel Kyzer, "Palestinian Boy Upset by Father's Arrest Garners International Media Attention" [video], *Haaretz*, August 5, 2010, available at http://www.haaretz.com/news/national/video-palestinian-boy-upset-by-father-s-arrest-garners-international-media-attention-1.306155.

4 **enjoy military parity:** Warren Bass, *Support Any Friend: Kennedy's Middle East and the Making of the U.S.-Israel Alliance* (New York: Oxford University Press, 2003), 149.

4 **Palestinian refugee issue:** In describing Gaza as occupied, I am following the Central Intelligence Agency, which declares, the "West Bank and Gaza Strip are Israeli-occupied." As the CIA explains, "Israel still controls maritime, airspace, and most access to the Gaza Strip; and it enforces a restricted zone along the border inside Gaza" from which Palestinians are barred entry. [Central Intelligence Agency, "Gaza Strip," *The World Factbook*, last updated June 14, 2011, available at https://www.cia.gov/library/publications/the-world-factbook/geos/country template_gz.html.] Critics note that the Arab League offer demanded "a just solution to the Palestinian Refugee problem to be agreed upon in accordance with UN General Assembly Resolution 194," a resolution that says "refugees wishing to return to their homes and live at peace with their neighbours should be permitted to do so at the earliest practicable date." But the words "agreed upon," which give Israel a veto over refugee return, effectively neuter that UN resolution. ["The Arab League 'Peace Plan,'" Jewish Virtual Library, March 27, 2002, available at http://www.jewishvirtuallibrary.org/jsource/Peace/arabplan .html; United Nations General Assembly, "194 (III). Palestine—Progress Report of the United Nations," United States Information System on the Question of Palestine, December 11, 1948, available at http://domino.un.org/unispal.nsf/0/c758572b78d1cd0085256bcf0077e51a?OpenDocument.]

4 **only country in the Middle East:** Martin van Creveld, "Israel Doesn't Need the West Bank to Be Secure," *The Jewish Daily Forward*, December 15, 2010, available at http://forward.com/articles/133961/; International Institute for Strategic Studies, "Chapter 7: Middle East and North Africa," *Military Balance* 2011 111.1 (2010): 235–82.

4 **ensure religious liberty:** "The Jewish Population of the World," Jewish Virtual Library, 2010, available at http://www.jewishvirtuallibrary.org/jsource/Judaism/jewpop.html.

5 ***The Times* of London:** Jonathan Sacks, "The Future of European Jewry," *The Jerusalem Post*, June 16, 2011, available at http://www.aish.com/jw/s/The_Future_of_European_Jewry.html.

5 **Of the last six editors of *The New York Times*:** Josh Nathan-Kazis, "The Jewish Woman with Journalism's Biggest Job," *The Jewish Daily Forward*, July 1, 2011, available at http://www.forward.com/articles/139013/.

5 **According to polling by Harvard political scientist:** Robert D. Putnam and David E. Campbell, *American Grace: How Religion Divides and Unites Us* (New York: Simon & Schuster, 2010), 505–6.

5   **Abraham Foxman, declared:** Remarks by Abraham H. Foxman, ADL Man of Achievement Award Dinner, "Anti-Semitism Becoming More Acceptable," November 23, 2009, available at http://www.adl.org/main_Anti_Semitism_Domestic/Indiana_Achievement_Address.htm.

5   **Eric Cantor devoted his entire speech:** Confidential Reporter, "The Anti-Obama: Eric Cantor's AIPAC Speech," *Foreign Confidential,* March 22, 2010, available at http://chinaconfidential.blogspot.com/2010/03/anti-obama-eric-cantors-aipac-speech.html.

5   **"Is it 1939?":** Malcolm Hoenlein, "Is it 1939? Assessing the State of World Jewry," *The New York Jewish Week,* Calendar of Events, available at http://wjc701.www49.a2hosting.com/event/malcolm-hoenlein-%E2%80%9C-it-1939-assessing-state-world-jewry%E2%80%9D; Malcolm Hoenlein, "Back to the Future: Is It 1938 Again?" in William B. Helmreich, Mark Rosenblum, and David Schimel, eds., *The Jewish Condition: Challenges and Responses, 1938–2008* (New Brunswick, N.J.: Transaction Publishers, 2007), 3.

6   **the Jews slaughtering seventy-five thousand souls:** Esther 8:3–9:16 (New JPS Version).

7   **researchers at Brandeis:** Charles Kadushin and Elizabeth Tighe, "How Hard Is It to Be a Jew on College Campuses," *Contemporary Jewry* 28, no. 1 (2008): 1–20, available at http://bir.brandeis.edu/bitstream/handle/10192/23260/CJ02kadush.pdf?sequence=1.

7   **Jewish students frequently befriend Muslims:** See, for instance, the negative responses by American Jewish college students to anti-Muslim images shown them in focus groups by pollster Frank Luntz. [Frank Luntz, "Israel in the Age of Eminem," The Andrea and Charles Bronfman Philanthropies, March 2003, 34, 38–40, available at http://www.policyarchive.org/handle/10207/bitstreams/10395.pdf.]

8   **with tear gas, rubber bullets:** B'Tselem, "Show of Force: Israeli Military Conduct in Weekly Demonstrations in a-Nabi Saleh," September 2011, available at http://www.btselem.org/download/201109_show_of_force_eng.pdf; Lior Yavne, "Backyard Proceedings: The Implementation of Due Process Rights in the Military Courts in the Occupied Territories," Yesh Din, December 2007, available at http://www.yesh-din.org/userfiles/file/Reports-English/BackyardProceedingsfullreportEng.pdf.

9   **Israel-Syrian peace:** "Olmert Sent Message to Syria via Erdogan: Israel," Reuters, July 13, 2008, available at http://www.reuters.com/article/2008/07/13/us-israel-syria-turkey-idUSL1334760120080713; Alon BenDavid, "Despite Heron Deal, Israel and Turkey at Odds," Military.com, February 4, 2010, available at http://www.military.com/features/0,15240,210185,00.html.

9   **subsidized hundreds of thousands:** Israel Ministry of Foreign Affairs, "Camp David Accords," September 17, 1978, available at http://www.mfa.gov.il/MFA/Peace+Process/Guide+to+the+Peace+Process/Camp+David+Accords.htm; David D. Kirkpatrick and Isabel Kershner, "Egypt and Israel Back Away from Diplomatic Crisis," *The New York Times,* August 20, 2011, available at http://www.nytimes.com/2011/08/21/world/middleeast/21egypt.html; Roee Nahmias, "Moussa: Peace Treaty 'Untouchable,'" YNet News, September 17, 2011, available at http://www.ynetnews.com/articles/0,7340,L-4123332,00.html.

10 **"If ye oppress not the stranger":** Jeremiah 7:5–7 (New JPS Version).

1. The Crisis in Israel

11   **"Tension between values":** Alexander Yakobson and Amnon Rubinstein, *Israel and the Family of Nations: The Jewish Nation-State and Human Rights* (New York: Routledge, 2009), 125.

12   **"no privileged voice in the state":** Theodor Herzl, *Old New Land*, trans. Lotta Levensohn, introduction by Jacques Kornberg (Princeton, N.J.: Markus Wiener Publishers, 1997), 67, xv.

12   **"enough for us":** Ibid., 66, 68.

12   **"there are other views among us":** Ibid., 66.

12   **had persecuted them:** Shlomo Avineri, "Utopia: The Sequel," *Haaretz*, May 3, 2010, available at http://www.haaretz.com/weekend/magazine/utopia-the-sequel-1 .287853.

12   **"Only then is Zion truly Zion!":** Herzl, *Old New Land*, 139.

12   **"stranger be at home among us":** Ibid., 276.

12   **dream come true:** Ibid.

12   **demanding a state in Palestine:** Avineri, "Utopia: The Sequel."

13   **"to the best of their ability":** Ahad Ha'am, *Al Parashat Derakhim: Kovets Ma'amarim*, trans. David Myers (Berlin: Jüdische Verlag, 1921), xxi–xxii.

13   **"But a Venice":** Herzl, *Old New Land*, xvii.

13   **"complete equality of social and political":** Israel Ministry of Foreign Affairs, "The Declaration of the Establishment of the State of Israel," May 14, 1948, available at http://www.mfa.gov.il/MFA/Peace%20Process/Guide%20to%20the%20Peace %20Process/Declaration%20of%20Establishment%20of%20State%20of%20Israel.

13   **"shocked by the deeds":** Tom Segev, *1949: The First Israelis* (New York: Free Press, 1986), 26.

13   **shot them dead:** Ibid., 72.

14   **Arab countries to which they fled:** Asem Khalil, "Palestinian Nationality and Citizenship: Current Challenges and Future Perspectives," Euro-Mediterranean Consortium for Applied Research on International Migration (Fiesole, Italy: European University Institute, 2007), 23–33, available at http://cadmus.eui.eu/dspace/ bitstream/1814/8162/1/CARIM%20RR-2007-07.pdf.

14   **under martial law:** Ilan Peleg and Dov Waxman, *Israel's Palestinians* (New York: Cambridge University Press, 2011), 50.

14   **in the direction of Herzl's dream:** On the treatment of Arab Israelis in the early years of the state, see Ian Lustick, "Zionism and the State of Israel: Regime Objectives and the Arab Minority in the First Years of Statehood," *Middle Eastern Studies* 16, no. 1 (January 1980), 127–43.

14   **apparent refusal to offer peace:** On the ambiguities of the Arab League's famed 1967 "Khartoum Resolution," see Avi Shlaim, *The Iron Wall: Israel and the Arab World* (New York: W. W. Norton, 2001), 258–60.

14   **Israel's Arab citizens:** Even deciding what to call Arab citizens of Israel is politically fraught. According to a 2009 poll by the University of Haifa's Sammy Smooha, 39 percent of Arab Israelis call themselves some variation of "Israeli Arab," 42 percent call themselves some variation of "Israeli Palestinian," and another 17 percent call themselves simply "Palestinian" or "Palestinian Arab." While Smooha's polling shows that the linguistic trend is clearly toward some version of "Palestinian" rather than "Arab," I use the latter term so as to clearly delineate

those Arabs who live inside Israel's 1967 lines from those in the occupied territories. [Sammy Smooha, "Arab-Jewish Relations in Israel: Alienation and Rapprochement," *Peaceworks* (December 2010): 67, available at http://www.usip.org/files/resources/PW67_Arab-Jewish_Relations_in_Israel.pdf.]

15 **They maintain their own:** Yakobson and Rubinstein, *Israel and the Family of Nations*, 119.

15 **By 1988, it was 15 percent:** Peleg and Waxman, *Israel's Palestinians*, 34.

15 **sympathize with those adversaries:** According to 2010 polling by the Pew Research Center, 27 percent of Arab Israelis felt favorably toward Hezbollah while 50 percent felt unfavorably. For Hamas, the figures were 21 percent favorable and 58 percent unfavorable. [Pew Research Center, "Little Enthusiasm for Many Muslim Leaders: Mixed Views of Hamas and Hezbollah in Largely Muslim Nations," Pew Global Attitudes Project, February 4, 2010, available at http://pewglobal.org/2010/02/04/mixed-views-of-hamas-and-hezbollah-in-largely-muslim-nations/.]

15 **"primarily neglectful and discriminatory":** Jewish Agency for Israel, "The Official Summation of the Or Commission Report," Fall 2003, available at http://www.jafi.org.il/JewishAgency/English/Jewish+Education/Compelling+Content/Eye+on+Israel/Current+Issues/Society+and+Politics/Or+Commission+Report.htm.

16 **20 percent of Israel's population:** Peleg and Waxman, *Israel's Palestinians*, 41.

16 **A 2010 study:** Dina Kraft, "Separate but Not Equal," *Moment* Magazine, September/October 2010, available at http://www.momentmag.com/Exclusive/2010/10/Feature-Arab_Israel.html.

16 **in their governing coalitions:** Freedom House, "Freedom in the World 2011—Israel," May 12, 2011, available at http://www.unhcr.org/refworld/docid/4dcbf51923.html.

16 **some Bedouin, do:** Peleg and Waxman, *Israel's Palestinians*, 23.

16 **only Jews, instant citizenship:** Israel Ministry of Foreign Affairs, "Acquisition of Israeli Nationality," August 20, 2001, available at http://www.mfa.gov.il/MFA/MFAArchive/2000_2009/2001/8/Acquisition%20of%20Israeli%20Nationality.

16 **state's dominant ethnic group:** Yakobson and Rubinstein, *Israel and the Family of Nations*, 127–28, 144.

16 **Being a Jewish state does not:** Benjamin Netanyahu has made a small effort toward remedying this inequity. In 2010, he backed a $214 million economic development plan for Arab Israeli communities. ["Israel Launches Economic Plan for Israeli Arab Towns," BBC News, March 21, 2010, available at http://news.bbc.co.uk/2/hi/8576282.stm.]

16 **Israel's declaration of independence:** Israel Ministry of Foreign Affairs, "The Declaration of the Establishment of the State of Israel."

16 **sit in the Israeli cabinet:** For instance, the Ashkenazi ultra-Orthodox party Agudath Israel—which in 2008 merged with another Ashkenazi ultra-Orthodox party, Degel HaTorah, to form United Torah Judaism—has sat in governing coalitions despite being non-Zionist. [Rabbi Avner Zarmi, "Agudath Israel May Be Non-Zionist, But It Supports Israel and Its People," *The Wisconsin Jewish Chronicle*, August 16, 2002, available at http://www.jewishchronicle.org/article.php?article_id=1548.]

17 **married by a minister or imam:** In 2010, the Knesset carved out a small exception to this rule for those few Israelis who are not classified as belonging to any religious group. [Amnon Meranda, "Knesset Approves 'Thin' Civil Marriage Bill," YNet News, March 16, 2010, available at http://www.ynetnews.com/articles/0,7340, L-3863253,00.html.]

17 **He introduced affirmative action:** Leslie King, "From Pronatalism to Social Welfare? Extending Family Allowances to Minority Populations in France and Israel," *European Journal of Population* 17, no. 4 (2001): 305–22, available at http://www.jstor.org/pss/20164160; Amnon Be'eri-Sulitzeanu, "Israel's Arab Citizens and the State: Is the Relationship Changing?" Mideast Peace Pulse Blog at IPF, May 11, 2009, available at http://www.israelpolicyforum.org/blog/israels-arab-citizens-and-state-relationship-changing; Yitzhak Reiter, "Israel and Its Arab Minority," Jewish Virtual Library, May 2009, available at http://www.jewishvirtuallibrary.org/jsource/isdf/text/reiter.html; Yair Ettinger, "Arabs Too Will Mourn," *Haaretz*, October 17, 2002, available at http://israelblog.theisraelforum.org/Articles/Arabs_too_will_mourn_him.html; Yakobson and Rubinstein, *Israel and the Family of Nations*, 114.

18 **ethnocracy:** While the Israeli political geographer Oren Yiftachel, who has popularized the term "ethnocracy," uses it to describe all of Israel, I believe that designation does not take sufficient account of Israel's genuinely democratic features within its 1967 lines. Thus, I use the phrase to refer only to Israeli governance in the occupied territories.

18 **Palestinians are not:** Since the beginning of the Oslo peace process in 1993, Palestinians have periodically voted in elections for the Palestinian Authority (PA). But the PA is nothing close to a sovereign state. It administers a noncontiguous territory within borders controlled by Israel. It lacks its own currency and although under Oslo the PA is supposed to enjoy control over both civil and security functions in "Area A" of the West Bank, even here Israeli forces retain the right to arrest Palestinians and bring them before an Israeli military court. [On Israeli jurisdiction throughout the West Bank, see Sharon Weil, "The Judicial Arm of the Occupation: The Israeli Military Courts in the Occupied Territories," *International Review of the Red Cross* 89, no. 866 (June 2007): 395–419.]

18 **hard-to-obtain—permit:** "Checkpoints," Jerusalem Media and Communications Center, March 2, 2011, available at http://www.jmcc.org/fastfactspag.aspx?tname=44; B'Tselem, "Background on the Restriction of Movement," available at http://www.btselem.org/freedom_of_movement.

19 **fewer than 1 percent are found innocent:** B'Tselem, "Dual System of Law," http://www.btselem.org/settler_violence/dual_legal_system; Lior Yavne, "Backyard Proceedings."

19 **population inside the green line:** Eyal Hareuveni, "By Hook and by Crook: Israeli Settlement Policy in the West Bank," B'Tselem, July 2010, available at http://www.btselem.org/Download/201007_By_Hook_and_by_Crook_Eng.pdf; Foundation for Middle East Peace, "Israeli Settler Population, 1972–2006," available at http://www.fmep.org/settlement_info/settlement-info-and-tables/stats-data/comprehensive-settlement-population-1972–2006; Peace Now Settlement Watch Team, "West Bank and Jerusalem Map," January 2011, available at http://peacenow.org.il/eng/sites/default/files/settlements_map_eng.pdf; Nadav Shragai and *Haaretz* Correspondent,

"Settler Population Growing Three Times Faster Than Rest of Israel, Study Says," *Haaretz*, December 15, 2008, available at http://www.haaretz.com/news/settler-population-growing-three-times-faster-than-rest-of-israel-study-says-1.259550.

19 **a single Jewish settler:** Akiva Eldar (chief political columnist and editorial writer for *Haaretz*) in discussion with the author, November 24, 2010.

19 **halfway across the West Bank:** Joshua Hammer, "I'm a Realist," *The New York Review of Books* 57, no. 5 (March 25, 2010), available at http://www.nybooks.com/articles/archives/2010/mar/25/im-a-realist/.

19 **They share the same:** Idith Zertal and Akiva Eldar, *Lords of the Land: The War over Israel's Settlements in the Occupied Territories, 1967–2007*, trans. Vivian Eden (New York: Nation Books, 2007), xv, 51, 113, 312; B'Tselem, "Forbidden Roads: Israel's Discriminatory Road Regime in the West Bank," August 2004, available at http://www.btselem.org/download/200408_forbidden_roads_eng.pdf; Central Intelligence Agency, "The World Factbook: West Bank," last updated on September 28, 2010, available at https://www.cia.gov/library/publications/the-world-factbook/geos/we.html; "Peace Now Asks Egged to Halt Bus Lines to Illegal W. Bank Outposts," *Haaretz*, December 12, 2007, available at http://www.haaretz.com/news/peace-now-asks-egged-to-halt-bus-lines-to-illegal-w-bank-outposts-1.235062; Associated Press, "West Bank Train Line Plan Draws Palestinian Ire," *The Jerusalem Post*, November 26, 2010, available at http://www.jpost.com/Headllines/Article.aspx?id=196913.

19 **"the heart of our country":** Tovah Lazaroff, "PM: Ariel Is the 'Capital of Samaria,'" *The Jerusalem Post*, January 29, 2010, available at http://www.jpost.com/Israel/Article.aspx?id=167225.

19 **Many Israeli maps:** Akiva Eldar and *Haaretz* Correspondent, "PM Olmert Backs Tamir Proposal to Add Green Line to Textbooks," *Haaretz*, December 5, 2006, available at http://www.haaretz.com/news/pm-olmert-backs-tamir-proposal-to-add-green-line-to-textbooks-1.206288; Hana Levi Julian, "Harsh Debate on Tamir's Green Line Map," Arutz Sheva, December 18, 2006, available at http://www.israelnationalnews.com/News/News.aspx/117697; "Dutch Watchdog Criticizes Israeli Tourism Website for Blurring Borders," *Haaretz*, September 30, 2010, available at http://www.haaretz.com/news/diplomacy-defense/dutch-watchdog-criticizes-israeli-tourism-website-for-blurring-borders-1.316495; "Israel Map," Israeli Tourism and Recreation Website, available at http://www.infotour.co.il/israel_map.html; Isabel Kershner, "Elusive Line Defines Lives in Israel and the West Bank," *The New York Times*, September 6, 2011, available at http://nytimes.com/2011/09/07/world/middleeast/07borders.html?_r=1&pagewanted=all.

19 **"The moment of truth":** "Haaretz Q&A/Avraham Burg Answers Readers' Questions on Anti-Semitism in the Modern World," *Haaretz*, April 4, 2011, available at http://www.haaretz.com/news/national/haaretz-q-a-avraham-burg-answers-readers-questions-on-anti-semitism-in-the-modern-world-1.354054.

20 **no more Jewish settlers live there:** See footnote tagged "Palestinian Refugee Issue" in Introduction.

20 **50 percent higher than Israel's Jews:** Central Intelligence Agency, "The World Factbook: Israel," last updated November 9, 2010, available at https://www.cia.gov/library/publications/the-world-factbook/geos/is.html; Central Intelligence Agency, "The World Factbook: West Bank," last updated November 9, 2010, available at

https://www.cia.gov/library/publications/the-world-factbook/geos/we.html; Central Intelligence Agency, "The World Factbook: Gaza Strip," last updated October 27, 2010, available at https://www.cia.gov/library/publications/the-world-factbook/geos/gz.html.

20 **suicide as a Jewish state:** Israel's declaration of independence does not actually use the word "democracy." But the concept is implicit in its promise of "complete equality of social and political rights" and its promise that the "Arab inhabitants of the State of Israel" will enjoy "full and equal citizenship and due representation in all its provisional and permanent institutions." [Israel Ministry of Foreign Affairs, "The Declaration of the Establishment of the State of Israel."]

20 **Some on the far left yearn for that day:** See, for example, Ali Abunimah, *One Country: A Bold Proposal to End the Israeli-Palestinian Impasse* (New York: Metropolitan Books, 2006).

20 **Ehud Barak and Ehud Olmert:** In 2007, Ehud Olmert declared, "If the day comes when the two-state solution collapses, and we face a South African–style struggle for equal voting rights (also for the Palestinians in the territories), then, as soon as that happens, the state of Israel is finished." [Barak Ravid, David Landau, Aluf Benn, and Shmuel Rosner, "Olmert to *Haaretz*: Two-State Solution, or Israel Is Done For," *Haaretz*, November 29, 2007, available at http://www.haaretz.com/news/olmert-to-haaretz-two-state-solution-or-israel-is-done-for-1.234201.] In February 2010, Ehud Barak warned that if "millions of Palestinians cannot vote, that will be an apartheid state." [Rory McCarthy, "Barak: Make Peace with Palestinians or Face Apartheid," *The Guardian*, February 2, 2010, available at http://www.guardian.co.uk/world/2010/feb/03/barak-apartheid-palestine-peace.]

20 **"become all one thing or all the other":** Abraham Lincoln, "A House Divided," delivered June 16, 1858, Springfield, Illinois, available at http://www.americanrhetoric.com/speeches/abrahamlincolnhousedivided.htm.

20 **"in the end the territories will hold us":** Gershom Gorenberg, *The Accidental Empire: Israel and the Birth of the Settlements* (New York: Times Books, 2006), 320.

21 **not present at trial:** B'Tselem, "Torture and Abuse Under Interrogation," available at http://www.btselem.org/english/torture/torture_by_gss.asp; Dan Izenberg, "High Court: No Remand Hearings Without Suspect's Presence," *The Jerusalem Post*, February 11, 2010, available at http://www.jpost.com/Israel/Article.aspx?id=168513.

21 **"constitutional revolution":** Gidon Sapir, "The Israeli Constitutional Revolution—How Did It Happen?" *Selected Works of Gidon Sapir*, February 2008, available at http://works.bepress.com/gidon_sapir1/.

21 **challenged cherished myths:** See, for instance, Segev, *1949*; Benny Morris, *The Birth of the Palestinian Refugee Problem, 1947–1949* (New York: Cambridge University Press, 1998); Avi Shlaim, *Collusion Across the Jordan: King Abdullah, the Zionist Movement and the Partition of Palestine* (New York: Columbia University Press, 1988).

21 **"have become routine":** B'Tselem, "Background on Violence by Settlers," available at https://gimmetruth.wordpress.com/2010/10/04/settlers-set-fire-to-mosque-in-west-bank-and-a-lesson-in-us-media/, accessed on October 4, 2010; Chaim Levinson, "Two Palestinian Cars Torched, Scrawled with 'Price Tag' Graffiti," *Haaretz*, April 16, 2010, available at http://www.haaretz.com/news/two-palestinian-cars

-torched-scrawled-with-price-tag-graffiti-1.284426; Barak Ravid, "Netanyahu: Settlers' Price Tag Policy Is Unacceptable," *Haaretz*, March 8, 2011, available at http://www.haaretz.com/news/diplomacy-defense/netanyahu-settlers-price-tag -policy-is-unacceptable-1.347941.

21 **"price tag" policy:** Aviel Magnezi, "West Bank Demolitions Prompt Riots, Arrests, 'Price Tag' Missions," YNet News, July 26, 2010, available at http://www.ynetnews .com/articles/0,7340,L-3925135,00.html; B'Tselem, "5 Sept. '11: Suspected 'Price Tag' Attack in Qusra Following Demolition of Houses in Migron Outpost," September 5, 2011, available at http://www.btselem.org/violence-settlers/5-sept-2011-suspected -price-tag-attack-qusra-following-demolition-of-houses-migron.

22 **have their homes bulldozed:** Chaim Levinson, "Two Palestinians Indicted for Fogel Massacre," *Haaretz*, June 6, 2011, available at http://www.haaretz.com/print -edition/news/two-palestinians-indicted-for-fogel-massacre-1.366181;   Ahiya Raved, "Fogel Family Murderer Gets 5 Life Sentences," YNet News, September 13, 2011, available at http://www.ynetnews.com/articles/0,7340,L-4121856,00.html; B'Tselem, "Restriction of Movement: Curfew," available at http://www.btselem.org/ freedom_of_movement/curfew; B'Tselem, "House Demolitions as Punishment," available at http://www.btselem.org/punitive_demolitions.

22 **2011 study by Yesh Din:** Yesh Din, "Law Enforcement upon Israeli Civilians in the West Bank," February 2011, available at http://www.yesh-din.org/userfiles/file/data-sheets/Final%20Data%20Sheet%20Law%20Enforcement%202011%20ENG.pdf.

22 **"the settlers are the sovereign":** "Who Is the Sovereign Here?" *Haaretz*, September 15, 2008, available at http://www.haaretz.com/print-edition/opinion/who-is-the -sovereign-here-1.253810.

22 **The settler was later made:** Larry Derfner, "A Rabbi's Fatwa," *Jewish Journal*, March 23, 2000, available at http://www.jewishjournal.com/articles/item/a_rabbis_fatwa _20000324/; Ori Nir, "Short History of Israeli Right-Wing Terrorism," Peace Now, November 13, 2009, available at http://peacenow.org/entries/short_history_of_ israeli_right_wing_terrorism; correspondence with Ori Nir (spokesman for Americans for Peace Now), August 25, 2010; Efrat Weiss, "Protest: Gays Acting Like Beasts," YNet News, October 31, 2006, available at http://www.ynetnews.com /articles/0,7340,L-3321676,00.html.

22 **In 2002, Hebrew University classics lecturer:** Neri Livney, "So What's It Like Being Called an Israel-Hater?" *Haaretz*, March 16, 2010, available at http://www .haaretz.com/print-edition/news/so-what-s-it-like-being-called-an-israel-hater-1 .264809; Hadani Ditmars, "Peace Offerings," *New Internationalist*, no. 422, available at http://www.newint.org/features/special/2009/05/01/israel-palestine/; correspondence with Ori Nir, August 25, 2010; Yuval Yoaz, "Above the Law," [Hebrew] *Haaretz*, January 26, 2006, available at http://www.haaretz.co.il/misc/ 1.1078063, trans. Elisheva Goldberg; correspondence with Amiel Vardi, October 13, 2010.

22 **"his leftist collaborators":** Efrat Weiss, "Marzel to Cabinet: Kill Left-Wing Leader," YNet News, March 20, 2006, available at http://www.ynetnews.com/articles/0,7340 ,L-3230185,00.html.

22 **Marzel currently:** Maayana Miskin, "Ben-Ari Faces Off with Leftist Critic," Arutz Sheva, July 31, 2011, available at http://www.israelnationalnews.com/News/News .aspx/146258.

22 **members of the dovish group Peace Now:** Hana Levi Julian, "'Peace Now' Head Goes to War over Rabbi's Sabbath Message," Arutz Sheva, August 29, 2008, available at http://www.israelnationalnews.com/News/News.aspx/127395; Yisrael Rosen, "Morality Requires: Hurt Hostile Population," YNet News, June 22, 2006, available at http://www.ynetnews.com/articles/0,7340,L-3266113,00.html.

22 **anyone who killed a member of Peace Now:** Efrat Weiss, "Jerusalem: Professor Ze'ev Sternhell Lightly Wounded by Pipe Bomb," YNet News, September 25, 2008, available at http://www.ynetnews.com/articles/0,7340,L-3601841,00.html; Jonathan Lis, "Dichter: Jewish Terrorists Tried to Murder Professor Zeev Sternhell," *Haaretz*, September 26, 2008, available at http://www.haaretz.com/print-edition/news/dichter -jewish-terrorists-tried-to-murder-professor-zeev-sternhell-1.254664.

22 **"an evil wind of extremism":** Karin Laub, "Olmert Decries 'Evil Wind of Extremism' in Israel," *USA Today*, September 28, 2008, available at http://www.usatoday .com/news/topstories/2008-09-28-1405682050_x.htm.

23 **small minority of settlers:** According to a 2010 study by the Harry S. Truman Institute at the Hebrew University, 21 percent of West Bank settlers say they would resist the evacuation of settlements by "all means," including violating the law. [Harry S. Truman Institute for the Advancement of Peace, "Israeli Poll #(31) 1–14 March 2010," available at http://truman.huji.ac.il/upload/truman_site_poll_31_ March2010.pdf.]

23 **"the backing of part of the [settler] leadership":** Amos Harel, "IDF West Bank Commander: Rightist Violence Encouraged by Settler Leaders," *Haaretz*, October 2, 2008, available at http://www.haaretz.com/print-edition/news/idf-west-bank -commander-rightist-violence-encouraged-by-settler-leaders-1.254818.

23 **"martyrs of the Holocaust":** Sefi Rachlevsky, "A Racist, Messianic Rabbi Is the Ruler of Israel," *Haaretz*, July 1, 2001, available at http://www.haaretz.com/print -edition/opinion/a-racist-messianic-rabbi-is-the-ruler-of-israel-1.370554; Nadav Shragai, "Top Yesha Rabbi Says Jewish Law Forbids Renting Houses to Arabs," *Haaretz*, March 19, 2008, available at http//www.haaretz.com/news/top-yesha -rabbi-says-jewish-law-forbids-renting-houses-to-arabs-1.241799.

23 **punishable by death:** Rachlevsky, "A Racist, Messianic Rabbi Is the Ruler of Israel"; Ami Pedahzur and Arie Perliger, *Jewish Terrorism in Israel* (New York: Columbia University Press, 2009), 98–110, available at http://cup.columbia.edu/book /978-0-231-15446-8/jewish-terrorism-in-israel/excerpt.

23 **Since then, Israel's internal security:** Zertal and Eldar, *Lords of the Land*, 445.

23 **Seventy percent of Jewish Israelis:** Asher Arian, Tamar Hermann, Yuval Lebel, Michael Philippov, Hila Zaban, and Anna Knafelman, "Auditing Israeli Democracy: Democratic Values in Practice," Israel Democracy Institute, November 2010, available at http://www.idi.org.il/sites/english/SectionArchive/Documents/ Auditing_Israeli_Democracy_2010.pdf.

23 **befriend an Arab:** Mina Zemach, "Attitude Survey Results: Social-Political Identities of Israeli Youth," in Hagar Tzameret-Kertcher, ed., *All of the Above: Identity Paradoxes of Young People in Israel* (Herzliya: Friedrich-Ebert-Stiftung, 2010), 79.

23 **allowed to run for the Knesset:** Or Kashti, "Poll: Half of Israeli High Schoolers Oppose Equal Rights for Arabs," *Haaretz*, March 11, 2010, available at http://www .haaretz.com/print-edition/news/poll-half-of-israeli-high-schoolers-oppose-equal -rights-for-arabs-1.264564.

23 **avoid renting apartments to Arabs:** Harry S. Truman Institute for the Advancement of Peace Press Release, "Joint Palestinian Israeli Poll, November–December 2010," Poll #34, available at http://truman.huji.ac.il/poll-view.asp?id=368.

24 **dominating as fully human:** On Israel's use of home demolitions and its restrictions on Palestinians living in the Jordan Valley, see "Statistics on House Demolitions (1967–2010)," Israeli Committee Against House Demolitions, available at http://www.icahd.org/?page_id=5508; B'Tselem, "Dispossession and Exploitation: Israel's Policy in the Jordan Valley and the Northern Dead Sea," May 2011, available at http://www.btselem.org/download/201105_dispossession_and_exploitation_eng.pdf; Amira Hass, "IDF Destroys West Bank Village After Declaring It Military Zone," *Haaretz*, July 21, 2010, available at http://www.haaretz.com/print-edition/news/idf-destroys-west-bank-village-after-declaring-it-military-zone-1.303098.

24 **"between master and slave":** David Grossman, *The Yellow Wind*, trans. Haim Watzman (New York: Farrar, Straus and Giroux, 2002), 40.

24 **Research by the Hebrew University social psychologist:** Ifat Maoz and Clark McCauley, "Explaining Support for Violating Out-Group Human Rights in Conflict: Attitudes Toward Principles of Human Rights, Trust in the Out-Group, and Intergroup Contact," *Journal of Applied Social Psychology* 41, no. 4 (April 2011): 891–905, available at http://onlinelibrary.wiley.com/doi/10.111/j.1550-1816.2011.00740.x/abstract.

24 **democracy as Israel's most important value:** Truman Institute, "Israeli Poll #(31)."

25 **the very people old enough:** Dahlia Scheindlin, "Final Report (Public Opinion and Focus Group)," Kulanana Society Building Initiative, February–March 2010, available at http://kulanana.org.il/h/?p=1408&lang=en.

25 **the "golden age":** The term comes from University of Haifa professor Sammy Smooha. [Smooha, "Arab-Jewish Relations in Israel."]

26 **less than 31 percent:** Ibid.

26 **killing thirteen Arab citizens:** Peleg and Waxman, *Israel's Palestinians*, 93–94.

26 **spiked to 24 percent in 2009:** Smooha, "Arab-Jewish Relations in Israel."

26 **arrested on suspicion of raising money for Hamas:** Ilene R. Prusher, "Israeli Arab's Rising Voice of Opposition," *The Christian Science Monitor*, October 26, 2006, available at http://www.csmonitor.com/2006/1026/p06s01-wome.html.

26 **he praised Hezbollah:** "Balad MKs Praise Hizbollah Resistance," *The Jerusalem Post*, September 15, 2006, available at http://www.jpost.com/Israel/Article.aspx?id=34947.

26 **"enemy within":** Mossawa Center, "One Year for Israel's New Government and the Arab Minority in Israel," April 27, 2010, available at http://www.mossawa.org/files/files/File/Reports/2010/Netanyahu%20Final.pdf.

26 **He spent a brief period of his youth:** Lily Galili, "Lieberman Was Involved in Radical Right Kach Movement," *Haaretz*, February 4, 2009, available at http://www.haaretz.com/print-edition/news/lieberman-was-involved-in-radical-right-kach-movement-1.269330.

26 **amending Israel's Basic Law:** This prohibition is currently the result of a decree by Israel's interior minister. To prevent the Supreme Court from using the Basic Law to overturn it, Lieberman's allies want to amend the Basic Law itself. ["Israeli Segregation/The End of the Road for the 'Jewish AND Democratic' Model?" Promised Land Blog, December 18, 2009, available at http://www.promisedlandblog.com/?p=2026.]

26 **anti-Zionist Arab parties:** Gershom Gorenberg, *The Unmaking of Israel* (New York: Harper, 2011), 212; Aviad Glickman, "Arab Parties Disqualified from Elections," YNet News, January 12, 2009, available at http://www.ynet.co.il/english/articles/0,7340,L-3654866,00.html.

27 **In the mock voting:** Yotam Feldman, "Lieberman's Anti-Arab Ideology Wins Over Israel's Teens," *Haaretz*, February 5, 2009, available at http://www.haaretz.com/news/elections/lieberman-s-anti-arab-ideology-wins-over-israel-s-teens-1.269489.

27 **"to live together":** Mossawa Center, "One Year for Israel's New Government and the Arab Minority in Israel."

27 **from moving in:** Roi Maor, "Knesset Passes Segregation Law," +972, March 22, 2011, available at http://972mag.com/knesset-passes-segregation-law/; Dr. Nimrod Luz, "Knesset to Pass 'Separate but Equal' Communities Bill," +972, March 21, 2011, available at http://972mag.com/"knesset-to-pass-separate-but-equal-communities-bill-tomorrow/.

27 **endorsed a law removing Arabic:** Jonathan Lis, "Lawmakers Seek to Drop Arabic as One of Israel's Official Languages," *Haaretz*, August 4, 2011, available at http://www.haaretz.com/print-edition/news/lawmakers-seek-to-drop-arabic-as-one-of-israel-s-official-languages-1.376829; Jonathan Lis, "Kadima Lawmakers Retract Support for Bill Scrapping Arabic as Official Language in Israel," *Haaretz*, August 5, 2011, available at http://www.haaretz.com/print-edition/news/kadima-lawmakers-retract-support-for-bill-scrapping-arabic-as-official-language-in-israel-1.377031.

27 **"Jews over Arabs in all walks of life":** "A Bad Knesset for Israel," *Haaretz*, July 23, 2010, available at http://www.haaretz.com/print-edition/opinion/a-bad-knesset-for-israel-1.303535.

28 **"a speaker should be prohibited":** Tamar Hermann, "The Israeli Democracy Index 2011," trans. Karon Gold and Zvi Ofer, Israel Democracy Institute, 2011, available at http://www.idi.org.il/events1/Events_The_President's_Conference/2011/Documents/democracy%20english.pdf.

28 **"the Israeli public is not":** Or Kashti, "Poll: Majority of Israel's Jews Back Gag on Rights Groups," *Haaretz*, April 28, 2010, available at http://www.haaretz.com/news/national/poll-majority-of-israel-s-jews-back-gag-on-rights-groups-1.285120.

28 **Israeli human rights organizations:** J. J. Goldberg, "Rightists Target New Israel Fund over Grantees' Goldstone Testimony," *The Jewish Daily Forward*, January 31, 2010, available at http://blogs.forward.com/jj-goldberg/124750/#ixzz1WWDctfAB; Didi Remez, "Nahum Barnea: How US Jewish Leaders Stepped In to Block the Knesset Anti-NIF Bill," *Coteret*, February 5, 2010, available at http://coteret.com/2010/02/05/nahum-barnea-how-us-jewish-leaders-stepped-in-to-block-the-knesset-anti-nif-bill/; Zeev Sternhell, "The Obligation of a True Patriot," *Haaretz*, February 19, 2010, available at http://www.haaretz.com/print-edition/opinion/the-obligation-of-a-true-patriot-1.263621.

28 **The result was a bill:** Dan Izenberg, "Cabinet Backs Bill to Register NGOs Funded by Foreign States," *The Jerusalem Post*, February 15, 2010, available at http://www.jpost.com/Israel/Article.aspx?id=168725; Mitchell Plitnick, "Knesset Attempt to Cripple Israeli Civil Society," *The Third Way: Finding Balance in Mideast Analysis*, February, 28, 2010, 339–41, available at http://mitchellplitnick.com/2010/02/28/knesset-attempt-to-cripple-israeli-civil-society/.

28 **special tax on Israeli human rights groups:** "Netanyahu Backs Laws to Limit Donations to Israeli Human Rights Organizations," *Haaretz*, November 8, 2011, available at http://www.haaretz.org/print-edition/news/netanyahu-backs-laws-to -limit-donations-to-israeli-human-rights-organizations-1.394256.

28 **Grossman, Amos Oz, and A. B. Yehoshua:** Lahav Harkov, "Anti-Boycott Bill Becomes Law After Passing Knesset," *The Jerusalem Post*, July 11, 2011, available at http://www.jpost.com/DiplomacyAndPolitics/Article.aspx?id=228896; Boaz Fyler, "Yehoshua, Oz, Grossman Back Boycott of Ariel," YNet News, August 30, 2010, available at http://www.ynetnews.com/articles/0,7340,L-3946485,00.html.

28 **his party was banned:** Israel Ministry of Foreign Affairs, "The Kach Movement— Background," March 3, 1994, available at http://www.mfa.gov.il/MFA/Government/ Law/Legal%20Issues%20and%20Rulings/THE%20KACH%20MOVEMENT%20 -%20BACKGROUND%20-%2003-Mar-94.

29 **did not disavow its substance:** "General Debate of the 65th General Assembly: H. E. Mr. Avigdor Lieberman, Deputy Prime Minister and Minister of Foreign Affairs," Permanent Mission of Israel to the United Nations, September 28, 2010, available at http://israel-un.mfa.gov.il/statements-at-the-united-nations/general -assembly/315-ga65gd28092010; Natasha Mozgovaya and Barak Ravid, "Netanyahu: Israel, Palestinians Can Reach Mideast Peace in a Year," *Haaretz*, September 28, 2010, available at http://www.haaretz.com/news/diplomacy-defense/netanyahu -israel-palestinians-can-reach-mideast-peace-in-a-year-1.316220; Liel Kyzer, "Rights Group Asks Netanyahu to Vow Not to 'Transfer' Arab Citizens," *Haaretz*, October 14, 2010, available at http://www.haaretz.com/print-edition/news/rights -group-asks-netanyahu-to-vow-not-to-transfer-arab-citizens-1.318959; Libby Friedlander (Director of the International Relations Department at the Association for Civil Rights in Israel) in discussion with the author, March 25, 2011.

29 **"nightmare into an operational plan":** Denis Staunton, "Is Oath a Step Towards the Transfer of Arabs?" *The Irish Times*, October 18, 2010, available at http://www .irishtimes.com/newspaper/opinion/2010/1018/1224281343072.html.

29 **"will soon have to make":** Daniel Gordis, *Saving Israel: How the Jewish People Can Win a War That May Never End* (Hoboken, N.J.: John Wiley, 2009), 159–62.

29 **A 2010 poll:** Arian, Hermann, Lebel, Philippov, Zaban, and Knafelman, "Auditing Israeli Democracy."

29 **"begin to see a monster":** Boaz Okon, "Draw Me a Monster," *Yediot Aharonot*, June 22, 2010, trans. by *Coteret*, available at http://coteret.com/2010/06/23/yediots -legal-affairs-editor-on-the-emergence-of-apartheid-and-fascism-in-israel/.

2. The Crisis in America

31 **October 22, 1992:** Harry Katz, "The Complete Unexpurgated AIPAC Tape," *The Washington Times*, October 22, 1992, available at http://www.wrmea.com/backissues /1292/9212013.html.

32 **AIPAC functions:** The story is also retold at Congregation Bonai Shalom, "Keeping the Dream Alive—Yom Kippur Morning 5765," October 2006, available at http:// www.bonaishalom.org/index.php?id=140.

32 **they find even less:** Writing about American Jewish leaders in the 1960s and 1970s, the American Jewish Committee's Steven Bayme, one of the shrewdest observers of American Jewish life, notes, "Frequently the same individuals who so vigorously

asserted their Jewish commitments in Washington and the American public square generally lacked the language to explain to their own children in the privacy of their own homes why leading a Jewish life might be important." [Steven Bayme, "American Jewry Confronts the Twenty-First Century," in Manfred Gerstenfeld and Steven Bayme, *American Jewry's Comfort Level: Present and Future* (Jerusalem: Jerusalem Center for Public Affairs, 2010), 23.]

32 **When Israel subsidizes Jews:** Jonathan Lis, "Israeli Minister Admits State Subsidizes Public Transportation for Settlers," *Haaretz*, July 26, 2011, available at http:// www.haaretz.com/news/national/israeli-minister-admits-state-subsidizes-public -transportation-for-settlers-1.375420; Maher Abukhater, "West Bank: Israeli Military Court Sentences Palestinian Nonviolence Activist to Prison," *Los Angeles Times*, October 11, 2010, available at http://latimesblogs.latimes.com/babylon beyond/2010/10/west-bank-israeli-military-court-sends-palestinian-non-violence -activist-to-prison.html; Haaretz Service and the Associated Press, "Military Court Convicts West Bank Palestinian Activist of Incitement," *Haaretz*, August, 24, 2010, available at http://www.haaretz.com/news/diplomacy-defense/military -court-convicts-west-bank-palestinian-activist-of-incitement-1.310007; Mark Weiss, "Israel Parliament Passes Anti-Boycott Bill," *The Telegraph*, July 11, 2011, available at http://www.telegraph.co.uk/news/worldnews/middleeast/israel/ 8631088/Israel-parliament-passes-anti-boycott-bill.html.

33 **Israeli F-15s flying over Auschwitz:** Aliza Davidovit, "Meet Man with World's Toughest Job," *Lifestyles*, August 15, 2007, available at http://www.wnd.com /?pageId=43052.

33 **desperately poor slum:** Economic conditions in the Gaza Strip have improved of late, as more goods have flowed across its borders with both Israel and Egypt. Still, a July 2011 study by the United Nations Conference on Trade and Development reports that unemployment stands at 47 percent, and 52 percent of Gazans remain "food insecure." As the United Nations Relief and Works Agency notes, the former figure is among the highest in the world. [United Nations Conference on Trade and Development, "Report on UNCTAD Assistance to the Palestinian People: Developments in the Economy of the Occupied Palestinian Territory," July 15, 2011, available at http://www.unctad.org/en/docs/tdb58d4_en.pdf; Salem Ajluni, "Labor Market Briefing: Gaza Strip Second-Half 2010," United Nations Relief and Works Agency, April 2011, available at http://www.unrwa.org/userfiles/201106083557.pdf.]

33 **as have American Jews:** This progressive impulse is not uniform. It expresses itself most strongly on cultural issues like abortion and gay rights, less strongly on questions of economic redistribution. For two sophisticated analyses, see Steven M. Cohen and Charles S. Liebman, "American Jewish Liberalism: Unravelling the Strands," *Public Opinion Quarterly* 61, no. 3 (Fall 1997): 405–30, available at http:// www.bjpa.org/Publications/details.cfm?PublicationID=11947 and Steven M. Cohen, Sam Abrams, and Judith Veinstein, "American Jews and the 2008 Presidential Election: As Democratic and Liberal as Ever?" Berman Jewish Policy Archive, New York University Wagner, October 20, 2008, available at http://bjpa.org/Publications/details.cfm?PublicationID=2444.

33 **give their money to the poor:** Jews have voted Democratic in every presidential election since 1924. ["Jewish Vote in Presidential Elections," Jewish Virtual

Library, 2011, available at http://www.jewishvirtuallibrary.org/jsource/US-Israel/jewvote.html.]

33 **In 2008, they supported Barack Obama:** According to exit polls, Obama won 78 percent of the Jewish vote, 70 percent of the gay and lesbian vote, 67 percent of the Hispanic vote, 56 percent of the female vote, 47 percent of the white Catholic vote, and 34 percent of the white Protestant vote. [Lisa Keen, "Gays Mostly Vote Democratic, Figures Show," *Bay Area Reporter*, November 27, 2008, available at http://www.ebar.com/news/article.php?sec=news&article=3522; Mark Hugo Lopez, "How Hispanics Voted in the 2008 Election," Pew Hispanic Center, November 7, 2008, available at http://pewresearch.org/pubs/1024/exit-poll-analysis-hispanics; Kent Garber, "Behind Obama's Victory: Women Open Up a Record Marriage Gap," *U.S. News & World Report*, November 5, 2008, available at http://www.usnews.com/news/articles/2008/11/05/behind-obamas-victory-women-open-up-a-record-marriage-gap.html; Pew Forum on Religion and Public Life, "How the Faithful Voted," November 10, 2008, available at http://pewforum.org/Politics-and-Elections/How-the-Faithful-Voted.aspx.]

34 **In 2004, when asked:** North American Jewish Data Bank, "2004 Annual Survey of American Jewish Opinion," 2004, available at www.jewishdatabank.org/Archive/N-AJC-2004-Data_Summary.pdf.

34 **American Muslims themselves:** "Muslim Americans: Faith, Freedom, and the Future," Abu Dhabi Gallup Center, August 2011, available at http://www.abudhabigallupcenter.com/148778/REPORT-BILINGUAL-Muslim-Americans-Faith-Freedom-Future.aspx.

34 **Zionism through his Americanism:** Melvin I. Urofsky, *Louis D. Brandeis: A Life* (New York: Pantheon Books, 2009), 408.

34 **"American ideals of the twentieth century":** Ibid., 411.

34 **poor neighborhoods in the United States:** Michael Brown, "Henrietta Szold's Progressive American Vision of the *Yishuv*," in Allon Gal, ed., *Envisioning Israel: The Changing Ideals and Images of North American Jews* (Detroit: Wayne State University Press, 1996), 76.

35 **the minimum wage:** Melvin I. Urofsky, *A Voice That Spoke for Justice* (Albany: State University of New York Press, 1982), 40–41, 98.

35 **"Zionism and liberalism, Judaism and America":** Jeffrey Shandler, "Producing the Future: The Impresario Culture of American Zionism Before 1948," in Deborah Dash Moore and S. Ilan Troen, eds., *Divergent Jewish Cultures: Israel and America* (New Haven, Conn.: Yale University Press, 2001), 56.

35 **"Zionism has been defined as a form of American liberalism":** Moore and Troen, "Introduction," in *Divergent Jewish Cultures*, 8. Mark Raider adds that before World War II, "the basic thrust of the American Jewish outlook vis-à-vis Palestine was shaped by," among other things, "a predominantly liberal and progressive worldview." [Mark A. Raider, "Idealism, Vision, and Pragmatism: Stephen S. Wise, Nahum Goldmann and Abba Hillel Silver in the United States," in *Nahum Goldmann: Statesman Without a State* (Albany: State University of New York Press, 2009), 148.]

35 **Railing against "the undemocratic":** Naomi W. Cohen, *American Jews and the Zionist Idea* (New York: Ktav, 1975), 27.

35 **"The time is come":** Urofsky, *A Voice That Spoke for Justice*, 130.

35   **aspirations of the local Arab population:** Urofsky, *Louis D. Brandeis*, 731–32; Urofsky, *A Voice That Spoke for Justice*, 286; Baila Round Shargel, "American Jewish Women in Palestine: Bessie Gotsfeld, Henrietta Szold, and the Zionist Enterprise," *American Jewish History* 90 (June 2002): 141–60; Daniel P. Kotzin, *Judah L. Magnes: An American Jewish Non-Conformist* (Syracuse, N.Y.: Syracuse University Press, 2010).

36   **Silver echoed three years later:** Urofsky, *A Voice That Spoke for Justice*, 279; Raider, "Idealism, Vision, and Pragmatism," 147. Bemoaning his failure to win support among American Jews, Jabotinsky told the Labor Zionist thinker Berl Katznelson in 1939, "You have America, the rich Jews. I have only Polish Jewry and now it is gone. I have lost the game!" [Raider, "Idealism, Vision, and Pragmatism," 148.] This changed somewhat in the 1940s as knowledge of the murder of Jews in Europe and rising anger at British restrictions on immigration to Palestine led some American Jews to sympathize with Jabotinsky's militant tactics. But after Israel's creation in 1948, Labor Zionism became hegemonic in the United States once again. [Rafael Medoff, *Militant Zionism in America: The Rise and Impact of the Jabotinsky Movement in the United States, 1926–1948* (Tuscaloosa: University of Alabama Press, 2002), 131, 215–16.]

36   **"appeared to depart from the principle":** American Jewish Committee, "In Vigilant Brotherhood: The American Jewish Committee's Relationship to Palestine and Israel," 1964, 5, available at http://www.ajcarchives.org/ajcarchive/DigitalArchive .aspx.

36   **"Arabs can hardly be expected to accept":** Nahum Goldmann, *The Autobiography of Nahum Goldmann: Sixty Years of My Life*, trans. Helen Sebba (New York: Holt, Rinehart and Winston, 1969), 304.

36   **"any sect or body of citizens":** Anti-Defamation League, "History of the Anti-Defamation League, 1913–2000," 2001, available at http://www.adl.org/ADLHistory /print_adl_history.asp.

36   **on the board of the NAACP:** J. J. Goldberg, *Jewish Power: Inside the American Jewish Establishment* (New York: Basic Books, 1996), 316.

36   **or the Department of Justice:** Ibid., 122.

36   ***Brown v. Board of Education:*** Marianne R. Sanua, *Let Us Prove Strong: The American Jewish Committee, 1945–2006* (Waltham, Mass.: Brandeis University Press, 2007), 49.

36   **"affecting the American Negro":** Michael E. Staub, *Torn at the Roots: The Crisis of Jewish Liberalism in Postwar America* (New York: Columbia University Press, 2002), 48–49.

37   **obscure and nearby bankrupt:** I. L. Kenen, *Israel's Defense Line: Her Friends and Foes in Washington* (Buffalo, N.Y.: Prometheus Books, 1981), 198, 251. As the historian Jack Wertheimer notes, "AIPAC became a powerful organization only during the 15 years after the Yom Kippur War." ["Jewish Organizational Life in the United States Since 1945," *American Jewish Yearbook 1995*, 56.]

37   **$15 million in fifteen minutes:** Cohen, *American Jews and the Zionist Idea*, 139.

37   **A small congregation in Oklahoma:** Sanua, *Let Us Prove Strong*, 143.

37   **bookkeepers could not keep up:** Cohen, *American Jews and the Zionist Idea*, 138–39.

37   **Between 1968 and 1971:** Chaim Waxman, "American Jewish Identity and New Patterns of Philanthropy," in Allon Gal, Athena S. Leoussi, and Anthony Smith,

The Call of the Homeland: Diaspora Nationalisms, Past and Present (Boston: Brill, 2010), 101.

38 **equating Zionism with racism:** Shlomo Avineri, "Israel-Russia Relations," *Carnegie Endowment Report*, April 2001, available at http://www.carnegieendowment.org/publications/index.cfm?fa=view&id=659.

38 *The Real Anti-Semitism in America*: Arnold Forster and Benjamin R. Epstein, *The New Anti-Semitism* (New York: McGraw-Hill, 1974); Nathan and Ruth Ann Perlmutter, *The Real Anti-Semitism in America* (New York: Arbor House, 1982), 80.

38 **"to render them victims anew":** Forster and Epstein, *The New Anti-Semitism*, 16.

39 **"continued presence in the world today":** Peter Novick, *The Holocaust in American Life* (New York: Houghton-Mifflin, 1999), 132.

39 **In 1973, the ADL:** Anti-Defamation League, "History of the Anti-Defamation League, 1913–2000."

39 **In 1980, the ADL's Oscar Cohen:** Novick, *The Holocaust in American Life*, 156.

39 *Holocaust* **to every member of Congress:** Ibid.

39 **first nationwide study:** Marianne R. Sanua, "AJC and Intermarriage: The Complexities of Jewish Continuity, 1960–2006," *American Jewish Yearbook 2007*, 11–12, 14–15, available at http://www.ajcarchives.org/AJC_DATA/Files/AJYB703 .CV.pdf.

39 **"confronting the organized Jewish community":** David Singer, "Living with Intermarriage," *Commentary* 68, no. 1 (July 1979), available at http://www.commentary magazine.com/viewarticle.cfm/living-with-intermarriage-6143.

40 **"don't pay much attention to history":** Novick, *The Holocaust in American Life*, 187.

40 **experiencing the trauma firsthand:** As the historian Rona Sheramy documents, a "connection between identification with victims of the Holocaust and a sense of responsibility to the Jewish people (whether through defense of Israel or a refusal to intermarry) became increasingly prevalent throughout the 1970s." [Rona Sheramy, "Defining Lessons: The Holocaust in American Jewish Education" (doctoral dissertation, Brandeis University, 2001), 57, 86.]

40 **"truth of their vulnerability":** Perlmutter and Perlmutter, *The Real Anti-Semitism in America*, 61.

40 **Jewish charities began redirecting:** Steven M. Cohen and Leonard J. Fein, "From Integration to Survival: American Jewish Anxieties in Transition," *Annals of the American Academy of Political and Social Science* 480 (July 1985): 81–82, available at http://ann.sagepub.com/content/480/1/75.

40 **Zionist education program in Israel:** Lawrence Grossman, "Transformation Through Crisis: The American Jewish Committee and the Six-Day War," *American Jewish History* 86, no. 1 (1998): 32, 52.

40 **culminate in its dissolution:** "A Victim of Madoff and Changing Priorities, the American Jewish Congress Calls It Quits," *The Jewish Daily Forward*, July 21, 2010, available at http://www.forward.com/articles/129542/.

41 **"feel your own pain":** Milton Himmelfarb, "In the Light of Israel's Victory," *Commentary* 44, no. 4 (October 1967): 57.

41 **In the presidential elections of 1972 and 1976:** "Jewish Vote in Presidential Elections," Jewish Virtual Library, 2011.

41 **American Jews donating to Jewish groups sharply fell:** Waxman, "American Jewish Identity and New Patterns of Philanthropy," in Gal, Leoussi, and Smith, *The Call of the Homeland*, 90–91; Manfred Gerstenfeld and Steven Bayme, "Interview with Jack Wertheimer: The Fragmentation of American Jewry and Its Leadership," in *American Jewry's Comfort Level*, 120; Jack Wertheimer, "Current Trends in American Jewish Philanthropy," *American Jewish Yearbook 1997*, 4, 81, available at http://www.ajcarchives.org/AJC_DATA/Files/1997_3_SpecialArticles.pdf.

42 **conservative donors and used AIPAC's ties:** Goldberg, *Jewish Power*, 200–202, 222. AIPAC's budget, which was only $300,000 in 1973, ballooned to $15 million by 1993. [Jack Wertheimer, "Jewish Organizational Life in the United States Since 1945," 56; Peter Beinart and Hanna Rosin, "AIPAC Unpacked: The Real Story of Tom Dine," *The New Republic*, September 20 and 27, 1993, 22.]

42 **its top staffer:** For several years in the 1990s, Hoenlein served as associate chairman for the annual fund-raising dinner for Bet El, one of the most radical settlements in the West Bank. He later said that his name had been listed without his permission. But at Bet El's fund-raising dinner in 2010, Hoenlein was a featured speaker. [Dan Fleshler, *Transforming America's Israel Lobby: The Limits of Its Power and the Potential for Change* (Washington, D.C.: Potomac Books, 2009), 77; "Malcolm Hoenlein at Bet El Dinner 12-5-10" [video], available at http://www.youtube.com/watch?v=KmwMNaoDmto.]

42 **"majority of their fellow Jews":** Goldberg, *Jewish Power*, 74, 218–19. In 1991, another Jewish journalist, Milton Goldin, called the American Jewish groups "a Potemkin community." Former *Jewish Week* Washington correspondent James Besser describes "a communal leadership that is less and less in touch with the community as a whole." [James Besser, "Goodbye, or 'Those 24 Years Sure Went By Quickly," *The Jewish Week*, June 16, 2011, available at http://www.thejewishweek.com/blogs/political_insider/goodbye_or_those_24_years_sure_went_quickly; Wertheimer, "Current Trends in American Jewish Philanthropy," 5.]

42 **described Israel as a victim-state:** In 1982, the American Jewish Congress called for Israel to withdraw from Lebanon. In 1987, it criticized Prime Minister Yitzhak Shamir for not participating in an international peace conference and warned that "in the long run [the occupation] can only corrupt the values which are associated with the Jewish state." [Steven T. Rosenthal, *Irreconcilable Differences? The Waning of the American Jewish Love Affair with Israel* (Hanover, N.H.: Brandeis University Press, 2001), 72, 94.]

42 **48 percent of American Jews were "often troubled":** Goldberg, *Jewish Power*, 216.

42 **In 1986, 63 percent:** Mark P. Cohen, "American Jewish Response to the Palestinian Uprising," *Journal of Palestine Studies* 17, no. 4 (Summer 1988): 100, available at http://www.jstor.org/stable/2537293.

43 **halting settlement growth:** Rosenthal, *Irreconcilable Differences?*, 111, 162; Fleshler, *Transforming America's Israel Lobby*, 109.

43 **bring a peace deal:** Fleshler, *Transforming America's Israel Lobby*, 112.

43 **the mass of American Jews are to the left of the organizations:** For a sense of American Jewish opinion on Israel, and the way that question design can influence the response, see the American Jewish Committee's annual surveys between 2000 and 2011 [AJC, "Publications—Surveys," available at http://www.ajc.org/site/c.ijITI2PHKoG/b.846741/k.8A33/Publications__Surveys/apps/nl/newsletter3.asp.]

and J Street's 2009, 2010, and 2011 polls [J Street, "National Survey of American Jews," February 28–March 8, 2009, available at http://www.jstreet.org/files/images/ J_Street_Survey_March_2009_Final_Results.doc; J Street, "National Survey of American Jews," March 2010, available at http://www.jstreet.org/page/new poll-of -american-jews-views-israel; and J Street, "National Survey of American Jews," July 2011, available at http://jstreet.org/polling-of-american-jews/.]

43 **Jewish organizations were at least broadly representative:** In the 1995 edition of his book *Community and Polity*, Daniel J. Elazar wrote that "a great change taking place in American Jewish community life is the decline in membership of the mass-based Jewish organizations." [Daniel J. Elazar, *Community and Polity: The Organizational Dynamics of American Jewry* (Philadelphia: Jewish Publication Society, 1995), 265.] Steven Cohen and Jack Wertheimer have noted that Jewish membership organizations witnessed a 20 percent decline in membership in the 1990s alone. [Stephen M. Cohen and Jack Wertheimer, "Whatever Happened to the Jewish People," *Commentary* 121, no. 6 (June 2006): 36, available at http://www .bjpa.org/Publications/details.cfm?PublicationID=2101.]

43 **"American Jewish peerage":** Urofsky, *A Voice That Spoke for Justice*, 216.

43 **they set the agenda:** In Jack Wertheimer's words, "ever growing percentages of Jewish philanthropy are contributed by a continually declining number of Jewish givers." [Wertheimer, "Current Trends in American Jewish Philanthropy," 81.]

44 **"Or understand what it means":** *Jewish Moments in the Morning with Nachum Segal*, Guests Malcolm Hoenlein and Rabbi Benjamin Yudin [radio], first broadcast June 5, 2009, by JM in the AM 91.1 fm 90.1 fm, produced by Nachum Segal, available at http://wfmu.org/playlists/shows/31710.

44 **"characterized as a sort of plutocracy":** Yossi Beilin, *His Brother's Keeper: Israel and Diaspora Jewry in the Twenty-First Century* (New York: Schocken Books, 2000), 191.

44 **"window dressing":** Former ADL official in discussion with the author, December, 17, 2010. Speaking about Jewish organizations more generally, former Washington correspondent for the New York *Jewish Week* James Besser remarks that the fact that "domestic activism has diminished and become less uniformly liberal [is] the result of a number of factors—starting with the fact that getting into the pro-Israel game is far and away the best way for Jewish organizations to raise money." [Besser, "Goodbye, or 'Those 24 Years Sure Went By Quickly.'"]

44 **"anti-Semite behind every door":** Former ADL official in discussion with the author, January 3, 2011.

44 **"the end game is always Israel":** American Jewish Committee regional representative in discussion with the author, September 1, 2011.

44 **What donors are "interested in is Iran":** Former staffer at the American Jewish Committee in discussion with the author, January 11, 2011.

44 **the Jewish Telegraphic Agency reported:** "A Victim of Madoff and Changing Priorities, the American Jewish Congress Calls It Quits."

45 **"I had dinner with so and so":** Tom Dine (former AIPAC executive director) in discussion with the author, January 10, 2011.

45 **it was denied meetings:** Nathan Guttman, "J Street: Pro-Peace, but Still Trying to Prove It's Pro-Israel," *The Jewish Daily Forward*, October 14, 2009, available at http://www.forward.com/articles/116704/; Laura Rozen, "Israeli Foreign Ministry

Snubs J-Street-Led Codel," Politico, February 17, 2010, available at http://www.po
litico.com/blogs/laurarozen/0210/Israeli_Deputy_FM_snubs_JStreetled_Codel
.html; Hadar Susskind (former vice president of policy and strategy, J Street) in
discussion with the author, September 7, 2011.

45   **"They feel it's a betrayal":** Former ADL official in discussion with the author,
January 3, 2011.

45   **Britain canceled a trip to the West Bank:** Marcus Dysch, "JLC Forced to Scrap
First West Bank Visit," *Jewish Chronicle Online*, January 20, 2011, available at
http://www.thejc.com/node/43949.

45   **"I felt like I had never been to Israel before":** "Alumni Testimonials," *Encounter*,
available at http://www.encounterprograms.org/program/alumni-testimonials.

46   **"Arab says wealth, oil and Islam":** Frank Luntz, "America 2020: How the Next
Generation Views Israel," The Israel Project, 40.

46   **have swimming pools:** Former American Jewish Committee staffer in discussion
with the author, January 11, 2011.

46   **fulfill their stated missions:** AJC, "Who We Are," available at http://www.ajc.org
/site/c.ijITI2PHKoG/b.789093/k.124/Who_We_Are.htm;   Anti-Defamation
League, "History of the Anti-Defamation League, 1913–2000."

46   **improving the lives of Arab Israelis:** Inter-Agency Task Force on Israeli Arab Issues, "Our Mission," available at http://www.iataskforce.org/members.

46   **"chill Israel's democratic political debate":** David A. Harris and Doug Lieb, "NY
Jewish Week Publishes AJC Op-Ed on Avigdor Lieberman," *New York Jewish Week*,
February 27, 2009, available at http://www.ajc.org/site/apps/nlnet/content2.aspx?
c=ijITI2PHKoG&b=2818295&content_id=%7B9C51735D-9223–461C-9E5C-310E7B1
E2BC7%7D&notoc=1.

46   **"may infringe on basic democratic rights":** ADL Press Release, "Knesset Anti-
Boycott Law May Infringe on Basic Democratic Rights," July 12, 2011, available at
http://adl.org/PresRele/IslME_62/6084_62.htm.

46   **created a widely praised curriculum:** ADL, "Curriculum Connections," available
at http://www.adl.org/education/curriculum_connections/spring_2005/.

46   **"morally indefensible":** Keith O'Brien, "ADL Local Leader Fired on Armenian
Issue," *The Boston Globe*, August 18, 2007, available at http://www.boston.com/
news/local/articles/2007/08/18/adl_local_leader_fired_on_armenian_issue/;
Jennifer Siegel, "Armenian Genocide Debate Exposes Rifts at ADL," *The Jewish
Daily Forward*, August 22, 2007, available at http://www.forward.com/articles/
11470.

46   **condemned anti-Muslim bigotry:** Abraham H. Foxman, "Norwegian Attacks
Stem from a New Ideological Hate," *The Washington Post*, July 29, 2011, available
at http://www.washingtonpost.com/opinions/norwegian-attacks-stem-from-a-new
-ideological-hate/2011/07/28/gIQAhxy8hI_story.html.

47   **religious freedom of Muslims must bow:** ADL Press Release, "Statement on Islamic Community Center Near Ground Zero," July 28, 2010, available at http://www
.adl.org/PresRele/CvlRt_32/5820_32.htm.

47   **the community center near Ground Zero:** David Harris, "Build the Cordoba
Center?" *The Huffington Post*, August 2, 2010, available at http://www.huffingtonpost
.com/david-harris/build-the-cordoba-center_b_667893.html.

47 **population is smaller than Muslim leaders claim:** David Harris, "In the Trenches: 'Nearly Seven Million'?" *The Jerusalem Post*, June 17, 2009, available at http://www.ajc.org/site/apps/nlnet/content2.aspx?c=ijITI2PHKoG&b=5264477&ct=7136285.

47 **strengthen the U.S.-Israel "relationship":** AIPAC, "Our Mission," available at http://www.aipac.org/en/about-aipac/our-mission; Conference of Presidents of Major American Jewish Organizations, "Who We Are: About the Conference," available at http://www.conferenceofpresidents.org/content.asp?id=52.

47 **Lieberman's rise was an internal Israeli matter:** Nathan Guttman, "Jewish Leaders Largely Silent on Lieberman's Role in Government," *The Jewish Daily Forward*, February 18, 2009, available at http://www.forward.com/articles/103178/.

48 **evangelist John Hagee:** "John Hagee at AIPAC 2007" [video], JerusalemOnline, available at http://video.google.com/videoplay?docid=-5755055312928744516; Terry Gross, "Pastor John Hagee on Christian Zionism, Katrina," NPR, September 18, 2006, available at http://www.npr.org/templates/story/story.php?storyId=90508742.

3. Should American Jews Criticize Israel?

49 **"I'm not a citizen [of Israel]":** Foxman said this even though the ADL has, on occasion, criticized Israeli policy. [Rachel Donadio, "Israel's Beilin Rips U.S. Jews for Undercutting P.A. Chief: 'Does the ADL Have Another Partner for Me?'" *The Jewish Daily Forward*, December 8, 2000, available at http://www.webshells.com/adlwatch/news20.htm.]

50 **"Israeli democracy should decide":** Glenn Frankel, *Beyond the Promised Land: Jews and Arabs on the Hard Road to a New Israel* (New York: Simon & Schuster, 1994), 222.

50 **frequently criticize:** See for example, ADL Press Release, "ADL Calls on Swedish to Abandon Initiative to Adopt Palestinian Position on Jerusalem," December 2, 2009, available at http://www.adl.org/PresRele/IslME_62/5665_62.htm; AJC Press Release, "AJC Calls Brazil, Argentina Recognition of Palestinian State Unhelpful and Counterproductive," December 6, 2010, available at http://www.ajc.org/site/apps/nlnet/content2.aspx?c=ijITI2PHKoG&b=849241&ct=8953965.

51 **"free and fair":** Aaron D. Pina, "Palestinian Elections," CRS Report for Congress, February 9, 2006, available at http://www.fas.org/sgp/crs/mideast/RL33269.pdf. http://www.fas.org/sgp/crs/mideast/RL33269.pdf.

51 **Without settler votes:** Oren Yiftachel, "The Shrinking Space of Citizenship: Ethnocratic Politics," in Joel Beinin and Rebecca L. Stein, eds., *The Struggle for Sovereignty: Palestine and Israel, 1993–2005* (Stanford, Calif.: Stanford University Press, 2006), 165. In Israel's 2009 elections, Likud won twenty-seven Knesset seats and the more centrist Kadima party won twenty-eight. Because right-leaning parties in general won more seats than centrist and left-leaning ones, Netanyahu was given the right to form a government. Since Likud relies more heavily than Kadima on settler support, a vote held only inside the green line might have decreased Likud's tally to twenty-six and increased Kadima's to twenty-nine, which might have forced Israel's president to give Kadima's Tzipi Livni the opportunity to form a government instead of Netanyahu. [David Makovsky, "Imagining the Border: Options for Resolving the Israeli-Palestinian Territorial Issue," The Washington Institute for Near East Policy, available at http://www.washingtoninstitute.org/

pubPDFs/StrategicReport06.pdf; Nitzan Goldberger, "West Bank Settler Voting Trends, 2006 and 2009," Settlement Report 19, no. 4 (July/August 2009), available at http://www.fmep.org/reports/archive/vol.-19/no.-4/west-bank-settler-voting -trends-2006-and-2009; "National Election Results," Central Election Committee of the 19th Knesset, available at http://www.knesset.gov.il/elections18/heb/results/ main_Results.aspx.]

51 **not join the lynch mob:** On the organized American Jewish community's campaign against Israel's "delegitimization," see Martin Raffel and Michael Kotzin, "Intro-ducing the Israel Action Network," *The Jerusalem Post*, October 26, 2010, available at http://www.jpost.com/Opinion/Op-EdContributors/Article.aspx?id=192892; James Besser, "Jewish Federations Join Fight Against Israel Delegitimization, but Is That Smart?" *The Jewish Week*, October 26, 2010, available at http://www.the jewishweek.com/blogs/political_insider/jewish_federations_join_fight_against_ israel_delegitimization_smart.

51 **Shlomo Avineri has observed:** Shlomo Avineri, "No One Is Questioning Israel's Legitimacy," *Haaretz*, June 29, 2011, available at http://www.haaretz.com/print -edition/opinion/no-one-is-questioning-israel-s-legitimacy-1.370169.

51 **12 percent answered yes:** Shibley Telhami, "2010 Arab Public Opinion Poll: Results of Arab Opinion Survey Conducted June 29–July 20, 2010," Brookings, August 5, 2010, available at http://www.brookings.edu/reports/2010/0805_arab_opinion_ poll_telhami.aspx.

51 **exercise in Israel's delegitimization:** See, for instance, the American Jewish International Relations Institute's paper, "AJIRI's Strategy Can Foil the Hijacking of the UN to Delegitimize Israel," available at http://ajiri.us/strategy/.

52 **"coexist with it":** Reuters, "Abbas: Palestinians Have No Wish to Isolate Israel," *Haaretz*, May 27, 2011, available at http://www.haaretz.com/news/diplomacy-defense/ abbas-palestinians-have-no-wish-to-isolate-israel-1.364481.

52 **"settlements are not the impediment [to peace]":** ADL, "The Problem Isn't Settle-ments," available at http://www.adl.org/peace/ad.asp.

53 **"agreed upon" settlement:** "The Arab League 'Peace Plan.'"

53 **eighty-nine-page "Guide for Activists":** ADL, "Israel: A Guide for Activists," 2010, available at http://www.adl.org/israel/advocacy/advocacy_guide_facts_updated.pdf.

53 **"Draw arrows":** Frank Luntz, "Israel Project's 2009 Global Language Dictionary," April 2009, available at http://fedgeno.com/documents/israel-projects-2009-global -language-dictionary.pdf.

53 **several new documents:** See, for instance, Hamas's March 2006 National Unity Government Program draft, which calls for "cooperating with the international community for the purpose of ending the occupation and settlements and achiev-ing a complete withdrawal from the lands occupied [by Israel] in 1967," or Prime Minister Ismail Haniyeh's March 27, 2006, delivery of the cabinet platform, in which he praises the Arab League's 2002 offer to recognize Israel and expresses a desire for "Palestinian geographical unity and the need to link the two halves (West Bank and Gaza) of the homeland politically, economically, socially, and culturally so that the region enjoys calm and stability during this phase." [Khaled Hroub, "A 'New Hamas' Through Its New Documents," *Journal of Palestine Studies* 35, no.4 (Summer 2006): 6–27, available at http://www.palestine-studies.org/jour nals.aspx?id=7087&jid=1&href=fulltext.]

53 **Hamas will accept the results:** In May 2010, Meshal declared, "If Israel withdraws to the borders of 1967, it doesn't mean that it gives us back all the land of the Palestinians. But we do consider this as an acceptable solution to have a Palestinian state on the borders of 1967 . . . the Palestinian state will have a referendum and the Palestinian people will decide. We in Hamas will respect the decision of the Palestinian majority." ["Hamas Leader Khaled Meshaal," *Current Affairs—Charlie Rose Middle East Journal*, May 28, 2010, available at http://www.livedash.com/transcript/charlie_rose/918/KQED/Monday_May_31_2010/316361/]. In November 2010, Haniyeh stated, "We accept a Palestinian state on the borders of 1967, with Jerusalem as its capital, the release of Palestinian prisoners, and the resolution of the issue of refugees. . . . Hamas will respect the results (of a referendum) regardless of whether it differs with its ideology and principles." [Reuters, "Hamas Vows to Honor Palestinian Referendum on Peace with Israel," *Haaretz*, December 1, 2010, available at http://www.haaretz.com/news/diplomacy-defense/hamas-vows-to-honor-palestinian-referendum-on-peace-with-israel-1.328234.]

53 **barely any acknowledgment:** A rare exception is a November 15, 2010, op-ed by the American Jewish Committee's director of communications, which mentions in passing Meshal's recent statement of support for a two-state solution, but dismisses it because it contradicts the Hamas charter. By that standard, American Jewish groups should reject Prime Minister Netanyahu's talk about a two-state solution as well, since it contradicts the explicit opposition to a Palestinian state in the Likud platform, most recently reaffirmed in 2006. [Kenneth Bandler, "The Hamas Image Makeover Lacks Substance," *The Jerusalem Post*, November 15, 2010, available at http://www.jpost.com/Opinion/Op-EdContibutors/Article.aspx?id=195469; Knesset, "Likud—Platform," available at http://www.ynetnews.com/articles/0,7340,L-3064466,00.html; Benjamin Netanyahu, "Likud," March 13, 2006, available at http://www.ynetnews.com/articles/0.7340,L-3227271,00.html.

54 **racial discrimination:** United Nations General Assembly, "World Conference Against Racism, Racial Discrimination, Xenophobia, and Related Intolerance: Conference Themes—Draft Declaration Note by the Secretary General—A/CONF.189/4," August 20, 2001, available at http://www.unhchr.ch/huridoca.nsf/(Symbol)/A.CONF.189.4.En?Opendocument.

54 **"bias against the Jewish state":** AIPAC, "AIPAC Deeply Disappointed in Choice of Robinson as Freedom Medal Nominee," August 4, 2009, available at http://www.aipac.org/~/media/Publications/Policy%20and%20Politics/Press/AIPAC%20Statements/2009/08/AIPACDeeplyDisappointedOverRobinson04Aug09.pdf.

54 **"anti-Israel bias":** ADL, "Statement on 2009 Presidential Medal of Freedom Recipient Mary Robinson," August 3, 2009, available at http://www.adl.org/PresRele/UnitedNations_94/5575_94.htm.

54 **thus angering Syria and Iran:** "World Conference Against Racism, Racial Discrimination, Xenophobia, and Related Intolerance: Declaration," United Nations, January 2, 2002, available at http://www.un.org/WCAR/durban.pdf; "Mixed Emotions as Durban Winds Up," BBC News, September 8, 2001, available at http://news.bbc.co.uk/2/hi/africa/1530976.stm; Adrienne Bryan and Katie White, "A Conversation with Mary Robinson," *Stanford Journal of International Relations* 11, no. 2 (Spring 2010): 71–73, available at http://www.stanford.edu/group/sjir/pdf/Robinson_11.2.pdf; Eric Fingerhut, "Israel Supporters Rip White House Honor for

Robinson," *Jewish Review*, available at http://www.jewishreview.org/wire/Israel
-supporters-rip-White-House-honor-for-Robinson. AIPAC's statement opposing
Robinson's award not only failed to mention her role in expunging the language
about racial discrimination, but referred to the Durban Conference's "final outcome document that equated Zionism with racism," even though the final document did no such thing. [AIPAC, "AIPAC Deeply Disappointed in Choice of
Robinson as Freedom Medal Nominee."]

54   **"When I see something like this, I am a Jew":** Cheri Brown, "Letters to the Editor:
'I Am a Jew,'" *The Washington Post,* August 17, 2009, available at http://www.wash
ingtonpost.com/wp-dyn/content/article/2009/08/16/AR2009081601698.html;
Bryan and White, "A Conversation with Mary Robinson," 71–73; Chris McGreal,
"I Am a Jew, Robinson Tells Racism Protesters," *The Guardian,* August 31, 2001,
available at http://www.guardian.co.uk/world/2001/aug/31/race.unitednations.

54   **joint statement in Robinson's defense:** "Israeli Human Rights Groups Back Robinson Pick," JTA, August 10, 2009, available at http://jta.org/news/article/2009/08/
10/1007154/israeli-human-rights-groups-back-robinson-pick.

54   **"a radical stream of Islam":** "Transcript: January 9, 2009," *Bill Moyers Journal,*
available at http://www.pbs.org/moyers/journal/01092009/transcript4.html; "Exchange Between Bill Moyers and Abraham Foxman of the Anti-Defamation
League," PBS, January 16, 2009, available at http://www.pbs.org/moyers/journal/
blog/2009/01/exchange_between_bill_moyers_a.html.

55   **"lacking [in] objectivity and impartiality":** Ali Gharib, "U.S.-Based Leading
Rights Group Denies Improprieties," IPS, July 16, 2009, available at http://ipsnews
.net/news.asp?idnews=47685; Kenneth Roth, "Human Rights Watch Applies Same
Standards to Israel, Hamas," *Haaretz,* October 26, 2009, available at http://www
.hrw.org/en/news/2009/10/26/human-rights-watch-applies-same-standards-israel
-hamas; Fred Abrahams, "Human Rights Watch Plays No Favorites in Probes,"
JTA, September 3, 2009, available at http://www.hrw.org/en/news/2009/09/03/human
-rights-watch-plays-no-favorites-probes.

55   **said largely the same thing:** James Traub, "Does Abe Foxman Have an Anti-Anti-
Semite Problem," *The New York Times,* January 14, 2007, available at http://www
.nytimes.com/2007/01/14/magazine/14foxman.t.html; Ravid, Landau, Benn, and
Rosner, "Olmert to *Haaretz*: Two-State Solution, or Israel Is Done For"; McCarthy,
"Barak: Make Peace with Palestinians or Face Apartheid."

55   **"borderline anti-Semitic":** ADL Press Release, "ADL Calls Amnesty International
Report 'Bigoted, Biased, and Borderline Anti-Semitic,'" August 23, 2006, available
at http://www.adl.org/PresRele/IslME_62/4878_62.htm; Amnesty International,
"Israel/Lebanon—Under Fire: Hizbullah's Attacks on Northern Israel," September
2006, available at http://www.amnesty.org/en/library/asset/MDE02/025/2006/en
/8b297b53-d3f6-11dd-8743-d305bea2b2c7/mde020252006en.pdf.

55   **"educated and an anti-Semite":** Ron Kampeas, "Meeting and Tweeting: Freedom Group's Director Says It All—in 140 Characters or Less," JWeekly.com,
March 4, 2010, available at http://www.jweekly.com/article/full/41560/meeting
-and-tweeting-federation-groups-director-says-it-all-in-140-characte/; Andrew
Sullivan, "Something Much Sadder," *The Atlantic,* February 10, 2010, available at
http://www.theatlantic.com/daily-dish/archive/2010/02/something-much-sadder/
190550/.

55 **"Most of the current attacks on Israel and Zionism":** Abraham Foxman, *Never Again? The Threat of the New Anti-Semitism* (New York: HarperCollins, 2003), 21.

56 **America imposes sanctions:** Arshad Mohammed, "Obama Widens U.S. Sanctions on North Korea," Reuters, August 30, 2010, available at http://www.reuters.com/article/idUSTRE67T3BX20100831; Ross Colvin, "Obama Says New U.S. Sanctions on Iran Toughest Ever," Reuters, July 2, 2010, available at http://www.reuters.com/article/idUSTRE66001Z20100702; U.S. Department of State, "Burma (Myanmar) Country Specific Information," available at http://travel.state.gov/travel/cis_pa_tw/cis/cis_1077.html; Bill Trott, "Obama Extends U.S. Sanctions Against Zimbabwe," Reuters, March 5, 2009, available at http://www.reuters.com/article/idUS-TRE5241BT20090305; U.S. Department of State, "U.S.-Sudan Relations," available at http://sudan.usembassy.gov/ussudan_relations.html.

58 **"On a daily basis":** Jodi Ochstein (former assistant to the director of government and national affairs in the ADL's Washington office) in discussion with the author, November 23, 2010.

4. Is the Occupation Israel's Fault?

59 **implicitly comparing:** David A. Harris, "Letter from a Centrist," February 28, 2005, in David A. Harris, ed., *In the Trenches: Selected Speeches and Writings of an American Jewish Activist,* Volume 4: 2004–2005 (Hoboken, N.J.: Ktav Publishing House, 2006), 128.

59 **"right to live in Paris or Washington":** Michael Massing, "Deal Breakers," *American Prospect,* March 11, 2002, available at http://prospect.org/article/deal-breakers.

60 **said they would allow:** In recent years, Palestinian leaders have repeatedly stated that Jews—as opposed to Israelis—would be free to live in a Palestinian state. ["Israeli Settlers on the West Bank: Might Some Stay?" *The Economist,* July 21, 2011, available at http://www.economist.com/node/18988684?story_id=18988684&fsrc=rss; Brent Gardner-Smith, "Palestinian Prime Minister: Jews Would Be Welcome in Future State," *Aspen Daily News,* July 4, 2011, available at http://www.aspendailynews.com/section/home/135325; Oren Dorell, "Palestinian Officials Foresee Secular, Pluralistic State," *USA Today,* September 15, 2011, available at http://www.usatoday.com/news/world/story/2011–09–15/palestinians-foresee-secular-state/50419552/1.]

60 **"Jerusalem is not a settlement":** AIPAC, "AIPAC Policy Conference 2010: Howard Kohr" [video], available at http://www.aipac.org/PC/webPlayer/mon_kohr10.asp.

60 **never considered part of Jerusalem:** On the legal status of Palestinians in East Jerusalem, see B'Tselem, "Legal Status of East Jerusalem and Its Residents," available at http://www.btselem.org/jerusalem/legal_status. On Jerusalem's historical boundaries, see "Jerusalem and Its Environs," Terrestrial Jerusalem, available at http://www.t-i.org.il/Portals/26/2011-06-29_A3-double-spread_web01.pdf. For the locations of the East Jerusalem neighborhood Har Homa, which is closer to Bethlehem than to the Old City, or Kafr Aqb, which is closer to Ramallah than to the Old City, see Ir Amim, "Greater Jerusalem 2009," available at http://www.ir-amim.org.il/Eng/_Uploads/dbsAttachedFiles/GreaterJerusalem2009Eng.pdf.

61 **"security buffer":** Luntz, "Israel Project's 2009 Global Language Dictionary," 62.

61 **won the war in six days:** Martin van Creveld, "Israel Doesn't Need the West Bank

to Be Secure," *The Jewish Daily Forward*, December 24, 2010, available at http://www.forward.com/articles/133961; Tareq Y. Ismael and Andrej Kreutz "Russian-Iraqi Relations: A Historical and Political Analysis," *Arab Studies Quarterly* (Fall 2001), available at http://findarticles.com/p/articles/mi_m2501/is_4_23/ai_80966042/; Kenneth Pollack (Director, Saban Center for Middle East Policy, the Brookings Institution) in discussion with the author, October 6, 2011.

62 **did not have in 1967:** Clayton Swisher, *The Truth About Camp David* (New York: Nation Books, 2004), 320, 323; Isabel Kershner, "The PA's Abu Ala: 'I Warned of Catastrophe,'" *The Jerusalem Report*, July 16, 2001, 13, 16; Gilead Sher, *The Israeli-Palestinian Peace Negotiations, 1999–2001: Within Reach* (New York: Routledge, 2006), 62, 107–8, 110, 138; Bernard Avishai, "A Plan for Peace That Still Could Be," *New York Times Magazine*, February 7, 2011, available at http://www.nytimes.com/2011/02/13/magazine/13Israel-t.html?pagewanted=all.

62 **"no longer an eastern front":** Gal Luft, "All Quiet on the Eastern Front: Israel's National Security Doctrine After the Fall of Saddam," Saban Center for Middle East Policy at the Brookings Institution, March 2004, available at http://www.brookings.edu/fp/saban/analysis/luft20040301.pdf.

62 **every inch of Israel:** Creveld, "Israel Doesn't Need the West Bank to Be Secure."

63 **sparks international outrage:** United Nations Office for the Coordination of Humanitarian Affairs (OCHA), "The Humanitarian Impact of the Barrier," last updated August 2008, available at http://www.ochaopt.org/documents/Barrier_Report_July_2008.pdf.

63 **"Before I go to bed":** International Crisis Group, "Squaring the Circle: Palestinian Security Reform Under Occupation," *Middle East Report* 98 (September 7, 2010): 37, available at http://www.crisisgroup.org/~/media/Files/Middle%20East%20North%20Africa/Israel%20Palestine/98%20Squaring%20the%20Circle%20—%20Palestinian%20Security%20Reform%20under%20Occupation.ashx.

64 **a public position:** J. J. Goldberg, "A Palestinian State Even the Securocrats Accept," *The Jewish Daily Forward*, September 15, 2011, available at http://www.forward.com/articles/142822.

64 **"Israel can easily afford":** Creveld, "Israel Doesn't Need the West Bank to Be Secure."

65 **"spurned every offer":** David Harris, "Hineni! Here I Am!" *In The Trenches—The Jerusalem Post*, September 13, 2011, available at http://blogs.jpost.com/content/hineni-here-i-am?msource=DAHBlog35&tr=y&auid=9479940.

65 **cheaper to live beyond:** Foundation for Middle East Peace, "The Socioeconomic Status in the Settlements Is Higher Than the Israeli Average," December 2009, available at http://www.fmep.org/analysis/analysis/the-socioeconomic-status-in-the-settlements-is-higher-than-the-israeli-average; Gorenberg, *The Unmaking of Israel*, 112.

66 **actively abetted it:** In the words of Gemal Helal, the Arabic language translator on the Clinton administration's Middle East team, "The Palestinians never fulfilled their part. For eight or nine years all they did was whine and complain. Hamas and Palestinian Islamic Jihad always threatened Israel and said that they did not believe in Resolutions 242 and 338, and yet the Palestinians were in bed with both of these groups! Also, the Palestinians never educated their people on coexisting with Israel. For eight years they were supposed to collect their weapons—they never did.

The Palestinians were also supposed to outlaw people who call for the destruction of Israel—they never did. I think that this was because Arafat wanted to have the 'armed struggle option.'" [Swisher, *The Truth About Camp David*, 159.]

66 **Barak had refused:** Donadio, "Israeli's Beilin Rips U.S. Jews for Undercutting P.A. Chief"; Ron Pundak, "From Oslo to Taba: What Went Wrong," *Survival* 43, no. 3 (August 2001), available at http://web.comhem.se/jakub/adebattarkiv/pundak.html; Akiva Eldar, "They Just Can't Hear Each Other," *Haaretz*, March 11, 2003, available at http://israelblog.theisraelforum.org/Articles/They_just_cant_hear_each_other.html.

66 **embittered Palestinians:** Hareuveni, "By Hook and by Crook."

66 **percentage of Palestinians who believed:** Khalil Shikaki, "Palestinians Divided," *Foreign Affairs* 81, no. 1 (January/February 2002): 89–105, available at http://www.foreignaffairs.com/articles/57622/khalil-shikaki/palestinians-divided.

66 **plausible deniability:** Charles Enderlin, *Shattered Dreams: The Failure of the Peace Process in the Middle East, 1995–2002*, trans. Susan Fairfield (New York: Other Press, 2003), 187; Jerome Slater, "What Went Wrong? The Collapse of the Israeli-Palestinian Peace Process," *Political Science Quarterly* 116, no. 2 (Summer 2001): 182, available at http://www.psqonline.org/?redir=%2F99_article.php3%3Fbyear%3D2001%26bmonth%3Dsummer%26a%3D01free; Robert Malley and Hussein Agha, "Camp David: The Tragedy of Errors," *New York Review of Books,* August 9, 2001, available at http://www.nybooks.com/articles/archives/2001/aug/09/camp-david-the-tragedy-of-errors/?pagination-false; Benny Morris, "Camp David Negotiations 2000" [video], available at http://www.youtube.com/watch?v=rpAQmAV_ZpM.

66 **less generous:** In assessing Barak's offer, it is important to remember that even Labor Party leaders like Yitzhak Rabin and Shimon Peres, the architects of Oslo, had not imagined it leading to a Palestinian state, and certainly not one including Jerusalem. Thus, while Barak's offer was indeed unprecedented, that is partly a testament to the vast gap between Israeli and Palestinian expectations when Oslo began. [Shlomo Ben-Ami, *Scars of War, Wounds of Peace: The Israeli-Arab Tragedy* (London: Weidenfeld and Nicolson, 2005), 220, 233, 247.]

66 **an area one-ninth as large:** Dennis Ross, *The Missing Peace: The Inside Story of the Fight for Middle East Peace* (New York: Farrar, Straus and Giroux, 2004), 688; Swisher, *The Truth About Camp David*, 295; Agha and Malley, "Camp David: The Tragedy of Errors."

67 **halves of the West Bank:** In the words of Barak's former foreign minister Shlomo Ben-Ami, "There is no doubt that settlements like Maale Adumim and Ariel make the problem of contiguity, the question of contiguity . . . of the Palestinian state something that is very, very difficult to imagine." ["Discussing the Palestine Papers Part I" (video), Al Jazeera, January 23, 2011, available at http://www.youtube.com/watch?v=YbsI2DVqTPM.]

67 **another 25 percent:** Ross, *The Missing Peace*, 689; Sher, *Within Reach*, 106; Slater, "What Went Wrong?"; Swisher, *The Truth About Camp David*, 295; Enderlin, *Shattered Dreams*, 184; Akram Hanieh, "Special Document: The Camp David Papers," *Journal of Palestine Studies* 30, no. 2 (Winter 2001): 82, 93–94, available at http://www.palestine-studies.org/files/pdf/jps/2759.pdf.

67 **"If I were a Palestinian":** "Fmr. Israeli Foreign Minister: 'If I were a Palestinian, I Would Have Rejected Camp David,'" *Democracy Now: The War and Peace Report,*

February 14, 2006, available at http://www.democracynow.org/2006/2/14/fmr_ israeli_foreign_minister_if_i.

67 **"did Yasser Arafat respond":** Dennis Ross, "Camp David: An Exchange: Dennis Ross and Gidi Grinstein, reply by Hussein Agha and Robert Malley," *The New York Review of Books*, September 20, 2001, available at http://www.nybooks.com/articles /archives/2001/sep/20/camp-david-an-exchange/. On this point, Ross and his intellectual adversary, former Clinton administration National Security Council staffer Rob Malley, agree. In Malley's words, the Palestinians failed "to present a cogent and specific counterproposal of their own." [Agha and Malley, "Camp David: The Tragedy of Errors."]

67 **but not the Temple Mount:** Sher, *Within Reach*, 62, 95, 108; Swisher, *The Truth About Camp David*, 323, 325; Martin Indyk, *Innocent Abroad: An Intimate Account of American Peace Diplomacy in the Middle East* (New York: Simon & Schuster, 2009), 334, 338; Jerome M. Segal, "The Palestinian Peace Offer," *Haaretz*, October 1, 2001, available at http://peacelobby.org/HaaretzOctober1001.htm; Menachem Klein, *The Jerusalem Problem: The Struggle for Permanent Status* (Gainesville: University Press of Florida, 2003), 67; Kershner, "The PA's Abu Ala: 'I Warned of Catastrophe,'" 13, 16; Eldar, "They Just Can't Hear Each Other."

67 **betray Muslims worldwide:** Sher, *Within Reach*, 105–6; Enderlin, *Shattered Dreams*, 179; Swisher, *The Truth About Camp David*, 295; Segal, "The Palestinian Peace Offer"; Kershner, "The PA's Abu Ala: 'I Warned of Catastrophe,'" 16; Robert Malley, "Fictions About the Failure at Camp David," *The New York Times*, July 8, 2001, available at http://www.nytimes.com/2001/07/08/opinion/fictions-about-the-failure-at -camp-david.html?pagewanted=all&src=pm.

68 **sovereignty over the Temple Mount:** In Sher's words, "I was under the impression that in return for Israeli flexibility on formulations that could have satisfied the Palestinians' need for appearances, the Palestinians would not have demanded the actual exercise of the Right of Return into Israel." [Sher, *Within Reach*, 62.] As former Israeli deputy foreign minister Yossi Beilin has noted about the Geneva Accords that he signed with PLO official Yasser Abed Rabbo in 2003, "The heart of the agreement is the concession of sovereignty over the Temple Mount to the Palestinians in exchange for Israeli sovereign discretion over the number of refugees admitted to Israel, with the rest free to settle in the Palestinian state." [Jerome Slater, "Web Letter: Jerome Slater Responds to Michael Walzer," *Dissent,* July 6, 2011, available at http://www.dissentmagazine.org/atw.php?id=490.] For additional perspectives on the Israeli and Palestinian positions on refugees at Camp David, see Swisher, *The Truth About Camp David*, 282; Indyk, *Innocents Abroad*, 334; Enderlin, *Shattered Dreams*, 181, 198.

68 **lacked the moral authority:** Shikaki, "Palestinians Divided."

68 **oft-repeated claim:** ADL, "Mr. President—The Problem Isn't Settlements, It's Arab Rejection."

68 **avoid grave domestic strife:** Sher, *Within Reach*, 98, 106, 138; Swisher, *The Truth About Camp David*, 318; Enderlin, *Shattered Dreams*, 184, 188.

68 **difficult for Israel to defend:** Sher, *Within Reach*, 95; Klein, *The Jerusalem Problem*, 67; Jerome M. Segal, "The Palestinian Peace Offer"; Kershner, "The PA's Abu Ala: 'I Warned of Catastrophe,'" 13; Eldar, "They Just Can't Hear Each Other."

69 **"kept coming back":** Avishai, "A Plan for Peace That Could Still Be."

69 **"destroyer of the Oslo":** Swisher, *The Truth About Camp David*, 151.

69 **reject this story:** Henry Siegman, "Sharon and the Future of Palestine," *The New York Review of Books*, December 2, 2004, available at http://www.nybooks.com/articles/archives/2004/dec/02/sharon-and-the-future-of-palestine/.

69 **more than 50 percent:** Shikaki, "Palestinians Divided."

69 **"by force":** Jeremy Pressman, "The Second Intifada: Background and Causes of the Israeli-Palestinian Conflict," *Journal of Conflict Studies* 23, no. 2 (Fall 2003): 128, available at http://www.lib.unb.ca/Texts/JCS/Fall03/pressman.pdf.

70 **one thousand Israeli police:** Swisher, *The Truth About Camp David*, 380–83; Jane Perlez, "US Envoy Recalls the Day Pandora's Box Wouldn't Shut," *The New York Times*, January 29, 2001, available at http://www.nytimes.com/2001/01/29/world/us-mideast-envoy-recalls-the-day-pandora-s-box-wouldn-t-shut.html?pagewanted=all&src=pm; Pressman, "The Second Intifada," 118.

70 **Israeli air force helicopters:** Enderlin, *Shattered Dreams*, 290–92; Sher, *Within Reach*, 166.

70 **Arafat . . . acquiesced:** Shikaki, "Palestinians Divided"; Pressman, "The Second Intifada," 132; Perlez, "US Envoy Recalls the Day Pandora's Box Wouldn't Shut."

70 **descent into bloodshed:** George J. Mitchell (chairman), Javier Solana, Warren B. Rudman, Thorbjoern Jagland, and Suleyman Demirel, "Mitchell Report," April 30, 2001, available at http://www.bitterlemons.org/docs/mitchell.html.

70 **"an explosion":** Pressman, "The Second Intifada."

71 **Western Wall and the Temple Mount:** Sher reprints the Clinton parameters on pages 197–200 of *Within Reach*.

71 **virtually meaningless:** Swisher, *The Truth About Camp David*, 39–402; Ross, *The Missing Peace*, 753–58.

71 **he insisted that Israel:** Jonathan Rynhold, "Making Sense of Tragedy: Barak, the Israeli Left and the Oslo Process," *Israel Studies Forum* 19, no. 1 (Fall 2003): 15; Robert Malley (former special assistant to President Clinton for Arab-Israeli Affairs and director for Near East and South Asian Affairs) in discussion with the author, June 14, 2011.

71 **publicly denounced the talks:** David Makovsky, "Taba Mythchief," *The National Interest* (Spring 2003), available at http://findarticles.com/p/articles/mi_m2751/is_2003_Spring/ai_99377581/?tag=content;col1; Sher, *Within Reach*, 226; Enderlin, *Shattered Dreams*, 341, 352; Ben-Ami, *Scars of War, Wounds of Peace*, 272.

71 **help Barak politically:** Swisher, *The Truth About Camp David*, 335–50; Enderlin, *Shattered Dreams*, 321.

72 **"bears responsibility":** Aaron David Miller, *The Much Too Promised Land: America's Elusive Search for Arab-Israeli Peace* (New York: Random House, 2008), 296–97.

72 **"in Israeli hands forever":** Indyk, *Innocents Abroad*, 339. Robert Malley, Special Assistant to President Clinton for Arab-Israeli Affairs, echoes the point, noting that "we often hear about Ehud Barak's unprecedented offer and Yasser Arafat's uncompromising no. Israel is said to have made a historic, generous proposal, which the Palestinians, once again seizing the opportunity to miss an opportunity, turned down. In short, the failure to reach a final agreement is attributed, without notable dissent, to Yasser Arafat. . . . As orthodoxies go, this is a dangerous one." [Malley and Agha, "Camp David: The Tragedy of Errors."]

72 **"but it's false":** Boaz Gaon and Jonathan Gurfinkel, "Charge of the Left Brigade," *Haaretz*, March 25, 2011, available at http://www.haaretz.com/weekend/magazine /charge-of-the-left-brigade-1.351789.

73 **long considered a burden:** At America's urging, Sharon agreed to dismantle four small West Bank settlements as part of the Gaza withdrawal. [Jonathan Rynhold and Dov Waxman, "Ideological Change and Israel's Disengagement from Gaza," *Political Science Quarterly* 123, no. 1 (2008): 28, available at http://www.baruch .cuny.edu/wsas/academics/political_science/documents/IdeologicalChangeandIs rael.pdf.]

73 **"removed indefinitely":** Ari Shavit, "Top PM Aide: Gaza Plan Aims to Freeze the Peace Process," *Haaretz*, October 6, 2004, available at http://www.haaretz.com/ print-edition/news/top-pm-aide-gaza-plan-aims-to-freeze-the-peace-process-1 .136686.

73 **"Bantustans":** Akiva Eldar, "People and Politics/Sharon's Bantustans Are Far from Copenhagen's Hope," *Haaretz,* May 13, 2003, available at http://www.haaretz.com /print-edition/features/people-and-politics-sharon-s-bantustans-are-far-from -copenhagen-s-hope-1.10275; Zertal and Eldar, *Lords of the Land*, 423.

73 **"network of bypass roads":** Ben-Ami, *Scars of War, Wounds of Peace*, 297.

74 **two-state solution:** Khalil Shikaki, "The Polls: What the Palestinians Really Voted For," *Newsweek*, February 6, 2006, available at http://www.newsweek.com/2006/02 /05/the-polls-what-the-palestinians-really-voted-for.html.

74 **election manifesto:** Hroub, "A 'New Hamas' Through Its New Documents"; Chris McGreal, "Hamas Drops Call for Destruction of Israel from Manifesto," *The Guardian*, January 12, 2006, available at http://www.guardian.co.uk/world/2006/ jan/12/israel.

74 **2002 peace offer:** Hroub, "A 'New Hamas' Through Its New Documents."

74 **"I speak of":** "Q&A with Hamas Leader Khaled Meshaal," Reuters, January 10, 2007, available at http://www.reuters.com/article/idUSL1046412720070110.

74 **Hamas would accept:** "Charlie Rose with Hamas Leader Khaled Meshaal." Meshal also declared his support for a Palestinian state in the West Bank and Gaza and praised the 2002 Arab Peace Initiative in a 2008 interview with Al Jazeera. ["Talk to Jazeera—Khaled Meshaal, Part 1" [video], March 5, 2008, available at http:// www.youtube.com/watch?v-O8TTjb54GzM&feature=related.]

75 **Palestinians in refugee camps:** Reuters, "Hamas Vows to Honor Palestinian Referendum on Peace with Israel."

75 **decades-long cease-fire:** Yitzhak Benhorin, "Hamas: Ceasefire for Return to 1967 Border," YNet News, January 30, 2006, available at http://www.ynet.co.il/english/ articles/0,7340,L-3207845,00.html; Amira Hass, "Haniyeh: Hamas Willing to Accept Palestinian State Within 1967 Borders," *Haaretz*, November 9, 2008, available at http://www.haaretz.com/news/haniyeh-hamas-willing-to-accept-palestinian -state-with-1967-borders-1.256915; Gil Ronen, "Hamas's Mashaal 'Sent Obama a Letter Offering 30 Year Truce,'" Arutz Sheva, November 30, 2008, available at http://www.israelnationalnews.com/News/News.aspx/128619.

75 **before Palestinian voters:** Scott Wilson, "Hamas Sweeps Palestinian Elections, Complicating Peace Efforts in Mideast," *The Washington Post*, January 27, 2006, available at http://www.washingtonpost.com/wp-dyn/content/article/2006/0126/

AR2006012600372.html; "Israel Must Accept New PA Gov't, Abbas Says," YNet News, February 2, 2007, available at http://www.ynetnews.com/articles/0,7340,L -3363770,00.html; AFP, "Poll Shows Palestinians Want National Unity Government," *The Daily Star*, March 14, 2006, available at http://www.dailystar.com.1b/ News/Middle-East/Mar/14/Poll-shows-Palestinians-want-national-unity-govern- ment.ashx#axzz1alizQmP8; Jerusalem Media and Communications Centre (trans.), "President Abbas' Speech Before the UN General Assembly," Miftah.org, September 22, 2006, available at http://www.miftah.org/Display.cfm?DocId=11519 &CategoryId=18.

75   **oddly analogous:** Knesset, "Likud—Platform"; Benjamin Netanyahu, "Likud"; Jonathan Lis, "Netanyahu in Favor of Referendum Prior to Signing Peace Deal," *Haaretz*, October 20, 2010, available at http://www.haaretz.com/news/diplomacy -defense/netanyahu-in-favor-of-referendum-prior-to-signing-peace-deal-1 .314855.

75   **"every new Israeli government":** Ben-Ami, *Scars of War, Wounds of Peace*, 213.

76   **backfired when Hamas won:** David Rose, "The Gaza Bombshell," *Vanity Fair*, April 2008, available at http://www.vanityfair.com/politics/features/2008/04/ gaza200804; "Hamas Coup in Gaza," *The International Institute for Strategic Studies* 13, no. 5 (June 2007), available at http://www.iiss.org/publications/strategic -comments/past-issues/volume-13-2007/volume-13-issue-5/hamas-coup-in-gaza/.

76   **punish Gazans for electing:** Israeli leaders said explicitly that their purpose in instituting the blockade was not merely to prevent Hamas and other terrorist groups from importing arms but also "to keep the Gazan economy on the brink of collapse." [Reuters, "Wikileaks: Israel Aimed to Keep Gaza Economy on Brink of Collapse," *Haaretz*, January 5, 2011, available at http://www.haaretz.com/news/ diplomacy-defense/wikileaks-israel-aimed-to-keep-gaza-economy-on-brink-of -collapse-1.335354.]

76   **blockade shattered its economy:** International Monetary Fund, "West Bank and Gaza: Economic Performance and Reform Under Conflict Conditions," September 15, 2003, 13, 37–38, available at http://www.imf.org/external/pubs/ft/med/2003/eng /wbg/wbg.pdf.

76   **garbage trucks stopped running:** John Ging, "The Humanitarian Emergency in Gaza 'A Shocking and Shameful Situation,'" International Development Commit- tee, House of Commons, April 30, 2008, available at http://www.unrwa.org/etem plate.php?id=389.

76   **but not the former:** Nathan Brown, "The Green Elephant in the Room: Dealing with the Hamas Party-State in Gaza," Carnegie Endowment for International Peace, June 2009, available at http://www.carnegieendowment.org/publications/ index.cfm?fa=view&id=23225; Lawrence Wright, "Captives," *The New Yorker*, No- vember 9, 2009, available at http://www.newyorker.com/reporting/2009/11/09 /091109fa_fact_wright.

76   **launching them as well:** On the dramatic reduction in rocket fire starting in July 2008 and ending that October, see "Summary of Rocket Fire and Mortar Shelling in 2008," Intelligence and Terrorism Information Center at the Israel Intelligence Heritage & Commemoration Center (IICC), 2009, 6, available at http://www .terrorism-info.org.il/malam_multimedia/English/eng_n/pdf/ipc_e007.pdf.

76   **cease-fire began to unravel:** Congressional Research Service, "Israel and Hamas: Conflict in Gaza (2008–2009)," January 15, 2009, 6, available at http://www.law .umaryland.edu/marshall/crsreports/crsdocuments/R40101_01152009.pdf.

77   **280 schools, some of which:** Wright, "Captives."

77   **post-traumatic stress disorder:** UNDP Programme of Assistance to the Palestinian People, "One Year After Report: Gaza, Early Recovery and Reconstruction Needs Assessment," May 2010, 32, available at http://www.undp.ps/en/newsroom/ publications/pdf/other/gazaoneyear.pdf.

77   **screaming when they heard:** Wright, "Captives."

77   **grow hysterical:** Eli Ashkenazi and Mijal Grinberg, "Study: Most Sderot Kids Exhibit Post-Traumatic Stress Symptoms," *Haaretz*, January 17, 2008, available at http://www.haaretz.com/news/study-most-sderot-kids-exhibit-post-traumatic -stress-symptoms-1.237438; Meital Yasur-Beit Or, "Sderot: Traumatized Kids Have Nowhere to Run," YNet News, November 13, 2006, available at http://www.ynet news.com/articles/0,7340,L-3327799,00.html.

77   **permitted far less rocket fire:** Israel Security Agency, "2009 Annual Summary— Data and Trends in Palestinian Terror," available at http://www.shabak.gov.il/Site CollectionImages/english/TerrorInfo/reports/terrorreport2009_en.pdf; "News of Terrorism and the Israeli-Palestinian Conflict," Meir Amit Intelligence and Terrorism Information, September 28–October 4, 2011, available at http://www .terrorism-info.org.il/malam_multimedia/English/eng_n/pdf/ipc_e229.pdf.

77   **eased the blockade:** Atilla Somfalvi, "Cabinet: All Non-Military Items Can Enter Gaza Freely," YNet News, July 20, 2010, available at http://www.ynetnews.com/ articles/0,7340,L-3907978,00.html.

77   **"access to sufficient food":** United Nations Conference on Trade and Development, "Report on UNCTAD Assistance to the Palestinian People: Developments in the Economy of the Occupied Palestinian Territory," July 15, 2011, available at http://www.unctad.org/en/docs/tdb58d4_en.pdf. The United States Agency for International Development defines food security as "both physical and economic access to sufficient food to meet their dietary needs for a productive and healthy life." [Jennifer Coates, Anne Swindale, and Paula Bilinsky, "Household Food Insecurity Access Scale (HFIAS) for Measurement of Food Access: Indicator Guide," USAID, August 2007, 5, available at http://www.fantaproject.org/downloads/pdfs /HFIAS_v3_Aug07.pdf.]

77   **remains Gaza's occupying power:** Central Intelligence Agency, "Gaza Strip"; "A Guide to the Gaza Closure: In Israel's Own Words," Gisha, September 2011, available at http://www.gisha.org/UserFiles/File/publications/gisha_brief_docs_eng_ sep_2011.pdf; Wright, "Captives."

5. THE JEWISH PRESIDENT

80   **denounced McCarthyism:** Edward K. Kaplan, *Spiritual Radical: Abraham Joshua Heschel, 1940–1972* (New Haven, Conn.: Yale University Press, 2007), 5, 221– 235, 311.

80   **"all are responsible":** Abraham Joshua Heschel, *The Prophets* (Philadelphia: Jewish Publication Society of America, 1969), 16.

80   **Wolf's background:** Grace Wolf (wife of Rabbi Arnold Jacob Wolf) in discussion with the author, June 30, 2010.

80 **He brought Martin Luther King Jr.:** Arnold Jacob Wolf, "Civil Rights" and "The Negro Revolution and Jewish Theology" from *Unfinished Rabbi: Selected Writings of Arnold Jacob Wolf*, ed. Jonathan S. Wolf (Chicago: Ivan R. Dee, 1998), 81, 84; Grace Wolf in discussion with the author, June 30, 2010.

80 **antiwar sermons:** Dave Newbart, "Activist Led State's Oldest Synagogue, Marched with King, Had His Bar Mitzvah Last Year—at 83," *Chicago Sun-Times*, December 25, 2008, 42; "Arnold Jacob Wolf Has Passed Away," *Daily Kos*, December 25, 2008, available at http://www.dailykos.com/story/2008/12/25/1218/3519/257/677059.

80 **gagged and shackled man:** Grace Wolf in discussion with the author, June 30, 2010; Martha Minow (dean of the faculty of law at Harvard Law School), in discussion with the author, January 17, 2011; University of Chicago, "Arnold Wolf, 1924–2008," December 27, 2008, available at http://uchicagolaw.typepad.com/faculty/2008/12/arnold-wolf-19242008.html.

80 **"One should not believe":** Arnold Jacob Wolf, "Calumny and Dissent," *Pathfinder: News and Information from Temple Solel* 13, no. 17 (April 15, 1970).

81 **"The core teaching of the Torah":** Trevor Jensen, "Rabbi Arnold Wolf, 1924–2008: Led 2 Prominent Reform Jewish Congregations," *Chicago Tribune*, December 25, 2008, available at http://articles.chicagotribune.com/2008-12-25/news/0812240848_1_congregations-reform-judaism-jewish.

81 **anguish into a crusade:** Kaplan, *Spiritual Radical*, 462.

81 **mortgaged the synagogue's building:** Wolf, "Breira and Dissent in American Jewry," in Wolf, *Unfinished Rabbi*, 146.

81 **fire employees:** Alexander Cockburn and James Ridgeway, "Doves, the Diaspora and the Future of Israel," *The Village Voice*, March 7, 1977, 2.

81 **Rabbinical Assembly denied:** Although he had led a Reform congregation, Wolf joined the Conservative movement's Rabbinical Assembly while serving as the Jewish chaplain at Yale, during a time when he was experimenting with Conservative Judaism and its greater emphasis on ritual observance. At the time, the Rabbinical Assembly allowed members to affiliate with other streams of Judaism. [Jonathan Wolf (son of Rabbi Arnold Jacob Wolf) in discussion with the author, January 26, 2011; Rabbi Eugene Borowitz (professor of education and Jewish religious thought at the Hebrew Union College) in discussion with the author, January 26, 2011; George Vecsey, "Rabbinical Meeting Rejects 2 Nominees," *The New York Times*, May 6, 1977, available at http://query.nytimes.com/mem/archive/pdf?res=F50614FC3A5D167493C4A9178ED85F438785F9.]

81 **Members of Meir Kahane's:** Cockburn and Ridgeway, "Doves, the Diaspora and the Future of Israel," 1.

81 **"must be democratic and egalitarian":** Breira, "Proceedings of Breira's First Annual Membership Conference," February 20–22, 1977, 7.

82 **"still remain":** Wolf, "The Shoah" and "Overemphasizing the Holocaust," in Wolf, *Unfinished Rabbi*, 195, 197,199.

82 **"a Zionism that sees":** Arnold Jacob Wolf, "On the Dialectics of Zionism," in *Perspectives on Jews and Judaism: Essays in Honor of Wolfe Kelman*, ed. Arthur A. Chiel (New York: Rabbinical Assembly, 1978), 483.

82 **"I love Israel as the Prophets did":** "Rabbi Arnold Wolf," in *A Dream of Zion: American Jews Reflect on Why Israel Matters to Them*, Jeffrey K. Salkin, ed. (Woodstock, Vt.: Jewish Lights Publishing, 2007), 145.

82 **"embedded in the Jewish world":** Pauline Dubkin Yearwood, "Obama and the Jews," *The Chicago Jewish News*, October 24, 2008, available at http://www.chicago jewishnews.com/story.htm?id=252218&sid=212226.

83 **Obama answered the call:** Ryan Lizza, "The Agitator: Barack Obama's Unlikely Political Education," *The New Republic*, March 19, 2007, available at http://www .tnr.com/article/the-agitator.

83 **power base in black Chicago:** David Remnick, *The Bridge: The Life and Rise of Barack Obama* (New York: Alfred A. Knopf, 2010), 132–33, 173–75.

83 **latter-day civil rights movement:** Jonathan Kaufman, "For Obama, Chicago Days Honed Tactics," *The Wall Street Journal*, April 21, 2008, available at http://online.wsj .com/article/SB120873956522230099.html; Remnick, *The Bridge*, 117, 135, 180.

83 **Obama helped to soothe:** Jodi Kantor, "In Law School, Obama Found Political Voice," *The New York Times*, January 28, 2007, available at http://www.nytimes. com/2007/01/28/us/politics/28obama.html?adxnnl=1&pagewanted=1&adxnnlx= 1297364496-ws6I8eGUBre9py5C8m9zSw.

84 **stood slightly to Obama's left:** David Remnick, *The Bridge*, 207.

84 **"pretty much the same way":** Former *Harvard Law Review* editor in discussion with the author, July 13, 2010.

84 **led by Arnold Jacob Wolf:** Gabrielle Birkner, "Rabbi Arnold Wolf, 84, Was Progressive Leader," *The Jewish Daily Forward*, December 31, 2008, available at http://www.forward.com/articles/14849; Andrew Ferguson, "Mr. Obama's Neighborhood," *The Weekly Standard* 13, no. 38 (June 16, 2008), available at http:// www.weeklystandard.com/Content/Public/Articles/000/000/015/197wxqsf.asp? page=1.

84 **hegemonically liberal:** Remnick, *The Bridge*, 284; Natasha Mozgovaya, "Some Chicago Jews Say Obama Is Actually the 'First Jewish President,'" *Haaretz*, November 13, 2008, available at http://www.haaretz.com/print-edition /features/some-chicago-jews-say-obama-is-actually-the-first-jewish-president -1.257204.

84 **black and white professionals:** Wolfgang Saxon, "Julian H. Levi, 87, Influential Advocate of Urban Renewal," *The New York Times*, October 19, 1998, available at http://query.nytimes.com/gst/fullpage.html?res=9B02E1DB1E31F93 AA25753C1A960958260; *Encyclopedia of Chicago*, "Urban Renewal," available at http:// encyclopedia.chicagohistory.org/pages/1295.html; Ferguson, "Mr. Obama's Neighborhood."

84 **challah bread:** Dayo Olopade (journalist and student at Yale Law School) in discussion with the author, July 4, 2010.

84 **Obama's own daughters:** Yearwood, "Obama and the Jews"; Marissa Brostoff, "At Synagogue Overlooking Obama's House, Blacks and Jews Live Side by Side," *Haaretz*, December 10, 2008, available at http://www.haaretz.com/jewish-world/ news/at-synagogue-overlooking-obama-s-house-blacks-and-jews-live-side-by -side-1.258812.

84 **earliest and most prominent:** Lynn Sweet, "McCain Misleading Public in Role Ayers Played in Obama Political Career," *Chicago Sun-Times*, October 15, 2008, available at http://blogs.suntimes.com/sweet/2008/10/ayers_alone_did_not_ launch_oba.html.

84 **"'What state are you'":** Brostoff, "At Synagogue Overlooking Obama's House, Blacks and Jews Live Side by Side"; Susan Saulny, "House for Sale Comes with a View: The Obamas," *The New York Times*, September 14, 2009, available at http://www.nytimes.com/2009/09/15/us/15chicago.html.

84 **"interfaith, left, liberal, integrationist":** "Mr. Obama's Neighborhood," *The Jerusalem Post*, February 15, 2010, available at http://www.jpost.com/home/article.aspx?id=118057.

85 **not just that as a state senator:** Grace Wolf in discussion with the author, January 26, 2011; Arnold Jacob Wolf, "My Neighbor Barack," *Jews for Obama*, 2008, available at http://jews4obama2008.wordpress.com/my-neighbor-barack-by-arnold-jacob-wolf/.

85 **Catholic Theological Union:** Grace Wolf in discussion with the author, June 30, 2010; Catholic Theological Union, "Effective Leaders for the Church," available at http://www.ctu.edu/alumni.

85 **Khalidi regularly came to KAM Isaiah:** Rashid Khalidi (professor of modern Arab studies at Columbia University) in discussion with the author, February 9, 2011.

85 **"teacher who changed my life":** Legal Services Corporation, "LSC Vice Chair Said to Be Potential Supreme Court Nominee," April 16, 2010, available at http://www.lsc.gov/media/newsletters/2010/lsc-updates-april-16-2010.

85 **The two reconnected:** Martha Minow in discussion with the author, January 17, 2011, and March 10, 2011.

85 **Wolf performed the ceremony:** Newton Minow in discussion with the author, September 14, 2010.

85 **give Obama a job:** Remnick, *The Bridge*, 200.

85 **bridge to many:** Newton Minow in discussion with the author, September 14, 2010; Yearwood, "Obama and the Jews."

86 **"almost threw me out":** Newton Minow in discussion with the author, September 14, 2010, and March 1, 2011.

86 **advisory council of J Street:** Chicago Peace Now, "Chicago Jewish and Palestinian Leaders Unite to Support Mideast Peace Accords," December 2, 2003, available at http://articles.chicagotribune.com/2002-10-17/news/0210170256_1_west-bank-and-gaza-israeli-jews-israeli-arabs; J Street, "Advisory Council," available at http://jstreet.org/supporters/advisory_council; Gideon Remba (former president and director of Chicago Peace Now, an affiliate of Americans for Peace Now) in discussion with the author, February 10, 2011.

86 **"failing to distinguish between":** Newton Minow, "Israel Must Leave Gaza, West Bank to Survive," *Chicago Tribune*, October 17, 2002, available at http://articles.chicagotribune.com/2002-10-17/news/0210170256_1_west-bank-and-gaza-israeli-jews-israeli-arabs; Newton Minow, "Voice of the People," *Chicago Tribune*, June 6, 2010, available at http://www.chicagotribune.com/news/opinion/ct-vp-0606voicelettersbriefs-20100606,0,4905034,full.story.

86 **Judge Abner Mikva:** Newton Minow in discussion with the author, September 14, 2010.

86 **tutored him on Chicago politics:** Remnick, *The Bridge*, 217, 342, 352.

86 **director of religious education:** Grace Wolf in discussion with the author, January 26, 2011; Rachel Mikva in discussion with the author, February 18, 2011.

86 **Wolf's views on Israel:** J Street, "J Street Rabbinic Cabinet," available at http://www.jstreet.org/page/rabbis-and-cantors.

87 **"Netanyahu speaks excellent English":** Abner Mikva (former U.S. congressman and White House counsel) in discussion with the author, September 14, 2010.

87 **"We abhor the continuing occupation":** David Suissa, "Eva's Peace Process," *The Huffington Post*, May 24, 2010, available at http://www.huffingtonpost.com/david_suissa/evas-peace-process_b_584952.html.

87 **"sophistry":** Josh Nathan-Kazis, "Prominent Jewish Liberals Answer the JCall," *The Jewish Daily Forward*, May 19, 2010, available at http://www.forward.com/articles/128182/.

87 **Bettylu Saltzman:** Remnick, *The Bridge*, 224.

87 **new city on Israel's southern coast:** Philip M. Klutznick with Sidney Hyman, *Angles of Vision: A Memoir of My Lives* (Chicago: Ivan R. Dee, 1991), 164–7, 186–9, 249, 354.

87 **in the 1970s:** Ibid., 157, 355.

88 **"opposition and revolt":** Ibid., 307.

88 **Yasser Arafat's PLO:** Ibid., 386–88.

88 **"They lambasted him":** Bettylu Saltzman (liberal activist and daughter of Philip Klutznick) in discussion with the author, July 26, 2010.

88 **organized a boycott:** Klutznick, *Angles of Vision*, 387–88; James Klutznick (real estate developer and son of Philip Klutznick) in discussion with the author, February 15, 2011.

88 **even publicly mentioned:** A longtime observer of Jewish Chicago in discussion with the author, March 16, 2011.

88 **letter in Percy's defense:** Bettylu Saltzman in discussion with the author, July 26, 2010.

88 **other progressive Israeli groups:** Ibid.

88 **advisory council of J Street:** J Street, "Advisory Council"; Gideon Remba in discussion with the author, February 10, 2011.

89 **became a conduit:** Remnick, *The Bridge*, 224; Yearwood, "Obama and the Jews."

89 **rally against the Iraq War:** Remnick, *The Bridge*, 343–44; J Street, "Advisory Council"; Barack Obama, "October 2002 Speech: Against Going to War with Iraq," CommonDreams.org, February 28, 2008, available at http://www.commondreams.org/archive/2008/02/28/7343; Bettylu Saltzman in discussion with the author, July 26, 2010.

89 **David Axelrod:** Remnick, *The Bridge*, 225.

89 **win white votes:** Ibid., 364–65.

89 **"Obama was very much a part":** David Axelrod in discussion with the author, January 10, 2011.

89 **donated to the New Israel Fund:** New Israel Fund official in discussion with the author, January 21, 2011.

89 **impressed Axelrod:** David Axelrod in discussion with the author, January 10, 2011.

89 **reportedly told a Palestinian American:** Larry Cohler-Esses, "Obama Pivots Away from Dovish Past," *The Jewish Week*, March 9, 2007, available at http://www.thejewishweek.com/features/obama_pivots_away_dovish_past.

90 **361 members of the House:** "House Denounces UN Misuse of International Court on Security Fence," Jewish Virtual Library, July 15, 2004, available at http://www.jewishvirtuallibrary.org/jsource/US-Israel/hres713.html; "The Five Questions,"

The Chicago Jewish News, March 12, 2004, available at http://chicagojewishnews.com/story.htm?sid=1&id=181907.

90 **obtained a rewrite:** Jewish activist in discussion with the author, March 24, 2011.

90 **"found myself unable to distinguish":** Barack Obama, *The Audacity of Hope: Thoughts on Reclaiming the American Dream* (New York: Crown, 2006), 322.

90 *The Yellow Wind:* In 2011, the White House told reporters that Obama was reading another book of Grossman's, his novel *To the End of the Land.* [Jeffrey Goldberg, "Obama on Zionism and Hamas," *The Atlantic*, May 12, 2008, available at http://www.theatlantic.com/international/archive/2008/05/obama-on-zionism-and-hamas/8318; Maya Sela, "David Grossman Doubts Arab States' Good Intentions," *Haaretz*, August 22, 2011, available at http://www.haaretz.com/print-edition/news/david-grossman-doubts-arab-states-good-intentions-1.379924.]

91 **"line of Peace Now":** Cohler-Esses, "Obama Pivots Away from Dovish Past"; White House official in discussion with the author, July 14, 2010.

91 **British rule in Kenya:** Remnick, *The Bridge*, 99–101, 104, 112–14, 247.

91 **parishioner in the church:** On Wright's views of Israel, see Richard Cohen, "Obama's Farrakhan Test," *The Washington Post*, January 15, 2008, available at http://www.washingtonpost.com/wp-dyn/content/article/2008/01/14/AR2008011402083_pf.html; Daniel Treiman, "Jeremiah Wright: Israel Is to Judaism as Flavor Flav Is to Christianity," JTA, January 23, 2011, available at http://blogs.jta.org/telegraph/article/2011/06/23/3088272/jeremiah-wright-israel-is-to-judaism-as-flavor-flav-is-to-christianity; "Rev. Jeremiah Wright Anti-Israel Comments" [video], May 27, 2008, available at http://www.youtube.com/watch?v=M-EBc2xaz44.

91 **"I learned that partly":** Goldberg, "Obama on Zionism and Hamas."

92 **"how much more open":** Ami Eden, "Obama Reaches Out to Jewish leaders," JTA, February 25, 2008, available at http://blogs.jta.org/politics/article/2008/02/25/999226/obama-reaches-out-to-jewish-leaders.

92 **"not as open":** Lynn Sweet, "Obama Tells Philadelphia Jewish Leaders He Would Not Sit Down with Hamas," *Chicago Sun-Times*, April 16, 2008, available at http://blogs.suntimes.com/sweet/2008/04/obama_tells_philadelphia_jewis.html.

92 **"unless you adopt an unwavering":** Eden, "Obama Reaches Out to Jewish Leaders."

92 **"Like Abraham?" he asked:** "Obama: 'Unshakable Commitment to the Security of Israel,'" *Neurotic Democrat*, October 14, 2008, available at http://neuroticdemocrat.com/2008/10/obama-unshakable-commitment-to-the-security-of-israel/.

93 **more establishment views:** Newton Minow in discussion with the author, March 1, 2011; Remnick, *The Bridge*, 224, 379; Melissa Harris, "Chicagoan to Head Pro-Israel Group," *Chicago Tribune*, March 21, 2010, available at http://articles.chicagotribune.com/2010-03-21/business/ct-biz-0321-confidential-rosy--20100321_1_pro-israel-aipac-steve-rosen; Bradley Burston, "Key Obama Backer, Confidante Alan Solow Tipped to Head U.S. Jewry's Top Body," *Haaretz*, December 22, 2008, available at http://www.haaretz.com/jewish-world/news/key-obama-backer-confidante-alan-solow-tipped-to-head-u-s-jewry-s-top-body-1.259954.

93 **told Obama he agreed:** Newton Minow in discussion with the author, September 14, 2010; Abner Mikva in discussion with the author, September 14, 2010; Jewish activist in discussion with the author, March 24, 2011.

93 **No Jewish communal leaders:** Jodi Kantor, "Next Year in the White House: A Seder Tradition," *The New York Times*, March 27, 2010, available at http://www

.nytimes.com/2010/03/28/us/politics/28seder.html?ref=jodikantor; Abner Mikva in discussion with the author, September 14, 2010; Eric Lesser (former special assistant to White House Senior Adviser David Axelrod) in discussion with the author, September 8, 2010, April 30, 2011, and October 16, 2011.

94 **"with matzah ball soup"**: Former Democratic Party official and Jewish organization executive in discussion with the author, March 23, 2011.

94 **"risky steps for peace"**: Jennifer Siegel, "Internal Memo Takes on Obama's Mideast Approach," *The Jewish Daily Forward*, January 23, 2008, available at http://www.forward.com/articles/12543/.

94 **"concern over the zeitgeist"**: Anshel Pfeffer, "Hoenlein: Obama's Spirit of Change Could Harm Israel," *Haaretz*, February 13, 2008, available at http://www.haaretz.com/print-edition/news/hoenlein-obama-s-spirit-of-change-could-harm-israel-1.239219; an official at a Jewish organization in discussion with the author, March 10, 2011; Matthew Berger, "Palin Disinvited from Iran Protest Rally," NBC News, September 18, 2008, available at http://firstread.msnbc.msn.com/_news/2008/09/18/4424232-palin-disinvited-from-iran-protest-rally; Anne E. Kornblut and Juliet Eilperin, "Steering the McCain Campaign, a Lot of Old Bush Hands," *The Washington Post*, September 22, 2008, available at http://www.washingtonpost.com/wp-dyn/content/story/2008/09/22/ST2008092200078.html.

94 **call Obama "anti-Israel"**: Congressional staffer who works on Israel policy in discussion with the author, March 15, 2011; Former Obama campaign adviser in discussion with the author, May 11, 2011; Malcolm Hoenlein in discussion with the author, October 24, 2011.

94 **partisan favoritism:** Source close to AIPAC, in discussion with the author, October 18, 2011.

94 **"knew where AIPAC was"**: Congressional staffer in discussion with the author, March 15, 2011, and March 23, 2011.

94 **At a rooftop reception:** Former Democratic Party official in discussion with the author, March 12, 2011, and March 23, 2011.

95 **skewed younger and less observant:** Jennifer Siegel, "Jews Follow Trend, Split Vote for Dems," *The Jewish Daily Forward*, February 6, 2008, available at http://www.forward.com/articles/12623/; National Jewish Democratic Council, "The Jewish Vote in Recent Presidential Primaries and Caucuses," available at http://njdc.typepad.com/jewishvoteexit.pdf.

95 **"nobody is suffering more"**: Thomas Beaumont, "Obama Urges More Compassion in Mideast," Politico, March 12, 2007, available at http://www.politico.com/news/stories/0307/3082.html; Justin Elliott, "Obama's Israel Shuffle," *Mother Jones*, February 1, 2008, available at http://motherjones.com/politics/2008/02/obamas-israel-shuffle.

95 **"heavy and tough"**: "Prepared Text of Barack Obama's Speech for the AIPAC Foreign Policy Forum," *Chicago Sun-Times*, March 2, 2007, available at http://blogs.suntimes.com/sweet/2007/03/obamas_aipac_speech_text_as_pr.html.

95 **retract it the following day:** "Senator Barack Obama, AIPAC Policy Conference 2008," June 4, 2008, available at http://www.imra.org.il/story.php3?id=39525; Glenn Kessler, "Obama Clarifies Remarks on Jerusalem," *The Washington Post*, June 5, 2008, available at http://voices.washingtonpost.com/44/2008/06/obama-backtracks-on-jerusalem.html.

95 **hired a former AIPAC staffer:** Ami Eden, "Obama Taps L.A. Federation, Former

AIPAC Official," JTA, July 15, 2008, available at http://blogs.jta.org/politics/article/2008/07/15/999418/obama-taps-la-federation-former-aipac-official.

95 **(later reversed):** Ido Rosenzweig and Yuval Shany, "IDF Revokes House Demolition Order Due to Doubts Whether Act of Violence Was Terror Attack," Israeli Democracy Institute, August 2, 2010, available at http://www.idi.org.il/sites/english/ResearchAndPrograms/NationalSecurityandDemocracy/Terrorism_and_Democracy/Newsletters/Pages/24th%20Newsletter/4/4.aspx; Chaim Levinson, "'08 Tractor Rampage Ruled Drug-Induced, Not Terror Attack," *Haaretz*, December 1, 2010, available at http://www.haaretz.com/print-edition/news/08-tractor-rampage-ruled-drug-induced-not-terror-attack-1.328125; Isabel Kershner, "Construction Vehicle Attack in Israel," *The New York Times*, July 23, 2008, available at http://www.nytimes.com/2008/07/23/world/middleeast/23israel.html; "Tractor Rampage Driver Killed in Jerusalem," CBS News, July 22, 2008, available at http://www.cbsnews.com/stories/2008/07/22/world/main4281220.shtml.

95 **"say that" in public:** Former Obama campaign adviser in discussion with the author, March 4, 2011.

96 **attacked Obama foreign policy adviser:** Troutfishing, "Tracing the Anti-Obama Smears: The GOP Connection," Daily Kos, March 14, 2008, available at http://www.dailykos.com/story/2008/3/14/111857/479/438/476537.

96 **not an adviser:** Richard Baehr and Ed Lasky, "Samantha Power and Obama's Foreign Policy Team," *American Thinker*, February 19, 2008, available at http://www.americanthinker.com/2008/02/samantha_power_and_obamas_fore_1.html; Eli Lake, "Obama's Brain Trust Taking Shape," *The New York Sun*, February 21, 2008, available at http://www.nysun.com/national/obamas-brain-trust-taking-shape/71580/.

96 **in months:** Ed Lasky, "Barack Obama and Israel," *American Thinker*, January 16, 2008, available at http://www.americanthinker.com/2008/01/barack_obama_and_israel.html; Lake, "Obama's Brain Trust Taking Shape."

96 **Israel bore part of:** Ed Lasky, "Barack Obama's Middle East Expert," *American Thinker*, January 23, 2008, available at http://www.americanthinker.com/2008/01/barack_obamas_middle_east_expe.html; Helene Cooper, "One Adviser Among Many, Under Lights over Israel," *The New York Times*, March 15, 2008, available at http://www.nytimes.com/2008/03/15/us/politics/15web-cooper.html.

96 **arrived in his inbox:** Former Democratic Party official and Jewish organizational executive in discussion with the author, March 22, 2011; White House official in discussion with the author, February 18, 2011, and June 17, 2011; Robert Malley (Middle East and North Africa program director at the International Crisis Group) in discussion with the author, February 18, 2011; Martin Peretz, "Can Friends of Israel—and Jews—Trust Obama? In a Word, Yes," *The New Republic*, January 31, 2008, available at http://www.tnr.com/article/politics/can-friends-israel-and-jews-trust-obama.

96 **personally dovish views:** Jennifer Siegel, "Barack Obama Steps Up Bid for Jewish Backing," *The Jewish Daily Forward*, March 9, 2007, available at http://www.forward.com/articles/10306/; Eric Fingerhut, "Dan Shapiro Joins Obama Full-Time," JTA, August 19, 2008, available at http://blogs.jta.org/politics/article/2008/08/19/999454/dan-shapiro-joins-obama-full-time; former campaign adviser in discussion with the author, February 15, 2011.

97   **the domestic pressures:** Akiva Eldar, "Obama Mulls Ex-Ambassador to Israel, Daniel Kurtzer, as Special Mideast Envoy," *Haaretz*, December 2, 2008, available at http://www.haaretz.com/print-edition/news/obama-mulls-ex-ambassador-to-israel-daniel-kurtzer-as-special-mideast-envoy-1.258623; "U.S. Ambassador: Terror Will Return," YNet News, March 25, 2005, available at http://www.ynetnews.com/articles/0,7340,L-3063263,00.html; Daniel C. Kurtzer and Scott Lasensky, *Negotiating Arab-Israeli Peace: American Leadership in the Middle East* (Washington, D.C.: United Institute of Peace Press, 2008), 44, 53, 57; former Democratic Party official and Jewish organization executive in discussion with author, March 23, 2011.

97   **"may displease many":** Ed Lasky, "Obama's New Foreign Policy Advisor Daniel Kurtzer," *American Thinker*, April 10, 2008, available at http://www.americanthinker.com/2008/04/obamas_new_foreign_policy_advi.html.

97   **"They didn't send him":** Washington Middle East insider in discussion with the author, February 18, 2011.

97   **Ross marginalized Kurtzer:** Former State Department official in discussion with the author, February 11, 2011; former campaign adviser in discussion with the author, March 4, 2011; Indyk, *Innocent Abroad*, 24; Miller, *The Much Too Promised Land*, 204–5.

97   **"melitz yosher":** Nathan Guttman, "Latest Chapter in Mideast Tension Is Dennis Ross vs. George Mitchell," *The Jewish Daily Forward*, January 21, 2011, available at http://www.forward.com/articles/134642/.

98   **reassuring Israel, rather than:** In the words of Ross's Clinton administration deputy, Aaron David Miller, Ross possessed "a deep conviction that if you couldn't gain Israel's confidence, you had zero chance of erecting any kind of peace process. And to Dennis, achieving this goal required a degree of coordination with the Israelis, sensitivity toward their substantive concerns, and public defense of their positions." [Miller, *The Much Too Promised Land*, 205.]

98   **offshoot of AIPAC:** M. J. Rosenberg, "Does PBS Know That 'The Washington Institute' Was Founded by AIPAC?" *The Huffington Post*, April 12, 2010, available at http://www.huffingtonpost.com/mj-rosenberg/does-pbs-know-that-washin_b_533808.html.

98   **placed less blame:** Ross, *The Missing Peace*, 690–710; Malley and Agha, "Camp David: The Tragedy of Errors"; Ross, "Camp David: An Exchange"; Aaron David Miller, "Israel's Lawyer," *The Washington Post*, May 23, 2005, available at http://www.washingtonpost.com/wp-dyn/content/article/2005/05/22/AR2005052200883.html; Miller, *The Much Too Promised Land*, 267, 243, 252; Indyk, *Innocent Abroad*, 339.

98   **transformed Ross into a favorite:** Former Middle East campaign adviser in discussion with the author, February 15, 2011.

98   **"tilted too much":** Kurtzer and Lasensky, *Negotiating Arab-Israeli Peace*, 61.

98   **discrepancy between his views:** Former campaign adviser in discussion with the author, March 4, 2011.

98   **"Dennis Ross was the biggest tool":** Jewish organization executive in discussion with the author, March 23, 2011.

98   **Among the elderly:** Former Obama campaign official in discussion with the author, February 18, 2011.

99   **"what's going to happen":** Yearwood, "Obama and the Jews."

6. THE MONIST PRIME MINISTER

100 **jawbone of an ass:** Ze'ev Jabotinsky, *Samson the Nazarite* (London: M. Secker, 1930).

101 **Joshua and King David:** Eran Kaplan, *The Jewish Radical Right: Revisionist Zionism and Its Ideological Legacy* (Madison: University of Wisconsin Press, 2005), 37.

101 **"seek justice":** Kaplan, *The Jewish Radical Right*; 37 Isaiah 1:17 (New JPS Version).

101 **"childish humanism":** Shlomo Avineri, *The Making of Modern Zionism* (New York: Basic Books, 1981), 164.

101 **"humanistic teachings":** Kaplan, *The Jewish Radical Right*, 34–35.

101 **liberal or socialist principles:** Ehud Luz, "The Moral Price of Sovereignty: The Dispute About the Use of Military Power Within Zionism," *Modern Judaism* 7, no. 1 (February 1987): 67–68.

101 **"Two basic aspirations":** Kaplan, *The Jewish Radical Right*, 33.

102 **"There is no other morality":** Ze'ev Jabotinsky, "The Iron Wall," Jabotinsky Institute in Israel, April 11, 1923, available at http://www.jabotinsky.org/multimedia/upl_doc/doc_191207_49117.pdf.

102 **nineteenth-century liberal:** Kaplan, *The Jewish Radical Right*, 15, 20; Ze'ev Jabotinsky, "The Arab Angle—Undramatized," in *The Jewish War Front* (London: G. Allen & Unwyn, 1940), available at http://www.jabotinsky.org/multimedia/upl_doc/doc_191207_140807.pdf.

102 **"we call 'monism' ":** Gideon Shimoni, *The Zionist Ideology* (Hanover, N.H.: Brandeis University Press, 1995), 243.

102 **"Let the stranger":** Herzl, *Old New Land*, 276.

102 **"but a Venice":** Ibid., xvii.

102 **praised the Boers:** Kaplan, *The Jewish Radical Right*, 116–17.

102 **Ukrainian nationalist movement:** Avineri, *The Making of Modern Zionism*, 170.

103 **"untainted by any universalist":** Yaacov Shavit, *Jabotinsky and the Revisionist Movement, 1925–1948* (Totowa, N.J.: Frank Cass, 1988), 21.

103 **"Every native population":** Jabotinsky, "The Iron Wall."

103 **best rendered in Latin script:** Kaplan, *The Jewish Radical Right*, 146–47.

103 **"thank God for that":** David J. Goldberg, *To the Promised Land: A History of Zionist Thought from Its Origins to the Modern State of Israel* (New York: Penguin Books, 1996), 181.

103 **"minimum of interference":** Shavit, *Jabotinsky and the Revisionist Movement*, 245–46.

103 **"five hundred years behind us":** Jabotinsky, "The Iron Wall."

103 **"Only among the Right":** Shavit, *Jabotinsky and the Revisionist Movement*, 231, 247.

104 **modern-day Jordan:** Kaplan, *The Jewish Radical Right*, 191.

104 **wavered on transfer:** Shimoni, *The Zionist Ideology*, 370; Kaplan, *The Jewish Radical Right*, 48; Shavit, *Jabotinsky and the Revisionist Movement*, 263–64, 266–67; Benny Morris, *The Birth of the Palestinian Refugee Problem Revisited* (New York: Cambridge University Press, 1988), 45; Jabotinsky, "The Arab Angle—Undramatized"; Nur Masalha, *Expulsion of the Palestinians: The Concept of "Transfer" in Zionist Political Thought, 1882–1948* (Washington, D.C.: Institute for Palestine Studies, 1992), 29, 148–49.

104 **more troubled by it:** As Ehud Luz writes, Labor Zionists "perceived military power as a necessary tool which must be used carefully for limited purposes." This view

"implies that any admiration or glorification of power for its own sake is invalid." [Luz, "The Moral Price of Sovereignty," 75.]

105 **"not ashamed of Deir Yassin"**: Segev, 25, 89.

105 **Vladimir Jabotinsky cabled:** Medoff, *Militant Zionism in America*, 48.

105 **called** *Zionews*: Ben Caspit and Ilan Kfir, *Netanyahu: The Road to Power*, trans. Ora Cummings (Secaucus, N.J.: Birch Lane Press, 1998), 19–20.

105 **"The prowess of Jewish youth"**: "A Timely Warning," *Zionews*, July 1944, 9.

106 **"full and total justice of"**: Benzion Netanyahu, "Jabotinsky's Place in the History of the Jewish People," address delivered at the University of Haifa, January 13, 1981, 4, 9.

106 **"an utter impossibility"**: "Hitler Crosses the Thames," *Zionews*, February 1944, 8; "Palestine, Partition, and Partition Plans," Jewish Virtual Library, available at http://www.jewishvirtuallibrary.org/jsource/judaica/ejud_0002_0015_0_15344.html.

106 **"the beginning of the end"**: Jason Epstein, "Personal History," *Tablet*, July 6, 2010, available at http://www.tabletmag.com/news-and-politics/38335/personal-history.

106 **"You don't return land"**: Noam Sheizaf, "Netanyahu's Father Discusses the Peace Process: Excerpts from the Exclusive *Maariv* Interview (Part I)," Promised Land Blog, April 3, 2009, available at http://www.promisedlandblog.com/?p=803; Noam Sheizaf, "Netanyahu's Father Discusses the Peace Process: Excerpts from the Exclusive *Maariv* Interview (Part II)," Promised Land Blog, April 3, 2009, available at http://www.promisedlandblog.com/?p=824.

107 **trying to kill British police:** "Shadows of Civil War," *Zionews*, July 1944, 10.

107 **called himself a fascist:** "The War for Achimeir's Release Continues" [Hebrew], *Hayarden*, May 22, 1934, trans. Sahar Segal.

107 **in Achimeir's honor:** Christopher Hitchens, "The Iron Wall," Salon, April 13, 1998, available at http://www1.salon.com/col/hitc/1998/04/nc_13hitc2.html.

107 **Palestine's Arabs in Iraq:** Medoff, *Militant Zionism in America*, 94–95.

107 **"far-reaching plan"**: "The American Resettlement Committee," *Zionews*, September/October 1943, 11.

107 **"to Arabia, Iraq, Syria"**: Benzion Netanyahu, *Five Founding Fathers of Zionism* [Hebrew], trans. Dana Rapoport (Tel Aviv: Yediot Achronot, 2003), 210.

107 *"they will run away from here"*: Sheizaf, "Netanyahu's Father Discusses the Peace Process (Part I)."

108 **"hatred for the stranger"**: B. Netanyahu, "The 'Facts' of 'Life,'" *Zionews*, July/August 1943, 31.

108 **"Ishmael, the wild man of the desert"**: "Words and Deeds," *Zionews*, September/October 1943, 8.

108 **"perpetual war"**: Sheizaf, "Netanyahu's Father Discusses the Peace Process (Part I)."

108 **but withholding food:** Ibid.

109 **"psychobabble"**: Nicholas Goldberg, "Is This a New Benjamin Netanyahu?" *Los Angeles Times*, April 5, 2009, available at http://www.latimes.com/news/opinion/commentary/la-oe-goldberg5-2009apr05,0,6013418.story.

109 **"Bibi's father had a substantial"**: Martin Regg Cohn, "His Father's Son," *Toronto Star*, July 5, 1998, F1.

109 **"huge influence on him"**: Dan Ephron, "The Unlikely Peacemaker," *Newsweek*, August 28, 2010, available at http://www.newsweek.com/2010/08/28/can-netanyahu-make-peace-with-the-palestinians.html.

109   **"He worries":** Jeffrey Goldberg, "The Point of No Return," *The Atlantic*, September 2010, available at http://www.theatlantic.com/magazine/archive/2010/09/the-point-of-no-return/8186.

109   **anxiety about his father's:** Caspit and Kfir, *Netanyahu*, 259.

109   **before withdrawing Israeli troops:** "Netanyahu: America Is Easy to Push Around"[Hebrew], trans. Daniel Charles, Israeli Channel 10, July 9, 2010, available at http://news.nana10.co.il/Article/?ArticleId=731025&sid=126.

109   **"From you I've learned, father":** Sheizaf, "Netanyahu's Father Discusses the Peace Process (Part I)."

110   **"acute sense of what mankind should be":** Benjamin Netanyahu, *A Durable Peace: Israel and Its Place Among the Nations* (New York: Grand Central Publishing, Kindle Edition, 2009), 355, 358–59, 368, 372; Benjamin Netanyahu, *A Place Among the Nations: Israel and the World* (New York: Bantam Books, 1993).

110   **"worse than [Neville] Chamberlain":** Rory McCarthy, "Profile: Benjamin Netanyahu," *The Guardian*, February 11, 2009, available at http://www.guardian.co.uk/world/2009/feb/11/binyamin-netanyahu-profile.

110   *"judenrein"* **West Bank:** Benjamin Netanyahu, *A Durable Peace*, 6, 168, 200.

111   **Meinertzhagen's "remarkable character":** Ibid., 53, 61, 60.

111   **"wild beast of a man":** Al Jazeera Transparency Unit, "Meeting Minutes: Saeb Erekat and George Mitchell, September 24, 2009," Al Jazeera, available at http://www.ajtransparency.com/en/document/4861.

111   **"The Arabs know only force":** Caspit and Kfir, *Netanyahu*, 139.

111   **"peace is a coin":** Benjamin Netanyahu, *A Durable Peace*, 330.

111   **Facebook group that urged boycotting:** Amy Teibel, "Yair Netanyahu, Israeli Prime Minister's Son, Creates Facebook Ruckus with Arab, Muslim Posts," *The Huffington Post*, June 24, 2011, available at http://www.huffingtonpost.com/2011/06/24/yair-netanyahu-israeli-prime-minister-son-facebook-posts-arab-muslim-_n_883805.html.

112   **Jews pleaded with:** Benjamin Netanyahu, *A Durable Peace*, 95, 154.

112   **Netanyahu's historical account is silly:** See, for instance, Morris, *The Birth of the Palestinian Refugee Problem* (Cambridge: Cambridge University Press, 2004), 59; *Benny Morris: Palestinian Nakba (part 4)* [video], December 8, 2009, available at http://www.youtube.com/watch?v=9nmzzaG55Z4&NR=1; Michal Ben-Josef Hirsch, "From Taboo to the Negotiable: The Israeli New Historians and the Changing Representation of the Palestinian Refugee Problem," *Perspectives on Politics* 5, no. 2 (June 2007): 241–58, available at http://www.jstor.org/stable/20446422.

112   **coercing "Israeli Arabs":** Uzi Arad, "Swap Meet—Trading Land for Peace," *The New Republic*, November 28, 2005, available at http://www.tnr.com/article/trading-land-peace.

112   **Netanyahu has not publicly repudiated:** Caspit and Kfir, *Netanyahu*, 174; Natasha Mozgovaya and Barak Ravid, "Netanyahu: Israel, Palestinians Can Reach Mideast Peace in a Year," *Haaretz*, September 28, 2010, available at http://www.haaretz.com/news/diplomacy-defense/netanyahu-israel-palestinians-can-reach-mideast-peace-in-a-year-1.316220; Timothy William Waters, "The Blessing of Departure—Exchange of Populated Territories, The Lieberman Plan as an Abstract Exercise in Demographic Transformation," Social Science Research Network, January 21, 2007, available at http://papers.ssrn.com/sol3/papers.cfm?abstract_id=958469.

112 **Association for Civil Rights in Israel:** Ben Hartman, "Prisons Service Holds Drills Dealing with All Scenarios," *The Jerusalem Post*, October 14, 2010, available at http://www.jpost.com/Israel/Article.aspx?id=191308; Liel Kyzer, "Rights Group Asks Netanyahu to Vow Not to 'Transfer' Arab Citizens," *Haaretz*, October 14, 2010, available at http://www.haaretz.com/print-edition/news/rights-group-asks-netan yahu-to-vow-not-to-transfer-arab-citizens-1.318959; Libby Friedlander (director of the International Relations Department at the Association for Civil Rights in Israel) in discussion with the author, March 25, 2011.

113 **ethnic group's birth rate:** Larry Derfner, "Rattling the Cage: A Bigot Called Bibi," *The Jerusalem Post*, January 3, 2007, available at http://www.jpost.com/Opinion/ Columnists/Article.aspx?id=46930.

113 **"mistaken in calling Bibi a bigot":** Ron Dermer, "Right of Reply: The Nerve of Bibi," *The Jerusalem Post*, January 8, 2007, available at http://www.jpost.com/ Opinion/Op-EdContributors/Article.aspx?id=47402.

113 **"he would expose his goals":** Noam Sheizaf, "Netanyahu's Father Discusses Bibi's Character, Childhood: Excerpts from the Exclusive *Maariv* Interview (Part III)," Promised Land Blog, April 5, 2009, available at http://www.promisedlandblog.com /?p=832#more-832.

114 **"truncated ghetto-state":** Benjamin Netanyahu, *A Durable Peace*, 5–6.

114 **"It is against my principles":** Caspit and Kfir, *Netanyahu*, 131–33, 191; Netanyahu, *A Durable Peace*, 279–319.

114 **"an enormous lie":** Colin Shindler, *The Land Beyond Promise: Israel, Likud and the Zionist Dream* (New York: I. B. Tauris, 1995), 285.

114 **attacked Oslo at length:** Benjamin Netanyahu, *Fighting Terrorism: How Democracies Can Defeat the International Terrorist Network* (New York: Farrar, Straus and Giroux, 2001), 99–120.

115 **would have lost by five points:** Caspit and Kfir, *Netanyahu*, 198, 229; Swisher, *The Truth About Camp David*, 5; Oren Yiftachel, "The Shrinking Space of Citizenship," 165.

115 **familiarity with American culture:** Caspit and Kfir, *Netanyahu*, 24, 36, 75.

116 **also developed friendships:** Ibid., 97, 108, 184; Jonathan Broder, "Bibi's American Friends," Salon, June 18, 1996, available at http://www1.salon.com/news/news960618 .html; Nathan Guttman, "Israel Lobby Rapped for Supporting Arabs," *The Jewish Daily Forward*, November 21, 2007, available at http://www.forward.com/articles /12079/; Connie Bruck, "The Brass Ring: A Multibillionaire's Relentless Quest for Global Influence," *The New Yorker*, June 30, 2008, available at http://www.new yorker.com/reporting/2008/06/30/080630fa_fact_bruck#ixzz1Lb8r8jKL; Matthew Dorf, "Is Irving Moskowitz a Hero or Just a Rogue?" JTA, September 26, 1997, available at http://www.jweekly.com/article/full/6673/is-irving-moskowitz-a-hero -or-just-a-rogue/; Barak Ravid, "Report: U.S. Jewish Leader Met Assad with Message from Netanyahu," *Haaretz*, January 3, 2011, available at http://www.haaretz .com/news/diplomacy-defense/report-u-s-jewish-leader-met-assad-with-message -from-netanyahu-1.335030.

116 **celebrity among activist American Jews:** Caspit and Kfir, *Netanyahu*, 128.

116 **even his ex-wife:** Ibid., 154, 183–84; Lawrence Cohler-Esses, "Lauder's Proposed Serb Deal Eyed," *The Jewish Week*, February 26, 1999, available at http://www

.thejewishweek.com/features/lauder%E2%80%99s_proposed_serb_deal_eyed; Ofri Hani, "Funded by U.S. Neocons, Think Tank Researchers Now Carving Israeli Policy," *Haaretz,* May 18, 2009, available at http://www.haaretz.com/jewish -world/news/funded-by-u-s-neocons-think-tank-researchers-now-carving-israeli -policy-1.276236; Lawrence Cohler-Esses, "Likud's Tangled Charity Web," *The Jewish Week,* February 19, 1999, available at http://www.thejewishweek.com/features/ likud%E2%80%99s_tangled_charity_web.

116 **consultant Arthur Finkelstein:** Caspit and Kfir, *Netanyahu,* 227, 229, 231.

116 **Netanyahu has denied:** Asher Wallfish, "Private Affair Held in Knesset Hall," *The Jerusalem Post,* June 27, 1991, 10.

116 **The move sparked Palestinian rioting:** Caspit and Kfir, *Netanyahu,* 9, 260–61; Barton Gellman, "Israelis, in Nighttime Move, Open Temple Mount Tunnel," *The Washington Post,* September 25, 1996, A25, available at http://www.highbeam.com /doc/1P2-794420.html.

117 **Netanyahu urged members of Congress:** Barton Gellman, "At the Crossroads: Part 2 of 2," *The Washington Post Magazine,* May 26, 1996, W15; Rowland Evans and Robert Novak, "Faxes from Jerusalem," *The Washington Post,* July 10, 1995, A17.

117 **banning direct U.S. assistance to the Palestinians:** Hillel Kuttler, "Congress Seeks Tight Rules on Aid to PA," *The Jerusalem Post,* June 15, 1995, 2.

117 **Conference did not issue:** Larry Yudelson, "Hoenlein Slow to Support Peace Process," JTA, July 19, 1994, available at http://www.shmoozenet.com/yudel/ mtarchives/1994_07.html.

117 **plot a response:** Longtime Jewish organizational official in discussion with the author, December 29, 2010.

117 **began finding excuses:** Colette Avital (former Israeli consul general in New York) in discussion with the author, May 6, 2011, May 10, 2011, and October 24, 2011; Malcolm Hoenlein in discussion with the author, October 24, 2011.

117 **"sucking at the teat of Likud":** Robert Dreyfuss, "AIPAC from the Inside: Part 1: Isolating Iran," *PBS Frontline,* June 11, 2011, available at http://www.pbs.org/wgbh /pages/frontline/tehranbureau/2011/06/aipac-from-the-inside-1-isolating-iran .html.

117 **"like pulling teeth":** Fleshler, *Transforming America's Israel Lobby,* 66.

118 **endorsed Dole's bill:** Gellman, "At the Crossroads: Part 2 of 2," W15; Neal M. Sher, "Why No Outrage from Community as Bush Ignores Embassy Pledge?" Political Mavens.com, January 18, 2007, available at http://politicalmavens.com/index.php /2007/01/18/why-no-outrage-from-community-as-bush-ignores-embassy-pledge/; Akiva Eldar, "Jerusalem and the Yitzhak Rabin Legacy," *Foreign Policy,* May 18, 2010, available at http://mideast.foreignpolicy.com/posts/2010/05/18/jerusalem _and_the_yitzhak_rabin_legacy; Akiva Eldar, "Obama's Defeat Will Definitely Not Be Netanyahu's Victory," *Haaretz,* November 1, 2010, available at http://www .haaretz.com/print-edition/opinion/obama-s-defeat-will-definitely-not-be -netanyahu-s-victory-1.322217; Marilyn Henry, "Unclear Stand," *The Jerusalem Post,* September 19, 1995, 6.

118 **replaced by Howard Kohr:** Matthew Dorf, "AIPAC Head of 2 Years Resigns Amid Mystery over Reason Why," JTA, May 31, 1996, available at http://www.jweekly.com /article/full/3343/aipac-head-of-2-years-resigns-amid-mystery-over-reason-why/.

118   **"waiting for Bibi to ascend":** Beinart and Rosin, "AIPAC Unpacked," 22.

118   **"to interpret the accords":** Glenn Kessler, "Netanyahu: 'America Is a Thing You Can Move Very Easily,'" *The Washington Post*, July 16, 2010, available at http://voices.washingtonpost.com/checkpoint-washington/2010/07/netanyahu_america_is_a_thing_y.html.

118   **"never be a Palestinian state":** Enderlin, *Shattered Dreams*, 53.

118   **hostility as an excuse:** Dani Korn, *Public Policy in Israel: Perspectives and Practices* (Lanham, Md.: Lexington Books, 2002), 82.

118   **constitute "his tribe":** Ross, *The Missing Peace*, 461, 492.

119   **atmosphere of distrust:** Pundak, "From Oslo to Taba," 33–34; Don Peretz, "The 1998 Wye River Memorandum: An Update," Jerusalem Fund, July 29, 1999, available at http://www.thejerusalemfund.org/ht/display/ContentDetails/i/2180/pid/v; Enderlin, *Shattered Dreams*, 51; Hareuveni, "By Hook and by Crook"; Tovah Lazaroff, "Settlers Hopeful Netanyahu Will Boost Housing Construction," *The Jerusalem Post*, April 1, 2009, available at http://www.jpost.com/Israel/Article.aspx?id=137798.

119   **fell from 44 to 30 percent:** Shikaki, "Palestinians Divided."

119   **rationale for shirking Israel's:** For instance, as Caspit and Kfir note, "From the moment he assumed office, however, Netanyahu did all he could to delay the peace process . . . Netanyahu demanded that the PLO publicly rescind the Palestinian charter which, in fact, had already been rescinded in 1996 at the Palestinian National Council in Gaza." [Caspit and Kfir, *Netanyahu*, 258.]

119   **would receive substantially more:** David Makovsky, "Beyond Hebron . . . The Future Is Now," *The Jerusalem Post*, December 13, 1996, 8; Ross, *The Missing Peace*, 205–6; Israeli Ministry of Foreign Affairs, "Israeli-Palestinian Interim Agreement on the West Bank and the Gaza Strip," September 28, 1995, available at http://www.mfa.gov.il/MFA/Peace%20Process/Guide%20to%20the%20Peace%20Process/THE%20ISRAELI-PALESTINIAN%20INTERIM%20AGREEMENT; Israel Ministry of Foreign Affairs, "The Israeli-Palestinian Interim Agreement—Annex I," September 28, 1995, available at http://www.mfa.gov.il/MFA/Peace+Process/Guide+to+the+Peace+Process/THE+ISRAELI-PALESTINIAN+INTERIM+AGREEMENT+-+Annex+I.htm#append1.

119   **dramatically reduced the land:** Akiva Eldar, "The Oslo Accords Are All But Dead," *Haaretz*, July 4, 2011, available at http://www.haaretz.com/print-edition/opinion/the-oslo-accords-are-all-but-dead-1.371234.

120   **additional 1 percent:** Israel Ministry of Foreign Affairs, "PM Netanyahu Presents Wye Memorandum to Cabinet," November 5, 1998, available at http://www.mfa.gov.il/MFA/MFAArchive/1990_1999/1998/11/PM+Netanyahu+Presents+Wye+Memorandum+to+Cabinet+-.htm; Israel Ministry of Foreign Affairs, "The Wye River Memorandum: Background and Main Points," October 23, 1998, available at http://www.mfa.gov.il/mfa/peace%20process/guide%20to%20the%20peace%20process/the%20wye%20river%20memorandum-%20background%20and%20main%20poin.

120   **a halfhearted effort:** Ross, *The Missing Peace*, 463, 468.

120   **resigned his ministership in disgust:** Enderlin, *Shattered Dreams*, 66.

120   **five ministers abstained:** Ross, *The Missing Peace*, 468.

120   **"it is better to give two percent":** "Netanyahu: America Is Easy to Push Around."

120 **"sufficient territorial depth":** Netanyahu, *A Durable Peace*, 343.

121 **cantons would not constitute a state:** Benjamin Netanyahu, "A Real Peace Plan for Israel," *The Wall Street Journal*, December 7, 1993, A16; Netanyahu, *A Durable Peace*, 344, 347–48; Herb Keinon, "'Allon Plus'—A Rejected Plan Is Resurrected," *The Jerusalem Post*, June 6, 1997, 2; Geoffrey Aronson, "Settlement Monitor," *Journal of Palestine Studies* 27, no. 1 (Autumn 1997): 126–28; Larry Derfner, "Netanyahu Offers Guidelines," *Cleveland Jewish News*, June 13, 1997; Caspit and Kfir, *Netanyahu*, 195; Neill Lochery, *The Difficult Road to Peace: Netanyahu, Israel and the Middle East Peace Process* (Reading, UK: Ithaca Press, 1999), 49–50; Ben-Ami, *Scars of War, Wounds of Peace*, 218; Laura Drake, "A Netanyahu Primer," *Journal of Palestine Studies* 26, no. 1 (Autumn 1996): 61–62.

121 **"No Palestinian alive":** Ross, *The Missing Peace*, 361.

121 **against the "iron wall":** Jabotinsky, "The Iron Wall."

121 **"cause it enormous pain":** Sheizaf, "Netanyahu's Father Discusses the Peace Process (Part I)."

121 **"they would accept it if":** Binyamin Netanyahu, "The Alternative Is Autonomy," *The Jerusalem Post*, April 8, 1994, 4A.

121 **"saw Bibi as a kind of speed bump":** Miller, *The Much Too Promised Land*, 273–74.

122 **"Bibi had any real interest":** Ross, *The Missing Peace*, 360.

122 **"Not one inch":** James D. Besser, "Netanyahu Takes Hard Right Turn in DC," *The Jewish Week*, January 28, 1998, available at http://www.thejewishweek.com/features/netanyahu_takes_hard_right_turn_dc; Steven Erlanger, "Netanyahu, in U.S., Woos Conservatives," *The New York Times*, January 20, 1998, available at http://www.nytimes.com/1998/01/20/world/netanyahu-in-us-woos-conservatives.html.

122 **"an affront to Mr. Clinton":** Craig Unger, "American Rapture," *Vanity Fair*, December 2005, available at http://www.vanityfair.com/politics/features/2005/12/rapture200512.

122 **"public ultimatum":** Hillel Kuttler, "Pulling Back from the Precipice," *The Jerusalem Post*, May 15, 1998, 13; Thomas W. Lippman, "Clinton Pressure on Israel Attacked," *The Washington Post*, May 7, 1998, A1.

122 **conservative allies went along:** James D. Besser, "Lost in Desert? Jewish Leaders Fear the Impact of President Clinton's Trip to the Gaza Strip," *Baltimore Jewish Times*, December 11, 1998, 0.

122 **"can be easily swayed":** "Netanyahu: America Is Easy to Push Around."

123 **"hit them":** Ibid.

123 **Dore Gold, outlined:** Jerusalem Center for Public Affairs, "Defensible Borders for Peace," 2008, available at http://www.defensibleborders.org/.

123 **director general of the Yesha Council:** Ephron, "The Unlikely Peacemaker."

123 **focus on "economic peace":** Isabel Kershner, "In Israel, Rice Faces Limited Prospects for Peace Process," *The New York Times*, November 7, 2008, available at http://www.nytimes.com/2008/11/07/world/middleeast/07mideast.html; Aluf Benn, "Netanyahu May Be a Latter-Day Gorbachev," *Haaretz*, August 27, 2010, available at http://www.haaretz.com/weekend/week-s-end/netanyahu-may-be-a-latter-day-gorbachev-1.310509; Ephron, "The Unlikely Peacemaker."

123 **"divided into a collection":** Lionel Barber and Tobias Buck, "Vision of Palestine

at Odds with the World," *Financial Times*, October 6, 2008, available at http://www.ft.com/intl/cms/s/0/267a9d3a-93c4-11dd-9a63-0000779fd18c.html#axzzleTYjlFS7.

7. THE CLASH

124   **"unwavering pro-Likud approach":** Eden, "Obama Reaches Out to Jewish Leaders."

124   **"just a liar and a cheat":** Swisher, *The Truth About Camp David*, 8.

125   **he was a pragmatist:** Dore Gold (President, the Jerusalem Center for Public Affairs) in discussion with the author, October 24, 2011.

125   **reached out to the Arab world:** Source who has worked with Likud in the past, in discussion with the author, October 11, 2011.

125   **"Obama's passive approach":** Yoram Ettinger, "Obama, McCain and Israel," YNet News, September 27, 2008, available at http://www.ynetnews.com/articles/0,7340,L-3602766,00.html; Jonathan Rynhold, "Labor, Likud, the 'Special Relationship' and the Peace Process, 1988–1996," in Ephraim Karsh, ed., *From Rabin to Netanyahu: Israel's Troubled Agenda* (London: Frank Cass, 2001), 256.

125   **"McCain's priorities":** Michael Oren, "The U.S.-Israel Partnership: Forks in the Road," *Journal of International Security Affairs*, no. 15 (Fall 2008), available at http://www.securityaffairs.org/issues/2008/15/oren.php.

125   **criticism grew so blatant:** Democratic strategist in discussion with the author, March 25, 2011.

125   **testament to the gulf:** Marc Stanley, "Op-Ed: Why Jews Voted for Obama," JTA, November 5, 2008, available at http://jta.org/news/article/2008/11/05/1000800/op-ed-why-jews-voted-for-obama.

126   **Obama administration's commitment:** Administration official in discussion with the author, August 18, 2011.

126   **report calling on Israel:** Mitchell, Solana, Rudman, Jagland, and Demirel, "The Mitchell Report."

126   **scrupulously "evenhanded":** James Besser, "Mitchell as Envoy Could Split Center," *The Jewish Week*, January 21, 2009, available at http://www.thejewishweek.com/features/mitchell_envoy_could_split_center.

126   **"to split the blame":** Lenny Ben-David, "The George Mitchell Appointment: The Tactics of 'Symmetrical Negotiations' May Not Work in 'Asymmetrical Conflicts,'" *Jerusalem Issue Briefs* 8, no. 19 (January 2009), available at http://jcpa.org/JCPA/Templates/ShowPage.asp?DBID=1&LNGID=1&TMID=111&FID=442&PID=0&IID=2839.

126   **"Swiss were neutral":** Ben Smith, "U.S. Foreign Policy: Who's in Charge?" Politico, January 23, 2009, available at http://www.politico.com/news/stories/0109/17811.html.

126   **security cooperation:** Nathan Thrall, "Our Man in Palestine," *The New York Review of Books*, October 14, 2010, available at http://www.nybooks.com/articles/archives/2010/oct/14/our-man-palestine/; International Crisis Group, "Squaring the Circle."

127   **Israeli domestic politics:** Kurtzer and Lasensky, *Negotiating Arab-Israeli Peace*, 31–32, 44.

127   **"it was apartheid":** Former senior State Department official in discussion with the author, March 31, 2011.

127   **never heard Clinton:** Beltway insider in discussion with the author, March 2, 2011.

127   **proposed "economic peace":** Ethan Bronner and Noam Cohen, "Israeli Candidate Borrows a (Web) Page from Obama," *The New York Times*, November 14, 2008, available at http://www.nytimes.com/2008/11/15/world/middleeast/15bibi.html; Barber and Buck, "Vision of Palestine at Odds with the World"; Benn, "Netanyahu May Be a Latter-Day Gorbachev."

128   **"reality on the ground":** "Ron Dermer on Netanyahu's Approach to Peace —II" [video], May 3, 2009, available at http://www.youtube.com/watch?v=n7ImG109csE &feature=related.

128   **"I don't see that":** "*Haaretz* Interviews Uzi Arad," *Haaretz*, July 10, 2009, available at http://niqnaq.wordpress.com/2009/07/10/haaretz-interviews-uzi-arad.

128   **refused to endorse:** "Obama Presses Netanyahu over Two-State Plan," BBC News, May 18, 2009, available at http://news.bbc.co.uk/2/hi/8055105.stm.

128   **"we were very close":** Avishai, "A Plan for Peace That Could Still Be."

128   **Together, the White House reasoned:** Administration official in discussion with the author, August 18, 2011.

129   **actually agreed to one:** Prime Minister Ariel Sharon's government did attach fourteen "reservations" to its acceptance of the Road Map, but since reservation number nine stated, "There will be no involvement with issues pertaining to the final settlement. Among issues not to be discussed: settlement in Judea, Samaria and Gaza (*excluding a settlement freeze* and illegal outposts)" [my emphasis], the United States government believed that Israel had, in fact, accepted a settlement freeze. [U.S. State Department, "A Performance-Based Roadmap to a Permanent Two-State Solution to the Israeli-Palestinian Conflict," April 30, 2003, available at http://www.mfa.gov.il/MFA/Peace+Process/Guide+to+the+Peace+Process/ A+Performance-Based+Roadmap+to+a+Permanent+Two-Sta.htm; "Israeli Cabinet Statement on Road Map and 14 Reservations," Jewish Virtual Library, May 25, 2003, available at http://www.jewishvirtuallibrary.org/jsource/Peace/road1 .html.]

129   **National security adviser James Jones:** Amos Harel and Avi Issacharoff, "Israel Fears Scathing U.S. Report on Its West Bank Policies," *Haaretz*, July 22, 2008, available at http://www.haaretz.com/print-edition/news/israel-fears-scathing-u-s -report-on-its-west-bank-policies-1.250211.

129   **endorsing the Road Map:** Nathan Guttman, "Emanuel's Record on Israel Is More Dovish Than the Headlines Suggest," *The Jewish Daily Forward*, November 20, 2008, http://www.forward.com/articles/14608/.

129   **had coddled Israel:** Source who has worked with Likud in the past in discussion with the author, October 11, 2011.

129   **Obama's chief of staff refused:** Stanley Greenberg (Democratic pollster) in discussion with the author, September 19, 2011.

129   **close observers noticed:** Former Middle East campaign adviser in discussion with the author, February 15, 2011.

129   **dialogue with Hamas:** Daniel Levy, "Bipartisan Foreign Policy Leaders on Annapolis Conference," *Prospects for Peace*, October 10, 2007, available at http://www .prospectsforpeace.com/2007/10/bipartisan_foreign_policy_lead.html.

129   **hostility to U.S. troops:** James A. Baker and Lee H. Hamilton, "The Iraq Study

Group Report," USIP, March–November 2006, available at http://media.usip.org/reports/iraq_study_group_report.pdf.

129   **coauthor was Ben Rhodes:** Carol E. Lee, "Obama's Foreign Policy Voice, Speechwriter Ben Rhodes," Politico, May 18, 2009, available at http://www.politico.com/news/stories/0509/22588_Page3.html.

129   **push deeply unrealistic:** Former senior administration official who worked closely with George Mitchell in discussion with the author, March 1, 2011, and March 7, 2011; administration official in discussion with the author, August 18, 2011.

130   **"peace process to Iran":** Massimo Calabresi, "Still Waiting for Obama's Iran Diplomacy," *Time*, February 2, 2009, available at http://www.time.com/time/nation/article/0,8599,1876362,00.html.

130   **"will not be involved":** Laura Rozen, "Why State's Having a Hard Time Explaining Dennis Ross's Job," *Foreign Policy*, February 26, 2009, available at http://thecable.foreignpolicy.com/posts/2009/02/25/why_the_diplomats_are_having_a_hard_time_explaining_dennis_rosss_job.

130   **Whether Ross abided:** Former senior administration official who worked closely with George Mitchell in discussion with the author, March 1, 2011; administration official in discussion with the author, August 18, 2011.

130   **"not build more settlements":** The White House Office of the Vice President, "Remarks by the Vice President at the Annual Policy Conference of the American Israel Public Affairs Committee," May 5, 2009, available at http://www.whitehouse.gov/the_press_office/Remarks-By-The-Vice-President-At-The-Annual-Policy-Conference-Of-The-American-Israel-Public-Affairs-Committee/.

130   **Obama declared, "Settlements":** The White House Office of the Press Secretary, "Remarks by President Obama and Prime Minister Netanyahu of Israel in Press Availability," May 18, 2009, available at http://www.whitehouse.gov/the_press_office/Remarks-by-President-Obama-and-Israeli-Prime-Minister-Netanyahu-in-press-availability/.

130   **"throw me under the bus":** Well-placed Israeli in discussion with the author, October 5, 2011.

130   **topple his government:** Associate of Netanyahu in discussion with the author, January 16, 2012.

131   *Hussein* **Obama:** Well-placed Israeli in discussion with the author, May 11, 2011, and October 5, 2011; Dore Gold in discussion with the author, October 24, 2011; Ron Dermer in discussion with the author, October 25, 2011.

131   **accommodate a new child:** Benjamin Netanyahu, "Address by PM Netanyahu at Bar-Ilan University," June 14, 2009, available at http://www.mfa.gov.il/MFA/Government/Speeches+by+Israeli+leaders/2009/Address_PM_Netanyahu_Bar-Ilan_University_14-Jun-2009.htm.

131   **help of government subsidies:** Akiva Eldar, "Peace Now: 'Natural Growth'—Israel's Trick for West Bank Expansion," *Haaretz*, May 17, 2009, available at http://peacenow.org/entries/archive6217; Lara Friedman, "Top 6 Bogus Arguments for Opposing Extension of the Settlement Moratorium (or for Adding Loopholes)," *Settlements in Focus* 6, no. 5 (July 29, 2010): 3, available at http://peacenow.org/entries/bogus_arguments_for_opposing_extension_of_freeze.

131   **Even George W. Bush:** Elliott Abrams, "Hillary Is Wrong About the Settlements," *The Wall Street Journal*, June 26, 2009, available at http://online.wsj.com/article/

SB124588743827950599.html; Elliott Abrams, "The Settlement Freeze Fallacy," *The Washington Post*, April 8, 2009, available at http://www.washingtonpost.com/wp -dyn/content/article/2009/04/07/AR2009040703379.html; Charles Krauthammer, "The Settlements Myth," *The Washington Post*, June 5, 2009, available at http://www .aish.com/jw/me/48969261.html; Israel Ministry of Foreign Affairs, "Letter from US President George W. Bush to Prime Minister Ariel Sharon," April 14, 2004, available at http://www.mfa.gov.il/MFA/Peace+Process/Reference+Documents/ Exchange+of+letters+Sharon-Bush+14-Apr-2004.htm; Ed Rettig, "AJC Mideast Briefing: Building Trust with Israel," July 25, 2009, available at http://www.ajc.org/ site/apps/nlnet/content2.aspx?c=ijITI2PHKoG&b=2818295&content_id= {A1DE490B-ADFA-4822-96A1-020EB3EF9197}&notoc=1.

132 **left them open to charges of collaborating:** International Crisis Group, "Squaring the Circle"; Gidi Weitz and Yanir Yagna, "Former Shin Bet Chief: Abbas Is Against Terror, but Not Because He Loves Israel," *Haaretz*, October 26, 2011, available at http://www.haaretz.com/news/diplomacy-defense/former-shin-bet-chief-abbas-is -against-terror-but-not-because-he-loves-israel-1.392126.

132 **"last nail in Abu Mazen's":** Al Jazeera Transparency Unit, "Meeting Minutes," February 27, 2009, available at http://www.ajtransparency.com/files/4449.pdf.

132 **considered him a Muslim:** New America Foundation, "Israel National Survey," December 10, 2009, available at http://asp.newamerica.net/sites/newamerica.net/ files/profiles/attachments/NAF.Israel.Survey.pdf.

133 **Israel's public television:** Akiva Eldar in discussion with the author, February 27, 2011.

133 **"strong desire to":** AIPAC, "Netanyahu Backs Two-State Solution, Reiterates Is- rael's Commitment to Peace," June 15, 2009, available at http://www.aipac.org/~/ media/Publications/Policy%20and%20Politics/AIPAC%20Analyses/Issue %20Memos/2009/06/AIPAC_Memo_Netanyahu_Backs_Two_State_Solution_ Reiterates_Israels_Commitment_to_Peace.pdf.

133 **recognize it as a Jewish state:** "Address by PM Netanyahu at Bar-Ilan University"; "Treaty of Peace Between the State of Israel and the Hashemite Kingdom of Jordan," Israel Ministry of Foreign Affairs, October 26, 1994, available at http://www.mfa.gov .il/MFA/Peace%20Process/Guide%20to%20the%20Peace%20Process/Israel-Jordan %20Peace%20Treaty; "Peace Treaty Between Israel and Egypt," Israel Ministry of Foreign Affairs, March 26, 1979, available at http://www.mfa.gov.il/MFA/ Peace+Process/Guide+to+the+Peace+Process/Israel-Egypt+Peace+Treaty.htm.

133 **capital in East Jerusalem:** Hussein Ibish (senior fellow at the American Task Force on Palestine), in discussion with the author, October 4, 2011; Slater, "Web Letter: Jerome Slater Responds to Michael Walzer."

133 **"[the Palestinians] will never accept":** Amit Segal, "Netanyahu's Father Reveals the Secret" [video], Mako—Channel 2 News, July 8, 2009, available at http://www .mako.co.il/news-military/politics/Article-77cd5b4ae4b5221006.htm, trans. Ari Leifman.

134 **"defensible borders," a phrase:** "Netanyahu Presents His 'Allon-Plus' Final Status Map," *Settlement Report* 7, no. 4 (July–August 1997), Foundation for Middle East Peace, available at http://www.fmep.org/reports/archive/vol.-7/no.-4/netanyahu -presents-his-allon-plus-final-status-map. For a detailed discussion of "defensible borders," as understood by a think tank with close ties to Netanyahu, see Jerusalem

Center for Public Affairs, "Defensible Borders for Peace," 2008, available at http://www.defensibleborders.org/.

134   **"We tried withdrawal":** "Address by PM Netanyahu at Bar-Ilan University."

134   **reissued in electronic form:** Netanyahu, *A Durable Peace*, 305.

135   **administration to work "privately":** "AIPAC-Backed Letter Gets 329 House Signatures," JTA, May 28, 2009, available at http://www.jta.org/news/article/2009/05/28/1005474/aipac-backed-letter-gets-329-house-signatures.

135   **"strongest supporters among Jewish":** Tony Karon, "Despite Jewish Concerns, Obama Keeps Up Pressure on Israel," *Time*, July 14, 2009, available at http://www.time.com/time/world/article/0,8599,1910376,00.html.

135   **"weight on solving":** Abraham Foxman, "A Point of View: After Meeting with Obama, What's Next?" *The Jerusalem Post*, July 16, 2009, available at http://cgis.jpost.com/Blogs/foxman/entry/after_meeting_with_obama_what.

135   **"not yield to the pressure":** Ron Kampeas, "Duking It Out over Christian Support for Israel," JTA, September 17, 2009, available at http://blogs.jta.org/politics/article/2009/09/17/1007958/duking-it-out-over-christian-support-for-israel.

135   **"demonstrating—with actions":** Brookings Saban Center, "Senator John Kerry: Restoring Leadership in the Middle East," March 4, 2009, available at http://www.brookings.edu/events/2009/~/media/Files/events/2009/0304_leadership/0304_leadership.pdf.

135   **"taken aback":** Former congressman Robert Wexler in discussion with the author, March 21, 2011; Paul Woodward, "US Presses Israel to Halt Settlement Growth Entirely," *The National*, May 25, 2009, available at http://www.thenational.ae/news/us-presses-israel-to-halt-settlement-growth-entirely; Bernie Becker, "The Early Word: Pollution and Proliferation," *The New York Times*, May 19, 2009, available at http://thecaucus.blogs.nytimes.com/2009/05/19/the-early-word-pollution-and-proliferation/.

135   **"members feel very uncomfortable":** Democratic strategist in discussion with the author, March 8, 2011.

136   **"you need to win":** Congressional staffer who works on Israel policy in discussion with the author, March 15, 2011.

136   **"scared to death":** Former campaign adviser in discussion with the author, February 15, 2011.

136   **"they were terrified":** Former campaign adviser in discussion with the author, Winter 2010.

136   **receive tax deductions:** Daniel Kurtzer in discussion with the author, December 15, 2010, and March 8, 2011.

136   **United States would not veto:** Washington Middle East policy expert in discussion with the author, February 10, 2011.

136   **not only supported a UN resolution:** Thomas Graham Jr., "Letter to the Editor: An Earlier Israeli Raid, When Reagan Was President," *The New York Times*, June 12, 2009, available at http://www.nytimes.com/2010/06/13/opinion/l13reagan.html?scp=8&sq=osirak%20reagan&st=cse; Donald Neff, "Israel Bombs Iraq's Osirak Nuclear Research Facility," *Washington Report on Middle East Affairs*, June 1995, available at http://www.washington-report.org/component/content/article/162–1995-june/7823-israel-bombs-iraqs-osirak-nuclear-research-facility

.html; Israel Ministry of Foreign Affairs, "Statement by Prime Minister Begin on U.S. Measures Against Israel," December 20, 1981, available at http://www.mfa.gov .il/MFA/Foreign%20Relations/Israels%20Foreign%20Relations%20since$201947/ 1981-1982/91%20Statement%20by%20Prime%20Minister%20Begin%20on%20US %20Measure.

136 **George H. W. Bush's administration:** Rory McCarthy, "US Gives Abbas Private Assurances over Israeli Settlements," *The Guardian*, April 29, 2010, available at http://www.guardian.co.uk/world/2010/apr/29/israel-settlement-building-peace -talks.

136 **Pentagon had demanded:** Ze'ev Schiff, "Don't Return Drones to China, U.S. Tells Israel," *Haaretz*, December 22, 2004, available at http://www.haaretz.com/print -edition/news/don-t-return-drones-to-china-u-s-tells-israel-1.144880; P. R. Kuma- raswamy, "At What Cost Israel-China Ties?" *Middle East Quarterly* 13, no. 2 (Spring 2006), available at http://www.meforum.org/926/at-what-cost-israel-china -ties.

136 **refused to veto a 2009 resolution:** Ron Kampeas, "Livni, Lacking Baggage, Would Find Friends in Washington," JTA, February 10, 2009, available at http://www.jta .org/news/article-print/2009/02/10/1002916/livni-lacking-baggage-would-find -friends-in-washington?TB_iframe=true&width=750&height=500; Ed Pilking- ton, "US Abstains as UN Security Council Backs Israel-Gaza Ceasefire Resolu- tion," *The Guardian*, January 8, 2009, available at http://www.guardian.co.uk/world /2009/jan/09/usforeignpolicy-unitednations.

137 **helped dethrone Shamir:** Ross, *The Missing Peace*, 84.

137 **Ross to the National Security Council:** Ben Smith, "NSC Names Ross Senior Director," Politico, June 26, 2009, available at http://www.politico.com/news/stories/ 0609/24221.html.

137 **could not hire them both:** Former Democratic Party official and Jewish organiza- tional executive in discussion with the author, March 22, 2011; former Obama campaign adviser in discussion with the author, March 4, 2011.

137 **power struggle between Ross:** Steven J. Rosen, "The Left vs. the Center on the Obama Mideast Team," *Middle East Forum*, July 31, 2009, available at http://www .meforum.org/blog/obama-mideast-monitor/2009/07/the-left-vs-the-center-on -the-obama-mideast-team.

138 **"telling politicians why":** Washington Middle East policy expert in discussion with the author, February 10, 2011.

138 **"settlement construction in 2009":** Al Jazeera Transparency Unit, "Meeting Min- utes: Saeb Erekat—David Hale, September 16, 2009," Al Jazeera, available at http:// www.ajtransparency.com/files/4835.pdf.

138 **"Of course you could":** Al Jazeera Transparency Unit, "Meeting Minutes: Saeb Erekat and David Hale, September 17, 2009," Al Jazeera, available at http://www .ajtransparency.com/en/document/4827.

138 **"essential for normal life":** "Palestinians Shun Israeli Settlement Restriction Plan," BBC News, November 25, 2009, available at http://news.bbc.co.uk/2/hi/8379868 .stm; Lara Friedman, "The Settlements Moratorium—A Six-Month Accounting," *Settlements in Focus* 6, no. 4 (June 14, 2010), available at http://peacenow.org/en tries/settlements_moratorium_six-month_accounting.

139 **laying more foundations:** Zvi Singer, Danny Adino Ababa, and Itamar Eichner, "Settlement Construction Spree Preceded Freeze," *Yediot Aharonot*, December 8, 2009, trans. by *Coteret*, available at http://coteret.com/2009/12/08/yediot-settlement -construction-spree-preceded-freeze; Amos Harel, "Settlers Have Been Working for Months to Undermine Construction Freeze," *Haaretz*, November 27, 2009, available at http://www.haaretz.com/misc/article-print-page/analysis-settlers -have-been-working-for-months-to-undermine-construction-freeze-1.3310?trailingPath=2.169%2C2.225%2C2.226%2C.

139 **the year of the "freeze":** Hagit Ofran, "Intensive Construction in Every Other Settlement," Peace Now, December 23, 2010, available at http://peacenow.org.il/eng /content/intensive-construction-every-other-settlement; Peace Now, "Peace Now Report: Summary of Construction in the West Bank in 2008," January 21, 2009, available at http://www.ochaopt.org/documents/opt_prot_peacenow_settlement _construction_annual_2008.pdf.

139 **Bahrain had considered opening:** Jonathan Prince (former State Department director of strategic communication in discussion with the author, March 1, 2011, and March 7, 2011.

139 **Saudi Arabia:** Hussein Ibish in discussion with the author, March 7, 2011.

139 **But when they saw:** Obama administration official in discussion with the author, March 2, 2011.

139 **"unprecedented":** Avi Issacharoff and Barak Ravid, "In Jerusalem, Clinton Hails 'Unprecedented' Israeli Settlement Concessions," *Haaretz*, November 1, 2009, available at http://www.haaretz.com/news/in-jerusalem-clinton-hails-unprecedented -israeli-settlement-concessions-1.5060.

139 **"because we failed":** Al Jazeera Transparency Unit, "Meeting Minutes: Saeb Erekat and George Mitchell, October 2, 2009," Al Jazeera, available at http://transparency .aljazeera.net/document/4844.

139 **not launch high-profile:** Al Jazeera Transparency Unit, "Meeting Summary: Saeb Erekat and George Mitchell, October 1, 2009," Al Jazeera, available at http://trans parency.aljazeera.net/files/4842.pdf.

139 **"need to get flustered":** Ben Smith and Laura Rozen, "U.S. Officials: Mideast Talks on Track," Politico, September 24, 2009, available at http://www.politico.com/news /stories/0909/27540.html.

139 **"Obama was a paper tiger":** Akiva Eldar in discussion with the author, February 27, 2011.

140 **neighborhood of Gilo:** Lara Friedman and Danny Seidemann, "Bibi Goes Nuclear on Jerusalem Settlements," Americans for Peace Now, November 17, 2009, available at http://peacenow.org/entries/bibi_goes_nuclear_on_jerusalem_settle- ments; Isabel Kershner, "Plan to Expand Jerusalem Settlement Angers U.S.," *The New York Times*, November 17, 2009, available at http://www.nytimes.com/2009/ 11/18/world/middleeast/18mideast.html.

140 **Har Homa, which particularly:** Lara Friedman, "With New Tenders, Bibi Goes Nuclear on Jerusalem (Again)," available at Americans for Peace Now, December 29, 2009, http://peacenow.org/entries/bibi_goes_nuclear_on_jerusalem_ again.

140 **Finally, in early March:** Hussein Ibish in discussion with the author, March 8, 2011.

140 **"or prejudice the outcome":** Janine Zacharia, "Biden Visits Middle East; Israel and Palestinians Agree to Indirect Talks," *The Washington Post*, March 9, 2010, available at http://www.washingtonpost.com/wp-dyn/content/article/2010/03/08/AR2010030801989.html.

140 **"condemn[ed] the decision":** The White House Office of the Vice President, "Statement by Vice President Joseph R. Biden, Jr.," March 9, 2010, available at http://www.whitehouse.gov/the-press-office/statement-vice-president-joseph-r-biden -jr; "Biden Says Palestinians Deserve 'Viable' State," YNet News, March 10, 2010, available at http://www.ynetnews.com/articles/0,7340,L-3860713,00.html; Laura Rozen, "Biden Israel Speech Invites," Politico, March 9, 2010, available at http://www.politico.com/blogs/laurarozen/0310/Biden_Israel_speech_invites.html.

140 **Biden gave a conciliatory:** The White House Office of the Vice President, "Remarks by Vice President Biden: The Enduring Partnership Between the United States and Israel," March 11, 2010, available at http://www.whitehouse.gov/the-press-office/remarks-vice-president-biden-enduring-partnership-between-united-states-and -israel.

140 **the Israelis promised:** Administration official in discussion with the author, August 18, 2011.

140 **Clinton harangued:** Mark Landler, "Clinton Rebukes Israel on Housing Announcement," *New York Times*, March 12, 2010, available at http://www.nytimes.com/2010/03/13/world/middleeast/13diplo.html.

140 **called it "an insult":** Harry Siegel, "Ax: Israel Announcement 'An Insult,'" Politico, March 14, 2010, available at http://www.politico.com/blogs/politicolive/0310/Axel-rod_Israeli_settlements_an_affront.html.

141 **courtesy of a joint press conference:** Laura Rozen and Ben Smith, "After Meeting, Deafening Silence," Politico, March 23, 2010, available at http://www.politico.com /news/stories/0310/34914.html.

141 **"Bibi's coalition's red lines":** Laura Rozen, "Fierce Debate on Israel Underway Inside Obama Administration," Politico, March 28, 2010, available at http://www.politico.com/blogs/laurarozen/0310/Fierce_debate_on_Israel_underway_inside _Obama_administration.html.

141 **"a ruthless campaign":** Close observer of the Obama administration in discussion with the author, March 15, 2011.

141 **wary of doing so:** Washington Middle East expert in discussion with the author, February 10, 2011; official at a Jewish organization in discussion with the author, March 10, 2011.

141 **hurting donations:** Democratic strategist in discussion with the author, March 8, 2011.

141 **"to defuse current tensions":** Stephanie Condon, "Schumer: Obama's Israel Policy 'Counter-Productive,'" CBS News, April 23, 2010, available at http://www.cbsnews .com/8301-503544_162-20003254-503544.html.

141 **"least pro-Israel president":** Washington Middle East expert in discussion with the author, March 1, 2011.

141 **Israeli officials called:** Source close to the White House in discussion with the author, June 3, 2011.

141 **gave way to direct talks:** Daniel Seidemann (attorney, founder and director of Terrestrial Jerusalem) in discussion with the author, March 10, 2011; former senior

administration official who worked closely with George Mitchell in discussion with the author, March 1, 2011.

142   **safeguard Israeli security:** Dore Gold in discussion with the author, October 24, 2011.

142   **refused to read the documents:** Saeb Erekat (chief Palestinian negotiator) in discussion with the author, October 19, 2011; source close to the White House in discussion with the author, June 3, 2011; senior administration official in discussion with the author, June 17, 2011; administration official in discussion with the author, August 18, 2011; former senior administration official who worked closely with George Mitchell in discussion with the author, March 7, 2011; Dan Ephron, "16 Hours in September," *Newsweek*, December 11, 2010, available at http://www.news week.com/2010/12/11/exclusive-details-on-mideast-peace-negotiations.html; Didi Remez, " 'Rejectionist Front': *Maariv* Details Netanyahu's Refusal to Directly Negotiate with PA," *Coteret*, January 3, 2011, available at http://coteret.com/2011/01/03/rejectionist-front-maariv-details-netanyahus-refusal-to-directly-negotiate-with -pa/; Lara Friedman, "Obama, Abbas, and Calling the 'Direct Talks' Bluff," *Foreign Policy*, July 30, 2010, available at http://mideast.foreignpolicy.com/posts/2010/07/30/obama_abbas_and_calling_the_direct_talks_bluff.

142   **no more public fights:** Administration official in discussion with the author, August 18, 2011.

143   **margin between Jews and other:** Frank Newport, "Muslims Give Obama Highest Job Approval; Mormons, Lowest," Gallup, August 27, 2010, available at http://www .gallup.com/poll/142700/muslims-give-obama-highest-job-approval-mormons -lowest.aspx.

143   **76 percent of the Jewish vote:** A different poll by the Republican Jewish Coalition found the Democratic candidate in Pennsylvania, Joe Sestak, winning only 62 percent of the Jewish vote. But it reached that lower number by polling only Jews who were affiliated with synagogues, a population that leans further right than the Jewish population overall. [Ron Kampeas, "First Sign of the New U.S. Political Reality—Bibi's Swagger," JTA, November 8, 2010, available at http://jta .org/news/article/2010/11/08/2741656/first-sign-of-the-new-us-political-reality -bibis-swagger.]

143   **"screwed up the messaging":** Herb Keinon, "Emanuel to Rabbis: US 'Screwed Up,' " *The Jerusalem Post*, May 16, 2010, available at http://www.jpost.com/International/Article.aspx?id=175654.

143   **a precondition for talks:** A Washington-based Jewish organizational official in discussion with the author, March 15, 2011.

143   **"the manifestations of the change":** Keinon, "Emanuel to Rabbis."

144   **never request another extension:** Laura Rozen, "Benjamin Netanyahu Takes U.S. Offer to His Cabinet," Politico, November 14, 2010, available at http://www.politico .com/news/stories/1110/45095.html; Guttman, "Latest Chapter in Mideast Tension Is Dennis Ross vs. George Mitchell."

144   **"for more than 40 years":** Daniel Kurtzer, "With Settlement Deal, U.S. Will Be Rewarding Israel's Bad Behavior," *The Washington Post*, November 21, 2010, available at http://www.washingtonpost.com/wp-dyn/content/article/2010/11/19/AR2010111903000.html.

8. The Humbling

145 **White House abandoned its effort:** Former senior administration official who worked closely with George Mitchell in discussion with the author, March 7, 2011.

145 **"The new Republican majority":** Laura Rozen, "Before Clinton Meeting, Cantor's One-on-One with Bibi," Politico, November 11, 2010, available at http://www.politico .com/blogs/laurarozen/1110/Before_Clinton_meeting_Cantors_oneonone_with _Bibi_.html.

146 **borrowed from:** Associated Press, "Palestinians Target Settlements in UN Resolution," *The Jerusalem Post*, December 29, 2010, available at http://www.jpost.com/ MiddleEast/Article.aspx?id=201456&R=R3; Dan Ephron, "The Wrath of Abbas," *Newsweek*, April 24, 2011, available at http://www.thedailybeast.com/newsweek/ 2011/04/24/the-wrath-of-abbas.html.

146 **cared about their own plight:** Administration official in discussion with the author, August 18, 2011.

146 **the Obama administration promised:** Ibid.

146 **The White House denied:** Ephron, "The Wrath of Abbas."

147 **Anti-American protests broke out:** Harriet Sherwood, "Palestinians Plan 'Day of Rage' After US Vetoes Resolution on Israeli Settlements," *The Guardian*, February 20, 2011, available at http://www.guardian.co.uk/world/2011/feb/20/palestinians -day-rage-us-veto; Joel Greenberg, "Palestinians Protest U.S. Veto of Resolution Condemning Israel's Settlement Policy," *The Washington Post*, February 20, 2011, available at http://www.washingtonpost.com/wp-dyn/content/article/2011/02/AR 2011022002203.html.

147 **in September to request international:** Ali Swafata, "Arab League to Seek U.N. Seat for Palestinian State," Reuters, May 28, 2011, available at http://www.reuters .com/article/2011/05/28/us-palestinians-israel-arabs-idUSTRE74R10A20110528.

148 **too ferocious to bear:** White House official in discussion with the author, June 17, 2011; administration official in discussion with the author, August 18, 2011.

148 **the statehood bid:** Ibid.

148 **invited Netanyahu to address:** JTA, "Boehner to Invite Netanyahu to Address Congress," *The Jewish Week*, April 14, 2011, available at http://www.thejewishweek .com/news/national/boehner_invite_netanyahu_address_congress; Laura Rozen, "Obama and Netanyahu Meet Amid Tensions," The Envoy, May 20, 2011, available at http://news.yahoo.com/blogs/envoy/obama-netanyahu-meet-amid-tensions -204042879.html; Helene Cooper, "Obama and Netanyahu, Distrustful Allies, Meet," *The New York Times*, May 19, 2011, available at http://www.nytimes.com/2011/05/20/ world/middleeast/20policy.html?pagewanted=all.

148 **"more influence on Capitol Hill":** Administration official in discussion with the author, July 14, 2010.

149 **they left the Israel section blank:** White House official in discussion with the author, June 17, 2011.

149 **wanted Obama to rule out:** Ibid.

149 **rampant in the Israeli press:** Washington insider in discussion with the author, September 27, 2011.

150 **"unrealistic to expect":** Israel Ministry of Foreign Affairs, "Letter from US President George W. Bush to Prime Minister Ariel Sharon."

150   **violation of the tradition:** Herb Keinon, "Analysis: What Rankled Netanyahu in the Obama Speech," *The Jerusalem Post*, May 20, 2011, available at http://www.jpost .com/DiplomacyAndPolitics/Article.aspx?id=221485.

150   **"The international community is tired":** White House Office of the Press Secretary, "Remarks by the President on the Middle East and North Africa," U.S. State Department, May 19, 2011, available at http://www.whitehouse.gov/the-press-office/ 2011/05/19/remarks-president-middle-east-and-north-africa.

150   **"we can deal positively":** Reuters, "Abbas: Palestinians Have No Wish to Isolate Israel," *Haaretz*, May 27, 2011, available at http://www.haaretz.com/news/diplomacy -defense/abbas-palestinians-have-no-wish-to-isolate-israel-1.364481.

151   **"Netanyahu expects":** "Statement by PM Netanyahu on Address by US President Obama," May 19, 2011, available at http://www.mfa.gov.il/MFA/Government/Com- muniques/2011/PM_Netanyahu_US_President_Obama_speech_19-May-2011.htm.

151   **better translated as:** Ron Dermer (aide to Prime Minister Netanyahu) in discussion with the author, October 25, 2011.

151   **construction in Har Homa:** Christi Parsons, Paul Richter, and Edmund Sanders, "A Blunt Push for Peace," *Los Angeles Times*, May 20, 2011, available at http://arti cles.latimes.com/2011/may/20/world/la-fg-obama-mideast-20110520.

151   **private meeting:** Associated Press, "Netanyahu: 1967 Lines Indefensible," YNet News, May 20, 2011, available at http://www.ynetnews.com/articles/0,7340,L-4071641,00 .html.

151   **"can't go back to those indefensible":** "Obama Gets Netanyahu Israeli History Lecture. Transcript." *Chicago Sun-Times—The Scoop from Washington*, May 20, 2011, available at http://blogs.suntimes.com/sweet/2011/05/obama_gets_netanyahu_ israeli_h.html.

152   **"the dignity of the office":** Administration official in discussion with the author, June 17, 2011.

152   **expressed their deep displeasure:** Associate of Netanyahu in discussion with the author, January 16, 2012.

152   **White House refused:** Administration official in discussion with the author, June 17, 2011.

152   **the word "expects":** Administration official in discussion with the author, October 4, 2011.

152   **president's supporters no instructions:** White House official in discussion with the author, June 17, 2011.

152   **One White House ally:** Source close to the White House in discussion with the author, June 3, 2011.

152   **"an ambush":** Josh Gerstein, "Barack Obama, Benjamin Netanyahu Meet Amid Fresh U.S.-Israeli Tension," Politico, May 20, 2011, available at http://www.politico .com/news/stories/0511/55362_Page3.html.

152   **Thirty senators:** Scott Wong, "Lieberman Rolls Out Pro-Israel Resolution," Po- litico, June 10, 2011, available at http://www.politico.com/blogs/glennthrush/0611/ Lieberman_rolls_out_proIsrael_resolution.html.

152   **his sister, a Hebrew school teacher:** Administration official in discussion with the author, June 17, 2011.

152   **gloating e-mails from American Jewish:** White House official in discussion with the author, June 17, 2011.

153   **"account for the changes"**: "Transcript of Obama's Remarks to AIPAC," Washington Wire, May 22, 2011, available at http://blogs.wsj.com/washwire/2011/05/22/tran script-of-obamas-remarks-to-aipac.

153   **a standing ovation:** AIPAC, "Senate Majority Leader Harry Reid (D-NV)," AIPAC Policy Conference: Speeches, May 21–22, 2011, available at http://www.aipac.org/PC/webPlayer/2011-monday-reid.asp.

153   **extensive polling:** Washington insider in discussion with the author, September 27, 2011.

154   **"strategic and national importance"**: "Transcript: Israeli Prime Minister Netanyahu Address to Congress," *The Washington Post*, May 24, 2011, available at http://www.washingtonpost.com/world/israeli-prime-minister-binyamin -netanyahus-address-to- congress/2011/05/24/AFWY5bAH_story.html.

154   **signaling them to stand:** Hadar Susskind in discussion with the author, September 23, 2011.

154   **"cartoon scene":** White House official in discussion with the author, June 17, 2011.

154   **"big-time Jewish problem":** John Heilemann, "The Tsuris," *New York*, September 18, 2011, available at http://nymag.com/print/?/news/politics/israel-2011-9/.

155   **"$10 million evaporated":** Adam Kredo, "The Best of Frenemies?—Reality Check on the President's 'Jewish Problem,'" *Washington Jewish Week,* June 1, 2011, available at http://washingtonjewishweek.com/main.asp?SectionID=4&SubSectionID =4&ArticleID=15017.

155   **not narrowed at all:** Frank Newport, "Jewish Support for Obama Down, but Not Disproportionately," Gallup, September 16, 2011, available at http://www .gallup.com/poll/149522/jewish-support-obama-down-not-disproportionately .aspx.

155   **time to get reelected:** Washington insider in discussion with the author, September 27, 2011; source close to the White House in discussion with the author, September 27, 2011.

155   **only effective validators:** David Paul Kuhn, "Obama Doesn't Have a 'Jewish Problem'—He Has a People Problem," *The Atlantic*, September 17, 2011, available at http://www.theatlantic.com/politics/archive/2011/09/obama-doesnt-have-a-jewish -problem-he-has-a-people-problem/245250; Jewish Democratic strategist in discussion with the author, September 23, 2011.

155   **"hardly remember . . . a better":** Ami Eden, "Axelrod: Barack Is Great for Israel. Just Ask Barak!" [video], JTA—Capital J, August 5, 2011, available at http://blogs.jta .org/politics/article/2011/08/05/3088870/axelrod-barack-is-great-for-israel-just-ask -barak.

155   **"never had a better friend":** "We've Never had a Better Friend Than President Obama" [video], BarackObama.com, September 16, 2011, available at http://www .barackobama.com/news/weve-never-had-a-better-friend-than-president -obama.

155   **transcript of Netanyahu praising:** "Netanyahu's Transcript Detailing Israel Embassy Evacuation in Egypt," Journal of a Business and Social Entrepreneur, September 12, 2011, available at http://blog.peaceworks.net/2011/09/netanyahus-transcript -detailing-israel-embassy-evacuation-in-egypt/.

156   **Israel against the world:** Laura Rozen, "Obama Envoys Hope 'Quartet Statement' Can Avert Palestinian UN Bid," The Envoy, September 14, 2011, available at http://

news.yahoo.com/blogs/envoy/obama-envoys-hope-quartet-statement-reduce-u -isolation-201333519.html; Daniel Levy, "America's Attempted Quartet Sophistry," *Foreign Policy*, July 22, 2011, available at http://mideast.foreignpolicy.com/posts /2011/07/22/palestine_israel_the_un_and_america_s_attempted_quartet_sophistry; Josh Rogin, "Team Obama Pushes New Quartet Statement to Avoid Palestinian U.N. Bid," *Foreign Policy*, September 16, 2011, available at http://thecable.foreign policy.com/posts/2011/09/16/team_obama_pushes_new_quartet_statement_to _avoid_palestinian_un_bid; Arshad Mohammed, "Issue of Israel as Jewish State Sank Quartet Moves," Reuters, September 26, 2011, available at http://uk.reuters .com/article/2011/09/26/uk-palestinians-israel-quartet-idUKTRE 78P1JB20110926.

156 **"sometimes I feel like":** Source close to the White House in discussion with the author, September 27, 2011.

157 **pushed ahead at the UN:** Administration official in discussion with the author, October 5, 2011; Saeb Erekat in discussion with the author, October 19, 2011.

157 **"lose an ally":** Turki Al-Faisal, "Veto a State, Lose an Ally," *The New York Times*, September 11, 2011, available at http://www.nytimes.com/2011/09/12/opinion/veto -a-state-lose-an-ally.html.

157 **"architect of Middle East peacemaking":** Helene Cooper and Steven Lee Myers, "Obama Rebuffed as Palestinians Pursue Statehood," *The New York Times*, September 21, 2011, available at http://www.nytimes.com/2011/09/22/world/obama -rebuffed-as-palestinians-pursue-un-seat.html?pagewanted=all.

157 **did not mention settlements:** Glenn Kessler, "The Education of President Obama," The Washington Post—The Fact Checker, September 22, 2011, available at http:// www.washingtonpost.com/blogs/fact-checker/post/the-education-of-president -obama-at-the-un/2011/09/21/gIQAmvwolK_blog.html.

158 **Obama perfectly echoed:** "Full Transcript of Obama's Speech at UN General Assembly," *Haaretz*, September 21, 2011, available at http://www.haaretz.com/news/ diplomacy-defense/full-transcript-of-obama-s-speech-at-un-general-assembly -1.385820.

158 **"appeared as though they were faxed":** Yitzhak Benhorin, "Obama Is Israel's Friend," YNet News, September 22, 2011, available at http://www.ynetnews.com/ articles/0,7340,L-4126147,00.html.

158 **among Jewish leaders:** Orly Azoulay, "Obama Courts Jewish Vote with UN Speech," Ynet News, September 22, 2011, available at http://www.ynetnews.com/articles/ 0,7340,L4125962,00.html.

158 **now gushed with praise:** Natasha Mozgovaya, "U.S. Jews Give Obama Mixed Reviews for 'Pro-Israel' UN Speech," *Haaretz*, September 22, 2011, available at http://www.haaretz.com/misc/article-print-page/u-s-jews-give-obama-mixed- reviews-for-pro-israel-un-speech-1.386043?trailingPath=2.169%2C2.216%2C2 .217%2C; AIPAC, "President Obama's Mideast Policy Speech: An Assessment," May 2011.

158 **"with both hands":** Mozgovaya, "U.S. Jews Give Obama Mixed Reviews."

158 **"great closing of the ranks":** "An Hour with Benjamin Netanyahu, Prime Minister of Israel" [video], *Charlie Rose*, September 26, 2011, available at http://www .charlierose.com/view/interview/11912.

158 **anti-Obama protests:** "Palestinians Blast Obama's UN Speech at West Bank Rally," *Haaretz*, September 22, 2011, available at http://www.haaretz.com/news/diplomacy-defense/palestinians-blast-obama-s-un-speech-at-west-bank-rally-1.386076.

158 **Palestinians now hated:** Larry Derfner, "Last Week at the UN, Israel Lost America," +972, September 24, 2011, available at http://972mag.com/last-week-at-the-un-israel-lost-america/23917/.

158 **United States could no longer serve:** Avi Issacharoff, "Abbas Will Head Home with Little to Show," *Haaretz*, September 23, 2011, available at http://www.haaretz.com/print-edition/news/abbas-will-head-home-with-little-to-show-1.386148.

159 **"Make me do it":** Amy Goodman, "Goodman: Make Obama Keep His Promises," *Seattle Post-Intelligencer*, January 21, 2009, available at http://www.seattlepi.com/opinion/396961_amy22.html; Max Pizarro, "Obama Coming to New Jersey," Politicker NJ, May 8, 2007, available at http://www.politickernj.com/obama-coming-new-jersey-8142.

9. The Future

160 **man in his sixties:** As of 2011, the ADL's Abraham Foxman was seventy-one, the Presidents' Conference's Malcolm Hoenlein was sixty-seven, the American Jewish Committee's David Harris was sixty-two, and AIPAC's Howard Kohr was fifty-six.

160 **"ADL's big supporters are eighty-year-olds":** Former ADL staffer in discussion with the author, April 29, 2011.

160 **"at the old-age home":** Prominent Jewish journalist in discussion with the author, December 20, 2010.

161 **Holocaust survivor:** ADL, "Biography of Abraham H. Foxman," available at http://www.adl.org/education/holocaust/foxman_bio.asp.

161 **children of Holocaust survivors:** Michael Freund, "Talking with Malcolm Hoenlein," Jewish Action Online, Spring 2007, available at http://www.ou.org/index.php/jewish_action/article/10099/; Subcommittee on State, Foreign Operations, and Related Programs, "Bio for Howard Kohr, Executive Director, AIPAC," available at http://appropriations.house.gov/_files/041411AIPACBio.pdf; ZOA, "National President Morton A. Klein," available at http://www.zoa.org/content/klein.asp.

161 **savagely beaten by Catholic boys:** Tom Dine in discussion with the author, January 10, 2011.

161 **twice detained by Soviet authorities:** AJC, "AJC Experts: David Harris," available at http://www.ajc.org/site/c.ijITI2PHKoG/b.817851/k.2E7F/AJC_Experts.htm.

161 **"it's not 1967 anymore, dude":** Jodi Ochstein in discussion with the author, November 23, 2010.

161 **share a laugh:** Former ADL staffer in discussion with the author, April 29, 2011, and June 10, 2011.

161 **"very serious problem":** Jacob B. Ukeles, Ron Miller, and Pearl Beck, "Young Jewish Adults in the United States Today," AJC, September 2006, available at http://www.ajc.org/atf/cf/%7B42D75369-D582-4380-8395-D25925B85EAF%7D/YoungJewishAdultsUS_102006.pdf.

162   **family pushing a stroller:** Samuel Heilman, *Sliding to the Right: The Contest for the Future of American Jewish Orthodoxy* (Los Angeles: University of California Press, 2006), 68–69.

162   **Orthodox get married younger:** Ukeles, Miller, and Beck, "Young Jewish Adults in the United States Today"; Chaim Waxman, "The Haredization of American Orthodox Jewry," *Jerusalem Letters*, February 15, 1998, available at http://www.jcpa .org/cjc/jl-376-waxman.htm.

162   **how dramatically the demography:** Jack Wertheimer, "The American Synagogue— Recent Trends and Issues," AJC, 2005, available at http://www.bjpa.org/Publications/ details.cfm?PublicationID=3178; Heilman, *Sliding to the Right*, 62–63.

162   **"Modern Orthodox," which means:** Heilman, *Sliding to the Right*, 76.

162   **more intensely committed to Israel:** As opposed to Europe, where many Ortho- dox Jews initially opposed a Jewish state created by human beings and not God, American Orthodox Jews, and especially American Modern Orthodox Jews, have been generally sympathetic to Zionism since the Zionist movement began. [Chaim Waxman (professor emeritus at Rutgers University) in discussion with the author, September 25, 2011.]

162   **Among Jews under forty:** Theodore Sasson, Charles Kadushin, and Leonard Saxe, "American Jewish Attachment to Israel: An Assessment of the 'Distancing' Hypothesis," Steinhardt Social Research Institute, February 2008, available at http://bir.brandeis.edu/bitstream/handle/10192/23015/IsraelAttach.030308.22.pdf? sequence=1.

163   **Orthodox Jewish schools where Israel:** Heilman, *Sliding to the Right*, 94.

163   **instilling devotion than critical thought:** In many American Jewish schools, the Israel curriculum is subcontracted to the David Project, which not only teaches students about the history of the Jewish state, but also teaches them how to advocate for it when they reach college. [The David Project, "Curriculum Online," available at http://www.thedavidproject.org/index.php?option=com_content& view=article&id=289:curriculum-outline&catid=8&Itemid=24; Alex Pomson, "A Sense of Distance Through the Classroom Window," *Contemporary Jewry* 30, no. 264 (2010), available at http://www.contemporaryjewry.org/resources/19 _pomson.pdf.]

163   **classes are named for Israeli cities:** The school is Ramaz on Manhattan's Upper East Side. The example of a clock set to Israeli time comes from the Ramaz middle school, June 4, 2011.

163   **Orthodox share of Americans who immigrate:** Shalom Z. Berger, Daniel Jacob- son, and Chaim I. Waxman, *Flipping Out—Myth or Fact: The Impact of the "Year in Israel"* (Brooklyn: Yashar Books, 2007), 17, 179, 181.

163   **denied permission to leave work:** Prominent Jewish journalist in discussion with the author, December 20, 2010.

163   **did not consistently serve kosher:** Keith Weissman (senior Middle East analyst in AIPAC's Foreign Policy Issues department from 1993 to 2005) in discussion with the author, March 13, 2011.

163   **first Orthodox president:** "OU Congratulates Its Long-Time Lay Leader Howard Tzvi Friedman on Swearing In as AIPAC President," March 7, 2006, available at http://www.ou.org/oupr/2006/friedman66.htm.

163   **AIPAC's . . . High School Summit:** Two former AIPAC student activists in discussion with the author, June 3, 2011, and June 4, 2011.

164   **close to twice the figure:** Ukeles, Miller, and Beck, "Young Jewish Adults in the United States Today."

164   **deny any commonality of interests:** Theodore Sasson, "The New Realism: American Jews' Views About Israel," AJC, June 2009, 14–15, available at http://www.ajc .org/atf/cf/%7B42d75369-d582–4380–8395-d25925b85eaf%7D/THENEWREALISM _SASSON.pdf.

164   **"Esau hates Jacob":** Orthodox educator in discussion with the author, March 10, 2011.

165   **God was punishing Asian governments:** Haaretz Service, "Eliyahu: Tsunami Was God's Punishment for Disengagement," *Haaretz*, January 31, 2005, available at http://www.haaretz.com/news/eliyahu-tsunami-was-god-s-punishment-for -disengagement-1.148753; Anshel Pfeffer, "Rabbi Mordechai Eliyahu—an Eloquent Racist," *Haaretz*, June 11, 2010, available at http://www.haaretz.com/print-edition/ news/anshel-pfeffer-rabbi-mordechai-eliyahu-an-eloquent-racist-1.295498; Zertal and Eldar, *Lords of the Land*, 395.

165   **"love and care toward every other Jew":** Rabbi Avi Berman, "Personal Reflections on a True Gadol," Orthodox Union, available at http://www.ou.org/index.php/ou/ print_this/70668/.

165   **too high a percentage:** Steward Ain, "Surprise! Jewish Charity Money Earmarked for Post-War Recovery in Israel Going to Arabs," *Jewish World Review*, October 12, 2006, available at http://www.jewishworldreview.com/1006/money_for_arabs .php3; Rebecca Spence, "Charity Hits Back in Feud over Arab Aid," *The Jewish Daily Forward*, October 20, 2006, available at http://www.forward.com/articles/ 5943/.

165   **publicly proposed disenfranchising:** Efrat Weiss, "Eitam: Expel Palestinians, Dismiss Arab MKs," YNet News, September 11, 2006, available at http://www .ynetnews.com/articles/0,7340,L-3302275,00.html; "14th Annual Dr. Manfred R. Lehmann Memorial Israel Day Concert," May 6, 2007, available at http://www .israeldayconcert.com/press/idc_poster_07.pdf.

165   **"'mutually responsible' for every other Jew":** Rabbi Pesach Lerner, "We Cannot Let a Yeshiva/Shul in Israel Be Destroyed," weekly e-mail update from National Council of Young Israel, May 25, 2010, available at http://www.youngisrael.org/ content/odyosef.cfm.

166   **"if they are allowed to grow":** Mohamad Alasmar, "Paying for the 'Price-Tag' Policy," *The Jerusalem Post*, August 19, 2010, available at http://new.jpost.com/ Opinion/Op-EdContributors/Article.aspx?id=185198; Noam Sheizaf, "Yitzhar Rabbi Publicly Supporting Attacks on Palestinians," Promised Land Blog, May 20, 2010, available at http://www.promisedlandblog.com/?tag=yitzhar; JTA, "Rabbi's Book Says Jews Can Kill Gentiles," November 9, 2009, available at http://www.jta .org/news/article/2009/11/09/1009034/rabbis-book-says-jews-can-kill-gentiles; Akiva Eldar, "U.S. Tax Dollars Fund Rabbi Who Excused Killing Gentile Babies," *Haaretz*, December 15, 2009, available at http://www.haaretz.com/print-edition/ features/akiva-eldar-u-s-tax-dollars-fund-rabbi-who-excused-killing-gentile-ba bies-1.2137.

166   **"Orthodox global village":** Berger, Jacobson, and Waxman, *Flipping Out*, 168.

166   **Yigal Amir took Rabin's life:** Shmulik Grossman, "Goldstein Legacy Continues," YNet News, February 26, 2010, available at http://www.ynetnews.com/articles/0,7340,L-3854982,00.html; Ehud Sprinzak, "Extremism and Violence in Israel: The Crisis of Messianic Politics," *Annals of the American Academy of Political and Social Science* 555 (January 1998): 121, 123, available at http://www.jstor.org/stable/1049215; Ehud Sprinzak, "Israel's Radical Right and the Countdown to the Rabin Assassination," in Yoram Peri, ed., *The Assassination of Yitzhak Rabin* (Stanford, Calif.: Stanford University Press, 2000), 124; Pedahzur and Perliger, *Jewish Terrorism in Israel*, 98–110.

167   **Schachter later apologized:** Matthew Wagner, "YU Rabbi Apologizes for Anti-Olmert Jab," *The Jerusalem Post*, March 10, 2008, available at http://www.jpost.com/International/Article.aspx?id=94527.

167   **Jewish law is silent:** Rabbi Joseph B. Soloveitchik, "On Israel, the Diaspora and Religious Issues," September 15, 1975, in Joseph B. Soloveitchik, *Community, Covenant and Commitment: Selected Letters and Communications*, ed. Nathaniel Helfgot (Jersey City, N.J.: Ktav, 2005), 236; Shalom Carmy, " 'The Heart Pained by the Pain of the People': Rabbinic Leadership in Two Discussions by R. Joseph B. Soloveitchik," *Torah u-Madda Journal* 13 (2005): 10, available at http://www.yutorah.org/lectures/lecture.cfm/715601/Rabbi_Shalom_Carmy/01_'The_Heart_Pained_by_the_Pain_of_the_People':_Rabbinic_Leadership_in_Two_Discussions_by_R_Joseph_B_Soloveitchik.

167   **giving back the Western Wall itself:** Rabbi Michael J. Broyde, "If I Forget Thee, O Jerusalem!" Hirhurim—Musings, December 5, 2007, available at http://hirhurim.blogspot.com/2007/12/if-i-forget-thee-o-jerusalem.html.

167   **"overrides the entire Torah":** Soloveitchik, "On Israel, the Diaspora and Religious Issues," 235.

167   **Soloveitchik warned that unless Mizrachi:** Chaim I. Waxman, "If I Forget Thee O Jerusalem . . . : The Impact of Israel on American Orthodox Jewry," in Chaim I. Waxman, ed., *Religious Zionism Post-Disengagement: Future Directions* (New York: Yeshiva University Press, 2008), 422, available at http://www.scribd.com/doc/31264057/Untitled.

167   **"any interest in any other religion:"** Heilman, *Sliding to the Right*, 58–59.

167   **sharp departure from Soloveitchik's:** Soloveitchik did support some barriers to intellectual exploration of the non-Jewish world. He opposed, for instance, theological dialogue between Jews and gentiles. Still, he himself read—and was influenced by—Christian theologians.

168   **still Modern Orthodox rabbis:** Among the most prominent such rabbis are Michael Melchior, the founder of the liberal Orthodox party, Meimad, and Rabbi Aharon Liechtenstein, rosh yeshiva of Yeshiva Har Etzion in the West Bank settlement of Alon Shvut.

168   **70 percent Orthodox:** James D. Besser, "Pulling It Off: Pro-Israel Rally at Capitol," *The Jewish Week*, April 19, 2002, available at http://www.thejewishweek.com/features/pulling_it_proisrael_rally_capitol.

168   **"innocent Palestinians are suffering":** Frank Rich, "The Booing of Wolfowitz," *The New York Times*, May 11, 2002, available at http://www.nytimes.com/2002/05/11/opinion/the-booing-of-wolfowitz.html?pagewanted=all&src=pm.

169   **troubled Jewish sociologists and philanthropists:** See, for instance, Stephen M. Cohen, "Ties and Tensions: The 1986 Survey of American Jewish Attitudes Toward Israel and Israelis," American Jewish Committee, 1987, available at http://www .bjpa.org/Publications/details.cfm?PublicationID=2704; Steven M. Cohen, "Ties and Tensions: An Update—The 1989 Survey of American Jewish Attitudes Toward Israel and the Israelis," American Jewish Committee, July 1989, available at http:// www.bjpa.org/Publications/details.cfm?PublicationID=167.

169   **than half as likely as other Americans:** Tom W. Smith, "Jewish Distinctiveness in America: A Statistical Report," AJC, April 2005, available at http://www.ajc.org/atf/ cf/%7B42D75369-D582-4380-8395-D25925B85EAF%7D/JewishDistinctiveness America_TS_April2005.pdf.

169   **For Jews marrying today:** Steven M. Cohen, "A Tale of Two Jewries: The 'Inconvenient Truth' for American Jews," Steinhardt Foundation for Jewish Life, November 2006, available at http://www.bjpa.org/Publications/details.cfm?PublicationID =2908; "Rates of Intermarriage," *The National Jewish Population Survey 2000–2001*, September 2003, available at http://www.jewishfederations.org/page.aspx?id=46253.

170   **McDonald's now serves:** McDonald's, "Elevating the Bagel to New Heights," available at http://www.mcdonalds.com/content/ca/en/menu/full_menu/breakfast/ bacon_egg_cheese_bagel.html.

170   **which she pronounced "choot-spa":** Natasha Lennard, "Michele Bachmann Can't Pronounce 'Chutzpah,'" War Room, July 14, 2010, available at http://www.salon .com/news/politics/war_room/2011/07/14/bachmann_yiddish_chutzpah.

170   **young Barack Obama read Saul Alinsky:** Peter Slevin, "For Clinton and Obama, a Common Ideological Touchstone," *The Washington Post*, March 25, 2007, available at http://www.washingtonpost.com/wp-dyn/content/article/2007/03/24/ AR2007032401152.html.

170   **"Israel occupies land belonging":** Steven M. Cohen and Ari Y. Kelman, "Beyond Distancing: Young Adult American Jews and Their Alienation from Israel," Jewish Identity Project of Reboot, 2007, available at http://www.bjpa.org/Publications/ details.cfm?PublicationID=326.

171   **Israeli government's account:** Theodore Sasson, Benjamin Phillips, Charles Kadushin, and Leonard Saxe, "Still Connected: American Jewish Attitudes About Israel," Brandeis University Cohen Center for Modern Jewish Studies, August 2010, available at http://www.schusterman.org/wp-content/uploads/Still-Connected -American-Jewish-Attitudes-About-Israel_August-2010.pdf.

171   **"Israel's destruction would be a personal tragedy":** Cohen and Kelman, "Beyond Distancing."

171   **"high" or "very high" salience:** Sam Abrams and Steven M. Cohen, "Israel Off Their Minds: The Diminished Place of Israel in the Political Thinking of Young Jews," Berman Jewish Policy Archive at NYU Wagner, October 27, 2008, available at http://www.bjpa.org/Publications/details.cfm?PublicationID=207.

171   **younger American Jews will become more attached:** See, for instance, Sasson, Phillips, Kadushin, and Saxe, "Still Connected."

171   **as you descend generationally:** Steven M. Cohen and Ari Y. Kelman, "Thinking About Distancing from Israel," *Contemporary Jewry* 30 (2010): 291, available at http://www.contemporaryjewry.org/resources/2_cohen_kelman.pdf.

171   **attachment to Israel over time collapses:** See, for instance, Jack Wertheimer, "Go

Out and See What the People Are Doing," *Contemporary Jewry* 30 (2010): 237, available at http://www.contemporaryjewry.org/resources/14_wertheimer.pdf; Sergio DellaPergola, "Distancing, Yet One," *Contemporary Jewry* 30 (2010): 185, available at http://www.contemporaryjewry.org/resources/7_dellapergola.pdf; Ariela Keysar, "Distancing from Israel: Evidence on Jews of No Religion," *Contemporary Jewry* 30 (2010): 200, available at http://www.contemporaryjewry.org/resources/9_keysar .pdf.

172   **clear "conventional wisdom":** "The Israel Attachment of American Jews: Assessing the Debate," *Contemporary Jewry* 30 (2010): 165, available at http://www.contemporary jewry.org/resources/5_kotler_berkowitz_ament.pdf.

172   **"We're losing them":** Nahum Barnea, "We're Losing Them," YNet News, March 17, 2010, available at http://www.ynetnews.com/articles/0,7340,L-3863066,00.html.

172   **number had almost quadrupled:** Marvin Schick, "A Census of Jewish Day Schools in the United States 2008–2009," Avi Chai Foundation, October 2009, available at http://avichai.org/wp-content/uploads/2010/06/Census-of-JDS-in-the -US-2008-09-Final.pdf; Marvin Schick, "A Census of Jewish Day Schools in the United States 2003–2004," Avi Chai Foundation, January 2005, available at http:// avichai.org/wp-content/uploads/2010/06/Census-of-JDS-in-the-US-2003–04 -Final.pdf.

173   **younger group were almost twice as likely:** Jack Wertheimer, "Generation of Change: How Leaders in Their Twenties and Thirties Are Reshaping American Jewish Life," Avi Chai Foundation, September 2010, available at http://bjpa.org/ Publications/details.cfm?PublicationID=6522.

173   **do not associate with any existing stream of Judaism:** See, for instance, Steven M. Cohen, J. Shawn Landres, Elie Kaunfer, and Michelle Shain, "Emergent Jewish Communities and Their Participants: Preliminary Findings from the 2007 National Spiritual Communities Study," S3K Synagogue Studies Institute, November 2007, available at http://www.bjpa.org/Publications/details.cfm?PublicationID=2828.

173   **there are roughly one hundred:** Elie Kaunfer (cofounder, rosh yeshiva, and executive director of Mechon Hadar) in discussion with the author, October 27, 2011.

173   **Every Friday night and Saturday morning:** While only 29 percent of adult members of American synagogues are under forty, they constitute 81 percent of participants in the independent minyanim. [Cohen, Landres, Kaunfer, and Shain, "Emergent Jewish Communities and Their Participants."]

173   **may begin establishing schools:** Mechon Hadar, "Fourth Independent Minyan Conference in Washington, D.C.," November 4–6, 2011, available at http://www .mechonhadar.org/imconference; Rabbi Elie Kaunfer in discussion with the author, June 10, 2011.

173   **level of religious literacy far beyond:** Forty percent of the participants in independent minyanim attended Jewish day school, compared to 15 percent of regular synagogue members. Sixty-five percent attended Jewish summer camp, compared to 39 percent of regular synagogue goers. [Cohen, Landres, Kaunfer, and Shain, "Emergent Jewish Communities and Their Participants."]

173   **raised Orthodox but desire greater intellectual openness:** The degree to which Orthodoxy will accommodate this yearning for greater equality for women is as yet unknown. The establishment of Yeshivat Chovevei Torah Rabbinical School in 1999—which advocates "open Orthodoxy"—marks an effort to reclaim Modern

Orthodoxy's engagement with the world and to create greater opportunities for women's religious participation. Chovevei's creation means that there is at least a small slice of the self-described Orthodox world whose values and sensibilities resemble those of the independent minyanim. Indeed, some rabbinical students at Chovevei Torah pray at Darkhei Noam, one of the more traditionally oriented independent minyanim. [Yeshivat Chovevei Torah, "History," available at http://www.yctorah.org/content/view/2/49/; student at Yeshivat Chovevei Torah in discussion with the author, April 14, 2011.]

173 **want greater religious commitment:** On the trend toward greater religious observance among committed young Reform Jews, see Sue Fishkoff, "Survey of Active Reform Jews: Under-40 Crowd More Observant," *Jewish Review*, December 7, 2007, available at http://www.jewishreview.org/node/9362.

174 **Jewish organizations that confront injustice:** For more about these organizations and the young Jews who join them, see Wertheimer, "Generation of Change." See also Shifra Bronznick and Didi Goldenhar, "Visioning Justice and the American Jewish Community," Nathan Cummings Foundation, March 2008, available at http://www.nathancummings.org/jewish/vj_final_0428.pdf.

174 **good works as an outgrowth of religious:** The 2008 "Visioning Justice and the American Jewish Community" study notes, "Many emergent spiritual communities and minyanim are making social justice a cornerstone commitment." [Bronznick and Goldenhar, "Visioning Justice and the American Jewish Community."]

174 **"religious traditionalism and social progressivism":** Cohen, Landres, Kaunfer, and Shain, "Emergent Jewish Communities and Their Participants," 4.

174 **"young nonestablishment leaders scoffed":** Wertheimer, "Generation of Change."

174 **"the civil rights movement":** Cohen, Landres, Kaunfer, and Shain, "Emergent Jewish Communities and Their Participants."

174 **"knows it has moral responsibility":** Elie Kaunfer, *Empowered Judaism: What Independent Minyanim Can Teach Us About Building Vibrant Jewish Communities* (Woodstock, Vt.: Jewish Lights Publishing, 2010), 4.

175 **members of independent minyanim marry other Jews:** Wertheimer, "Generation of Change."

175 **almost double the rate:** Ibid., 26.

175 **younger nonestablishment leaders believe:** Ibid., 16; Cohen, Landres, Kaunfer, and Shain, "Emergent Jewish Communities and Their Participants," 29.

176 **the young Jews refused:** Steven M. Cohen, "The Silence of the Jews—Personal Reflections on the Suppression of Israel Engagement," unpublished paper, July 30, 2011.

176 **views about Israel publicly:** Steven M. Cohen, "JTS Rabbis and Israel, Then and Now: The 2011 Survey of JTS Ordained Rabbis and Current Students," available at http://www.jtsa.edu/Documents/pagedocs/Communications/JTS_Rabbis_and_Israel_Then_and_Now_Sept_2_2011_(PDFl).pdf.

177 **compared to 56 percent of the older cohort:** Wertheimer, "Generation of Change," 15.

177 **" 'but Zionism doesn't mean anything to me' ":** Shai Held, "Redemptive Dreams, Stubborn Realities" [video], UStream, March 1, 2011, available at http://www.ustream.tv/recorded/13031537#utm_campaigne=synclickback&source.

177 **"doesn't interest me":** Ibid.

CONCLUSION

178   **"too small for the greatness":** Urofsky, *A Voice That Spoke for Justice*, 279, 369; Israel Ministry of Foreign Affairs, "Declaration of Establishment of the State of Israel."

179   **settler Israel as one and the same:** "Taxes/Decades of Tax Breaks for the Settler Population," *Haaretz*, September 25, 2003, available at http://www.haaretz.com/print-edition/business/taxes-decades-of-tax-breaks-for-the-settler-population-1.101212; Zertal and Eldar, *Lords of the Land*, xv, 51, 113, 312, 314.

179   **result might be civil war:** In his 2011 report, *Imagining the Border: Options for Resolving the Israeli-Palestinian Territorial Issue*, David Makovsky of the Washington Institute for Near East Peace outlines a map that would allow Israel to annex 80.01 percent of the settler population, the percentage that Ehud Barak demanded in 2000 and 2001. Makovsky achieves that by annexing Ariel, Immanuel, Kfar Adumim, Ofra, and Beit El. By way of explanation, he writes that "Bet El holds biblical resonance and, along with Ofra, is home to the national settler movement leadership. This has led many to speculate that annexing these two large communities is pivotal to reaching an overall agreement." The implication is that if Israel does not annex Ofra and Beit El, settler resistance to a two-state deal may be impossible to overcome. Barak himself shared a similar worry. According to his chief of staff, Gilead Sher, "one of Barak's greatest fears was the potential military confrontation with the settlers who would refuse to evacuate." This anxiety is also borne out by polling. In 2005, the year Israel removed fewer than ten thousand settlers from the Gaza Strip (a place far less biblically resonant than the West Bank), almost half of Israeli Jews told Israel's Institute for National Security Strategies that soldiers had the right to refuse orders to dismantle settlements. But while Makovsky's 80 percent map may seem reassuring to Israelis, its Israeli peninsulas deep in the West Bank almost certainly make it anathema to Palestinian leaders. By way of comparison, the 2003 Geneva Agreement—reached by former Israeli and Palestinian negotiators—permits Israel to annex only 55 percent of the settler population, and thus leaves not only Ofra and Beit El, but Ariel, Immanuel, and Kfar Adumim beyond Israel's borders. [David Makovsky, "Imagining the Border: Options for Resolving the Israeli-Palestinian Territorial Issue," Washington Institute Strategic Report, 2011, available at http://washingtoninstitute.org/pubPDFs/StrategicReport06.pdf; Yehuda Ben Meir and Dafna Shaked, "The People Speak: Israeli Public Opinion on National Security, 2005–2007," Institute for National Security Studies, May 2007, available at http://www.inss.org.il/upload/(FILE)1188302092.pdf; Palestinian Peace Coalition and Yes to an Agreement, "The Geneva Accord: Settlements," available at http://www.geneva-accord.org/mainmenu/settlements; Gilead Sher, *The Israeli-Palestinian Peace Negotiations, 1999–2001*, 98, 106, 138.]

180   **a single Palestinian, Arab:** AIPAC, "Breakout Sessions: Sunday I," AIPAC Policy Conference, 2011, available at http://www.aipac.org/pc/breakout1.asp; AIPAC, "Breakout Sessions: Sunday II," AIPAC Policy Conference, 2011, available at http://www.aipac.org/pc/breakout2.asp; AIPAC, "Breakout Sessions: Monday III," AIPAC Policy Conference, 2011, available at http://www.aipac.org/pc/breakout3.asp; AIPAC, "Breakout Sessions: Monday IV," AIPAC Policy Conference, 2011, available at http://www.aipac.org/pc/breakout4.asp.

180   **West Bank's water supply:** On the impact of annexing Ariel on access between the

northern and southern West Bank, see Makovsky, "Imagining the Border," Map 1. On the impact of large-scale annexations on Palestinian access to water, see Rami El Houry, "The Israeli-Palestinian Water Conflict," MUFTAH, October 22, 2010, available at http://muftah.org/?p=366.

181   **AIPAC and Malcolm Hoenlein have feted:** As Hoenlein told a Christians United for Israel crowd in 2006, "I have to admit to you that my rabbi complains that I mention Pastor Hagee more often in my speeches than I do him. I told him that I have a lot of rabbis but only one pastor. And I have developed a great affection for him [Hagee] especially since I came here four years ago and had the opportunity to watch and to help the creation of CUFI." ["Malcolm Hoenlein," October 23, 2006, available at http://www.youtube.com/watch?v=L2StBFl1c8k.]

182   **intermarriage rate among non-Orthodox:** Steven M. Cohen (research professor of Jewish social policy at Hebrew Union College–Jewish Institute of Religion) in discussion with the author, July 24, 2011.

182   **only 7 percent raise their children as Jews:** Steven M. Cohen, "A Tale of Two Jewries, 11.

183   **melting pot ideal is not as strong:** Of the world's large Diaspora communities, perhaps the only one whose assimilationist ethos rivals the United States' is Brazil, where Jews intermarry at close to the rate they do in the United States. [Clare Davidson, "Sao Paulo Broadcasts Jewish Pride in Portuguese," *The Jewish Daily Forward*, December 19, 2003, available at http://www.forward.com/articles/7337/#ixzz1Tze 90Sy7; Jewish People Policy Institute, "Annual Assessment 2010: Executive Report No. 7," 2011, 32, available at http://jppi.org.il/uploads/2010_Annual_Assessment .pdf.]

184   **but to Judaism itself:** Shaul Kelner, *Tours That Bind: Diaspora, Pilgrimage and Israeli Birthright Tourism* (New York: New York University Press, 2010), 5–6.

184   **show a rise in Jewish, and Zionist:** Leonard Saxe, Theodore Sasson, Shahar Hecht, Benjamin Phillips, Michelle Shain, Graham Wright, and Charles Kadushin, "Jewish Futures Project: The Impact of Taglit-Birthright, 2010 Update," Brandeis University, February 2011, available at http://www.brandeis.edu/cmjs/pdfs/jewish %20futures/Jewish.Futures.02.08.11.pdf.

184   **"very much open to question":** Chaim Waxman, "Beyond Distancing: Jewish Identity, Identification and America's Young Jews," *Contemporary Jewry* 30, nos. 2–3 (2010): 231, available at http://www.contemporaryjewry.org/resources/13_wax-man.pdf.

184   **the figure was 96 percent:** Steven M. Cohen and Laurence Kotler-Berkowitz, "The Impact of Childhood Jewish Education on Adults' Jewish Identity: Schooling, Israel Travel, Camping, and Youth Groups," *United Jewish Committee Report Series on the National Jewish Population Survey 2000–2001*, July 2004, available at http:// www.peje.org/docs/ImpactofJewishEducation.pdf.

185   **likelihood of marrying another Jew:** Cohen, "A Tale of Two Jewries," 14.

185   **between 18 and 25 percent of Jewish children attend Jewish schools:** Jewish People Policy Institute, "Annual Assessment 2010: Executive Report No. 7," 32–33; Ukeles, Miller, and Beck, "Young Jewish Adults in the United States Today," 25.

185   **Jewish schools are expensive:** Jack Wertheimer, "Who's Afraid of Jewish Day Schools?" *Commentary*, December 1999, 51, available at http://www.commentary magazine.com/article/whos-afraid-of-jewish-day-schools/.

185 **tuition averages $14,000 a year:** JTA, "Funding Jewish Education—a Self-Sustaining Solution," Jewish Education Service of North America, April 19, 2010, available at http://www.jesna.org/jewish-education-news-blog/item/726-op-ed -funding-jewish-education%E2%80%94a-self-sustaining-solution.

185 **less than a decade old:** Nadine Brozan, "Postings: Heschel School Expanding to West End Avenue and 60th Street: A High School Building for 300," *The New York Times*, November 18, 2001, available at http://www.nytimes.com/2001/11/18/reales-tate/postings-heschel-school-expanding-west-end-avenue-60th-street-high -school.html.

185 **rarely have significant endowments:** Jerome A. Chanes, "Hebrew Language Charter Schools Are a Bad Bargain," *The Jewish Daily Forward*, June 24, 2011, available at http://www.forward.com/articles/138654/#ixzz1RFOqyDo5; Avi Chai Foundation, "Securing Jewish Day Schools for Future Generations," May 3, 2011, available at http://avichai.org/2011/05/securing-jewish-day-schools-for-future-generations/; Wertheimer, "Who's Afraid of Jewish Day Schools," 52.

186 **educating a child in Jewish school:** As Jack Wertheimer notes, a 1999 study found that the average local federation allocates $530 per child to their local Jewish schools. According to a 2010 Jewish Telegraphic Agency article, Jewish school tuition averages $14,000. Thus, even assuming that allocations have increased since 1999, it is unlikely that the federations cover more than 5 percent of the cost of educating a Jewish child. [JTA, "Funding Jewish Education—a Self-Sustaining Solution"; Jack Wertheimer, "Talking Dollars and Sense About Jewish Education," Avi Chai Foundation, August 2001, 7, 9, available at http://avichai.org/wp-content/ uploads/2010/06/Dollars-Sense.pdf.

186 **require an endowment of more than $8 billion:** Wertheimer, "Talking Dollars and Sense About Jewish Education," 10; Jewish Federations of North America, "About Us," available at http://www.jewishfederations.org/about-us.aspx.

186 **government picks up part of the tab:** See, for instance, Paul Forgasz and Miriam Munz, "Australia: The Jewel in the Crown of Jewish Education," in Helena Miller, Lisa D. Grant, and Alex Pomson, eds., *International Handbook of Jewish Education* (New York: Springer Science+Business Media, 2011), 1125–40; "My School . . . Go Figure," *The Australian Jewish News*, March 11, 2011, available at http://www.jewish news.net.au/editorial-march-11-2011/19856; "Australia," *American Jewish Year Book* 98 (1998), available at http://www.ajcarchives.org/AJC_DATA/Files/1998 _12_Australia.pdf; Oliver Valins, Barry Kosmin, and Jacqueline Goldberg, "The Future of Jewish Schooling in the United Kingdom: Preface," Institute for Jewish Policy Research, December 31, 2002, available at http://www.jpr.org.uk/publications /publication.php?id=138; Uriel Heilman, "Two Schools in Argentina Provide Model for Jewish Education," JTA, August 27, 2009, available at http://www.jta .org/news/article/2009/08/27/1007494/argentina-schools-ort; Michael Brown, "Good Fences Do Not Necessarily Make Good Neighbors: Jews and Judaism in Canada's Schools and Universities," *Jewish Political Studies Review* 11, nos. 3–4 (Fall 1999), available at http://www.jcpa.org/cjc/cjc-brown-f99.htm; Jack Wertheimer, "The High Cost of Jewish Living," *Commentary*, March 10, 2010, available at http://www.commentarymagazine.com/article/the-high-cost-of-jewish-living; Erik H. Cohen, "Comparison of Attitudes, Behaviours, and Values of French Jewish Families with Children Enrolled in Jewish Day Schools and Other School

Systems," in A. Pomson and H. Deitcher, eds., *Jewish Day Schools, Jewish Communities: A Reconsideration* (Oxford, UK: Littman Library of Jewish Civilization, 2009), 207–21, available at http://www.bjpa.org/publications/details.cfm?PublicationID =4805.

186 **government will have to start doing the same:** Another option is charter schools, open to Jewish and non-Jewish students, which surmount church-state concerns by teaching the Hebrew language without teaching Judaism. Such schools now exist in Brooklyn, New York; East Brunswick, New Jersey; and Hollywood, Florida, and they are an intriguing and welcome development. Their limitation, from the perspective of Jewish continuity, is that many of the students are not Jewish, and even those who are gain no religious instruction. [Hebrew Language Academy School in Brooklyn, New York, available at http://www.hlacharterschool.org/; Hatikvah International Academy Charter School in East Brunswick, New Jersey, available at http://hatikvahcharterschool.com/; Ben Gamla Charter School in Hollywood, Florida, available at http://www.bengamla-charter.com/2009/index.php; Jonah Lowefeld, "How Jewish Are Hebrew Charter Schools?" JewishJournal.com, August 24, 2010, available at http://www.jewishjournal.com/cover_story/article/how_jewish _are_hebrew_charter_schools_20100824/.]

186 **liberal American Jews have vehemently opposed:** The Orthodox Union, by contrast, has supported government funding of religious schools since 1976. ["The United States of America," in *Encyclopaedia Judaica*, 2nd ed., ed. Michael Berenbaum and Fred Skolnik (Detroit: Macmillan Reference, 2007), 371.]

186 **local governments pay:** U.S. Department of Education Office of Elementary and Secondary Education, "Guidance on the Supreme Court's Decision in *Agostini v. Felton* and Title I (Part A) of the Elementary and Secondary Education Act," July 1997, available at http://www2.ed.gov/legislation/ESEA/feltguid.html.

187 **very little conclusive data on their impact:** Maggie Severns (program associate with the Education Policy Program at the New America Foundation) in discussion with the author, October 17, 2011.

187 **pass constitutional muster:** On the potential constitutionality of broader government support for secular education at religious schools, see State of New York, Office of the Attorney General, Advisory Committee on Non-Public Education, "Report on Non-Public Education," May 2002, available at http://www.ag.ny.gov/ media_center/reports/non_public_schools_report.pdf.

187 **A recent experiment in Cleveland:** George D. Hanus, "Jewish Education Economics 101," *The Philadelphia Jewish Voice*, July 2007, available at http://www.pjvoice.com /v25/25004tuition.aspx.

187 **the figure was 67 percent:** Cohen and Kotler-Berkowitz, "The Impact of Childhood Jewish Education on Adults' Jewish Identity," 10.

188 **informal survey by J Street U:** When J Street U director Daniel May conducted an informal poll of J Street student leaders in September 2011, he found that 54 percent had attended Jewish school. By contrast, a 2004 study by Steven M. Cohen found that the overall percentage of American Jews aged eighteen to thirty-four who had attended Jewish school was only 18 percent. [Daniel May in discussion with the author, September 28, 2011; Ukeles, Miller, and Beck, "Young Jewish Adults in the United States Today."]

189 **Barack Obama's "blocking back":** James Traub, "The New Israel Lobby," *The New*

York Times, September 9, 2008, available at http://www.nytimes.com/2009/09/13/magazine/13JStreet-t.html.

190 **global BDS campaign take no position:** Adam Horowitz and Philip Weiss, "The Boycott Divestment Sanctions Movement," *The Nation*, June 28, 2010, available at http://www.thenation.com/article/boycott-divestment-sanctions-movement?page=full.

190 **prominent figures in the BDS movement:** See, for instance, Omar Barghouti, "Putting Palestine on the Map: Boycott as Civil Resistance," *Journal of Palestine Studies* 35, no. 3 (Spring 2006), available at http://www.palestine-studies.org/journals.aspx?id=6804&jid=1&href=fulltext.

192 **the European Union now demands:** Yossi Sarid, "Time to Boycott the Settlements," *Haaretz*, July 10, 2011, available at http://www.haaretz.com/print-edition/news/time-to-boycott-the-settlements-1.372383.

192 **every Yom Kippur:** Isaiah 58:6 (New JPS Version).

193 **acclaimed authors like David Grossman:** Boaz Fyler, "Yehoshua, Oz, Grossman Back Boycott of Ariel," YNet News, August, 30, 2010, available at http://www.ynetnews.com/articles/0,7340,L-3946485,00.html; Sarid, "Time to Boycott the Settlements."

193 **Palestinian Authority itself advocates a boycott only:** Khaled Abu Toameh and Tovah Lazaroff, "PA Declares Mass Settlement Boycott," *The Jerusalem Post*, May 19, 2010, available at http://www.jpost.com/MiddleEast/Article.aspx?id=175923.

194 **already sanctioned:** U.S. Department of the Treasury, "Sanctions Program," last updated August 3, 2011, available at http://www.treasury.gov/resource-center/sanctions/Programs/Pages/Programs.aspx.

194 **Somalia, and Sudan:** United Nations Security Council Sanctions Committees, "Security Council Committee Established Pursuant to Resolution 1572 (2004) Concerning Cote d'Ivoire," available at http://www.un.org/sc/committees/1572/; United Nations Security Council Sanctions Committees, "Security Council Committee Established Pursuant to Resolution 1533 (2004) Concerning the Democratic Republic of the Congo," available at http://www.un.org/sc/committees/1533/; United Nations Security Council Sanctions Committees, "Security Council Committee Established Pursuant to Resolution 1737 (2006)," available at http://www.un.org/sc/committees/1737/; United Nations Security Council Sanctions Committees, "Security Council Committee Established Pursuant to Resolution 1636 (2005)," available at http://www.un.org/sc/committees/1636/; United Nations Security Council Sanctions Committees, "Security Council Committee Established Pursuant to Resolution 1718 (2006)," available at http://www.un.org/sc/committees/1718/; United Nations Security Council Sanctions Committees, "Security Council Committee Established Pursuant to Resolution 1591 (2005) concerning the Sudan," available at http://www.un.org/sc/committees/1591/; United Nations Security Council Sanctions Committees, "Security Council Committee Established Pursuant to Resolution 751/1907 (2009) concerning Somalia and Eritrea," available at http://www.un.org/sc/committees/751/.

194 **boycott the state of Arizona:** "Who Is Boycotting Arizona?" AZ Central, August 27, 2010, available at http://www.azcentral.com/business/articles/2010/05/13/20100513immigration-boycotts-list.html.

194 **Ehud Barak and Ehud Olmert, who have compared:** Ravid, Landau, Benn, and Rosner, "Olmert to *Haaretz*: Two-State Solution, or Israel Is Done For"; Rory McCarthy, "Israel Risks Apartheid-Like Struggle If Two-State Solution Fails, Says Olmert."

194 **seventeen West Bank companies to close:** Janine Zacharia, "Palestinians Turn to Boycott of Israel in West Bank," *The Washington Post*, May 16, 2010, available at http://www.washingtonpost.com/wp-dyn/content/article/2010/05/15/AR2010051501492.html.

195 **not granted this right by birth:** Uriel Heilman, "Golan Druze Seek Peace—and the Heights," JTA, September 28, 2006, available at http://www.jewishexponent.com/article/10803/Golan_Druze_Seek_Peace__and_the/; B'Tselem, "East Jerusalem: Legal Status of East Jerusalem and Its Residents."

196 **"you would slay":** Judah HaLevi, *The Kuzari*, trans. Hartwig Hirschfeld (London: George Routledge and Sons, 1905), 69.

Acknowledgments

Often while writing this book, I felt not only intellectually over-whelmed by its subject but emotionally overwhelmed as well. I value Jewish solidarity. I know that at times in our history, its absence has cost our people dearly. In my own life, I have felt its power. Again and again during this project, I asked myself: Am I conveying the devotion, reverence, love, and awe that I feel toward the Jewish people and the Jewish state, and not merely my anger at the policies that I believe threaten the Jewish future? Have I succeeded in being what Michael Walzer calls "a connected critic," a critic who does not judge coldly from on high but who feels empathy for, and attachment to, the community with whom he disagrees?

My life is intertwined with the institutions and attitudes I criticize. I have spoken before AIPAC, the Anti-Defamation League, and the American Jewish Committee, and I know many people who work at those organizations, people I admire. I have friends and family members who believe that God gave the land of Israel to the Jewish people, all of it, and who believe that the gentile world has not fundamentally changed in the last seventy years. I attend synagogues and send my children to schools where Israeli flags and pictures of the Kotel and Gilad Shalit dot the walls. For me, the American Jewish community and the uncritical Zionism it often champions are not remote. They are the world in which I live. I cannot imagine living anywhere else.

Still, as I waded into this project I found that there was much I did not understand. In my effort to do so, I benefited immeasurably from conversations with people who know more about Israel, America, Jewish identity, and the interactions among them, than I ever will. Among those people are Lee Altzil, Mark Baker, Bradley Burston, Steven M. Cohen, Hagai El-Ad, Akiva Eldar, Libby Friedlander, Lara Friedman, Dore Gold, Samuel Heilman, Shai Held, Hussein Ibish, Eli Kaunfer, Ari Leifman, Nicholas Lemann, Daniel Levy, Rachel Liel, David Makovsky, Chip Manekin, Mikhael Manekin, Daniel May, Yehuda Mirsky, Yousef Munnayer, David Myers, Ori Nir, David Remnick, Jonathan Rynhold, Dahlia Scheindlin, Daniel Seidemann, Chaim Seidler-Feller, Assaf Sharon, Noam Sheizaf, Henry Siegman, David Sloan, Daniel Sokatch, Carlo Strenger, Chaim Waxman, Dov Waxman, Ross Weiner, Jack Wertheimer, and Uri Zaki. They are joined by many people who spoke to me on condition of anonymity.

Some of the people mentioned above disagree passionately with the arguments of this book. That only makes me more grateful to them for having helped me nonetheless. Over the past year, I have been reminded, again and again, of the preciousness of relationships that cross ideological lines. I can think of little more hollow than a life in which the political overwhelms the personal and am privileged to have friends to my political right who feel the same way.

This book would have been impossible without three institutions. The first is the City University of New York, where Bill Kelly and Joe Rollins at the CUNY Graduate Center and Steve Shepard and Judith

Watson at the CUNY Journalism School have allowed me the privilege of being part of a remarkable academic community. Steve Shepard, in particular, has been an invaluable partner in thinking through this book, and I am deeply grateful for his encouragement and advice. The second institution is *The Daily Beast–Newsweek*, for whom I am privileged to write. In that capacity, I have worked with three extremely talented editors, Tina Brown, Edward Felsenthal, and Tom Watson, who have helped me nurture the ideas in this book in my columns and given me the time away from column writing to finish it. Third, I have had the privilege of being associated with the most intellectually vibrant think tank in Washington, the New America Foundation, and have benefitted greatly from the support of its leaders, Steve Coll, Rachel White, Andres Martinez, and Faith Smith.

Among the New America Foundation's greatest gifts have been three gifted young people who helped with the book's research. In the project's early stages, I was aided by Jamie Holmes, a talented young journalist who is well on his way to a successful writing career of his own. During the bulk of the project, I was assisted by Caroline Esser, an extraordinarily reliable, intelligent, cheerful collaborator. I shudder to think how difficult writing this book would have been without her. I was assisted in the final stages by Elisheva Goldberg, who embodies the combination of Jewish commitment, intellectual honesty, and moral integrity that we need from the people who will one day help lead American Jewry. With any luck, she will be among their ranks. In addition, I received research help from Benjamin Alter, Logan Bayroff, Daniel Charles, Ellen Degnan, Aliyah Donsky, Benjamin Elkind, Gabriel Fischer, Hannah Fishman, Benjamin Lewy, Yonah Lieberman, Jonah Newman, Mira Oreck, Dana Rapoport, Harry Samuels, Sahar Segal, Sarah Stillman, Aaron Weinberg, Micah Weiss, Chanan Weissman, Jessica Youseffi, and Simone Zimmerman.

I was also privileged to work with my agent, the formidable Tina Bennett, whose initial enthusiasm for this project was crucial to its inception, and with my editor at Times Books, Paul Golob, whose smart, careful, tough-minded comments made this a far better book than it would otherwise have been.

——+——

Finally, and most importantly, my family. My sister, Jean Stern, has been a wise and caring friend and counselor during the writing of this book. I hope that in some small way it positively influences the future not only for my children, Ezra and Naomi, but for their cousins, Sasha and Lila, as well.

My grandmother, Adele Pienaar, may not agree with everything in this book, but it was her life experience and love of Israel that helped inspire it, and no one has taught me more not just about Jewish fortitude, but about how to live a life of joy. Robert Brustein, my stepfather, offered thoughtful comments on the manuscript and typically warm-hearted encouragement and praise.

My father-in-law, Arthur Hartstein, has been an unflagging supporter of this project and a good-natured companion at many of the speaking events before Jewish audiences that helped shape the book's argument. My mother-in-law, Marlene Hartstein, has been a passionate supporter as well, even inquiring about the book's progress from the hospital, when she had every right to worry only about herself. My sister-in-law, Lieutenant Colonel Bonnie Hartstein, also offered an inspiring example of determination and grace in difficult circumstances. Among the many remarkable qualities of the family I was lucky enough to marry into, perhaps most impressive is their courage when life requires it most.

This book is dedicated to my parents, Doreen Beinart and Julian Beinart. They left Cape Town, South Africa, just before I was born, choosing harder lives for themselves so that their children could grow up in a nation whose future was not menaced by apartheid. The political challenge that faced apartheid South Africa and the political challenge that faces Israel today are vastly different. But what my parents brought with them from the beautiful, scarred land of their youth was a set of dual inclinations that informs every page of this book. On the one hand, they were products of tightly knit Jewish communities. From an early age, I sensed that my father and mother, in different ways, felt most truly at home—no matter where they were on the planet— when surrounded by yiddishkeit. Yet they taught my sister and me that Jewish commitment must be the wellspring of universal moral concern, not a refuge from it. I was raised on stories of Jews who arrived in South Africa never having seen a black person and yet—nourished by the ethical traditions they had learned in the shtetls of Lithuania— risked their lives so that black South Africans could be free. In those stories, my parents told me what kind of person, and what kind of Jew, they wanted me to be.

My wife, Diana, has again supported me in ways both intensely practical and deeply emotional. By taking a vast array of family responsibilities on her shoulders, she has given me something every author needs: uninterrupted time. But she has also supported my decision to undertake a project that she knew might complicate our lives. Often, she has been the one who has had to face the anxieties that my writing about Israel has aroused, and she has done so with the same combination of honesty, charisma, and fierce devotion that made me fall in love with her a decade ago.

Our children have borne the burden of this book as well. Too often, I have stolen the time to write it from them. Israel and the Jewish future have even intruded upon our conversations, sometimes in unexpected ways. Once, upon hearing that I was writing a book about Israel, Ezra, age five, asked when we would take him there. I replied by asking where in Israel he wanted to go. "Mount Sinai," he declared. Gingerly, I told him that Israel had given back the Sinai desert to Egypt. "Egypt?" he exclaimed in disgust. "They gave it to Pharaoh?" Hmm, I thought, perhaps this liberal Zionism thing is going to be harder than I thought.

For her part, Naomi, age three, told me that she is writing a book about *V'ahavta*, the verses that follow the *Shema*, the centerpiece of

Jewish morning and evening prayers. Among the most famous words in those verses are *v'shinantam l'vanekha*, "and you shall teach your children." I wrote this book, in part, to teach my children about the struggle for a democratic Israel, the struggle I believe will define the Jewish people in our age. I dearly hope that by the time Naomi and Ezra teach their children, it won't be too late.

Index

About the Author

PETER BEINART is the author of *The Icarus Syndrome* and *The Good Fight*. A former editor of *The New Republic*, he is a senior political writer for *The Daily Beast* and the editor in chief of Zion Square, a blog about Israel and the Jewish future at thedailybeast.com. He is an associate professor of journalism and political science at the City University of New York and a senior fellow at the New America Foundation. He lives with his family in New York City.